# Unmasking
# the Crimes
# of the Powerful

**PETER LANG**
New York • Washington, D.C./Baltimore • Bern
Frankfurt am Main • Berlin • Brussels • Vienna • Oxford

# Unmasking the Crimes of the Powerful

## SCRUTINIZING STATES & CORPORATIONS

EDITED BY
### Steve Tombs & Dave Whyte

PETER LANG
New York • Washington, D.C./Baltimore • Bern
Frankfurt am Main • Berlin • Brussels • Vienna • Oxford

**Library of Congress Cataloging-in-Publication Data**
Unmasking the crimes of the powerful : scrutinizing states and
corporations / edited by Steve Tombs, Dave Whyte.
p. cm.
Includes bibliographical references and index.
1. Commercial crimes. 2. Political corruption. 3. Criminal justice, Administration
of—Corrupt practices. 4. Corporations—Corrupt practices. 5. Power (Social
sciences). 6. Elite (Social sciences). 7. Social sciences—Research—Government
policy. 8. Communism and social sciences. I. Tombs, Steve. II. Whyte, David.
HV6768.U56   364.1—dc21   2003006447
ISBN 978-0-8204-5691-1


Bibliographic information published by **Die Deutsche Bibliothek**.
**Die Deutsche Bibliothek** lists this publication in the "Deutsche
Nationalbibliografie"; detailed bibliographic data is available
on the Internet at http://dnb.ddb.de/.

Cover art by Jai (uhc-collective.co.uk)
Cover design by Joni Holst

The paper in this book meets the guidelines for permanence and durability
of the Committee on Production Guidelines for Book Longevity
of the Council of Library Resources.

© 2003, 2009 Peter Lang Publishing, Inc., New York
29 Broadway, 18th Floor, New York, NY 10001
www.peterlang.com

Printed in Germany

*For Doreen Tombs, 3 May 1928–17 May 2003*

*For Iain and Isabel Whyte*

# Contents

FRANK PEARCE

# Foreword

## *Holy Wars and Spiritual Revitalization*

I write as Bush prepares the world for a further round of his assault on "the axis of evil," a self-determined, highly elastic, but notably quasi-religious turn of phrase. There is no little irony in the religious tone of much of Bush's rhetoric, used, as it is, to justify the slaughter or emiseration of hundreds of thousands of men, women, and children, whether through sanctions, acts of war or mass displacement. Of course, the USA—the engine of a globalizing neo-liberalism and the self-appointed guarantor of "freedom" and "democracy"—has always been extremely selective in its applications of its publicly stated principles when deciding which political regimes to attack, tolerate or actively support. The USA was born of European, and specifically English, imperialism. Europeans justified their presence and their expropriation of land in the Americas by the general Christian doctrine that God had given the world to mankind as a whole. The Spaniards further legitimated their claim by using the Papal Bull of Pope Alexander VI (Alejandro Borgia!) that gave the Spanish crown dominion over all lands 100 leagues west of the Azores not already subject to a Christian king. The English invoked a Protestant doctrine that property right came from fulfilling the biblical injunction to "multiply and replenish the earth and subdue it." This they did by sedentary farming, and, relatedly, putting in place regimes of private property. Since the "savage" native peoples "failed" to build houses and to mark the boundaries of their property, any land that they had previously used could be appropriated by barter or conquest. Current estimates of the pre-conquest population of the Americas is that it was between 80 and 120 million people and, by the eighteenth century, after extensive exposure to the European "civilizing process," the population of aboriginal peoples was less than 10 per cent of that number.

After the American War of Independence, it was not hard for the elite that ran a new country with such roots to assert its exclusive sphere of influence in the Americas nor to claim it had the "Manifest Destiny" to bring private property, Protestantism, and its version of democracy to other lands, whether they were nearby, like Mexico and Cuba, or distant but strategic states such as the Philippines. A similar rationale inspired USA involvement in World War I, which few would now see as much more than a struggle between rival imperialist powers. Then, while World War II was undoubtedly primarily between the Allies and the Axis powers, its more general course was marked by rivalry between Britain and the USA and by a more fundamental struggle between Britain and the USA against Russia. There is good evidence that strategic considerations about containing Russian power, rather than any calculation that their use would save American lives, played the key role in the decisions to drop the atomic bombs on Hiroshima and Nagasaki. Yet, at the same time, retribution—indeed, seemingly divine retribution—was at work, for, immediately after the first bomb was dropped, President Truman warned that if the Japanese leaders did not accept the surrender terms, "they may expect a rain of ruin from the air, the like of which has never been seen on this earth," and, in private, he thanked God that the bomb "has come to us instead of our enemies and we pray that he may guide us to use it in his ways and for his purposes." Nine years later, under Eisenhower's presidency, "In God We Trust" became America's national motto. During the cold war against Russia, when the USA led the "free world," the latter contained as many, if not more, dictatorships than democracies, and was marked more by poverty than affluence. Further, in that post-1945 period, the US has engaged in bombing campaigns against China, Korea, Guatemala, Indonesia, Cuba, Congo, Peru, Laos, Cambodia, Grenada, Libya, El Salvador, Nicaragua, Panama, Iraq, Sudan, Afghanistan, and Yugoslavia. Bush's recent pursuit of bin Laden, then Saddam Hussein, show how little concern he has for the principles of national and international criminal law: that a suspect is innocent until proven guilty, to be judged and tried by an independent and impartial legal system.

While each of these US governments may have imagined "itself to be actuated by purely 'political' or 'religious' motives" and thereby to have transformed "[t]he 'fancy' the conception of . . . their real practice . . . into the sole, determining and effective active which dominates and determines their practice" (Marx and Engels *The German Ideology*), we do not need to share this illusion. In this context, imperialist domination and expansionism seem to have been the major motivating factors, and religious ideologies, while important, have been somewhat secondary and something of a gloss. The crucial, and obvious, point here is that it is naive to take at face value claims by states that they are essentially democratic, that they are responsive to the needs of an informed citizenry, and that their societies are characterized by equality, either of opportunity or of condition. Yet to me it is astonishing that so many people, after so much critical work has been written, leave generally unchallenged the claim that America is a democracy and one founded fundamentally on Judaeo-Christian moral ideals. This may be a public conceit but, in practice, in so far as there is a practical religious morality and an eschatological faith, it is all in relation to "Mammon," the possession of money (as capital) and in the belief in the intrinsic good of possessing ever more. Such a capitalist fundamentalism is well caught by Karl Marx's sardonic comment in *The Economic and Philosophic Manuscripts of 1844:* "Money is the supreme good, therefore its possessor is good. Money, besides, saves me the trouble of being dishonest: I am therefore presumed honest." The accumulation and expansion of capital, and the preservation and extension of its conditions of existence, remain the major determinants of domestic and international state activities in societies with capitalist economies.

A commitment *not* to take the claims of the powerful at face value—rather, as this volume's title notes, to subject them to scrutiny—is one of the common elements that runs through the contributions that follow. What is both notable and depressing, though, is how unusual is this commitment, and the issues that follow from it. Why notable? Many of the reasons for the relative silencing of these arguments and commitments are set out in this text, but there are perhaps a number of additional points that might be made here. In the period from the late 1960s to the early 1980s, when critical scholarship was strong in the social sciences, and when Marxism played a significant role within this, critique meant engaging seriously with the positions held by one's opponents. In general, there was an expectation that positions with which one disagreed should be represented accurately and challenged conceptually, epistemologically, and empirically; it was also anticipated that an exchange might develop subject to the same "rules." While this was not always achieved in practice, it nevertheless constituted a regulative ideal. By implication, social theory and social analysis were collaborative enterprises. However passionately a position was held, there existed a real possibility of its modification, its development, its abandonment, and, sometimes, the development of surprising, and non-eclectic, syntheses. A disturbing aspect of current academic practice is that differing but rigorous interpretations of the nature of the social world and of theories and theorists are often simply *ignored,* at times crudely parodied, or simply, and contemptuously, dismissed. This is to no one's benefit and it seems important to find different ways of dealing with such disagreements.

One among a number of experiences of Steve Tombs and myself in this respect is illuminating. In 1990 and 1991, through the pages of the *British Journal of Criminology,* we had a curious exchange with Keith Hawkins regarding appropriate forms of regulatory enforcement. This was initiated by our article "Ideology, Hegemony and Empiricism: Compliance Theories of Regulation" in which we identified Hawkins as a key figure within a group of academics we termed "The Oxford School." The results of this exchange have been curious, for at least two reasons. First, because within the mass of work that has appeared since, either within or broadly sympathetic to the views of the Oxford School, our own position, developed in those articles, is often simply ignored, at best footnoted and passed over. Curious, second, because although the exchange is often referred to by other commentators on regulation, the position that we developed in those articles is consistently misrepresented, even by those who cite it approvingly! Thus our argument—that a corporation when acting as a sophisticated amoral calculator is aware of the distinction between long-term and short-term consequences, is sometimes caught within a disabling ideology, sometimes less than competent and, as an organization, is often wrought by conflicts—gets translated into the claim that corporations are coherent organizations with a consensus about goals and means and that as amoral calculators they focus only on immediate consequences, are omniscient and never make mistakes! Two points follow. First, this is a clear illustration of how deep incommensurabilities are displayed and negotiated, but also how positions can develop or shift in the context of a dialogue. Second, there is also an indication of the dominance of certain ways of looking at the world which do not even see the need to engage with alternative knowledge claims—there is no need, it seems, for "The Oxford School" to understand, and engage in dialogue with, its critics.

There seems to be little recognition that we were clearly drawing upon the work on hegemony of the Italian Marxist, Antonio Gramsci. This is particularly interesting because Gramsci explicitly makes the points, albeit in his case about national politics, that "a particular political act may have been an error of calculation on the part of the leaders of the dominant classes"; that the "principle of 'error' is a complex one: one may be dealing with an individual impulse based on mistaken calculations or equally it may be a manifestation of the attempts of specific groups or sects to take over hegemony within the directive grouping, attempts which may well be unsuccessful"; and, "that many political acts are due to internal necessities of an organizational character, that is they are tied to the need to give coherence to a party, a group, a society." This lack of recognition suggests that there is a broader issue at work here, namely the decline of familiarity with critical modes of thought in general, and Marxist social science in particular. This aspect of the recent trajectory of social science will have the most destructive long-term consequences on the prospects for a vibrant tradition of critical social science. There is now a whole generation of academics, from undergraduates to post-doctoral teachers and researchers, many of whom lack any basic training in Marxist concepts or modes of analysis. This in turn significantly reduces the likelihood of Marxist social science being produced and then published.

Thus, if criminology is, as Foucault said, a "garrulous discourse" noted for its "endless repetitions"—this "discipline" is, after all, a booming area—it is now so on much narrower ground than was the case in, say, the 1960s and 1970s. This is the case despite there being an abundance of sophisticated critiques of its pretensions to being a distinct discipline. In general, such pretensions demonstrate that it does not have its own social scientific 'problematic' but rather one given to it by sundry state apparatuses. How is it possible that its main practitioners are able simply to choose not to engage with these critiques?

Let me illustrate this with reference to a graduate/undergraduate course that I teach, "Towards a Sociology of Killing." Stunningly, the standard definition of murder, taken up uncritically in most criminology textbooks, is simply "unlawful killing" and, like the law, there is some presumption that such acts (and not so many others also leading to death), are *mala in se*. Then, the criminal statistics that are used follow state practice again by excluding from their coverage all manslaughter except non-negligent manslaughter—which means not analyzing most motor vehicle-related deaths, most "accidents" at work and occupationally induced illnesses. There are some exceptions, but the work that does exist on corporate crimes of violence is generally simply ignored. And even when these matters are addressed, commentators often remain within the parameters of the way in which the law has actually been implemented. For example, the Ford Pinto case is explored, but the grounds for treating the activities of the tobacco industry as engaging in reckless or negligent homicide or manslaughter during the 1970s—when they knew cigarette tobacco was highly carcinogenic, when they knew that nicotine was addictive and when they often implicitly aimed their advertising at very young people while publicly denying all three points—are usually ignored. Four million or more premature deaths will be the likely result of the addictions produced during this period, and there is every reason to define them as homicide or manslaughter. With notable exceptions, criminology teaching and writing also excludes failures by prison officers to fulfil their duties of care, failures that lead to the deaths of inmates; excessive force by the police is also treated as of marginal interest. True, there are books like Jack Katz's *Seductions of Crime* that show that it is not only police officers who engage in morally ambiguous killings, but even this interactionist text never frees itself from official definitions. State-sponsored violence in particular and state crimes in general are almost entirely absent from criminological discourses. The horrors of Nazism are generally also excluded from discussion—most of the Nazis' killing, after all, was actually legal—and excluded too are the genocides inflicted, in the name of Christianity, on the peoples of the Americas. Serial and spree killing are generally included but war is generally excluded, as is the question of the rationales for dropping the atomic bombs and what that might tell us about state terrorism. Killing people is always morally problematic, but the moral and sociological questions are confused by uncritical acceptance of the definitions of murder by either states or organized religions. As Herman and Julia Schwendinger pointed out in 1975, sociology and criminology cannot be morally neutral. As intellectual practices, they unavoidably have moral dimensions. Untheorized claims to neutrality implicitly endorse extant ideologies. Not surprisingly, my Sociology of Killing course finishes with an examination of the non-elitist implications of some of Nietzsche's perspectivalist interrogations for the question of the foundations of morality and the nature of responsibility. With Nietzsche, one wonders how it is that so many people still do not acknowledge that the Gods of Religion and the Gods of the State are dead.

There are no holy wars and if there is a spiritual revitalization, it is to be seen in the ethics and courage of those who challenge the different forms of domination in the world currently subject to a capitalist "globalization." These challenges are taking place on the streets, across the globe; and there is some evidence that, whilst not equivalents, they are also still taking place through critical analysis and argument. This book makes a significant contribution to this challenge.

# Acknowledgments

This book began its life in the summer of 1999, when we organized some special sessions at the British Criminology Conference in Liverpool on "researching the powerful." Since then, we have accumulated debts for support, friendship and insight in relation to this project that will no doubt overwhelm our memory. So, with apologies to those who should be here but are not, here goes with a series of thank yous. To David Bergman, Courtney Davis, Pete Gill, Chris Hamerton, and Charles Woolfson, all of whom, for professional or personal reasons, were not able to add contributions to this volume. To Gregg Barak for his incredible enthusiasm, encouragement and collegiality, and to Phyllis Korper for her patience and expertise—without either, no-one would be reading this. To the participants at the 2000 Lincoln Conference of the European Group for the Study of Deviance and Social Control, and in particular to Andrea Beckman, for hosting a workshop on issues relating to "researching the powerful." To the organizations and individuals with whom we have worked, upon whose energy and courage we have drawn over many years, and who struggle at the very sharpest end of power, we say thanks for the inspiration. Among them, we owe a particular debt to the Centre for Corporate Accountability, Greater Manchester Hazards, Liverpool's People Not Profit, Merseyside Hazards and Environment Centre and the OILC. To the contributors, who have endured with good grace and diligence flurries of e-mails interrupting months of silence; and for their contributions themselves, each of which stands as an important piece of work in its own right. It has been a pleasure to work with people we admire, many of whom have been a constant source of advice, encouragement, and inspiration. And to Frank Pearce, a good friend and comrade, who to the best of our knowledge pretty much invented the phrase "crimes of the powerful." It means a great deal in both personal and political terms that he agreed to write the foreword to this book. To our own friends and families—you know who you are—but especially to Jess, Pam and Patrick. And to each other—for this is but one project in a productive and long-term relationship that will continue for years to come. Keep on keeping on.

Steve Tombs and Dave Whyte

# Introduction

1    STEVE TOMBS
     AND DAVE WHYTE

# Scrutinizing the Powerful

*Crime, Contemporary Political Economy,*
*and Critical Social Research*

## Scrutinizing the Crimes of the Powerful

Crimes committed by states and corporations have far greater economic, physical and social costs than those associated with the "conventional" criminals who continue to represent the fixation of contemporary criminal justice systems. Indeed, contemporary criminology—the study of crime and criminal justice—even its most reactionary, conservative or state/administrative elements, does not dispute this fact. Yet this pressing aspect of social reality is generally ignored, or at best the subject of empty, gestural acknowledgment in current research, writing, and commentary on crime and criminal justice.

If the crimes of states and corporations are partly an effect of power, this is all the more remarkable given the fact that states and corporations play key roles in defining the laws which they so constantly violate. Crime and power are inextricably linked phenomena in a variety of often contradictory ways.

Throughout the world, corporations are key actors with enormous economic, political and social power. Some commentators have gone so far as to argue that multinational corporations are now replacing states as the most powerful forms of actors, a claim associated with some versions of economic globalization. The world looks increasingly like a place where corporate capital can roam in a relatively foot-loose fashion. However, if there have been real increases in the power of transnational capital, it would be a mistake to accept many of the "extravagant claims" (Perraton et al., 2001) of the globalization literature, or to see this as necessarily entailing the diminution of state power and the significance of state activity (Alvesalo and Tombs, 2001b; Pearce and Tombs, 2001). Rather than to view power as distributed in some zero-sum fashion between states *or* corporations—as many of the cruder exponents of economic globalization theses would have us believe—it is more accurate empirically, and certainly more plausible theoretically, to understand the relationships between corporations and states as much more complex and often symbiotic. In the latter view, the increasing social and economic power of corporations may not be at the expense of, but may actually augment, the power of particular national and local states.[1]

Now, as part of their struggle to secure and maintain an increasingly privileged position, it remains in the interests of the powerful that certain of their "activities" (a shorthand term used here for acts and omissions) be obscured, be as invisible, and remain as absent from the public gaze and scrutiny as possible. Indeed, it might be argued that *one of the key features and effects of power is the ability to operate beyond public scrutiny and thus accountability.* The corporate veil and (official) state secrecy are obvious manifestations of power, enjoyed by corporations and states respectively. To the extent that the relatively invisible and hence unaccountable activities of the powerful produce social harm, create a range of social problems, exacerbate inequalities in social life, and indeed even form distinct ways of social action, then we might reasonably expect such activities to be the object of academic work, critical or otherwise. This is far from the case.

Our interest in this volume is with research conducted within the discipline of criminology, and its related area, or sub-discipline, criminal justice. It is from this discipline that most of the contributors to this volume speak (even if many would not define themselves as criminologists).[2] Research conducted within the discipline of criminology has historically sidelined the study of corporate and state illegalities, a myopia that has remained even in the face of overwhelming evidence that, in both Britain and in the USA, the social and economic impact of corporate and state crimes upon their victims massively exceeds the corresponding impact of conventional crimes (see Reiman, 1998; Salmi, 1993; Slapper and Tombs, 1999).

The last-mentioned social fact is *acknowledged* in much contemporary criminology, though such acknowledgment tends to appear somewhat gesturally, as if mere recognition of the existence of corporate and state crimes is enough to bolster the integrity of criminological research. The truth of the matter is that, despite such token recognition of the crimes of the powerful, criminological research rarely takes these types of offences and offenders as an object of study. While we would suggest that the claim regarding the marginalization, indeed the virtual absence, of work around corporate and state crime within criminology is incontestable, we wish here to provide some brief empirical indicators of this relative absence. We begin with an attempt to document the relative lack of published work on corporate and state crime within mainstream criminology and criminal justice publishing.

First, a couple of quite stark observations. There are, quite simply, *no* textbooks published in Britain which are devoted to a study of state crime. Further, to the best of our knowledge, only four textbooks have ever appeared in Britain that focus upon "corporate crime" (Croall, 1992, 2001; Punch, 1996; Slapper and Tombs, 1999); all of these have appeared in the past ten years; and three of them deal with white-collar and corporate crimes, thus conflating what in our view are often quite different phenomena (see Croall, 1992, 2001; Punch, 1996).[3] There *is* a greater volume of academic work around both corporate and state crime in the USA, though it is difficult to judge the extent to which this is simply a function of the far greater scale of publishing there in general, or evidence of a greater academic interest in these areas. Even if the latter is the case, even if there is greater interest in corporate and state crime in the USA academy, then it is again incontestable that these types of crime remain peripheral to the issues which dominate academic criminology and criminal justice there.

Second, the reference to textbooks is in itself important, for the trend within the increasingly concentrated academic, and international, publishing industry (Barnett and Low, 1996; Schiffrin, 2000) is away from monographs and towards textbook publishing—a shift obviously based upon rational calculations of potential markets and sales (calculations themselves related to the expansion of higher education). This, then, militates against the likelihood of work on corporate and state crime appearing in book form. The reasons for this are simple and mutually supporting: given the marginal status of these substantive concerns within criminology and criminal justice, there are relatively few undergraduate and postgraduate courses which incorporate these issues in a thoroughgoing sense; thus there is only a small market for textbooks in these areas; while there remain few textbooks, the possibility of developing new courses in these areas—in an era in which textbooks are dominant as university and public libraries have increasingly fewer funds to stock a range of materials—is diminished.

Third, this lack of academic attention to corporate and state crime appears to be replicated in journal publishing across criminology and allied disciplinary areas, an observation confirmed by the data in Table 1.1. The data indicate that there remains a dearth of criminological research in state and corporate crime research being published in mainstream British criminology journals.

The journals sampled were the five journals that publish the work of UK academics in the disciplines of criminology and socio-legal studies. There are, of course, other journals that regularly publish research papers authored by UK academics in those fields, in particular, law journals (such as the *Modern Law Review*),

Table 1.1    Corporate and State Crime Content by Journal

| Journal (issues, 1991–2000 inclusive, unless stated) | State crime | Corporate crime | Total articles |
|---|---|---|---|
| *British Journal of Criminology* | 1 | 6 | 298 |
| *Howard Journal of Criminal Justice* | 3 | 2 | 216 |
| *Journal of Law and Society* | 10 | 16 | 266 |
| *Social & Legal Studies* (1992–2000) | 2 | 10 | 215 |
| *Theoretical Criminology* (1997–2000) | 1 | 2 | 63 |
| Total | 17 | 36 | 1058 |
| | (2%) | (3%) | (100%) |

sociology journals (such as *Sociology* or the *British Journal of Sociology*) or social policy journals (such as *Policy Studies* or *Critical Social Policy*). Academic work on state and corporate crime may also be found (albeit rarely) in journals that publish work from disciplines such as business and management studies, media/cultural studies, economics and politics. Since our concern at this point of our argument is with the dissemination of *criminological* research that is concerned with state and corporate crime, our analysis has deliberately excluded journals that publish substantially in other disciplines. Articles were sampled from all issues of each of the five above-mentioned journals over a 10-year period, 1991–2000 inclusive, with the exception of *Social & Legal Studies* and *Theoretical Criminology*, since those journals commenced publication in 1992 and 1997 respectively.

For the purpose of this sample, corporate crime and state crime are defined as commissions or omissions of the state or corporations that occur as a result of a breach of the criminal or administrative law that regulates the activities of public and government authorities and private business; or commissions and omissions by public and government authorities and private business which result in victimization for which legal redress is available to the victim (for debates on appropriate definitions of state and corporate crime see Slapper and Tombs, 1999; Green and Ward, 2000; and Ward and Green, 2000). Thus, although the definition of state crime and corporate crime that was used was structured by legal categories, it was also a broad one. Consistent with this definition, nine articles concerned with political "corruption" in state governments were included in the sample (for example, seven articles were included from a *Journal of Law and Society* special issue in 1996, as was Ruggiero's 1994 *Howard Journal* piece on political corruption in Italy, and Wing Lo's 1993 *Social & Legal Studies* article on political corruption in China). Institutional malpractice that is dealt with by legal remedy was also included (for example, Henhan's 2000 piece in the *Howard Journal* on the use of court procedures against the authorities by prisoners in the UK prison system). Institutional malpractice that is regulated internally (for example, sexual and racial discrimination in employment practices in public authorities) was omitted from the sample.

Selection was made on the basis that a *central theme* of the article was state or corporate crime as defined above. Thus, articles where state and corporate crimes were merely alluded to, mentioned in passing, or were peripheral to the main arguments contained in the narrative are not represented in the data (for example, work by Hillyard that discusses the normalization of emergency powers in Northern Ireland), since the substantive concern of this work is the *legal* abuse of power by state agents. The emergent literature on human rights legislation was omitted, since none of the articles published in the journals sampled were primarily concerned with current illegal state or illegal corporate practices.

Beyond the clearest conclusion of Table 1.1 — namely, that there remains a dearth of criminological research in state and corporate crime research being published in mainstream British criminology journals — some further observations are worth making. First, we should note that these data relate to the past decade, which would be the era in which we would most expect journal articles to be published in this area, given that all British *textbooks* on corporate crime have appeared during this period. Second, if we examine the data in a little more detail, it is particularly striking that literature on state crime (even broadly defined) is marginalized even relative to that on corporate crime. Moreover, the majority of the articles (9 of 17) that dealt with state crime were highly individualized accounts of political corruption in the UK and elsewhere. Third, articles on corporate crime tend, perhaps unsurprisingly given political debates on the subject over the past 10 years, to be concerned with regulatory structures and government policies for the regulation of corporations. One point that needs to be made here is that while the concerns of this latter work may be crucial to the understanding of corporate and state illegalities respectively, one effect of the negligible volume of literature in these subject areas is that ideas around the numerous problems thrown up in this literature remain relatively underdeveloped. Thus not only can we identify only a small volume of work published in these areas, but also, it should be added, the ability of this work to go beyond some fundamental and topical questions appears to be restricted by its lack of critical mass.

There are a whole series of consequences of this relative absence of corporate and state crime from academia and beyond, and we shall treat these in detail in this chapter, as will the contributors to the other chapters in this volume. One consequence is worth emphasis here, since it provides a rationale for this text. If one impact of the dearth of work is that the methods for researching powerful corporations and states are grossly underdeveloped, another effect is that there is very little experience for future researchers to draw upon as a methodological resource. There are no examples of texts organized around a sustained concern for methodological issues raised in the processes of "researching the powerful," either within criminology or indeed across social science. Neither is this vacuum in methodological work confined to Britain or Europe: it is a global phenomenon. At the same time, within criminology, but also across the broad spectrum of the social sciences, work which addresses questions of method and methodology is proliferating, a trend that is not surprising given the period of reflexivity which criminology in particular and social sciences in general seem to have entered.

Of course, there are places where some of the issues raised in this text are addressed, most notably in parts of Gordon Hughes's "The Politics of Criminological Research" (Hughes, 1996), and in a chapter of Vic Jupp's classic *Methods of Criminological Research* (Jupp, 1989). Further, in "The Political Economy of Socio-Legal Research," Hillyard and Sim (1997) examine the effects of recent socio-political changes in Britain on universities in general and socio-legal research in particular. However, while these chapters are deservedly well known and important reference points within criminology and criminal justice—we shall draw upon each of them in the course of this chapter—they contain highly truncated considerations of just some of the issues under examination; the very fact that these chapters are referred to so frequently indicates the need for a more sustained and comprehensive treatment of the issues they highlight.

So, we believe that the lacuna to which we are pointing—the absence of any sustained treatment of considerations of researching the crimes of the powerful—is a problematic one, for at least four reasons. First, from the point of view of thinking about how we can know about the social world, the activity of researching the powerful raises in peculiarly sharp form some of the problems highlighted in considerations of methods and methodologies. Second, such research also generates novel and particularly difficult problems for researchers; these include questions regarding the construction of research agendas within and beyond the academy, the regulation of funding, issues of access, and problems of disseminating research findings albeit within an environment which places emphasis on published "output." Third, the absence of any critical discussion of issues related to researching the crimes of the powerful is one further element of the marginalization of the broad range of topics within the rubric the "crimes of the powerful" itself. Finally, developing a methodological approach to researching the crimes of the powerful can illuminate not only the contexts for those crimes, but also the way in which states and corporations subtly (and not so subtly) evade scrutiny. By doing this, we can learn much about how power is maintained, how resistance to power is neutralized, and the prospects for more successful forms of resistance and counter-hegemonic struggle, not least through academic activity.

Of course, the terms "power" and "the powerful" are hardly unproblematic. We do not intend here to enter into a discussion of what constitutes power[4] or the powerful. But in our considerations of hegemony (below), and in the empirical and theoretical insights of the contributions that make up this text, there will be various forms of elaboration upon what power is and, more pointedly, how it "operates" (the term is used advisedly, since one common theme of this text is the significance of viewing power in structural terms, rather than simply in terms of agency). Further, we elide any discussion of who or what constitutes the powerful. Our objects of focus are states and corporations. We take it as self-evident that, in a relative sense, such entities are powerful. This is certainly the case if states and corporations are compared with the usual objects of criminological focus, namely lower-class individuals and groups. Historically, criminology has cast its gaze "downwards." Criminal justice, in contrast, is partially organized around a concern with the central institutions of a criminal justice system—classically, police, courts, prisons—many of which can be identified as parts of the state. Yet this concern has tended to be either descriptive or conducted from the point of view of a more effective functioning within taken-for-granted rationales, and, thus, the vast majority of criminal justice is uncritical; indeed, some have argued that it is an even more conservative area of enquiry than criminology *per se* (S. Cohen, 1981).

The contributions to this volume are grouped together in three sections, which explore the construction of "valid" knowledge surrounding the crimes of the powerful, the ways in which researchers have sought to challenge power and build an alternative knowledge of the criminal activities of states and corporations, and the ways in which an alternative knowledge is crucial to exposing those criminal activities. Linkages between states, corporations, and universities are explored at length in this extended introduction, which also seeks to set out the theoretical framework within which this work proceeds and to which it will contribute. We do not intend to engage in long definitional issues around what constitutes corporate or state "crimes" when we are speaking of the crimes of the powerful. These issues have been debated *ad nauseam,* the debates themselves acting as one obstacle to substantive work on the issues. Here we take broad definitions of each of these types of phenomena, though we retain a commitment to some legal standard, consciously avoiding a descent into "mere moralizing" (Shapiro, 1983).

In the remainder of this chapter, we attempt, first, to set out empirically the dimensions of the "problem" of subjecting corporations and states to critical scrutiny from the university in a neo-liberal era; and, second, to develop a theoretical framework within which the substantive issues highlighted by "researching the crimes of the powerful" can best be understood. In reference to a theoretical framework, however, we should emphasize that not all of the contributors would subscribe to all, or even to very much, of such a framework. For us, what we tentatively propose here presents the most useful set of tools for understanding the problems in and the praxis of researching the crimes of the powerful.

## Hegemony, Academics, and the Role of the University

In this section, we consider Gramsci's notion of hegemony with particular reference to the role of intellectuals, our concern being with intellectuals who engage in research generally, and in universities in particular.[5] The reading of Gramsci from which our concept of hegemony is drawn is a materialist one (Anderson, 1977; Morera, 1990; Sears and Morera, 1994). On this materialist reading, for a social order to be hegemonized, a leading fraction of the class that plays a key role in the extraction of the surplus in "the decisive nucleus of the economy" (Gramsci, quoted in Morera, 1990: 168) must successfully form a historical bloc. This involves persuading other members of that class, other dominating classes, and other professional groupings to accept its moral and political leadership and to both accept and contribute to its mode of governance. This bloc must be constituted, to some extent, in and through the state.

Further, members of a historical bloc expect their ideas, their understanding of the world, their specification of historical possibilities to become the general common sense so that subordinate classes will, to a considerable extent, formulate their interests within the categories of the dominant ideology (Gramsci 1971: 180–95). The ability of the members of the historical bloc to set this agenda will depend upon their degree of dominance over mainstream social institutions, including those involving education, communication, mental and physical health, political organization, the means of production (all involving disciplinary practices through which subjects are socially constituted, distributed to different tasks and empowered to fulfil these in an appropriate manner), and apparatuses of repression. Thus, hegemony involves "the entire complex of practical and theoretical activities within which the ruling class not only justifies and maintains its dominance, but manages to win the active consent of those over whom it rules" (Gramsci 1971: 244).

Consistent with our reading of the Gramscian notion of hegemony (see also Pearce and Tombs, 1998: 35–47, 247–79), we argue that the construction of this new hegemony relies not just on material power (the ability of capital and national states to distribute benefits and disadvantages), but also on moral and intellectual leadership, so that certain ideas become predominant to the extent that they seep into popular consciousness, ruling out alternatives, and integrating into the ranks of the (relatively) advantaged some "subordinate" groups while (often safely) consigning to economic and social marginalization and exclusion whole segments of populations (Pearce and Tombs, 1996). In particular, this hegemony seeks to organize off political agendas certain alternative ways of seeing or doing.

We should be clear that academic discourse plays a significant role here, and more generally in constructions of the "feasible" or "acceptable" (Snider, 1990, 2000; Tombs, 2002; also see Pearce and Tombs, 1998: 223–46). This process of construction is one that can take on a different character, depending upon the balance of social forces. Hegemonic superstructures (state institutions, the hegemonic bloc and economic alliances) and counter-hegemonic movements struggle to make ideological gains in what Gramsci called wars of maneuver and position (Gramsci, 1996: 229–39). These represented the political strategies used by the hegemonic bloc and were analogous to military tactics. Wars of position involve the consolidation of hegemony, in defense of which state organizations and the "complexes of associations in civil society" constitute "the 'trenches' and the permanent fortifications of the front" (Gramsci, 1996: 243). Wars of maneuver entail "frontal assaults on the state" (Forgacs, 1988: 224) and are best conceived as immediate and responsive attempts to disrupt hegemonic rule that arise from particular crises and moments of exposure for the state. Of course, the historical bloc has always to deal with the threat of counter-hegemonic movements. Since subordinate groups are never merely powerless, one would expect "the bloc" to work at fragmenting them, through repression, by creating divisions through limited reform with the selective incorporation of some personnel into the hegemonic bloc and some cultural symbols into its ideology. Hegemony always involves the fragmentation of counter-hegemonic groupings.

### Gramsci and the Intellectuals

The roles adopted by intellectuals (in this case, by academic researchers) in both wars of position and wars of maneuver ultimately depend upon the stability of the balance of social forces in any given social formation. To elaborate upon this point, we can, for example, distinguish between two roles of academic research. First, the product of academic research has a crucial role in the construction, manipulation and presentation of "common-sense" views of the world. As the dominant ideas of a society are promoted, disseminated, and reproduced, they bid, through a variety of means (not least, universities and research institutions), to reach popular consciousness. When these ideas gain popular acceptance beyond the confines of groups of intellectuals (Gramsci, 1996: 423), they are said to have become part of "common sense." That is, these ideas, no matter how flawed they may be, are accepted as an accurate view of the world, set of truths, "realities" and so on. Achieving the status of common sense for ideas that justify the conditions of subordination and make them appear natural is the aim of hegemonic ideological reconstruction. As such, this process corresponds most accurately to what Gramsci calls the war of position.

Second, academic research has a role in providing the means for particular social and economic groups to respond to particularly threatening situations/conditions as they arise. This role becomes acutely significant during moments of crisis for the hegemonic bloc, or at a micro level, during moments of exposure for particular fractions of capital and state institutions/departments. Invariably, crises in hegemony entail a shift from consent to coercion (Hall et al., 1978: 208–17). Increasingly, the hegemonic bloc is forced to seek an "authoritarian consensus" as "the masks of liberal consent and popular consensus slip to reveal the reserves of coercion and force on which the cohesion of the state and its legal authority finally depends" (ibid.: 217). As the masks of consent and consensus slip and hegemony is weakened by the crude resort to coercion, the moral and intellectual legitimacy of the state remains under siege. Since reliance upon force alone can only undermine the state's legitimacy and erode popular consent yet further, it is at this point that the intellectual resources of the state must be marshalled to provide the ideological substance for reasserting hegemonic rule. It is these phases of crisis that are fought out and resolved by the wars of maneuver. It is therefore during these phases that the reapportion of moral and intellectual authority assumes a *decisive* role in class struggle. In this sense, it is possible to argue that wars of maneuver raise the stakes in the ideological struggle between the state and counter-hegemonic movements, and place an even greater premium on the production of ideas that can be rehearsed to legitimize state strategies.

Thus, it is important to recognize that academic intellectuals play a central role *both* in the long-term process of common sense construction and manipulation and in responses to particular crises in the state and the hegemonic order. Also central to our reading of Gramsci is that the ideological formations that emerge during both wars of position and wars of maneuver are always related. The empirical claims and theoretical formulations that emerge during wars of maneuver to reinforce moral and intellectual authority always make reference to pre-existing common-sense understandings of the world. Equally, common-sense understandings of the world are modified and reformed by ideas that emerge during wars of maneuver.

Having made this point, we must note that the prevailing common sense cannot in any sense be viewed as a coherent and unified way of interpreting the world. Competing class interests and ideological struggles between class fractions render common sense, in Gramsci's words, "a chaotic aggregate of disparate conceptions" within which "one can find there anything one likes" (Gramsci, 1996: 422). Common sense is thus "an ambiguous, contradictory and multiform concept" (ibid.: 423). This is not to say that there are no rational, organized conceptual threads that have a decisive role to play in the construction of common sense. For the hegemonized order must always present itself as the most rational and complete social formation, indeed as the "natural" order of human organization. In capitalist social orders, this raises a multitude of contradictions, not least the contradiction between the interests of the collective and the individual, a contradiction that, according to Marx and Engels, is most clear in the formation of the state; in particular in the state's claim that it exists to represent the common interests of all individuals in society (Marx and Engels, 1970: 53).

It is within the contradictions posed by capitalist social orders that we find the greatest leverage for developing a counter-hegemonic knowledge. By exposing the contradictions inherent in common sense, and in particular the hegemonic discourses that seek to gain currency as common sense, counter-hegemonic struggles can seek most productively to build alternative views of the world: ultimately to construct a new common sense. The very process of presenting alternative understandings of social phenomena—for example, highlighting the scale, consequences and origins of various forms of production of social harms—has the potential to challenge hegemonic rule. All of the research included here is involved in exposing the crimes and harms committed by powerful states and corporations and thus may under certain conditions hold out prospects for destabilizing the (neo-liberal) capitalist social order.

### Universities and the Role of Intellectuals

Gramsci (1996: 3–23) distinguishes between two types of intellectuals: organic and traditional. He describes the former as those intellectuals who emerge to give the dominant hegemonic group "homogeneity and an awareness of its own function" (ibid.: 5) in the economic, social and political spheres. The latter are the categories of intellectuals that, despite the emergence of a new hegemonic order, retain their social position as intellectuals.

For traditional intellectuals, their apparent disconnection from the dominant social group, or from other economic groups—added to the apparent historical continuity that they retain—is proof positive of their political neutrality and ability to produce value-free intellectual work. Denying their role in the class warfare of position and maneuver, traditional intellectuals are idealized as organically linked to the institutional context within which they work: "these various categories of traditional intellectuals experience through an 'esprit de corps' their uninterrupted historical continuity and their special qualification, they thus put themselves forward as autonomous and independent of the dominant social group" (ibid.: 7). Thus, "the intellectuals think of themselves as 'independent,' autonomous, endowed with a character of their own, etc." (ibid.: 8).

In the case of universities, the institutional context that ensures historical continuity is the "academy." For many university teachers and researchers the "academy"—the institutional discipline of academic study—represents a higher loyalty that keeps them above the fray of class struggle.

Similarly, organic intellectuals may not recognize their role as partisan if it is not immediately tied to an economic group. In particular, the claim that state officials have no loyalty to any power bloc is a powerful one in most Western democracies. However, it is crucial to recognize that the idea of political neutrality is based upon a fetishized account of the state and of the sphere of politics.

> [S]ince the State is the concrete form of a productive world and since the intellectuals are the social element from which the governing personnel is drawn, the intellectual who is not firmly anchored to a strong economic group will tend to present the State as an absolute; in this way the function of the intellectuals is itself conceived of as absolute and pre-eminent, and their historical existence and dignity are abstractly rationalized. (Gramsci, 1996: 117)

In this sense, the range of groups of organic intellectuals—their scientific and technical role and their role as definers of the truth, and of the way we are supposed to understand the world and so on—are imagined as possessing an intellectual credibility that rises above the class divisions endemic to capitalist social orders. Their intellectual output is idealized as knowledge which gives rise to fundamental changes in social forces, as opposed to being the product of social change.

The separation of organic and traditional intellectuals is, for Gramsci, a formal one; in reality, the boundaries between those categories are blurred. For, as Nietzsche observed, "The old maids of academism and the technical modernisers march in different armies but to the same drum" (quoted in Ainley, 1998). Indeed, in the context of universities, it is not always the case that the intellectuals march in different armies. What academics actually do in many cases is act out simultaneously the roles of organic and traditional intellectuals. University-based researchers may conduct policy- or industry-useful research that can be deployed as part of the hegemonic political project, *and* at the same time may use this research as the basis of their general contribution to the academy, to academic bodies of knowledge and so on. In the case of universities, drawing a clear division between different types of intellectuals may not be possible under particularly advanced hegemonic orders. Thus, as Gramsci noted, "One of the most important characteristics of any group that is developing towards dominance is its struggle to assimilate and to conquer 'ideologically' the traditional intellectuals, but this assimilation and conquest is made quicker and more efficacious the more the group in question succeeds in simultaneously elaborating its own organic intellectuals" (Gramsci, 1996: 10). Rather than seeking a crude distinction or dichotomy between categories or types of intellectuals, Gramsci suggests that it is possible to measure the "organic quality" (ibid.: 12) of groups of intellectuals and their connectedness with the dominant (or, indeed other) economic group(s).

### Universities as Ideological Apparatuses

As Poulantzas reminds us, the separation between the public and private realm (and indeed state and civil society) is purely a juridical one, a distinction established by law (Poulantzas, 1970: 305). Thus, although some institutions are idealized as private, as part of civil society, they are more accurately viewed as simply part of the state ideological apparatuses. They may only be regarded as "private" in that they enjoy some measure of relative autonomy from the state. Universities are in this category, and are only distinguished from the formal structures of the state because of a relative autonomy that is largely derived from their assumed status as traditional (as opposed to organic) institutions. The growing research divisions of government departments and agencies can make no such claim: they are unambiguously ideological apparatuses at the heart of the state, albeit with their own traditions and history. But the role of other organizations that produce research is less distinguishable. Research institutes formally tied to corporations, freelance research consultancies and research think tanks allied to political interest groups all have features that distinguish them from having a direct relationship with the state. Not the least of these features is their function as a site of activity for organic intellectuals. Yet these are intellectuals that have all been trained in the universities; their work makes reference to and contributes to the same body of knowledge; their social status and political influence is maintained collectively via professional organizations and so on. In this sense, the distinction between state and civil society, between public and private spheres, is always blurred and ill-defined.

As we have noted, universities often assume an ideological role that has an organic relationship to the dominant economic group. Furthermore, they also perform a crude instrumental task for capital: they have, first and foremost, the role of training workers and managers for capital. This role is one that has been deemed too great a task for capital to assume single-handedly. As James O'Connor has pointed out, "The most expensive economic needs of capital as a whole are the costs of research, development of new products, new production processes . . . and, above all, the costs of training and retraining the labor force, in particular technical, administrative and non-manual workers." This role is of particular importance, since no single fraction of capital can afford to train its own workforce or divert the requisite proportion of profits into research and development (O'Connor, 1973, quoted in Smith, 1974: 160).

Universities have, for the last 600 years of their existence, been marked by a continual process of change, change that has been closely connected to—although not always prompted by—developments in the mode of social organization. The industrial revolution and the rise of a new ruling class ensured that universities would, to some extent, be transformed to produce the science and technology required by the new industries for organizing and developing the sphere of production. But this transformation of the universities did not occur without a protracted struggle. Indeed, resistance to the industrialists from within the universities and beyond was largely successful. In John Stuart Mill's inaugural lecture as rector of St. Andrews University in 1867, he summed up the position of the traditionalists: "There is a tolerable agreement about what a university is not. It is not a place of professional education . . . Their object is not to make skilful lawyers and physicians or engineers, but capable and cultivated human beings" (quoted in Sanderson, 1972: 5). The struggle between the increasingly powerful industrial capitalists on the one hand and the traditionalists on the other cannot be simplified as a distillation of the organic/traditional dichotomy. The traditionalists were not only defending the right of universities to provide a liberal education, but also defending the social structures that this university system maintained: structures that sustained the prominence of the propertied class. Thus, the successful cooption of the universities for providing the teaching and researching to be utilized directly by capital (as opposed to the traditionally dominant subjects, such as classics, mathematics and philosophy, that were deemed to be vocationally useless) did not begin until well into the nineteenth century. When the role of the university did begin to be transformed, it was based upon the rising acceptance of the utility value of education (and, of course, the expansion of industry) as a social good. Education that was relevant to industry had to be introduced into the universities if capitalism and British society were to advance and flourish.

The romantic ideal of the "ivory tower" has always been a highly fetishized one, a point Gramsci was at pains to stress. For him, the "concept of free-floating intellectuals, whose roles and functions appeared to have little directly to do with the productive sphere, state policy or political activity, was a myth" (Showstack-Sassoon, 2000: 18). The idea of research conducted within the context of universities as neutral, value-free and divorced from the partisan imperatives of economic forces is itself intellectual nonsense, particularly since the period of the emergence of capitalism (ibid.). Rejecting such preconceptions brings into sharp focus the claims of academic institutions to neutrality and objectivity.

It is the argument here that if this claim has ever reflected some degree of accuracy (and it has to the extent that there have always been pockets of learning in universities that were free to develop and promote counter-hegemonic knowledge), universities are increasingly exposed to the structured imperatives of the state and capital. This is not to romanticize or fetishize the idea that the university can act as a positive social force for change. Conceptually, this is not a particularly useful way to think about higher education or research more generally. The fact that critical and counter-hegemonic work emerges from the ideological apparatuses is not a function of the institutions themselves; it is always a result of protracted struggles (either within or beyond the institution) that create the space for this work. After all, as Bourdieu (1988) has argued, the reproduction and consecration of social inequalities is the primary function of all educational apparatuses. It is only by intellectualizing and creating a legitimizing terminology that explains away the structural inequalities of capitalism that the state can retain a mask of neutrality. Thus, universities play a key role in the mystification of the capitalist social order. In turn, universities can do this only by retaining their own mask of neutrality.

## Neo-Liberalism and the Entrepreneurial University

### *Taking the Universities to Market*

A dominant concern of this chapter is with the marketization of universities and the commodification of knowledge. By the former, we mean the various means by which universities are increasingly required to act as economic actors, both in external markets—as competitors for students, research funds, prestige, and so on—and through the development of internal markets, whereby courses, departments and so on become individual cost centers which are required to generate a surplus or perish, where there is competition for students (as a resource) at all levels, and where academics are increasingly required to generate income to meet their wage or salary (and often employed upon fixed-term contracts to add the necessary discipline in this enterprise). This compulsion towards acting as economic units has also been furthered by universities turning towards the business world for models, advice, prescriptions as to how to operate and be organized. By the commodification of knowledge, we mean the variety of shifts towards the production of knowledge as something to be traded as a commodity, with a realizable exchange value within some internal or external market (R. Barnett, 1994). To preempt our argument in summary form, if there has ever existed some relative independence of academic work from the political imperatives of the powerful, an independence somehow turned towards the advancement of an "objective" knowledge, then this has been under sustained attack both within and beyond universities in the era in which neo-liberalism has reached national and international hegemony.

As we have indicated, these trends towards marketization and commodification are not entirely new, nor should their emergence be viewed in an unfolding, unilinear fashion. For example, writing in 1961, E. P. Thompson developed a searing critique of the liberal academic, urging intellectuals to develop an "angry courage" to confront what he called the "encroaching authoritarianism of the Business Society, with its growing retinue of intellectual retainers" (E. P. Thompson, 1980: 10).[6] Then, in 1970, an analysis of Warwick University Ltd by Thompson and others cited the rise of a "business university," in whose development the regional business elite was seen to have played a central role.

Writing in the 1970s, Miliband charted the evolving relationship between capital, the state, and the universities, and noted the growing influence of the state and business interests: not only was the state more involved in the direction of the university, but "academics are also immeasurably more involved than ever before in the life of the state" (Miliband, 1973: 222).

Structurally, the marketization of research has been encouraged (and indeed deemed necessary) by political reforms in the funding regime for higher education. Over the past quarter of a century, links between university departments and corporate/state sponsors have developed in the context of a massive expansion of the higher education sector and, at the same time, steady cuts in state funding.

In the USA, this process of disinvestment has had a fundamental impact upon business-university relationships. As early as the mid-1970s it was estimated that about a third of the faculty in all USA universities had been involved in some form of corporate consultancy (Marrer and Patton, 1976, cited in Stankiewicz, 1986: 44). Yet the process of state disinvestment since the early 1970s has forced universities to attract ever-greater corporate funds (Soley, 1998: 230–31). This trend has occurred partly as a result of military disinvestment as the restructuring of the military-industrial complex has gradually reduced state funding for research (Geiger, 1992; Ovetz, 1996; and Rivers, 1998: 60). However, the story of the decline in state funding for research in the USA is not just the story of the changing imperatives of the military-industrial complex. In the fifteen years between 1980 and 1995 there was a drop of 43% in non-military state funding in the USA (Ovetz, 1996: 115). Commenting upon higher education in Canada, Newson and Buchbinder have noted that a similar program of disinvestment embarked upon in the late 1970s, following the liberal expansion of the universities in the 1960s, has prompted a severe funding crisis in recent years (Newson and Buchbinder, 1988: 11–22). The result in both countries has been a creeping entrepreneurialization of the universities based upon the expansion of research consultancies and joint ventures, ostensibly aimed at facilitating knowledge and technology transfer from the public sector to private corporations. Funding data analyzed by Slaughter and Leslie indicate that similar trends are unfolding in all Organisation for Economic Cooperation and Development (OECD) countries (Slaughter and Leslie, 1997, Appendix). Recently, higher education systems in locations as diverse as Australia (Slaughter, 1998), Mexico (Ovetz, 1996), New Zealand (Kelsey, 1998) and South Africa (Orr, 1997) have been forced to accept the conditions of essentially similar processes of marketization.[7]

In the UK, a similar regime of austerity forced universities increasingly to look beyond mainstream state funding, for alternative sponsors. Since 1979, the sector has been the subject of several waves of reductions in grants from central government (see, for example, Slaughter and Leslie, 1997: 41). Alongside these reductions in funding have occurred two equally significant developments: first, an opening up of universities to external market influences; second, attempts to introduce an era of mass higher education.

Between 1988/89 and 1993/94, the total number of full-time students in higher education had increased by 65% and part-time students by 35%. In the same period, staff numbers increased by less than 17% (Hillyard and Sim, 1997: 51–52). Student numbers are expected to continue to rise (HEFCE, 1999: 6), while Higher Education Funding Council for England (HEFCE) funding for both research and teaching is expected to rise only in line with inflation, allowing no increase in expenditure to deal with the projected increase in students. For example, the Dearing Report (Dearing, 1997) calculated that between 1976 and 1996 funding per student fell by just over 40% (Thomson, 2001: 6); between 1989 and 1997, Conservative governments reduced funding per student by 36% (ibid.).[8] Unsurprisingly, HEFCE has noted that higher education institutions across the sector are not generating the income necessary to keep pace with rising cost pressures and the need to reinvest in the institutions, and recently estimated that there was a shortfall in operating surplus of £252m across the sector (HEFCE, 1999: 3–4). By 1999, around 50 higher education institutions (30%) had fallen into debt (HEFCE, 1999). All of this confirms the fear of most people working in the sector that a regime of austerity is set to intensify, producing and reproducing pressure on higher education institutions to find other sources of funding for both research and teaching activities.

Research was not exempt from this program of austerity: between 1983 and 1999 public research funds declined by 20% in real terms (Monbiot, 2000b: 263). But more detailed scrutiny than a global figure for research funding across the university sector is important here. In the "old" university sector, between 1980 and 1990 external research grants and contracts as a proportion of total university income had risen from 15% to 23% (Phillips, 1994: 43). This trend is set to continue (HEFCE, 1999: 5).

Significantly the decade between the early 1980s and the early 1990s was characterized by a shift in resources from university block grants to funding provided through the research councils (Phillips, 1994: 45; also Williams, 1992). Indeed, patterns in total government funding of research and development during this period indicate an increasingly important role for the research councils: research council funding as a percentage of total government research and development spending rose from 12% in 1985/86 to 17% in 1990/91 (Salter and Tapper, 1994: 223). The political rationale for shifting funding into the research councils was largely to centralize control over the research conducted in universities. Thus, institutional autonomy regarding how central government research money was to be spent was eroded as the research councils extended control over and demanded accountability for funded projects. For the time being, we note that the marketization of the universities in this period was closely paralleled by a program of austere cuts, and an attempt to increase the dependency of universities on the research councils and external sources of research funding.

### New Labour and the Utility Value of Research

In recent years, the intensified regime of austerity that has swept through the social sciences and beyond has been a key tool in entrenching the principle of utility, and strengthening the reliance of academics upon mainstream sources of external funding dominated by policy or industrial requirements. Furthermore, there is much evidence to suggest that we are in the midst of a period where the quality of research is increasingly being downgraded as demands for work that has a utility value, an immediate relevance for the dominant power bloc, intensifies. This can be measured partly in terms of the loss of time for basic research, the lack of support personnel or the consumption of other academic resources due to pressure to meet the demands of fund holders (Menzies and Chunn, n.d.). Due to the insatiable demand for policy-useful, immediately utilizable research, we are witnessing the progressive downgrading of research that has a theoretical focus. Where research does have a theoretical focus, it will tend to be a highly conservative one: for example, it will place a higher use-value upon "safe," orthodox research, published in established mainstream journals (Harvie, 2000: 113–14). Indeed, the theoretical perspectives developed by research will tend towards those that lend legitimacy to the role and activities of states and corporations, and away from those that encourage alternative views of capitalist social organization. At the same time the highly refined research market operates on the basis of one internal logic: that this market must by necessity be ever more finely tuned to pro-business/pro-state ideals. Thus we may be witnessing a trend identified in a recent review of state/corporate/university relationships in the USA during the Cold War era: "in the short-term, power typically *selects* ideas . . . while in the long term ideas tend to *conform* to the realities of power" (C. Simpson, 1998a: xxix, emphases in original).

Thus, in the UK, while the current government may be less rhetorically hostile to social research (Lipsey, 2000), there is very little difference in the degree to which current and previous governments wish to see social science tied to government and industry's functional requirements. However, the election of a Labour Government in 1997, following the party leader's statement of the key issue facing the country as "education, education, education," did signify more than a simple rhetorical change for the social sciences: for example, a recent increase in the Economic and Social Science Research Council (ESRC) budget (of 15% in real terms over the next 3 years) compares with the last Labour Government's attack upon the Social Science Research Council (later changed to the ESRC) that equated to a real terms cut of 24% between 1976 and 1981 (Kogan and Kogan, 1983: 118). Lipsey's bold statement on the terms under which research will be funded and received into the fold by government is indicative of a much more pragmatic understanding of the contribution of research to the policy process. The current government's support for the ESRC is linked closely to a renewed government commitment to "evidence based policy" (ESRC, 1999: Chairman's Statement). If researchers want to be involved in the right type of research and tie themselves into government or research council-defined priorities, then being a social scientist at the moment can be a successful enterprise. While the ESRC's commitment has some welcome aspects, the signals which it sends, and indeed other recent messages from the ESRC and the government, do not augur well for critical social research, least of all that devoted to exposing the powerful to critical scrutiny.

Thus it seems that, if the international project of neo-liberalism was kickstarted at governmental level by the administrations of Thatcher and Reagan, the assumption of power by apparently "Left-of-Centre" (or at least centrist) governments under Blair and Clinton hardly disrupted its progress. In Britain, Labour's apparent capitulation to the twin logics of "structural dependence" and "no alternatives" (Hay, 1999) helps to explain the government's subjugation of political independence to the immediate demands of capital. In almost all spheres of social and economic activity, and at every opportunity, the Blair governments have acted upon a dogmatic pro-business stance.

In the context of education, Labour's evangelical business-friendliness has been applied vigorously: for Blair, "in the knowledge economy, entrepreneurial universities will be as important as entrepreneurial businesses, one fostering the other" (Blair, 1999). At the forefront of this commitment is the Foresight program, which brings together representatives from industry, government and the research base (largely the universities) ostensibly to maximize the role of the science base in maximizing future wealth creation and a better quality of life.[9] Foresight panels provide a forum for the incorporation of universities into the commercial strategies of the industrial sectors the panels represent, and in so doing, they draw the universities into a general promotion (rather than scientific scrutiny) of the profitability of the sector. This is not particularly surprising, given that there is a numerical dominance of corporate representatives on many of the panels. In addition, civil servants and academics are selected on the basis of their support for the general aims of promoting the industry in which they are involved.[10] Indeed, the general direction of the work taken on by the panels is one that rarely deviates from promoting the commercial success of the sector.

Yet, the effects of academic-business interactions seem rather one-sided. Far from boosting the resources available to universities, the experience of the USA has been that the growth of research parks and university/business consortia have not, despite the hype, been successful in producing profitable returns for the university sector. Indeed, these arrangements have often left universities in the red (Ovetz, 1996: 120). In the meantime, huge benefits accrue to private corporations: in terms of the training of managers and technical workers; in terms of the transfer of technology to the private sector; and in terms of the construction of ideologies and interpretations of the world consistent with the stability of capitalist social orders (indeed, with particular fractions of capital). Thus, the very idea that the marketization of research and, more generally, the entrepreneurialisation of the universities are based upon a flow of resources from business to the universities is little more than an illusion. Corporations are now obtaining far greater benefits from the universities for less money than ever before.[11] Yet this is the process that is used to justify programs of austerity in parts of the university that are deemed unprofitable or resistant to commercialization (ibid.: 126).

### Elites, Capital and Social Credibility

Given the evolving processes described in previous sections, it is reasonable to talk of a growing assimilation of the universities into the neo-liberal project. This is also encouraged via the key international economic and political institutions associated with this project.

For example, the World Bank, in a 1994 report on higher education, urged an international shift within nation-state higher education regimes from state funding to "multiple sources" of income, noting that "In short, higher education should resemble the United States model more closely" (Currie, 1998: 6–7). Thus it continues to undermine the public provision of education in countries undergoing "structural redevelopment," challenging the principle of higher education provision as a public good, and increasingly forcing states to commodify their universities. Included in the World Bank's prescriptive measures are introducing tuition charges for students, limiting the number of scholarships available to the poor, forcing down costs in universities, and encouraging private schooling (Kelsey, 1998: 53–54). In South Africa, for example, foreign advisers have been drafted into institutions to teach the principles of the "market university" (Orr, 1997; Kishun, 1998), principles that have militated against the development of research around topics of social justice and poverty (Orr, 1997: 63). The World Bank's version of the market university in many countries has created the conditions whereby "[t]he fragile storehouse of indigenous knowledge is almost destroyed, along with the major source of independent critique. Local research by independent academics is minimal" (Kelsey, 1998: 54). Recent developments in the World Trade Organisation (WTO) under the General Agreement on Trade in Services (GATS) threaten to force higher education systems across the world to open up to private capital investment from overseas. If the terms of GATS were implemented, publicly funded higher education systems would be deemed anti-competitive and the WTO could force states to privatize (ibid.). Many other institutions are, of course, involved in these processes. For example, the European Union (EU) recently announced that its Framework research program would be restructured to encourage greater collaboration between universities and industry (*Times Higher Education Supplement*, 3 December 2000). It is ironic that UK funding for the EU initiative is allocated by top-slicing government funding for universities (ibid.).

A further element of the domination of the ideas and the personnel of the hegemonic bloc is the growing number of appointments of senior university staff to the boards of large corporations in the USA.

In the UK, the Council for Industry and Higher Education (CIHE), an "independent" body comprising 32 heads of large companies and 12 heads of universities and colleges (Slaughter and Leslie, 1997: 41) emerged in the 1980s to become a significant forum for policy debate and formulation. Acting as a political lobbying organization, its primary function was to pressurize government to develop policy to improve links between universities and industry. The 1988 Education Reform Act closely followed the prescriptions of CIHE, as did subsequent government policy developments (see Edwards and Miller, 1998: 54–55). The act also consolidated the physical presence of corporate representatives in government: the new administrate bodies for higher education were to be formally dominated by business representatives. Corporate and state interests now abound across ESRC committees. University boards of governors are increasingly dominated by senior businesspeople. Vice-chancellors of universities are more likely to be involved in branches of the local state and to act as representatives of the public interest on the boards of public/private sector partnerships. The influence of private business interests in the formal management structures of universities is now institutionalized in the UK. Moreover, senior academics are increasingly recruited from industry and senior executives occupy influential government policy positions in higher education (see Muttitt and Lindblom, forthcoming, for one case study). Within the context of the higher education restructuring project, corporate representatives may find themselves in an increasingly receptive, business-friendly environment. In short, in the UK, representatives of business and industry are now not only well placed to wield influence at the level of the university and the emergent partnerships discussed above, but they are at the heart of the decision-making processes that initiate policy on higher education.

What is in this for capital? Such trends allow business organizations several opportunities: the carrying-out of high-quality research, subsidized both by students and by the taxpayer; influence over the supply of labor; increased prestige and marketing opportunities, whereby the legitimacy of business activity is increasingly and pervasively augmented; and an excellent location from which to respond to moments of crisis through ideological counter-offensives, not least through influencing the very direction of particular disciplines.[12]

An equally significant effect of the relationships developing between the universities and various sectors of capital for reasons of utility or social credibility has been the rising status that seems to be conferred upon corporate and external funding by universities themselves. In an increasingly competitive marketplace, universities vie with each other to attract limited sources of corporate and government funding. Therefore, the other side of the coin of the social credibility of capital is that capital in turn can enhance the credibility of the institutions that attract research capital. Of course, there may well exist some hierarchy of research funds in terms of perceived prestige, as has been argued in the case of the USA (Slaughter and Leslie, 1997: 137). However, it may also be that external research funding *per se* is valued indiscriminately. Thus, in the UK, one of the distinguishing—and most perverse—features of the Research Assessment Exercise (RAE) is that it rewards university departments for the *sheer volume* of corporate and other external funding secured. Capital, therefore, to some extent has the power to enhance the status and credibility of an institution simply by making a donation, funding a research project, setting up a research center, and so on.

Seeking the status and prestige conferred by business is related to other ways in which universities may seek acceptance within the business community. The coopting of universities into the framework of assumptions and values of the business community may be understood in this context. Moreover, as the new protagonists of entrepreneurial discipline, universities increasingly sound and act as if they are private companies. In some respects, the "university acting as business" syndrome appears to be endemic in the sector in the current period. Higher education in the UK was worth £9 billion to the exchequer in foreign exchange earnings in 1997. Around half of this was generated by recruiting students from abroad. A growing slice (around £250 million) comes from course franchises—largely unheard of 10 years ago—where colleges abroad are sold the rights to teach ready-made courses taught in British colleges and universities. In 1998, it was estimated that 140,000 students were enrolled on courses franchised from British universities (*Guardian*, 17 November 1998).

## *Austerity and Discipline*

The project of neo-liberal austerity forced upon the universities in the UK over the past three decades is one in which there have been real continuities between successive Conservative and Labour governments, and one which has at its heart a more generalized subordination of the non-measurable use values of research to quantifiable research value (Harvie, 2000: 104). The reach of neo-liberal market discipline into the universities heightened the requirement for a system quantifying research work. Such a system was essential to the operation of a disciplined "research market" (ibid.). This process is unfolding first as a result of the increasing tendency of university departments to rely upon corporate and state funding, and secondly, as a result of the establishment of a complex system of exchange value of research work through the Research Assessment Exercises which, since their inception in 1986, have facilitated the expansion of this market, a process that Hunt (1994) has described as the monetarization of intellectual labor. The effect of this process has been to tighten the grip of corporations and the state over definitions around what kind of knowledge is produced and how it is produced, and to push out to the margins research that is deemed to have a low market value.

Central to the regime of the market has been a continued restructuring of the academic labor market. In 1994/95, 60% of UK academics were employed on permanent contracts; by 1997/98, this figure had fallen to 55% (Harvie, 2000: 117). It is estimated that now only half of all academics in the UK are permanent (Chitnis and Williams, 1999). Of all academic appointments made in 1997/98, only 18% were on permanent contracts (Harvie, 2000: 117).

Of course, the restructuring project is claimed to be a necessary part of gearing up to the new demands of corporate and state-sponsored research. It allows the universities to draw from a labor market that is much more responsive to their contractual requirements and that has lower overheads. But perhaps more crucially, the subordination of research workers to the imperatives of the market plays a fundamental *disciplinary* role. We can identify five aspects of this process.

First, the rise in casualized and temporary posts may force researchers to seek funding wherever it is available. Since this is increasingly likely to be found in contract research, researchers may have little option but to conduct utility research. In 1998, 94.2% of research-only staff in universities were on casualized, fixed-term contracts (*Times Higher Education Supplement,* 20 November 1998). Thus, the expansion of the university sector may well be ushering in a new generation of researchers entirely dependent upon policy and commercial research projects.

Second, those researchers are less likely to be in a position to carve out space for developing autonomous research agendas outside the agendas of large grant-holders. The neutralization of critical research may be one result of casualization.

Third, casualization in universities is likely to produce increasing numbers of researchers that are relatively powerless, unorganized and atomized. The very conditions of security that allow workers in all industries to resist overbearing managerial regimes are therefore denied to the new generation of casualized researchers. To be blunt, "Say the wrong thing and you can be out of a job" (Crace, 2001).

Fourth, the entrepreneurialization of the universities has created a new binary divide that is closely related to the old one. The old polytechnic institutions, the new universities, receive only 7% of RAE-allocated resources (Chitnis and Williams, 1999). Since the old universities have successfully reasserted their control over state-allocated research funds, this leaves the new universities (if they want to conduct research) overwhelmingly reliant upon the "utility" sources. At the same time, lecturers (particularly in the new universities) are granted less time to conduct research. One effect of this is a further separation of the teaching and research roles of academics. Increasingly, specialist research centers are established to conduct the research and attract the revenue and take groups of academics out of teaching.

Fifth, the casualization of research in universities must be recognized more generally as a deskilling process that increasingly separates academics from the research they produce, akin to the classic Marxist process of alienation. As research (inside and outside universities) becomes increasingly managed by small elite groups of research capitalists, the researcher becomes less likely to have control over the whole process of inquiry (Harvie, 2000). The research process is increasingly characterized by a division of labor whereby researchers are given the task of completing atomized elements of the project: selecting problems and methods, sampling, conducting fieldwork, interpreting results and so on. And the way that the project is formed, the way it takes shape and what it looks like in various forms for dissemination may no longer be in the hands of the researcher, but in the hands of those who employ and manage the researcher.

## Criminology in the Service of the State?

To this point, we have mostly spoken about social science in general terms as opposed to focusing more specifically upon criminology and criminal justice. We must do so, however briefly, not least because to some extent these latter disciplines are quite peculiar. One set of reasons for this peculiarity of criminology (and, to an even greater extent, its more applied offspring, criminal justice) is that it has had since its very inception an extremely intimate, indeed subservient, relationship to the state. If this is generally true for social science as a whole, it is peculiarly marked in the case of criminology and criminal justice.

In a now famous passage, Foucault has claimed that "the *whole content* of criminology—with its 'garrulous discourse' and 'endless repetitions' —is to be explained with reference to its application by the powerful" (quoted in S. Cohen, 1981: 220):

> Have you ever read any criminology text? . . . They are staggering. And I say this out of astonishment, not aggressiveness, because I fail to comprehend how the discourse of criminology has been able to go on at this level. One has the impression that it is of such utility, is needed so urgently and rendered so vital for the working of the system, that it does not even need to seek a theoretical justification for itself, or even a coherent framework. It is entirely utilitarian. (Foucault, quoted in S. Cohen, 1981: 220)

For Garland, its relationship to power is a defining feature of criminology, which is "shaped only to a small extent by its own theoretical object and logic of inquiry. Its epistemological threshold is a low one, making it susceptible to pressures and interests generated elsewhere" (Garland, 1994: 28).

This intimate relationship between criminology on the one hand, and the demands of the state and power on the other, has seriously infected the character of British criminology, a character which is long-standing and relatively resistant to change (S. Cohen, 1981).[13] Even in the early 1980s it was suggested that British criminology was becoming even more pragmatic:

> [T]he Home Office Research Unit, the research branches of the prison department, the Metropolitan Police and allied state agencies have all expanded and become more pro-

fessional and productive. This is particularly notable given the decline of government support for social science research. In line with what happened in the United States over this decade [the 1970s], the content of this type of criminology has switched (and is likely to switch even more) in the direction of "criminal justice": that is to say, an exclusive concern with the operation of the system. Research deals mainly with matters of decision-making, manpower, evaluation and classification. (S. Cohen, 1981: 236)

Thus there are good reasons to suggest that the general shifts identified above—the marketization and commodification of knowledge—have worked upon academic criminology as much as, if not more than, on most other disciplines across and indeed beyond the social sciences. Rock, for example, examining the "Social Organization of British Criminology" (Rock, 1994; Rock and Holdaway, 1998), identifies the period of expansion of British higher education in the latter half of the 1980s as a crucial moment: it produced, among other things, a younger, smaller generation of criminologists that "came to preoccupy itself with hunting grants for empirical research'"(Rock, 1994: 135):

> [A] growing proportion of criminologists were becoming increasingly dependent on soft money, obliged to work on short-term contracts to supply research to order for government departments, statutory agencies, and voluntary organizations. (Rock and Holdaway, 1998: 9–10)

Moreover, the research agendas set by these professionals are heavily influenced by their acceptance of the growing problem of crime—and this is, by and large, crime as defined by the state (Rock and Holdaway, 1998: 7–9), about which we shall say more below.

These explicit links to state definitions of crime and to the notion of crime as a growing problem help to explain why criminology and criminal justice in the UK are currently in the midst of a boom period. Criminal justice and criminology degree programs are recruiting students (from both the criminal justice professions and schools and further education colleges) in large numbers. Two new UK-based journals publishing in the discipline have been launched in the last four years: *Theoretical Criminology* in 1997 and *Criminal Justice Policy* in 2000. Another measure of this "boom" in criminology is the exponential growth of Home Office funding for criminological research in recent years.

There is little evidence that the Home Office[14] Research Development Statistics (RDS) unit intends to redress the state/corporate crime lacuna that we discussed earlier in this chapter. Indeed, the Home Office's recent record in relation to investigating forms of serious crime which implicate powerful corporations or state servants is striking. A catalogue of Home Office research reports gives us a quantitative indication of this record (Home Office, 2002). The catalogue details a total of 571 research reports published by the Home Office since 1988 and still in print in April 2002.[15] Within this research output, there are 10 reports which deal with crimes *against* businesses, but none—*not one single report*—which deals with crimes which have been committed by legitimate businesses. Given the priority afforded to the rhetoric of "evidence-based policy," this is a glaring omission. The almost complete absence of research addressing serious state and corporate crime has continued even within the context of a steep rise in the total numbers of publications in recent years. Reports with publication dates of 1998 and 1999 number 116, whilst reports with publications dates of 2000 and 2001 total 221.[16]

Much of what has actually been a recent boom in Home Office funding, resulting in this proliferation of research reports, has occurred in response to the need to evaluate the activities of the growing numbers of local criminal justice "partnerships" (see Crawford, 1997, 1998; Hughes, 1998) and initiatives funded by the Crime Reduction Programme (Home Office, 2000a). Thus the external research budget of the Home Office RDS increased by over 500% in two years, from £2,754,000 in 1998/99 to £17,013,000 in 2000/01 (personal communication, RDS, 23 October 2000). The RDS personnel themselves attribute this increase in funding to the current government's enthusiasm for "evidence-led policy" (personal communication, RDS, 5 December 2000).

The detail of this budget suggests that this funding is actually much more tightly controlled and carefully targeted than should be the case on the basis of the open, pluralistic and responsive government suggested by the bureaucratese term "evidence-led policy." The largest single area of work that accounts for the huge increase in the RDS budget is the government's Crime Reduction Programme, a Home Office pool of funding worth £250m (made available after the 1998 government spending review) which is open to competitive bids from local crime prevention partnerships. The RDS is allocated £2.5m in running costs for the administration of the Crime Reduction Programme, and £9–£10m ring-fenced to fund projects in the program (ibid.), largely targeted at the evaluation and technical development of methods of situational crime prevention (for example, geographical information systems, closed-circuit television, and so on). A further £1.9m of the RDS budget is ring-fenced for drug research (Home Office, 2000b). Thus, it is apparent that almost every penny of the 500% increase in the RDS budget is allocated to policy areas that remain tightly organized around the crime reduction or war on drugs agendas. This is money that academics involved in criminological research are, in conditions of austerity, under intensifying pressure to bid for—in increasing numbers of cases, and either in fact or in effect, simply to secure employment.

## The Research Process

Our contention throughout this chapter is that the relative lack of scrutiny of corporate crime and state crime—indicated above—is not an inexplicable quirk.

Thus far, we have attempted to provide an explanation for these absences through macro-considerations whereby certain research questions are defined as useful, pressing and legitimate, others as futile, irrelevant or illegitimate. These considerations have been introduced at the level of hegemony and hegemony construction and then at the level of government policy towards higher education and social science research in general, and criminological research in particular. In this section, we turn to the micro-processes through which hegemony is constructed and reconstructed on a day-to-day, highly practical basis.

Our starting-point, then, following Hughes, Jupp, Lee and others, is that sponsors—by which we mean those who demand, support, recognize as legitimate, fund, facilitate and seek to disseminate—help to create research agendas. In this creation, as some questions are organized *onto* agendas, others are by definition organized *off* these agendas. Now, while some of this organizing is highly conscious on the part of individuals and organizations who sponsor research activity, it would be wrong to cast this process as simply—or even largely—one involving direct or conscious manipulation. Certainly, concerted agency on the part of individuals and institutions frequently takes place. But the key issue about the creation and reproduction of research agendas is much more fundamental than simply the hands-on control that the powerful are able to wield; rather, it is their by-and-large taken for granted nature. Certain questions seem "naturally" to fall within the boundaries of the legitimate, feasible and acceptable, and generally questions beyond those boundaries tend not to be raised, or if they are raised they are not taken seriously. This is, after all, one of the mechanisms by which the process of hegemony operates. In other words, while we do not dismiss the role of agency, we are talking about power operating in a structural fashion here.[17]

### Regulating Funding: The Construction of Feasible Enquiry

We wish to avoid the impression—and indeed such an impression is directly undermined in many of the contributions to this text—that what we have argued to this point renders funded research as having no value, or suggests that the funder is all-powerful. Neither is the case. We certainly need to be somewhat more sensitive here about how funded research is defined—the distinction drawn by Sanders (1997) between "policy-relevant" and "policy-led" or policy-driven research, where the former is much less problematic than the latter, seems to us to be a useful one. Nor should consideration of the power of funders obscure the fact that researchers do not always supply funders with what they want. Further, we should be wary of casting funders as a homogeneous group: for example, even state departments such as the Home Office and the Health and Safety Executive are far from being monolithic, undifferentiated entities, and they should not be cast as such.

Following Hughes (1996), we should also emphasize that we do not imply here that one can simply read off or assume certain effects from the existence of a particular funder. But at the same time, to explore the issue of funding is to argue that we at least need to ask who or what the funder of a particular piece of research is in order to evaluate it—even if, in terms of our more macro-level argument regarding the production and reproduction of research agendas congruent with the existent hegemonic compromise, the key issue is not individual funders but more the *overall* sources and directions of research funding.

It is therefore crucial to make a distinction between research that is conducted generally within the boundaries of acceptability and feasibility, and research that is conducted under highly prescriptive conditions. Following others, then, we would argue that almost two decades of Conservative government, followed by a new Labour administration which is firmly located within the problematic of neo-liberal political economy, have seen the terrain of acceptable academic discourse shift to the right (Hillyard and Sim, 1997). One of the consequences of this shift has been to place even upon critical work a greater demand for suggesting immediate and feasible reform rather than for conclusions of fundamental and societal critique. Further, as we have seen, the UK has been the site of considerable reordering of relationships between academic research and sources of funding. These have largely tended to render any form of critical, partisan social science in general, and criminology in particular, less rather than more likely.

The definitions of both feasible reform and utility are increasingly open to influence by those who provide funding for research. Indeed, the availability of funding affects not simply the use of the outcomes of research but the type of research that does (and does not) get done. In this context, the distinction between official and critical research becomes more significant (Harvey, 1990).

As we have argued in previous sections, under neo-liberal conditions, the tightening of government control over research agendas over the past two decades has had the effect of intensifying demand for utilizable and policy-relevant research findings. An intensifying demand for policy-relevant research findings has narrowed the scope for asking politically sensitive research questions, or for focusing upon more fundamental or long-term issues. One effect of this is that state-funded research projects increasingly tend to be empiricist and a-theoretical. This trend also has a constraining effect in terms of defining what is and what isn't possible to achieve, or even suggest, in terms of the reform or development of policy (Hillyard and Sim, 1997: 56–57).

Aside from these general points regarding funding, there are particular issues pertaining to possible funding of research into the illegal activities of the powerful. It is perhaps a truism to note that private capital is, all things being equal, not likely to be enthusiastic about sponsoring research into the activities of private corporations! Yet we also need to be clear that corporate crime research does not necessarily look particularly attractive from the viewpoint of state funders either. For when we are speaking of academic attention to corporate crime, it is also clear that we are speaking of attention directed to states and state agencies. This is much more than simply a reference to the effect of the state's regulatory functions. Rather, understanding corporate crime raises methodological, empirical and theoretical questions that lead us to enquire into state-capital relationships. Within capitalism, an economic order based upon private property with markets in capital and in labor, the limited liability corporation remains the main legal mechanism through which capital is brought together and interacts in various marketplaces. Thus, corporations are artificial entities created for the mobilization, utilization, and protection of capital within recent socio-historical state formations, entities whose very existence is provided for and maintained through the state via legal institutions and instruments, which in turn are based upon material and ideological supports. The corporate form and the state are thus inextricably linked. The nature, visibility and treatment of corporate crime can be approached only within a broader understanding of social constructions of crime and criminality, and in relation to the key role played in the development and maintenance of such constructions by states in general and key state institutions in particular.

Thus, critical attention to corporate crime entails critical attention to states.[18] If the research is itself funded by the state, then clear tensions are raised. Without descending into crude instrumentalism, it seems clear to us that certain implications do follow from state funding of academic research, implications which are of particular consequence for critical researchers. That the state does not relish the scrutiny of researchers who may present a particularly critical or even complex view of the role and activities of its institutions is no longer a controversial point. It has been well established through the experience of numerous researchers over the years, particularly in criminology (for example, Baldwin and McConville, 1977; Cohen and Taylor, 1977; Scraton et al., 1991; see also *The Guardian*, 4 July 1994). But we should also be aware that, on one front, the neo-liberal project has made significant gains in assimilating social research into the "official" or business-friendly policy environment which rewards anyone who is "one of us" (Hillyard and Sim, 1997: 58).[19]

Once a group of researchers, or a university "department," to use a generic term, enters into a funding relationship with a state department, a research council, or corporate grant holders, then it must accept that its research activities will, to some extent, be structured by those who hold the purse-strings (Whyte, 2000). For many university departments that rely upon external funding, their future success may be gauged by their ability to secure and retain financial support from government and corporate sources. Given the value currently placed by research councils upon the securing of research grants, loss of funding may also effectively have a "double" impact in terms of a department's ability to win funding from Research

Assessment Exercises. It follows that since loss of this funding may have implications for the long-term sustainability of a university department's research output, the "success" of a department's research may be measured ultimately by the degree to which funders are satisfied with the output. With this measure as a primary performance indicator, it may become difficult to distinguish between the role of management consultancies and the role of some groups of researchers in universities (see Whyte, 1999: 54–58).

Indeed, this whole process can generate a perverse relationship between means and ends in the context of academic research. The relationship between funding and research activity has generally been viewed as one whereby the funding is the means to secure the end, namely, the carrying out of the research project. We at least wish to suggest here, despite the fact that we have not yet attempted to subject this claim to empirical scrutiny, that the apparently increasing search for external funding on the part of academics may be reversing this research-funding relationship: that is, funding may no longer be the means to conducting research for some researchers; rather, the research may be seen as a means to the end which is securing funding. In the context of a higher education system where a variety of sources of income, beyond those attached to student recruitment, is desperately sought, where departments and individuals are assessed partly on the basis of the levels of income generated (whether internally, by management, or externally, via Research Assessment Exercises), and where fixed-term contracts seem to be increasingly prevalent, the pressure to see research income as an end is enormous. In other words, once a grant has been received there may be a tendency to become concerned less with the research activity at hand, and more with the need to secure *subsequent* funding. This perceived (indeed, for many researchers in universities, real) need may infect the nature and quality of the research being conducted, whether consciously or not.

### Regulating "Access": Power, Control, Exclusion

For criminologists, the most obvious methodological problem likely to be encountered is that of access to offenders and sites of offending. Of course, access to offenders is problematic for researchers of conventional crime. Yet in comparison with offenders or potential offenders in the context of corporate and state crime, conventional crime researchers are dealing with the relatively powerless, and this, whether we like it or not, renders such work immediately more feasible than dealing with, and seeking to focus upon, the relatively powerful. As Hughes has noted, studying relatively powerless groups is much more common than studying elite groups (G. Hughes, 1996: 77). One reason for this is that, quite simply, "the inner sanctum of the company boardroom and the senior management enclaves within corporate hierarchies still remain a largely closed and secretive world" (Reed, 1989: 79, quoted in Punch, 1996: 4). The same could be said for the corridors of the civil service and other parts of state and government, at both national and local levels. And if we accept the accuracy of this observation by Reed and its generalization to state bodies, then it should be apparent that the inner sanctum is likely to be even more tightly sealed from outside scrutiny when the aim of the outside researcher is to investigate actual or possible illegality.

Of course, access to such sanctums may be pursued. In the case of access to state or public bodies, gaining formal access can often be a highly proceduralized or legalistic affair (G. Hughes, 1996: 69). This is not to say that access is impossible. At least for reasons of legitimacy, state and public bodies may need to provide some rationale for denying access, though, as we shall see below, such rationales are hardly in short supply and often rather unconvincing. Moreover, this proceduralism often means that if access is secured, it may have highly restrictive effects—for example, the signing of the Official Secrets Act, or the requirement to make available for comment material prior to publication. On the other hand, private corporations are literally private entities to which the vast majority of us have no rights of access, making access to such sites much more difficult to secure.

Methods of generating data that do not rely upon the cooperation of corporations or the state, while highly preferable, are not always easy to identify. The study of the powerful can be greatly enhanced by the utilization of sources of data held and controlled by powerful organizations themselves. The availability of such data clearly varies over time, and from one nation-state to another. Certainly, in the context of the British state, this may cause particular problems. Historically, Britain has held, and still holds, the dubious honor of being the most secretive of all liberal democracies (Rogers, 1997; see also Leigh, 1980; Michael, 1982).

The state's self-defined role as the protector of the public/national interest allows it a great deal of leeway over what it wants researchers to see. Denial of access in the interests of "public safety," "the prevention and detection of crime," "national security," or even the "economic well-being of the nation" may be cited as formal reasons to preclude disclosure. These obstacles become more significant the greater the potential or perceived threat that is posed to state legitimacy by certain forms of social research.[20]

Of course, there is no obligation in the first instance for the state or for corporations to provide information on request. If such a request is declined, there is very little by way of legal remedy, save the very long and difficult (and for those reasons, rare) process of judicial review. Private corporations enjoy almost complete rights of ownership to information about their activities, save the requirement to submit the names and addresses of directors and basic annual financial returns to the public register at UK Companies House. In this sense, the very legal constitution of corporations is designed to avoid public disclosure of the details of their activities.

Further elements of power come into play in the consideration of requests for access. Relevant considerations may include who is making the request, so that issues of status are taken into account—it is a generalization, but one could argue that a researcher from Cambridge or Harvard is more likely to gain access to inner sanctums than is a researcher from Liverpool John Moores University. Ironically, issues of funding may also come into play. Again, it is reasonable to suggest that research with the backing of funding from the Home Office or the ESRC carries greater weight in securing access than research being carried out largely through departmental budgets or—even worse—from monies secured from some so-called "pressure group." Also likely to come into play are the background and credentials of the researcher. Certainly in attempts to gain access to certain parts of the state, there will be formal checking of individuals' histories. Researchers who are not deemed to be "safe" or "friendly" by those organizations to which they seek access face a series of tactics designed to frustrate and obstruct their inquiry and marginalize their viewpoint.

The point about all of these factors is that they are likely to militate against those wishing to conduct critical research—let alone research into the illegal activities of states and corporations—being able to secure the access they desire or require. *If* a researcher hails from an elite university as opposed to an old polytechnic or further education college; *if* a researcher has a grant from a state or quasi-state funding body; *if* a researcher is (and has been) committed to conducting research which is not to be used for "political" purposes;[21] *if* a researcher can show her or himself not to intend to be critical where others have been in the past, then all these factors are likely to help in securing access. Now, although this is a generalization, it is reasonable to say that *all* of these factors are more likely to characterize mainstream research, rather than critical work or research into corporate and state illegality.

Moreover, whether or not access is granted to social researchers, the opportunities afforded to corporations to obscure their structures, decision-making processes, lines of accountability, knowledge, and responsibility are socially and legally constructed in ways that limit, to say the least, opportunities for locating and understanding corporate illegality. As we have indicated above, one might think that the same observation could not be made of the state. Up to a point state structures are more transparent, so that access to people, records, statistics and so on should be easier. But in one sense this is becoming less the case. For what we have witnessed in Britain in the past 25 years or so is increasing complexity in state structures at both national and local levels. The proliferation of a range of nonelected bodies, the increasing trend to the appointment of nonelected individuals to formally accountable structures, the mushrooming of public-private partnerships and so on all make the job of locating responsibility (let alone acting upon it) much more difficult for researchers. More generally, these developments make it problematic to identify precisely what *constitutes* the state, which is in itself a problem for social research on the state.

This blurring of state boundaries throws a rather different light on the point made above, namely, that, since most government departments and state institutions have, as public authorities, some form of formal transparency in the form of public accountability, there tends to be more scope for scrutiny by research. With the exception of the limited registration information held at Companies House and the published annual accounts of quoted companies, there is no responsibility placed upon private corporations to disclose information. Information gathered by the government, such as compliance information or tax returns, is in the main protected by that most mercurial of catch-all clauses, "commercial confidentiality." In many of the areas of public service where the private sector has encroached, the clause of commercial confidentiality prevents disclosure of information that was previously publicly available. Thus, for example, details of contracts between the Prison Service and private companies that now run private jails may be hidden from the public—indeed, aspects of private prison management may even be withheld from state servants (see Sim et al., 1995). During the writing of this chapter, the authors requested from the Home Office RDS the names of institutions and consultants under contract to conduct research. The request was denied on grounds of commercial confidentiality (personal communication, 16 October 2000).

Where access *is* successfully negotiated, this can quickly reveal itself as more apparent than real. As Jupp (1989) notes, often within organizations there are hierarchies of gatekeepers to be negotiated, with hierarchies of power and authority distributed among them. Professor Hugh Pennington found precisely this after he was appointed by the government to lead an inquiry into an outbreak of e-coli in Lanarkshire (Scotland) which killed 18 people. He was given access to all relevant government-held documents, but later found that key reports that detailed the filthy conditions of abattoirs were withheld by civil servants keen to avoid rigorous criticism of the industry and of poor regulatory standards (*Daily Record,* 7 March 1997). Thus the problem of access does not end once you are "in"; it can be a continual process of negotiation and renegotiation. Formal access is often, then, only the beginning of securing real or adequate access (Jupp, 1989: 134). We suggest that while these are common issues, they are more starkly raised when the objects of research are the powerful. Certainly, the possibility of deliberate obfuscation on the part of the researched is greater where one is dealing with individuals who are often well-educated, possess highly developed social skills, are socialized into particular ideologies and cultures and so on.

All in all, gaining access is highly problematic. Of course, while methodological issues such as gaining access from the "outside," the role of gatekeepers and the cooperation of the researched are common across social research (Bryman, 1988), the extent to which they may, or do, prove problematic varies according to the context. Thus the argument being made here is that in general there are good reasons to expect it to be more difficult to research the relatively powerful, where such research involves access to the powerful themselves.

## Disseminating Research on the Crimes of the Powerful

We began this chapter with an indication of the dearth of published work within criminology and criminal justice around the crimes of the powerful. Our arguments thus far—regarding the nature of hegemony and hegemony construction, the roles of intellectuals and universities, the increasing marketization of universities and the commodification of "knowledge," the trends towards funding research of immediate utility and our observations upon the nature of the research process—all help to explain this dearth of work. However, there is a final set of issues to be considered here. For where research on the crimes of the powerful *is* successfully conducted, then there remains the problem of disseminating that knowledge, which for university academics usually entails the struggle to have that work published in some form.

If some of the processes of exclusion are conscious, some are more subtle. Thus, for example, Arrigo has referred, with echoes of the process of hegemony construction and maintenance, to "a suppressor effect." Given that part of the struggle of critical criminology "is with dominant ideologies and how they are sustained through various means of communication," and that the marginalization of critical as compared with mainstream criminology is one function of a "journal-industrial complex," he claims that there exists a

> general "suppressor" effect operating within and throughout the Academy, particularly when critical scholarship is repeatedly denied recognition and thus legitimacy in the leading periodicals of our discipline. This is the presence of hegemony in the academy. What counts as "serious" scholarship and, hence, what is actively engaged in by critical criminologists is, all too often, circumscribed by the "chilling effect" found in the seemingly systematic exclusionary practices enacted and sustained by the more prestigious periodicals of our field. (Arrigo, 2000: 1)

In short, both conscious and unconscious efforts and assumptions may operate—often in combination—to exclude certain forms of work from prestigious publications and thereby reinforce the illegitimacy of this work.

Of course, there are other, highly conscious, processes whereby academic work on corporate and state crimes is prevented from reaching a public audience. These include the threat or use of libel laws and resort to the use of the Official Secrets Act among other forms of legal action and censorship. Taking the issue of libel and other legal action on the part of the powerful designed to prevent publication which might expose their illegal activities, it is clear that recourse to law was part of a concerted effort by corporations to respond to the emergence of social activism and criticism in the late 1960s and the 1970s. This counterattack was itself facilitated by the general sociopolitical shift to the right in both Britain and North America (which in itself has inhibited corporate crime research). There is also reason to think that criminology will be the subject of legal control as much as—if not more than—any other field of social scientific study. For, as Carson has noted in relation to an attempt by the Australian attorney general to censor two papers presented at the 1996 Australian and New Zealand Society of Criminology Conference,

> Academic freedom in the field of criminology is perhaps even more problematic and more important than quite a few areas of academic endeavor because it's touching the State at a raw nerve. . . . Almost automatically, if we are studying crime, we are messing around with some of the most powerful constructs the State has at its disposal. (Carson, quoted in Presdee and Walters, 1998: 158)

Censorship of research findings remains a frequent state response to those who produce government-funded work that does not sit comfortably with government or departmental policy. Indeed, where the research is funded by government, censorship does not always require the threat of legal action. Several examples of "straight" censorship have been exposed in the UK media in recent years. A Department of Health–funded guide for employers on mental health and stress in the workplace (Cooper and Cartwright, 1995) was printed and ready for distribution, but was pulped on the instruction of government ministers because it contained the following offending statement: "Research has shown that working more than 48 hours a week doubles the rate of coronary heart disease" (Cooper and Cartwright, 1995: 12). The government was involved in a legal challenge to Europe's Working Time Directive, which sought to regulate working hours. In September 1994, *Guardian* reporter Alan Travis discovered that the Home Office had delayed, censored, postponed, or shelved no fewer than eight pieces of research because the results did not support government policy. Amongst this research was one report concluding that young black men were less likely to commit crime than their white counterparts, and another challenging the idea that asylum seekers tend to be economic rather than political immigrants (Travis, 1994). A report prepared by the European Union on torture and degrading treatment by UK police forces was censored by the government in January 2000. It was apparently the first of its kind to be published with passages blanked out. The material that was removed included details of the Metropolitan Police solicitors' advice on disciplining officers involved in cases of police brutality (Dyer, 2000).

Such considerations are also relevant in terms of corporate crime, which entails researching and confronting "powerful political and economic interests" (Kramer, 1989: 152). Certainly corporate crime researchers and activists have always faced the real or putative power of corporations. The potential use of libel laws in the USA was, after all, one reason behind Sutherland's decision to remove the names of offending companies and one chapter of case histories from the original version of *White-Collar Crime* (Geis and Goff, 1983: x–xi). The publication of Braithwaite's (1984) classic study, *Corporate Crime in the Pharmaceutical Industry*, was delayed for two years when managers whom he had interviewed used lawyers to haggle over "300 empirical claims that might be raised in court" (Punch, 1996: 44).

If we shift beyond the relatively conservative confines of the academy, we find that when faced with charges of criminality, corporations are hardly averse to flexing their not-inconsiderable muscle. Perhaps most famously, Hoffman-La Roche confronted the whistle-blower Stanley Adams with legal action, and despite the company being found guilty of the price-fixing to which he had drawn public attention, Adams was imprisoned for industrial espionage, was bankrupted, and lost his wife to suicide (Adams, 1984). Solicitor Louise Christian faced an 18-month investigation by the Law Society, following a complaint by Railtrack over a press release citing the company's "callous disregard for safety" following the Ladbroke Grove inquiry. Having been fully cleared of professional misconduct, she warned of a general use by powerful private interests of the disciplinary processes of the Law Society and Bar Council to silence or intimidate critics (Dyer, 2002). British Airways' campaign of dirty tricks—a euphemism for criminal attacks and espionage—against Virgin employees is well documented (Gregory, 1994). Even more recently, there has been an upsurge in the use of strategic lawsuits against public participation (Beder, 1997; Monbiot, 1997; Rowell, 1996; Vick and Campbell, 2001), which have been developed partly as a means of pre-empting even the need to resort to libel laws, which as McDonalds found in the celebrated "McLibel" case can be highly costly and, some would argue, ultimately counterproductive (Vidal, 1997).

In particular, corporations have become adept at launching propaganda campaigns to discredit and enforce the withdrawal of research findings by deploying resources that invariably dwarf the resources available to those who conduct critical research. A recent campaign by the tobacco company Philip Morris, said to be funded to the tune of $2m, operated with the express intention of discrediting a World Health Organization study of the effects of smoking upon health. The campaign sought consultants that would provide alternative scientific opinions, and then fed false information to the press about the findings of the study (see Bosely, 2000: 1). Similarly, a small number of academic experts recruited by the oil and coal mining industries have been at the head of a recent campaign to discredit dominant scientific opinion on the positive relationship between the use of fossil fuels and the greenhouse effect, a campaign which included the launching of an electronic scientific journal, to be called *World Climate Review* (Gelbspan, 1997: 3).

In addition to threats to the production of certain types of knowledge deemed commercially sensitive, ever-closer links between corporations and universities may also render certain research results politically sensitive. In a university department in which we have both worked, one academic received national news coverage for his (critical) comments on the senior management of a locally based corporation. The academic was, within hours of the broadcast, ordered by his head of department and by senior management of the university not to allow his research findings to reach media sources, or even to comment publicly on matters relating to his research interest without first gaining approval from the university press office. It was made clear that if this order was breached, he would face disciplinary proceedings. The corporation in question happened to be the largest single private funder of the university.

Of course, the use of a variety of highly developed extralegal techniques to stifle publicity and attack the credibility of critics has not only been directed at the research community. Far from it. Exposes by investigative journalists and film makers, campaigns by activist groups and trade unions are likely to meet counteroffensive tactics that include the use of corporate espionage, smear campaigns and enforced media silence, more often than not in breach of criminal law.[22] For all its sophisticated forms of operation, class power can work in very crude forms indeed.

The phenomena considered in this section all serve to make it less rather than more likely that a critical social science, let alone criminology, of corporate and state crime will be developed within Britain or the USA. The relative exclusion of published work from mainstream criminology texts and journals is another element of disciplinary boundary maintenance. The relative marginalization of work on corporate and state crime reinforces the construction of a discipline within which such issues are marginal or peripheral, and in this way minimizes the scrutiny to which the illegal activities of the powerful are subject. This emerging political economy of research will influence what work is done, where it is done, how it is done, who funds it, by whom it is done, why it is done, and what ends up being done with it. This new political economy does not bode well for a critical academic assault upon corporate and state crime. Yet such an assault is crucial.

## Conclusion: Scrutinizing the Crimes of the Powerful

We are not implying that the disciplinary effects of marketization and commodification have eradicated the space in which alternative research agendas can be developed. Certainly, as the contributions to this text demonstrate, there are good empirical reasons for resisting such a pessimistic conclusion. It is not the case that the effects of marketization under a new binary divide, if this is what we can call the division between specialist research institutions and teaching institutions, have created the same conditions in all institutions. In fact, this process is at different stages of advancement across the sector (see M. Edwards, 1998: 260) and there is still considerable space within higher education to conduct relatively "independent" research, particularly in departments that continue to preserve the link between teaching and research. Furthermore, as Epstein has noted, although critical research may not be having much of an impact upon the culture of universities, even under difficult conditions "a surprising number of faculty manage to sustain some connection to progressive activism outside the university" (Epstein, 2001: 201).

Of course, from the outset, the neo-liberal assault upon the universities in Western democracies has unfolded with little or no opportunity for participation in political debate in the public arena, or within internal university decision-making structures (Newson and Buchbinder, 1988). But this is not to say that the process of marketization of the universities has gone unchallenged. For example, in both the USA and Canada, organized student resistance won a series of victories in the 1990s in struggles to obstruct the rampant march of business through the universities. This resistance has been led by a series of newly emergent organizations such as the Student Environment Action Coalition (which investigates university environmental and health and safety records, and the environmental impact of industry-university partnerships), the War Research Information Service (linking campus protests during the Iraqi conflicts), and the National Coalition of Universities in the Public Interest (providing student organizations with information on military and industrial links to the university) (Ovetz, 1996: 136–42).[23] At the University of Wisconsin, opposition to a gagging clause introduced on the back of a Reebok college merchandise deal was successful. Reebok's clause preventing college staff and students from criticizing the company in public (Soley, 1998: 232) was dropped after a campaign to expose the company's appalling record on labor rights (Klein, 2000: 97). At the University of Texas-Austin, a campaign that linked up with community activists managed to prevent toxic waste dumping on a number of sites. Key to the campaign was the establishment of links with other groups struggling against the same corporation, Freeport McMoRan, in Louisiana, and in West Papua, Indonesia (Ovetz, 1996: 141). In other cases, academics have shown that it is possible to take on corporations that seek to gag them, and indeed win, not least through publicly exposing corporate censorship (Klein, 2000: 99–100).

In an empirical sense, then, the march of neo-liberalism through the universities is neither inevitable nor unstoppable. Moreover, in a theoretical sense, it is inconceivable that the marketization of the universities will proceed unobstructed. For one thing, as we argued above, the Gramscian concept of hegemony alerts us to the fact that dominance is never complete nor entirely secure, but always open to challenge and resistance. Given that corporations and the state continue to require a heavily subsidized publicly funded education system, it is likely the universities will continue to receive state subsidies for as long as they are required to perform a technological and educative role for capital. They will therefore be required, at one level, to account for the public subsidy that this entails. In this sense, the universities will remain an important site for struggle, and one where the contradictions inherent in the dominant representation of the function of universities as educative, independent, acting in the public interest, and so on can be regularly and effectively exposed.

Indeed, the very processes of marketization render explicit the contradictory nature of the university within capitalist social orders—particularly between the ways in which universities' existence is represented and/or legitimated, and in terms of the rather schizophrenic ways in which they, and the academic staff within them, act. Certainly, there are several closely related reasons which indicate why universities cannot *simply* act as unfettered subjects of the market in the way that some other commercial operations might.

First, universities, particularly older universities, have constructed for themselves long and proud histories, based upon reputations for the quality of their product, whether in terms of their teaching or their research. In this sense, there is reason to believe that the marketization of the universities has a limit; universities can never act as "pure" commercial concerns, responding to the demands of corporations, without losing control over the quality of their product. A university which attempted to act purely commercially would at some point find itself losing market share in terms of both students and research grants—and would, in any case, be unattractive for private capital since one of the key commodities that such capital buys from universities is precisely the reputation for, or claims to, relative independence, objectivity and so on.

Second, for all the drive towards utility in research activity and output, states themselves require universities to continue to meet ideological expectations of acting as "independent" voices, and thus require university research to air voices that are critical of existing social, economic and political arrangements. Thus, liberal claims of state neutrality dictate that some funding be granted to critical voices, even where these are voices of resistance, since the liberal state must at least be seen to be supporting and acting on behalf of those who claim to take seriously its ideals of greater social equality, social justice and democratic accountability.[24]

Third, universities, as publicly funded institutions, remain rather more vulnerable to public opinion than private corporations. This aspect of higher education institutions creates the space for critical debate. For example, in relation to the British American Tobacco (BAT)/Nottingham University case, public opposition was voiced by pressure groups such as Action on Smoking and Health and back-bench Members of Parliament. This opposition was effective enough to prompt a call from the government's PR Standards Council to boycott BAT-sponsored courses in other universities (*The Guardian,* 8 December 2000). Relatedly, the fact of continuing public funding for universities does still render them partially accountable, at least in principle. Even if we know that public bodies, including universities, can and do regularly evade accountability, we also know that they can be reformed to improve standards of accountability: this is much more difficult in the case of the private sector, where companies have a fiduciary duty to their shareholders, are subject to the unrelenting imperatives of the stock market, and resist external scrutiny via the corporate veil and claims of commercial confidentiality.

Fourth, as (partially) publicly funded bodies, universities still retain some ideological commitment to democratic forms of management and functioning, and there remain some structural features which reflect these commitments. One such aspect is the existence of tenure or tenure-type arrangements in various countries' higher education systems. A second is the continued existence of academic trade unions: it remains the case that unions are recognized and nationally agreed conditions of service operate throughout many higher education systems. A third aspect is the persistence of some form of employee representation on boards and management committees and other quasi-democratic governance structures. Now, this is not to claim that such arrangements are in practice or necessarily democratic, nor to deny that each has also been subject to considerable erosion; but it is to recognize that these structures persist, that they are worth defending (and, of course, seeking to extend) and that their existence is intimately related to the ideological cloth in which universities wrap themselves.

Notwithstanding these contradictions, this chapter has sought to document how the current trends that we are witnessing have the effect of closing down political debate. These trends also bring with them highly damaging implications for the quality of academic social inquiry more generally. The commodification of research is eroding the value of research that is rigorous, is thorough, and seeks to retain an objective distance from vested interest. It is the last point that is of most significance here. Once more, we wish to stress that those developments have implications for distinctions between traditional and organic intellectual work. Put bluntly, the organic quality of academic research is increasingly revealed in the relationship between researchers and their funders. This reinforces our earlier argument that the conditions under which academic researchers work are increasingly forcing us to make "organic" choices in terms of how our research seeks to engage in the "real" world. Certainly, the ability to act and cast oneself as a traditional intellectual has become diminished in the marketized, politicized world of the contemporary university. For us, there is a clear choice, as research becomes increasingly and organically tied to the imperatives of the powerful (via the use of contractual conditions and obligations and more loosely circumscribed hegemonic processes)—it has become yet more crucial for critical researchers to seek organic ties to counter-hegemonic movements. The following chapters each contribute to our understanding of what such counter-hegemonic activities, or intellectual work of resistance, entail, and we shall further address this issue in our concluding chapter, as well as considering the prospects of "success" for such a strategy.

In our view, this volume, taken together, may further such acts of resistance. Specifically, the chapters collected here seek to achieve a number of aims. First, throughout the chapters, contributors identify the key methodological, theoretical and epistemological problems entailed in researching crime and the powerful. One aim of this text is to emphasize the dynamic nature of these issues and problems. Second, the text aims to place methods and methodologies within a broader political economy of academic work. Third, the text seeks to identify and develop ways in which the obstacles to critical criminology and critical social science—in particular, work on crimes of states and corporations—might be overcome, and this is a task to which we return in the concluding chapter. Fourth, throughout the chapters, and in the conclusion, there is a sustained attempt to develop an argument for, and at least highlight some of the elements of, a partisan criminology. Within such a criminology, notions of value freedom are rejected yet demands of rigor are maintained, while historically dominant understandings of the role of academics and universities are challenged. Fifth, taken as a whole, the contributions here contribute to academic understandings of what power is, how power operates and who can legitimately be labelled "powerful."

By addressing these aims, this book seeks to map out the parameters of a political economy of researching the powerful, both delineating the major problems facing those who would subject the powerful to scrutiny, and beginning to identify concrete ways in which these problems might be overcome or circumnavigated. To this end, the book brings together material that is entirely original and has been prepared specifically for this volume. The content of the text has a genuinely international quality, drawing upon contributions that speak from experiences in Britain, Ireland, Spain, Finland, Turkey, Canada and the USA. Crucially, each contribution is based upon contemporary practical experience of, and critical reflection upon, attempts to research "the powerful." Taken together, the contributions represent valuable combinations of the empirical and the theoretical, the analytical and the prescriptive.

## Notes

1. This argument is developed at length in Pearce and Tombs, 2001.
2. We will refrain from referring to individual chapters in this introduction. Many of the issues that we raise are developed in detail in the chapters and in the conclusion to this volume.
3. To these four texts might be added the Ashgate collection, edited by David Nelken (Nelken, 1994a), which also reproduces the white-collar/corporate crime confusion.

4. There is an enormous literature on defining "power"; for a useful introduction, see Clegg, 1989.

5. Gramsci used the term "intellectuals" in a very broad sense (Showstack-Sassoon, 2000: 20–22). While recognition of this broad usage should inform any reading of Gramsci's arguments regarding intellectuals, it clearly includes "academics" and certainly does not preclude the analysis here.

6. Thanks to Joe Sim for reminding us of the anger and insight of Thompson's *Writing By Candlelight*.

7. For an excellent overview of these trends at the international level, see the papers collected in Currie and Newson, 1998.

8. In 1995, total spending on higher education was 0.7% of GDP, about half the Organisation for Economic Cooperation and Development (OECD) average (Barr, 2001a); the comparable figure for the USA was 2% (Barr, 2001b).

9. See http://www.foresight.gov.uk

10. For a case-study of the dominance of oil industry personnel on the relevant Foresight panels, see Muttitt and Lindblom, forthcoming: 42–43.

11. For example, higher education institutions in the UK carry out 981 research and development projects worth £67m per year on behalf of the oil industry. However, despite the fact that the oil companies benefit directly from this work, over 50% of these projects are funded by the taxpayer (Muttitt and Lindblom, forthcoming). It is rare for universities even to recoup their overheads from industry-sponsored research. In this context, the apparently philanthropic donations and scholarship funding given by corporations to universities (such as BP's £19.5m gift to Cambridge University in 1998, or British American Tobacco's £3.8m gift to establish a Centre for Corporate Responsibility at Nottingham University in 2000) are clearly worth much more to the corporate sector than to the universities. Ultimately universities are being willingly used as part of a broader project to restore profitability to private corporations

12. A classic example here is the emergence of the "law and economics" movement (see Soley, 1998; Snider, 2000). On the nature of such ideological offensives, see C. Simpson, 1998a, 1998b.

13. On which reading, the challenges to mainstream criminology of the labelling perspective, then of critical criminology in the late 1960s and 1970, leading to the formation of the National Deviancy Conference, were somewhat fleeting and, in the medium term, largely unsuccessful.

14. In the case of Scotland, the Scottish Executive (the former Scottish Office) occupies a similarly dominant position in terms of funding research. At the risk of obscuring significant nuances, we suggest that many of the observations made in this section regarding the Home Office could apply equally to the Scottish Executive in its role as research sponsor.

15. This figure does not include the Annual Criminal Statistics Publications and Supplementary tables produced by the Home Office, or other statistical publications listed as "miscellaneous."

16. The same provisos apply as noted in note 14.

17. For all the problems associated with his own "third dimension" of power, not least for its failure to transcend completely the problematic of human agency (see Clegg, 1989: 86–128), Lukes's (1974) critical discussion of agency-based theorizations of power is instructive on the distinction being made here.

18. This attention may be further encouraged, at least conceptually, by the obligations placed upon states through the Human Rights Act of 1998.

19. On the role of networks and/or the construction of schools of thought, and their ability to construct commonsense within a particular discipline, see Pearce and Tombs, 1990, 1991; C. Simpson, 1998a.

20. For example, when the Finnish Government reached a decision of principle in 1995 to reduce economic crime, it opened up much of its own data, personnel, and so on to extensive access to external researchers (Alvesalo and Tombs, 2002). What is of interest, of course, is that although the Finnish experience seems quite contrary to that in Britain or Ireland, one basic point holds—namely, that access is related to whether or not the state has defined a certain sphere of activity or phenomenon as an actual or potential crime problem.

21. For political, read counter-hegemonic; of course, conscious or unwitting support for the existent hegemonic compromise is rarely cast as "political."

22. For example on the McLibel case, see Vidal, 1997; on the 1984/85 UK miners' strike, see Milne, 1994; on the international tobacco industry see, P. Taylor, 1984; for a comprehensive collection of examples from the USA, see Stauber and Rampton, 1995.

23. Moments of crisis force the hand of the state, resulting in clear cracks in its attempts to maintain claims to academic independence and galvanizing resistance on the part of its opponents—note the post–September 11th efforts to "gag" critics of USA foreign and military policy.

24. We are grateful to Laureen Snider for noting the need to make such points explicit.

# Power, "Valid" Knowledge, and the Limits to Scrutiny

# Researching Corporate Crime

## Introduction

Many authors have traced the creation of the legal subject, investigating the development of the discursive foundation that makes criminalization and censure possible (for example, Smart, 1995). However, the creation of the discursive foundations that account for decriminalization, that make a subject less censurable or culpable, have been virtually ignored. This is not surprising given the horrific human costs of policies of condemnation and criminalization, the spiralling incarceration rates and the accelerating levels of desperation, distrust and fear they have spawned (Cayley, 1998; Snider, 1998). However, the reverse process, the normalizing or de-stigmatizing of a subject, is noteworthy partly because it is so rare. But it is also noteworthy because it has the potential to reveal the usually obscured economic, social, and political foundations of discourse, of knowledge claims, and of their acceptance or rejection. The replacement of the culpable executive or corporate criminal with the non-culpable, responsible, accidental corporate law-breaker, then, provides insight into crucial linkages between academic disciplines and their audience. It shows the role played by parties outside the university, those that benefit (or suffer) from the intervention of disciplinary "experts," in the development, acceptance and shaping of academic knowledge.

The links between power, knowledge, and discipline have been generally accepted, in both sociology and in the critical, Foucauldian theoretical components of criminology (if not the positivist/applied mainstream). Disciplinary knowledge builds up a discourse of self and other, knowledge claims by authorized knowers ("experts") offer moral maps of a subject as well as policy prescriptions on how that subject should be "handled." Like all knowledge claims, such claims benefit some perspectives, parties and interests, and weaken others. Since the invention of criminology several hundred years ago, most criminological work has constituted as primary criminal subject the racialized, poor, male youth. It has made claims about the character and motives of this subject and built elaborate models on the causes, cures and controls required. The last 20 years have seen the constitution, particularly in Anglo-American positivist criminology, of the predatory, self-maximizing, opportunistic criminal who is unable or unwilling to control his[1] antisocial impulses, or delay gratification of his every desire (Gottfredson and Hirschi, 1990; Herrnstein and Murray, 1994). Conversely, as indicated above, the last 20 years in the field of corporate crime have seen the demise of the wilful, greedy or careless corporate criminal in favor of the non-culpable, accidental, educable corporate subject. In academic research and in policy and law, the corporate criminal has been replaced by the high-minded, intelligent corporate executive who breaks laws, if at all, because of the arcane and obtuse organizational systems imposed on him by mindless bureaucrats of the state.

If these arguments are correct, if the ease or difficulty of researching the powerful is intimately connected to the interests that see themselves as benefiting (or suffering) from its knowledge claims and subjects, it should be possible to demonstrate these links empirically. This chapter sets out to do that, presenting a history of the rise and fall of knowledge claims that have constituted the corporate criminal. Specifically, it examines studies of corporate crime originating in American sociology and criminology from 1939 to 1999. The research focus is limited to the United States of America because it has been, throughout the time period discussed, the dominant player on the stage of world capitalism and, not coincidentally, in the invention, dissemination, and acceptance of knowledge as well. As the pre-eminent (and since 1989 the only) world power, economically, politically and militarily, and as chief model-monger and model-merchandizer (Braithwaite, 1994), American claims and actors have particular impact. America's public and private universities, its think tanks and research collectives, are the richest and (again, not coincidentally) the most prestigious in the world. Thus brilliant ideas or people, whatever their countries of origin, are routinely poached—that is, hired and appropriated—by American universities, think tanks, media, and industry. And American-sponsored ideas have a disproportionate influence all over the world, an influence exponentially increased in the 1980s and 1990s through global capitalism.

## Origins of the Punishable Corporate Subject

White-collar crime originated as an academic concept in Edwin Sutherland's now famous presidential address to the 1939 annual meeting of the American Sociological Society (later the American Society of Criminology).[2] Seeking to direct his colleagues away from their preoccupation with the crimes of the powerless (then, as now, the bulk of research money and attention in criminology went to study the petty thefts, assaults and drug habits of poor young males, then called juvenile delinquents), Sutherland's speech drew attention to the illegal acts committed by privileged business executives and corporations. Defining white-collar crime as "all offences committed by a person of respectability and high social status in the course of his [*sic*] occupation" (Sutherland, 1940: 1), the concept was contentious from the outset. At the time, Sutherland's formulation was attacked primarily on the grounds of positivism—it was not sufficiently "scientific" because it covered behaviors that were illegal but not outlawed by criminal statute, such as false advertising or anti-competitive practices. It was therefore too broad and subjective. Limiting the study of white-collar crime to those acts which violated existing criminal codes, as recommended by Tappan (1947) and others, was "objective" because such acts were *legislated* as crime by lawmakers, not merely *labelled* so by criminologists.

The underlying assumption of this critique, and of Sutherland's subsequent defense of his views, is that "crime" is a real thing that legislators, informed by science and law, discover. If they haven't discovered a particular act, it is therefore not crime. Sutherland argued against only one half of this equation, pointing out that power (not to mention self-interest, political lobbying, media-generated moral panic, and a myriad of other factors) sometimes prevented legislators from criminalizing the harmful acts of business. Thus the fact that anti-competitive practices and false advertising were *proscribed*, albeit through regulatory or administrative statute not criminal law, was sufficient to indicate the "real" intentions of legislators, and to justify studying these acts as criminal. Sutherland agreed with his critics that the study of white-collar crime had to be (and be seen as) scientific. Like most of the authorized knowers of his day (and many criminologists today), he accepted as an object of faith the tenet that only "scientific method" produced objective, value-free knowledge rather than politically or ideologically biased opinion.

The concept of corporate crime developed out of Sutherland's original claim and its allied conceptual ambiguities. The constitution of a corporate criminal was always opposed, even in its home discipline(s). Battles raged over what should count as white-collar crime, over the role of trust and of occupational status, and over which harms or antisocial acts should be included (Tappan, 1947; Simon and Eitzen, 1999; Nelken, 1994b; Shapiro, 1990). Some researchers insisted that interests— that is, the primary beneficiaries and victims of the act—should shape the conceptual categories (Coleman, 1989; Pearce, 1976; Snider, 1993). For these researchers, it was important to distinguish corporate or organizational crime from occupational or white-collar crime. Occupational crime looks at crimes, committed by employees or consumers, which victimize business—profitability, efficiency, and reputation are threatened when, for example, employees embezzle or falsify expense accounts. Corporate or organizational crime refers to illegal acts done by business to benefit business, committed with the intention of increasing profit levels, stock prices or reputation (or sometimes to stave off disaster, save face, retain income share, or postpone loss). In policy terms this means that initiatives to surveil, curb, sanction, or censure corporate crime will face vigorous business resistance while those against occupational crime will not.[3] In terms of the argument developed in this chapter, then, corporate crime is a much more counter-hegemonic concept than white-collar crime.

Other basic issues of classification and definition have been the cause of dispute. Many claim that corporate crime can be subdivided into two subfields, financial and social (Edelhertz, 1970; Cranston, 1982). Others argue that the key distinction is between offences that are morally wrong in themselves *(mala in se)* and those which are merely illegal *(mala prohibita);* or some argue for definitions that present all "social harms," all acts that offend against basic human rights, as corporate crime (Simon and Eitzen, 1999; Michalowski, 1985). Who gets studied/ counted as a corporate criminal? Is the essence of the offence abuse of trust, which situates causality at the individual level, or is it organizational complexity? Is the job status of the offender (the white-collar aspect) crucial (for example, Shapiro, 1990; Reiss and Tonry, 1993; Shover and Bryant, 1993)? Summing up the knowledge claims constituting white-collar crime, Shover concludes: "the insoluble conceptual disputes endemic to the study of white-collar crime . . . have slowed the pace and distorted the advancement of empirical research" (Shover, 1998: 49). Researching powerful actors and organizations through knowledge claims that cast their acts as criminal has been strongly resisted, then, even within the disciplines that invented the concepts.

## Methodology

The original aim of the study upon which this chapter is based was to identify all empirical studies of corporate crime published in US journals from 1939–99 (later extended to 2000) and to record the purpose, sources and amount of funding (if any), access, sample size, methodologies, mode(s) of analysis, and conclusions for each. Studies published in journals outside sociology and criminology, or authored by those whose primary discipline was not sociology or criminology, were excluded. Since the emphasis was on empirical rather than theoretical studies, and on criminology and sociology produced and funded in the United States, purely theoretical studies, chapter summaries, reviews of secondary literature, and all studies focused on or originating in countries outside the United States—Australia, Canada, New Zealand, and the countries of the European Union, including the United Kingdom—were ignored.[4] Since detailed funding information was consistently available only for studies published in the last 25 years, the discussion and analysis, in the end, highlights this period.

The initial searches asked for all published studies employing the term "corporate crime," in title or abstract, in works in sociology, criminology, and law published during the 1939–2000 period. This was done through WebSPIRS, a database network which accesses various databases (such as the Social Science index) separately or simultaneously. This was supplemented by searches using the term "white-collar crime," because many studies covered both kinds of offenders or failed to make a conceptual distinction between the two. Searches under corporate and/or white-collar crime produced 90 articles. After eliminating overlap (several studies appeared three or four times) and removing theoretical or definitional articles, literature reviews and non-American pieces, 33 records remained. Twenty of these were published in the 1990s—6 books, 1 discussion paper, 1 dissertation[5] and 12 journal articles; 10 in the 1980s—4 books, 3 journal articles, 3 dissertations; and 3 in the 1970s—1 journal article, 1 dissertation and 1 "other" (a paper prepared for the Rural Sociological Society).[6]

Working on the assumption that studies from the 1950s and 1960s were less likely to be electronically accessible, and that electronic searches would miss studies if the authors had not employed the magic terms "corporate," "white-collar" or "crime" in the title or abstract, an intensive, old-fashioned bibliographic literature search was then done. Senior scholars in the field of American corporate crime were contacted about sources and omissions (see acknowledgments). Edited collections and books (for example, Hochstedler, 1984; Szockyj and Fox 1996; Lofquist et al., 1997; Post, 1998; Tonry and Reiss, 1993; and Blankenship 1993), collections of conference papers (Schlegel and Weisburd, 1992; Geis et al., 1995; Pearce and Snider, 1995), miscellaneous collections on related themes such as political crime or critical theory (for example, Tunnel, 1993), and new analyses of earlier studies (for example, Lee and Ermann, 1999) were all searched.[7] When the studies themselves contained insufficient information and detail on funding or methodology, authors were contacted personally, usually via e-mail.[8]

The emphasis on empirical studies, and therefore on funded studies, is deliberate. When a discipline, sub-field, or knowledge claim falls from favor, funding sources decline. Massive quantitative empirical studies typically require huge budgets, lots of research assistants and (particularly today) heavy computer resources and time. If funding declines, such studies become increasingly difficult to do, forcing researchers wishing to remain in the field to adopt alternative strategies. Some utilize different methodologies, doing historical work, qualitative case studies or theoretical inquiries. Or they do quantitative work on a smaller scale, with smaller samples and less data.[9]

However, forced choices of this kind have costs. While funding, quantitative methodology and budget size have nothing to do with the quality of a particular study—superb studies of corporate crime have been done from many methodological angles, with and without external funding—claims legitimated by numbers have much greater credibility than those backed by "mere" words; they are more likely to be accepted as "facts" while word-based claims are denigrated as mere "arguments." Quantitative methodologies and large research budgets are the *sine qua non* of academic respectability, particularly valorized in countries where critical, theoretical traditions are weak—compare France, the land of Foucault and Lyotard, for example, to the United States. The articles published in the most prestigious American journals, such as the *American Sociological Review* and the *American Journal of Sociology*, reflect this predilection, and so do the research areas and methodologies of dominant American criminologists (the alpha males—and a few females—of the discipline) (Naffine, 1996). Scholars without outside funding, then, are more likely to be devalued by peers, department heads and deans. Without major research grants, such scholars have more trouble attracting and supporting graduate students. And, once it is clear that publication prospects in major journals are limited and research funding is virtually unavailable, a cycle of declining legitimacy and centrality is set in motion. Bright young graduate students and untenured faculty members notice which types of research and research areas attract dollars and prestige and which do not, and choose their specializations accordingly.[10] As Schrecker points out,

> If attracting substantial research funding from external sources is a significant determinant of promotion and tenure decisions within the academic world, the composition of academic departments will shift over time to emphasize specialties and normative orientations that are compatible with the priorities of external sources of funds. (Schrecker, 2001b: 37)

## Observations

### The Early Years

Because World War II focused attention and resources on the war effort, radar and the bomb, the natural sciences took precedence and few studies of white-collar or corporate crime were funded or published in the 1940s. In the 1950s, six studies appeared in American journals. Arguably the most important one was Edwin Sutherland's, first published in 1956 (Sutherland, 1977). Sutherland studied what he called the criminal careers of the 70 largest corporations in the United States since their founding, through an analysis of the 980 adverse decisions registered against them, an average of 14 offences per corporation. Here, for the first time, a senior academic at the top of his discipline, backed by the power and legitimacy of the "science" of criminology, forcefully applied the terms, concepts, and censures of crime to the corporation and its executives, constituting them as criminal. Prior to this, in the early 1950s, several studies were published which applied concepts of white-collar crime (derived from Sutherland's presidential address) to wartime situations. Business resistance to and violations of rationing laws or price controls, as well as business participation in black market trades, were examined by Clinard (1952), Hartung (1950) and Aubert (1952).[11] There was also Donald Cressey's now classic embezzlement study (Cressey, 1953) which asked why employees steal, and pioneered the concept of the "unshareable problem" as an explanatory mechanism. Newman (1953) published the first of many studies examining public opinion on and attitudes to white-collar crimes.

The 1960s saw the publication of Ralph Nader's *Unsafe at Any Speed* (Nader, 1965). This book had an important ideological impact because it signalled the rise of the consumer movement and consumer activism. As a crusading lawyer, Nader helped legitimize and popularize the idea that august senior executives in traditional, respectable, and profitable corporations may do harm, on purpose, to maximize profits. He is credited with showing that senior General Motors officials knew of the life-threatening design flaws of the Corvair, but decided to put the car on the market anyway. The culpability, venality, and criminality of management was underlined when Nader successfully sued General Motors for conducting a smear campaign against him—hiring spies to dig up or manufacture discreditable material. In US universities, conflict theories associated with William Chambliss, Richard Quinney and Austin Turk were developed, challenging the previously dominant conservative functionalist approaches, putting forth claims that law passage and enforcement were inherently political, and that power rather than consensus shaped law. Few studies of corporate crime appeared during the 1960s, largely because it takes up to a decade to produce publishing academics. Thus there is an inevitable time lag between an upsurge of activism and the emergence of knowledge claims of academic disciplines. However Gil Geis's now-classic study of the price-fixing conspiracy maintained by manufacturers of electrical appliances throughout the 1950s appeared in 1967 (Geis, 1967), signalling the advent of a new generation of critical scholars.

### The High Point

The largest and best-funded empirical studies of corporate crime in the United States were published in the 1970s. In 1976 the National Institute of Justice (NIJ) awarded Marshall Clinard and Peter Yeager a major grant to update Sutherland's 1956 study. Clinard and Yeager's study analyzed administrative, civil and criminal actions taken by 25 federal agencies against the 477 largest public corporations, and the 105 largest wholesale, retail, and service corporations (582 corporations in all), over a two-year period (1975 and 1976). The massive, rich, data thereby collected produced a number of influential publications (Clinard and Yeager, 1980; Clinard et al., 1979; Clinard and Yeager, 1978). This study marks the first, and thus far the only, federally funded empirical examination of all publicly available databases on corporate crime. As Szwajkowski and Figlewicz (1998) point out, it is "the only large-scale information source *ever* published" (1998: 174, emphasis in original). Thus scholars wanting to do empirical studies of corporate crime have been forced to return to this study—mining it for alternative explanations or unexplored connections—for almost two decades (see, for example, Cochran and Nigh, 1987).

While the Clinard and Yeager study was unique, this was not the only important grant awarded during this period. Herb Edelhertz received a major grant to study economic crime, part of it used to install Economic Crime Prosecution Units in local prosecutors' offices across the United States. Edelhertz also studied definitional issues and the methodologically crucial subject of data collection, sources and databases (Edelhertz, 1970; Edelhertz and Overcast, 1982; also Shapiro, 1980). Another large NIJ grant went to scholars at the University of Tennessee to study corporate crime and the regulation of surface coal mining (Shover, 1980; Lynxwiler et al., 1984; Shover et al., 1986). A pioneering study of the ways in which (some) corporate systems are criminogenic (Needleman and Needleman, 1979) was produced. A three-year National Institute of Mental Health (NIMH) grant in the sociology of social control (through Al Reiss at Yale) enabled Diane Vaughan to turn a case study of a Medicaid fraud perpetuated by Revco, originally a Ph.D. dissertation, into a book. Another dissertation, this one analyzing the Ford Pinto case, was completed by Beti Thompson (1981). The range, volume and quality of studies produced during this period—see the collections edited by Geis and Stotland (1980) or Hochstedler (1984)—are impressive indeed.

The 1970s saw corporate America and the political-military establishment challenged as never before (and certainly not since), through the combined force of the civil rights movement, Watergate, the pill, the New Left and the Vietnam War protests and defeat. In every institution, from the corporation to the family, from political parties to churches, authority and hierarchy were questioned. Culturally and socially, conformity was derided and protest, in popular music, dress, and film, became the norm. In the popular press, investigative and muckraking journalism became (for a very short time) fashionable, prestigious, and career-building. Mark Dowie (1977) published an influential piece based on a "smoking gun" memo, which purportedly showed that Ford executives put profits before human lives when they decided that it would be more costly to replace a badly positioned gas tank on Pinto automobiles than to pay off crash victims and survivors' families.[12] Harry Caudill used the language of crime to describe how coal mine owners maximized profits while causing hundreds of preventable deaths in mine disasters (Caudill, 1977). Leaked documents showing widespread bribery and corruption in multinational corporations and government agencies, revealed by the Watergate papers and subsequent official and unofficial investigations, stimulated popular (Blundell, 1976; McClintick, 1976) and academic studies in any number of disciplines (N. Jacoby, 1977; Seidler et al., 1977).

The 1970s also saw the initiation of an influential funding program on sentencing, a program which spawned several major works on corporate crime and law. What became known as the "Yale Studies in White-Collar Crime" began as a series of grants awarded to Stan Wheeler and Al Reiss, then at Yale, by the National Institute of Justice. While spin-off grants generated publications well into the 1980s, the projects initiated in the 1970s were most explicitly concerned with, and relevant to, the study of corporate crime. One of the most influential of these analyzed data on federal white-collar offences and offenders in major cities such as New York, Los Angeles, Atlanta, and Chicago, as well as a number of less-urban jurisdictions as well. Some of the more sociological authors looked at decision-making by prosecutors, district attorneys and regulatory officials (Wheeler et al., 1982); the more legally oriented looked at corporate liability and the judicial process (Mann et al., 1980).[13]

## The Mid-1980s and 1990s: Major Funded Studies

### *Sentencing Studies*

Since the 1970s very few empirical projects on corporate crime have been funded by major funding agencies in the United States. This is particularly notable at the federal level, where funding to investigate corporate crime, from crucial, prestigious bodies such as the National Institute of Justice, virtually dried up after Reagan came to power in 1980. As one eyewitness put it, the funding environment at the NIJ changed dramatically and virtually "overnight" (personal communication from Neal Shover, 27 June 2001). Sentencing studies, which were big in American criminology in the 1980s, constitute a partial exception to this—partial because the presence of corporate criminals in these studies was generally incidental, not central, to the research agenda. In the mid-1980s the White-Collar and Organized Crime Research Program of the National Institute of Justice provided funds to replicate the Wheeler study, albeit on a smaller scale (Benson et al., 1991, 1988; Benson and Walker, 1988). Other grants went for studies to compare federal white-collar offenders with traditional criminals. Wheeler, Weisburd, Waring and Bode (1988,

1991) compared those convicted of eight different federal offences with those convicted of two traditional federal offences, through pre-sentence investigation reports. A later study looked at the likelihood of white-collar criminals becoming repeat offenders and developing "criminal careers" (Weisburd, Chayet and Waring, 1990). Both studies used the original 1976–78 data set. While other large-scale empirical studies of sentencing were funded in the 1980s, and some of them included corporate offenders in their data, the main focus was on judicial discretion and sentence variation (Hagan et al., 1980; Hagan and Nagel, 1982; Hagan and Bumiller, 1983). Susan Shapiro apparently obtained NIJ funding for her analysis of sentencing and sanctioning by the US Securities and Exchange Commission (Shapiro, 1985, 1990).[14] While Shapiro's focus was also on discretion and lenience, she was definitely studying corporate offenders, those who own and trade stocks and bonds, and their engagement in corporate crime.

Sentencing studies were also funded through the US Sentencing Commission, a body set up to "rationalize" and systematize the huge, varied American criminal justice system. The major grant relating to corporate crime was received by Mark Cohen. Cohen and his team gathered data on all federal criminal prosecutions of corporations, for all types of social and financial corporate crime with the exception of antitrust offences, from 1984 to 1987. This yielded a total of 288 corporate offenders, a sample which comprised a full 30% of all non-antitrust cases at the time of the study (M. Cohen, 1989, 1991). The goal was to analyze whether sentencing practices in federal courts reflect the social harm caused by corporate crime. The authors had access to data on sentencing maintained by the Administrative Office of the US Courts (Administrative Office of the United States Courts Master File), by the Federal Probation Sentencing and Supervision Information System (FPSSIS), as well as access to any Pre-Sentence Investigation Reports (PSIs) filed. Using these records, the authors assigned each case a number which reflected their assessment of the harm (monetary, environmental, social) caused by the offence. The results, to no one's surprise, showed that the average fine assessed against corporations is considerably less than the monetary harm, at a ratio of .10 (M. Cohen, 1989: 658).

A study on sentencing reform that received no funding from the Sentencing Commission was done by William Lofquist (1992, 1993). Lofquist set out to examine the influence of economic (corporate) power on the deliberations and recommendations of the Sentencing Commission, with a particular focus on organizational probation. Organizational probation is a sanction which allows courts to interfere directly in the internal workings of a convicted corporation. In theory, it gives courts the power to force corporations to alter their chain of command and division of labor, making their organizational structure less criminogenic. This power was resisted by business, but approved by the Sentencing Commission nevertheless. Given "the weakness of Congressional authorization to the Sentencing

Commission, the opposition of business to organizational probation, and the historical reliance on market-based corporate crime controls" (Lofquist, 1992: Abstract), this approval is a surprising and unexpected result, and Lofquist set out to investigate why and how it happened, using documentary records and interviews with key personnel (Lofquist, 1992; see also Rodriguez and Barlow, 1999). Sentencing Commission personnel played no role in facilitating this study; indeed, they were strikingly uncooperative. To quote Lofquist: "I had absolutely no ties to the Sentencing Commission, received no money from them, and maintained a generally antagonistic relationship with many of the folks there while I was doing my research" (personal communication, 14 June 2000). Moreover the commission frustrated the author's original intention, which was to do follow-up case studies, by "repeatedly refus[ing] to release . . . the necessary information about corporations sentenced under the guidelines" (personal communication, 11 July 2001).

## Savings and Loan/Fraud and Bankruptcy Studies

The other area where major studies of corporate crime were funded came out of the Savings and Loan crisis—the collapse of the "thrifts," as Savings and Loans (S&L) institutions were called, which occurred when with the deregulation of federal laws governing them were changed in the early 1980s.[15] The largest grant went to a research team headed by Henry Pontell and Kitty Calavita at the University of California, Irvine.[16] After receiving a small seed grant from the university to examine secondary data sources such as government documents, congressional hearings, and news media accounts (Calavita and Pontell, 1991, 1990), the research team secured funds from the White-Collar and Organized Crime Research Program of the National Institute of Justice and launched a major study. Ninety-eight interviews were conducted with key enforcement and regulatory personnel in Washington, D.C., Florida, Texas and California. Statistical data on prosecutions, costs, and sanctions were gathered on 686 insolvent S&L institutions. The bulk of the study focused on California and Texas, the states with the highest number of bankrupt institutions and the highest dollar volume of losses (Calavita, Pontell and Tillman, 1997; Calavita, Tillman and Pontell, 1997; Pontell, Calavita and Tillman, 1994; Tillman et al., 1997; Tillman and Pontell, 1995).

The NIJ also awarded $83,160 to Davita Silfen Glasberg and Dan Skidmore from 1992 to 1995, to study the collapse of one specific institution, the Columbia Savings & Loan Association of Beverly Hills (Glasberg and Skidmore, 1998). The NIJ is also listed as a sponsoring agency for a grant received by Zimring and Hawkins (1993) for a survey of the S&L hearings and a discussion of their implications for legal and criminological theory. Finally, an unfunded S&L study was done by Mary Zey (1993), who argued that the 1980s saw a redistribution of wealth in the United

States that could be attributed, at least in part, to the disproportionate influence that corporations, investment bankers, and banks exercised over federal government policy. The converging interests of these key financial elites led, she claims, to banking deregulation, the S&L bailout, and other instances of "corporate welfare."

Following this (but independent of it), the state of California funded a study to investigate frauds against Medicaid. The grant was obtained by Robert Tillman, a co-author with Calavita and Pontell of the S&L studies (Tillman and Pontell, 1992). Using sentencing data as well as interviews, Tillman and Pontell investigated sentencing disparities between those convicted of defrauding Medicaid (usually high-status medical personnel, pharmacists and doctors), and those convicted of traditional forms of theft and fraud (usually working-class people). Tillman also received, "after many tribulations" (personal communication, 14 June 2000), a small grant from the National Institute of Justice to study health insurance fraud (Tillman, 1999).

None of the other white-collar studies funded by the Department of Justice during this period looked at corporate crime. Mock and Rosenbaum (1988) were funded to investigate industrial espionage, surveying 41 communications companies, 45 oil, gas, and mining companies, and 124 industrial and manufacturing companies on whether they had lost company secrets through theft. Although every search engine "found" this study when searching for "corporate crime," it is an investigation of crimes against corporations, not by them. Hamilton and Sanders (1996) received National Science Foundation grants of $114,482 and $99,456 to do comparative research on attitudes towards corporate crime in the United States, Russia and Japan. Cindy Alexander (1999) published a study in the *Journal of Law and Economics* (not a socio-legal or criminological venue) on reputational penalties suffered by corporations convicted of federal crime, looking at 78 public corporations in the United States from 1984 to 1990. This study was probably funded internally by the Department of Justice, where Alexander was apparently employed at the time. John Braithwaite, a senior and much respected Australian corporate crime scholar, conducted a large comparative study of nursing home regulation in England, Japan, Australia and the US (see Braithwaite, 1995). However, the money for this research was primarily Australian, albeit supplemented by funds from the American Bar Foundation. The NIJ is not listed or acknowledged in the Braithwaite study. In 1986 an interesting survey of occupational health and safety and environmental violations, accessed through the US Occupational Safety and Health Administration (OSHA) and Environmental Protection Agency (EPA) records, was published in *Human Relations,* a journal for business professionals. There are two points of interest here: first, it was apparently funded by a private management firm; and second, the authors eschewed the language of crime, calling the study "An Empirical Examination of the Causes of Corporate *Wrongdoing* in the United States" (Hill et al., 1992, emphasis added).

## *The Mid-1980s and 1990s: Other Studies*

Other notable investigations of corporate crime were published in the United States from 1985 to 2000, though they were produced with no significant external funding or major grants. The studies are all empirical investigations of corporate crime, and the scholars were (and are) distinguished in the field. Most were funded by seed grants (often internal), teaching release time, and research fellowships, often supplemented by the individual's academic salary. Thus it was the ingenuity, drive, and track record of the faculty members that made these studies possible, not sponsorship by American state funding agencies.

Some of the most empirically sophisticated studies of antitrust violations have been done by Sally Simpson and her colleagues (Simpson, 1992; 1986; 1987). Simpson examined data from the Federal Trade Commission's Case Decisions and the Commerce Clearing House Trade Cases *(The Blue Book)* on antitrust and trade violations, from 1927 to 1981, for 52 firms in seven basic manufacturing industries. Another study looked at 38 corporations charged with one or more serious antitrust violations between 1928 and 1981 to determine whether "sanction experience decreases the likelihood of a firm's reoffending" (Simpson and Koper, 1992: 347). In other words, they addressed a classic criminological problem, namely, do sanctions deter? More recently Simpson and her colleagues examined the interplay of individual and organizational factors in managerial decisions to break or comply with the law (Simpson et al., 1998; Simpson, 1997; Paternoster and Simpson 1996, 1993), this time using data gathered through questionnaires distributed to students in Masters of Business Administration programs at four universities. Simpson's studies are notable since they are all empirical, quantitative, and of high quality, observations reinforced by the fact that all were published in major, prestigious US journals. However Simpson was unable to obtain major funding for any of them, save through "summer support from my Chair to relieve me from teaching a class" (Simpson, personal communication, 7 June 2000).

This period also saw a series of important case studies being produced, again without significant external funding. Several researchers have looked at the Challenger disaster, the explosion that destroyed the American space shuttle in 1986 (Kramer, 1992). One of the most prolific researchers of this case is Diane Vaughan (1983, 1996, 1997, 1998). Although Vaughan won fellowships at the Centre for Socio-Legal Studies in Oxford (1986–87) and the American Bar Foundation (1988–89) to give her the time and academic space to write the Challenger study, as well as a 1996–97 National Endowment for the Humanities Fellowship from the Institute for Advanced Study after the Challenger book was out—and the book itself won a major award from the American Society of Criminology—no major federal grants funded her Challenger study.[17]

Studies of environmental crime have remained popular among students and scholars of corporate crime (H. Barnett, 1994, 1995; Yeager, 1991; Block, 1993). This fact reflects the continuing cultural and social significance of the environment, as entire species are wiped out, air and water are fouled, and habitats disappear under the relentless pressure of global, local and national capitalism. Throughout the 1980s and 1990s there was minimal funding support for such investigations. In spring 2000, however, the National Institute of Justice announced a new competition to fund research into "Corporate Environmental Compliance," the first since the 1970s.[18] Thus, most of the investigations of corporate environmental crime throughout this period were case studies.

Finally, a scattering of miscellaneous studies of corporate crime were published. Some studied corporate crime from a perspective within feminism, a social movement which became stronger, at least in academe, throughout the period. Thus there were studies of women as victims of corporate crime, through the manufacturing and promotion of silicon breast implants, or of unsafe birth control drugs and devices such as diethylstilbestrol (DES) (Chapple, 1998; see also Szockyj and Fox, 1996; or, for a Canadian overview, Peppin, 1995). There was one study that was international in scope. Gerber (1990) examined the efficacy and operation of the Nestlé Infant Formula Audit Commission, the regulatory agency set up by the World Health Organization following international outrage about the deaths of hundreds of thousands of Third World infants, who died from malnutrition or dysentery when their mothers switched from breast feeding to infant formula after receiving free samples of the latter. The only funding cited for this study was a 1989 seed grant from the University of Idaho (Gerber, 1990).

## Conclusions

The concept of white-collar crime was invented in the depths of the depression, when world capitalism (business) was politically, ideologically and economically at a low point. During the 1940s funding, media and scholarship focused on the battle to win World War II. In the 1950s and 1960s, a new enemy took shape (communism) and the Cold War ensued. Business regained much of the power and prestige it had lost during the depression, and profits and profit margins peaked. Keynesian economics dominated capitalist democracies in the developed world, and the welfare state was born, albeit with significant variations in quality, coverage, and cost. Unemployment and inflation were low. Following the emergence of the 1960s' protest movements, the late 1960s and 1970s saw all the institutions of the modern capitalist state challenged by an array of new social movements, particularly feminism and environmentalism. By the late 1970s, Japan and Germany were challenging American business hegemony, rates of surplus value began to decline, profit margins slipped, and high inflation and unemployment reappeared. The corporate counter-revolution of the 1980s and 1990s began. In the United States and the United Kingdom, neo-liberal regimes under Ronald Reagan and Margaret Thatcher were elected. Over the next 20 years, unions were attacked, welfare state programs downsized or eliminated, corporate tax rates cut, state enterprises privatized. Business profits multiplied, and unemployment, incarceration, and inequality soared. The social, economic, and political power of business peaked and the whole political spectrum shifted to the right (Marchak, 1991; Pearce and Tombs, 1998; Schrecker, 2001a).

The disciplinary trajectory of corporate crime in the United States follows a similar course: the concept was invented in the 1930s, but was quiescent through the 1940s and 1950s. Interest, legitimacy, and funding (while never generous) grew in the late 1960s, peaking in the 1970s. Major empirical studies were funded, notably Clinard and Yeager's investigation of corporate crime and the Sentencing/White-Collar Crime program at Yale. Interest and funding plummeted in the 1980s and 1990s. Economics, law and business became more than ever the favored disciplines in politics and policy venues, and in media, law and academe. In its hypotheses, methodologies, and conclusions, empirical work on corporate crime (when the term was still used) became more conservative. The two exceptions—the rash of sentencing studies in which corporate criminals were sometimes included, as government concern over judicial discretion peaked, and the funded research on the S&L disaster—might best be explained in terms of legitimacy on the one hand and the necessity for the stability of capitalist markets on the other. Few studies in American sociology and criminology today, funded or unfunded, problematize the executive as corporate criminal, or posit capitalism as criminogenic.[19]

The virtual absence of funding signifies the marginalization of corporate crime as a field. The dearth of funding contrasts sharply with the hundreds of grants and thousands of dollars devoted to studying the crimes of the powerless in the 1980s and 1990s, via gang or drug research. It is premature to conclude that corporate crime as an object of knowledge is dying in the United States, but few funding sources are available, and comparatively few new scholars are being produced, particularly in criminology.[20] While, as we have seen, some high-quality unfunded research on corporate crime continues, much of it is small-scale and qualitative, and much of it has been possible only because academics have been willing to subsidize research out of their own pockets. In addition, it has only been possible because university faculty, decades ago, won the right to pursue independent scholarship, to develop research agendas not reliant on the vagaries of state or marketplace. This autonomy is now seriously threatened. Most of the academics pursuing corporate crime in universities today have continuing appointments and tenure, which shield them from demands to produce only funded, "marketable" research. But with tenure disappearing and eight-month teaching contracts becoming the norm, today's graduate students and new faculty may not have the luxury of choice. Under this scenario, research agendas will increasingly reflect the world-views of the powerful, and reflect the priorities of government or industry.

Are there any signs of hope? Certainly, if many of the obstacles to researching the powerful are related to the cultural, economic, and political power of the subjects constituted by this research, then recent social movements opposing corporate capital are important, and may signify an end to quiescence. On the other hand, the post-September 11 period[21] has seen the revival of old-style militarism, the repression of dissent, and considerable reversion, in the dominant Western states, to the values and practices of the 1980s. It is much too early to predict how these struggles will play out over the next decade.

In addition one must consider the possibly irreversible implications of the structural changes that occurred in state agencies in the 1980s and 1990s. In many areas of corporate crime (with the notable exception of insider trading and some anti-trade law), regulations and regulatory officials have disappeared.[22] Many public records have been rendered inaccessible through privatization, or through conversion from criminal law (where records, while increasingly expensive to obtain, are defined as public) to civil law (where access is severely limited). The institutional memory, in some agencies and regulatory arenas, has been erased. Indeed, as argued by Hoberg (1998), the ideology and working assumptions of the civil service itself—in the United States, at least—have changed. The onus of proof, once on the private sector to demonstrate its right to the privilege of incorporation and limited liability (and the opportunities for wealth this brings), has shifted dramatically. Now the public sector must prove its right to intervene in the marketplace, to "interfere" with capital. The fall-back position and working philosophy of "public service" (the term has become an oxymoron, the calling demonized) requires the state to justify each and every regulation. The US law on "takings" would have regulatory agencies document and pay the full cost of every regulation passed! (Snider, 2000). The principle of "regulate if necessary" has increasingly shifted to "anything but regulation."[23]

Thus researchers who want to study the powerful face an escalating series of obstacles. New, large-scale empirical studies require significant funding; without it, only certain topics can be studied, and the academic legitimacy of the field (rightly or wrongly) quickly suffers. To reconstruct crime events from scratch is costly and time-consuming; researchers forced to gather empirical data on their own have to "reinvent the wheel" for every study (Szwajkowski and Figlewicz, 1998: 168). For example, even in the antitrust area (an area largely exempted from deregulation), those who would study violations face "the daunting task of collecting and organizing data from several distinct sources," each comprising "thick volumes of complaints, hearings, court procedures and decisions" (ibid.). And getting access to the internal records of a corporation to conduct such studies in the first place is difficult if not impossible.[24]

The private sector is unlikely to sponsor research to discover, document, or publicize its own harmful, antisocial acts. This blindingly obvious fact must be re-iterated because there is so much chatter about (and, apparently, belief in) the naive notion that the socially responsible corporation, the good corporate citizen, will automatically appear, flourish and multiply. Corporate crimes are committed, generally speaking, because they are profitable. The interests of business as a whole, on the macro level, lie in normalization, denial, and concealment.[25] Without public initiative and agency, corporate crime as a counter-hegemonic act, a way of thinking and seeing, a constitution of knowledge, data, and research, disappears. The fact that corporate dominance is increasingly aided and abetted by the modern nation-state under the guise of globalization or competitiveness is therefore very frightening. The virtual collapse of resistance to corporate power by the once (at least somewhat) liberal state threatens to reverse progress made, millimeter by millimeter, through centuries of struggle by many diverse groups—feminists, union activists, preachers, philanthropists, crusading politicians. Establishing the claim that markets are predatory, that corporate acts do cause real, lasting damage to lives, cultures, and environments, was bitterly resisted and hotly contested (Bliss, 1974; Carson, 1980a, 1980b; Paulus, 1974). Breaking the monopoly of the privileged over laws granting absolute rights to owners of private property, rights interpreted to mean that factory owners could determine all aspects of the work environment from meal breaks and ventilation to time-off (many decided all three were unnecessary frills) was a necessary first step to improving the lifestyle and life chances of working people (Carson and Martin, 1974; Bliss, 1974).[26] Such progress is threatened by the resurgence of ideas and policies that define health, working conditions, and knowledge as property, and citizenship as the right of an individual to purchase the cheapest possible consumer goods and to punish any person or state smaller and weaker than him/herself.

Researching crimes of the powerful, therefore, is more important than ever. There is no reason to believe that the "real" rate of corporate crime has declined.[27] On the contrary, antisocial, acquisitive, harmful acts committed by business have most likely increased. Why? The global economy and the internet have made corporate crime potentially more profitable than ever as the opportunities to make mind-boggling fortunes through fraud, deception, false advertising, and misleading claims have mushroomed. The pressure to profit-maximize has increased, executives now have to show higher profits each and every quarter to keep stock prices up and avoid takeover bids, and the agendas of finance capital reign supreme (Pearce, 1990; Tombs, 1996; S. Simpson, 1986, 1987). The weak, complacent, corporate-dependent nation-state, the dismantling or downsizing of regulation and the evisceration of unions make the chances of detection smaller than ever, and the large, powerful corporation can always employ the threat of disinvestment to block protective legislation, state prosecution, and sanctions. The world, after all, is now a capital-friendly zone. Finally, at the all-important micro level, when antisocial, harmful behaviors and those who engage in them are normalized in ideology and in law, such acts do not elicit shame. With collective responsibility an unfashionable idea and individualistic, me-first philosophies are ascendant, corporate executives are unlikely to shame themselves for corporate crime, or to experience shaming through their peers.[28] Downplaying research on corporate crime now is therefore particularly wrongheaded.

## Acknowledgments

I would like to thank Paula Curry for her excellent research assistance. Paula's familiarity with data bases, search engines and the intricacies of the MegaPac CD-ROM made this project feasible. In addition, this chapter owes a tremendous debt of gratitude to people such as Kitty Calavita, Gil Geis, Neal Shover, Sally Simpson, and Diane Vaughan for their insight, suggestions, and thoughtful critical evaluations. Others, particularly Robert Tillman and William Lofquist, provided additional information quickly and cheerfully. The time, effort, kindness, and professionalism of all of them allowed the completion of this project. This does not mean, of course, that any of them agree with my arguments or interpretations (or misinterpretations?) of their work. Nor are any of them responsible for studies I may have slighted or missed.

## Notes

1. Both the evil individual criminal and the accidental corporate offender are coded male. Empirically, males are over-represented at every stage of the criminal justice process from arrest to incarceration (Snider, 1998; Belknap, 2001). On the rare occasions when corporate criminals are sanctioned, males are over-represented there as well (Chapple 1998; Daly, 1989; Rynbrandt and Kramer, 1995; Szockyi and Fox 1996).
2. Thanks to Gil Geis for clarifying this point (e-mail communication, 5 February 2001). Professor Geis noted that the name of the organization was changed when someone noticed the acronym it formed. Some scholars today would argue that the original name at least provided truth in advertising.
3. This does not mean that private corporations always favor state action against employees who steal; they prefer to choose when to call upon criminal justice, and when to deal with white-collar crime privately.
4. This meant that all articles on the development of the legal category known in American law as "Corporate Homicide" were excluded (for example, Swigert and Farrell, 1980–81; Maakestad, 1981; Poveda, 1992). So were most of the studies done by prolific scholars of corporate crime based outside the United States, such as Frank Pearce (British/Canadian) and John Braithwaite (Australian).
5. Dissertations are not included in the final sample unless published in a venue surveyed by

this study. However, they are listed because they indicate birth or renewal of interest and activity in the field by the next generation of academics.

6. This search was quite different from that done by DiMento et al., 2000–2001. Their comprehensive and useful bibliography focuses on corporate crime liability, looking at materials from law, the social sciences, humanities, management, and business over the last century.

7. I am confident that the combination of the various search methods have produced a sufficiently comprehensive group of studies to lay the basis for the claims this chapter puts forth. However it is almost certainly the case that some studies have been missed.

8. Everyone contacted responded, often at length. Several gave very helpful comments on the research endeavor itself, and/or on earlier versions of this chapter.

9. Access is also implicated: researchers doing large-scale studies funded by prestigious agencies are harder for corporations and record-keeping agencies to turn away. So are researchers who come from prestigious academic institutions—and those with major research grants are more likely to be hired by prestigious, Ivy League universities.

10. This is not to imply that funded work *necessarily* has official or state backing, or that it is *necessarily* conservative in its objectives and conclusions.

11. Although Aubert's geographic focus was on Norway.

12. The Ford Pinto case was reanalyzed, and Dowie's interpretation of these events is intelligently disputed by Lee and Ermann, 1999.

13. There were several methodological/political problems with these studies. Because of the need for "objectivity," only convicted offenders were included in the sample. This meant that all putative offenders whose power, resources, contacts, and political clout allowed them to avoid prosecution, indictment, or sentencing, an unknown but certainly large number, were ignored in favor of the less powerful (or more egregious?) offenders at the final stage of the criminal justice "funnel."

14. The American Bar Foundation is also credited in her publications.

15. Prior to the collapse of Enron, this *was* the largest and most expensive set of corporate crimes ever to occur in the USA.

16. The University of California, Irvine, has become one of the most important centers for white-collar and corporate crime research in the United States, under the leadership, first, of Gil Geis and then Henry Pontell.

17. As Diane Vaughan pointed out, she and many others who do qualitative work in corporate crime do not typically apply for grants. This is partly because of the perception that "quantitative work gets funded and qualitative does not," and partly because work animated by grounded theory evolves as it progresses (personal communication, 22 June 2000 and 12 July 2001).

18. Since this predated the election of George Bush, his pro-business anti-environmental agenda and then his "War on Terrorism," the fate of this initiative is very much in doubt.

19. There are exceptions: see, for example, Calavita, Pontell and Tillman, 1997.

20. Indeed, the brain drain looks to be in the other direction, with graduate students who did theses in corporate crime migrating into better-funded areas of research, or areas where the publication chances are better.

21. While the bulk of the research for this paper was done in 2000–2001, the final edit is being done in February 2002.

22. Of course this is a generalization, one which must ultimately be demonstrated empirically on a case-by-case basis. However, as Hoberg, 1998; Doern, 1995a, 1995b; Doern and Wilks, 1998a, 1998b; and Schrecker, 2001b, demonstrate, structural change in many areas of the federal state, in Canada and the United States in particular, has been dramatic.

23. For discussion of occupational health and safety in the new "decoupled" workplace, particularly in Britain, see Tombs, 1996, 1999; and Woodiwiss, 1992. Studies on the replacement of environmental crime with permits and licences to pollute include Hoberg, 1998; Doern, 1995b. The issue of regulation versus de- or re-regulation following privatization in the UK has also been addressed by Pearce and Tombs (1998), Hogwood (1998), and Wilks (1998).

24. Jackall's (1988) attempts to gain access to study corporate ethics (a comparatively unthreatening topic) are illustrative.

25. The interests, values and actions of individual corporate executives and CEOs are not necessarily coterminous with structural agendas (Giddens, 1990, 1991; Beck et al., 1994).

26. That is, working people in the Western, first-world welfare state. The notion that this should apply globally is one of the ideas promoted by counter-hegemonic protesters and strongly resisted by states and their corporate masters.

27. Since all crime rates are social constructions, there is no real rate of corporate crime. However the term is used here to describe antisocial, harmful acts committed by corporations, that *would have been* labelled corporate crime in the past (see introduction to this chapter).

28. Without longitudinal data and empirical studies, how can we know?

# Researching Corporate Crime

## *A Business Historian's Perspective*

## Corporate Crime: A Lacuna in the Historiography of British Business

In 1999, I was asked by the Wellcome Trust to attend a "Technical Workshop on Tobacco Industry Documents" at the National Institutes of Health in Bethesda, Maryland. The conference involved tobacco industry archives, which had been produced in the aftermath of tobacco litigation in the USA. I had recently completed a history of the leading British asbestos producer, Turner & Newall (Tweedale, 2000), and had already read some of the published work on tobacco (the tobacco and asbestos industries having certain similarities as manufacturers of carcinogenic products). When I arrived in Washington, I found that the main subject of discussion was the British American Tobacco (BAT) archive at Guildford in Surrey, which BAT had created as part of a legal settlement brokered in Minnesota. Discussions of the skulduggery of BAT, already well publicized by Stanton Glantz (Glantz et al., 1996), featured heavily in the proceedings.

When I returned to Manchester, the first thing that greeted me on my desk was the program for the conference of the Association of Business Historians (ABH). Running across the top were the words: "sponsored by BAT." I asked the ABH president why BAT was supporting the conference and also questioned the suitability of BAT as a source of funding (it was the first time an ABH conference had carried any business sponsor's name). I never received a reply and I did not attend the conference. So I never did find out why the ABH had accepted sponsorship from a company well known (particularly in the USA) for providing scientific misinformation, attempting to curb freedom of speech, and misleading the House of Representatives—aside from manufacturing a carcinogen that kills 4 million people each year worldwide.

Gatherings of business historians, of course, are small-scale affairs; and BAT's sponsorship was a trivial matter set against its support for more high profile-events. However, the affair seemed to be symptomatic of the approach of business historians to the corporate world—in particular, their almost complete failure to address those areas of business activity that one might label corporate crime or misconduct.

I need to start with a disclaimer: these issues had hardly featured in my own work until the mid-1990s. Much of my output had been in mainstream business history, largely involving the history of technology, the analysis of individual companies, and the achievements of various entrepreneurs. Like most business historians, I drew my theoretical frameworks from America, where the emphasis was on the detailed analysis of business structures and corporate strategies. The result is history with an onward and upward theme, which is generally sympathetic to big business (in historian's parlance, Whig history). When I began work on the asbestos industry and Turner & Newall (T&N), prompted by my colleague, David Jeremy, who has long had an interest in ethical issues in business history, it soon became clear that the evidence would not support this comforting view of business. It was not that T&N was not a great success story—in fact, during the 1950s it was one of Britain's most profitable multinationals—but that its main product killed (and is still killing) thousands of individuals. It soon became apparent that T&N's actions (and those of other firms, such as Cape Asbestos) were such that if the UK had had any effective factory laws then the company directors involved would have been jailed for manslaughter. By the 1970s, if not earlier, asbestos had all the hallmarks of a rogue industry, one which (at its worst) often disregarded health and safety laws, suppressed scientific information, avoided paying compensation, violated anti-trust laws and irresponsibly injured thousands of individuals.

What was also striking was that there was no tradition of dealing with this type of subject-matter in business history. Business historians like to think that they are conversant with ethical issues—and indeed there has been some work on the interactions between religion and business—but in truth none of this has got to grips in any way with the capacity of companies and business leaders to behave badly, even criminally.

Business history thus lags behind other disciplines where the study of corporate criminality does have some foothold. For example, there are now journals of business ethics, courses on the subject and the literature is beginning to burgeon. Textbooks by Maurice Punch (1996) and by Gary Slapper and Steve Tombs (1999) have recently appeared. The Punch book provides a good overview of management and organizational misbehavior, using a case-study approach to discuss the Bank of Credit and Commerce International (BCCI), Bhopal, Guinness, thalidomide and so forth. Punch is very good at showing the discrepancy between the popular image of business as a highly respectable activity (what Punch describes as the "management myth") and what can happen behind the scenes—power struggles, rivalry, the manipulation of information and the pursuit of short-term ends. The Slapper and Tombs volume is more thematic and is particularly good on the theoretical and legal debates. Both draw on an extensive literature. However, their bibliographies are notably devoid of work by business historians—though Slapper and Tombs do cite in passing Leslie Hannah (1983) on the history of the corporate economy in the UK.

Since neither Punch nor Slapper and Tombs would describe themselves as experts in business history, one might suspect that this was an oversight. I conducted a literature search to find out. This soon produced plenty of books on corporate criminality, which often contained some history: Tom Bower (1991, 1996) on Robert Maxwell; Philip Knightley (1981; Knightley et al., 1980) on thalidomide and the meat-dealing Vesteys; Ivan Fallon and James Strodes (1983) on the car-maker DeLorean; Charles Raw (1971; Raw et al., 1977) on the finance companies International Overseas Services (IOS) and Slater Walker; Anthony Sampson (1977, 1982) on arms dealers and bankers; Geoffrey Hodgson (1984) and Adam Raphael (1994) on the insurers Lloyd's of London; and Martin Gregory (1994) on the Virgin and British Airways debacle. These books cover subjects as diverse as tax-dodging, bribery, pension fraud, corporate "dirty tricks," espionage, and scientific malfeasance. Some will be familiar to the general public because they were bestsellers or they were serialized in newspapers. All were written by freelance writers or journalists, not academic historians.

Surely, one imagines, more scholarly work is available on corporate crime. However, when I tried to expand the above list, I found only four titles! John Garrard (1987) on an obscure utilities scandal; George Robb (1992) on white-collar crime in England; Markham Lester (1995) on Victorian insolvency; and John Harris (1998) on Anglo-French industrial espionage. None of these books would count as mainstream business history: the late John Harris was an economic historian; Robb and Lester are professors of history; and Garrard is a social and political historian. To be sure, a little extra digging does capture slightly more business-history writing on shady business dealings. A few fraudsters, speculators and black sheep appear in the London School of Economics' *Dictionary of Business Biography:* Jabez Balfour (Cleary, 1984–86), Horatio Bottomley (Shaw, 1984–86), Clarence Hatry (Fanning, 1984–86), and Ernest Hooley (Richardson, 1984–86). Jeremy and Tweedale (1994) extended this coverage in a reference book on twentieth-century businessmen by profiling, *inter alia,* Peter Clowes, Asil Nadir, Ernest Saunders, John Poulson and Robert Maxwell. Jeremy (1998) includes a chapter on various forms of unethical business behavior in a recent textbook. And no one should ignore the work of Richard Davenport-Hines (1984), with his sharp eye for rogues and his flair for describing them.

However, this is clearly a meager list. I teach classes in business history that touch on business ethics and it is very difficult to cite traditional academic monographs. If one wants to use any literature in this field for teaching, then almost invariably one is citing the work of the Fleet Street "hacks." Think of any recent business crime or scandal and the media have covered it first, either through publications or through television documentaries. In 1992, George Robb had been moved to write that the "best work in business history is increasingly sensitive to the criminal aspects of its subject matter" (Robb, 1992: 6). Clearly, the trend, if it existed, did not continue. A striking feature of Davenport-Hines's work is that the business world he describes, with its backstairs fixing and dubious business morality, is so different from that depicted by most business historians.

To find the literature so scanty is odd. Maurice Punch has argued that one of the places one might expect to find corporate wrongdoing as an object of academic study would be in business schools. He found the exact opposite. Similarly, one might also expect that the subject would be of serious interest to business historians. After all, they have the necessary long-term perspective; they have a tradition of patient archival research (often combined with the requisite writing skills); and they examine a wide range of subject-areas that are relevant to corporate crime— management strategies, entrepreneurial behavior, ethics, government regulation and labor policies. Why, then, this lacuna?

I suspect that a business historian's defense might run as follows. First, campaigning journalism and moral outrage are a bad model for academic work, because as we know journalists and TV documentary-makers write for the railway bookstall and feed off scoops, single-case studies and sensation. Corporate crime is, anyway, a hazy subject that is probably incapable of definition and statistical analysis. Even if it exists, it plays only a marginal role in the economy, which is mostly conducted by honest businessmen and reputable companies. Moreover, most criminality is contemporary and therefore not "history."

These defenses do not stand up to closer scrutiny. The condescension that academic historians feel for freelancers and journalists is not always justified. Many books by journalists, though they often lack the scholarly apparatus of a university-press monograph, are first rate. Some of them have been best sellers and highly influential. Still one of the most insightful books on smoking is by a former BBC reporter, Peter Taylor (1984). He looked at the protective circle of politicians, advertisers and tobacco lobby groups that help perpetuate the profits of the tobacco firms. With Conservative politician Kenneth Clarke as BAT deputy-chairman, Margaret Thatcher as a Philip Morris consultant, and John Carlisle as head of the Tobacco Maufacturers' Association, this book is as relevant as ever. Taylor's efforts have been repeated more recently by journalists such as Peter Pringle (1998). The asbestos scandal first reached a wider audience in America due to the campaigning American journalist Paul Brodeur (1985) and a number of investigative reporters in Britain. One of the most revealing books on South African asbestos mining (and other mining industries there) is by the ex-*World in Action* journalist Laurie Flynn (1992). Often these books have a significant historical component and also tackle more general themes, such as corporate accountability, fraud and the ethics of capitalism.

Certainly, there are methodological problems in defining corporate malfeasance and this does present problems for business historians who are more aware than most that the concept has changed over time. Originally, the corporation, according to Lord Thurlow, had "no soul to be damned and no body to be kicked" (Lord Thurlow, quoted in Leigh, 1969: 4). For some considerable time, the law was framed to protect corporate liability and there were no corporate "crimes." But corporate accountability has been changed by Parliament and the courts to ensure that companies are now seen as entities capable of crime. Obviously, any definition should encompass any act committed by corporations (or business leaders) that is punished by administrative, civil or criminal law. Perhaps, too, this definition should be extended to include other acts which are morally reprehensible, according to either religious or moral codes, but have not been deemed as punishable or have escaped punishment. Either way, one feels that business historians should be able to construct a workable theoretical framework that allows them to explore ethical issues.

The empirical work that does exist on business crime shows that it is far from marginal; it also shows that it has deep *historical* roots. The term "white-collar crime" was coined in the 1940s by American sociologist Edwin Sutherland. Besides helping to define the term ("a crime committed by a person of respectability and high social status in the course of his occupation," Sutherland 1949: 9), Sutherland also tried to map its extent by examining the histories of the 70 largest corporations and logging their legal violations. All the corporations had been in court and had decisions against them, the average number being 14. Even if limited to criminal convictions, the data showed 60 corporations had an average of four convictions each—as Sutherland notes, this is defined by statute as "habitual" criminality. This pioneering work was belatedly duplicated on a larger sample of firms in the 1970s, which confirmed this picture of generalized criminality (Slapper and Tombs, 1999: 37–41). There is no comparable work by historians. Indeed, I have never seen Sutherland's work even referenced by a business historian. However, the historical studies conducted by Robb (1992) and Lester (1995) also paint a picture of Victorian society in which white-collar crime and financial chicanery were rife.

This evidence, too, tends to undermine the view that corporate skulduggery is too modern a phenomenon to be regarded as history. To be sure, many of the events are contemporary or very recent. However, business history has been pushing its center of gravity ever closer to the present day (largely in its search for relevance). Since many contemporary events shed light on the culture of the past, should not business historians do the same with corporate crime?

## Business Historians as Good Capitalists

There are other reasons why traditional business history finds it difficult to engage with the underbelly of capitalism. These relate to the academic roots of the subject and the outlook of business historians. Few of them (including this writer) have any direct experience of business—which may explain the tendency for historians to see business as a profession, and business life as largely filled with respectable professionals (which it manifestly is not). Whatever the reason, business-history writing (like criminology itself) has been overwhelmingly conservative, with business historians acting as "good" capitalists. Since the 1950s, when business history began to evolve as a speciality, the academic attitude to business leaders has been friendly, even reverential. Indeed, the avowed aim of one of the first practitioners of business history (T. S. Ashton at the London School of Economics, LSE) was to counterbalance what he saw (in the late 1950s) as the prevalent negative picture of industrialists. Not surprisingly, it is difficult to think of any economic historians who have been critics of capitalism—at least, none that have written business history. Even Sidney Pollard, with his radical and Marxist background, wrote very traditional business history. It was perhaps unfortunate (and perhaps revealing) that the LSE's most famous socialist economic historian—R. H. Tawney—was unsympathetic to business history. Overall, the ethos of business history was that the entrepreneur and business had been given a raw deal in the historical record.

This pro-business outlook was given a further push in the early 1980s, with the development of the business school ethos and the hegemony of American big business. Business historians hoped to position themselves within management faculties and business schools (thus following the American model). This looked as though it would solve a question that has always dogged the writing of history—what is it for? But business historians have found that business schools are generally not interested in history, and the work of business historians continues, with a few exceptions, to be ignored by academics in the field of management. This is hardly surprising, given the fact that most management academics view business history with as much puzzlement and suspicion as business historians view the work of management writers. But the management school outlook has been influential, particularly the gospel according to the Harvard Business School. Here the writings of business historian Alfred D. Chandler Jr. have been hugely influential. In a series of major works, Chandler (1962, 1977, 1990) has sought to explain the rise of American business largely in terms of its management and company structure. In doing so, Chandler—himself related to the American elite (his middle name is DuPont)—became the chief chronicler of American corporatism. American business has seen a logical progression towards large multi-divisional, hierarchical organizations, staffed by professional managers. In a mirror image of the economic events he writes about, Chandler's writings (which also seek to explain European business success/failure) have spread across the Atlantic and influenced a whole generation of British business historians.

Chandler aimed to avoid the distrust of big business that he believed characterized the work of his fellow historians, whose work had sorted industrial statesmen into "bad fellows or good fellows . . . [and] . . . agreed that they were bad" (Chandler 1977: 5). Consequently, ethics and corporate misconduct never intrude into Chandler's sanitized view of American economic history. Sidney Pollard noted that "In Chandler's world no one ever bribes an American judge or an Asiatic prime minister, no one ever sets private armed police or private armies on strikers, no one manipulates the stock exchange" (quoted in Jeremy, 2001). Most business historians, however, have found Chandler's world highly congenial, thus ensuring that business history mirrors the current ideology of free and unfettered enterprise. This can be seen by scanning the last 10 years' volumes of the leading journals in the field. *Business History Review (BHR),* published by the Harvard Business School, contained only a handful of articles that discussed the more contentious aspects of big (or small) business. A search of about 150 *Business History Review* articles between 1990 and 2000 produced only a few that are remotely connected with corporate misconduct: Bittlingmayer (1996), E. J. Balleisen (1996) and Christian (1999). Given the role that antitrust, illegal marketing practices, fraud, corporate malpractice and labor problems have played in US history this is an extraordinary omission. This deficiency is unfortunately not rectified in the monograph literature, which is similarly one-sided. The latest publication of the editor of *BHR* is a book that praises the career of an American business leader—a former dean of the Harvard Business School (McCraw and Cruikshank, 1999)!

*Business History,* the leading UK journal, shows a similar bias. No articles since about 1990 have discussed corporate misconduct, though two studies (Tweedale and Jeremy, 1999; Darby, 1997) have glanced upon it. Among the hundreds of book reviews, only three discussed business misbehavior: Garrard's (1987) study of the Salford gas scandal; Davis's (1998) biography of a corrupt American oilman; and Geoffrey Searle's study of Victorian economic morality, which contains a chapter on "criminal capitalism" (1998: 77–106). What, then, were the most popular subjects? The bulk of the coverage related to globalism, foreign direct investment and the management aspects of big business. Almost every issue of *Business History* during the 1990s had an article relating to multinationals and/or the work of Chandler, sometimes more; and in the "special" issues of this journal the tendency became even more pronounced. An enormous amount of time and effort has been spent in compiling lists of the biggest firms or the richest individuals; and in analyzing the roots of British economic decline. The emphasis is on economic performance, which has been rated according to profit, productive efficiency and entrepreneurial success/failure.

Not surprisingly, many contemporary concerns are simply not addressed in business history. Anyone who has lost money through pension fraud, has been mis-sold an endowment mortgage, or has fallen victim to an investment scandal will be aware that the financial world is not always a bastion of integrity. Each of these offences has been commonplace within UK financial services in the past fifteen years or so, each continues to be covered by the mass media, and each has affected literally millions of people on these islands. Thus, one might expect that the work of business historians would reflect, in part, these aspects of City life. Certainly, a few books have touched upon fraud and corruption. Edwin Green and Michael Moss (1982) have described the Royal Mail group debacle in the 1930s. The problems with insider dealing and fraud in the City and Stock Exchange surface briefly in recent studies by Michie (1999) and Kynaston (1999). But mostly, business historians have shied away from any detailed discussion of these issues. Finance remains a growth area in business history, but only because it is replete with the commissioned histories of banks and insurance companies (most recently Ferguson, 1999; Hannah and Ackrill, 2001; and Moss, 2000). Anyone curious about the historical dimensions of, say, the Lloyd's of London meltdown will find journalism and the web (www.lliarsoflondon.com) far more useful than the academic press. Business historians can sound pompous and naïve when discussing City dealings. In a commissioned history of Price Waterhouse (and with the concerns regarding that firm's performance as auditors of BCCI before him), one historian wrote: "most would agree that standards of professional conduct should have an enduring quality and that those promulgated by the Victorians largely pertain today" (E. Jones, 1995: 24).

Similarly, there is no tradition among business historians of writing and debating about the environment, corporate ethics, and the political and social problems of multinationals in the Third World. Let me give one example. When I was examining T&N's corporate structure, it soon became evident to me that in North America the company operated through a web of holding companies and nominee shareholdings. These arrangements gave T&N (which was engaged in illegal price-fixing and cartels in the USA) a measure of protection from US antitrust laws. Later these same arrangements would hinder the victims of asbestos disease when they tried to file claims against the company. A competitor of T&N, Cape Asbestos, had taken such arrangements to their logical conclusion in 1981 by using a dummy company in Liechtenstein, so that it could market asbestos in America without risk of litigation (Flynn, 1992: 194). The actions of the asbestos companies were a backdrop to events in South Africa, where a mixture of flagrant disregard for health and safety and human rights abuses have produced a major epidemic of asbestos-related diseases. BAT has been criticized for using shell company tactics when defending itself against court actions involving its US subsidiary, Brown & Williamson (Pringle, 1998: 204–6).

What I wanted to know from the business history literature was, to what extent was this typical? Had other companies used "shells" and offshore arrangements for similar ends? What about the situation in South Africa? Despite the wealth of material that is now published by business historians on multinationals, I was unable to find anything useful. The fact that multinationals might behave badly hardly seems to have occurred to business historians. On South Africa, business historians have published almost nothing, leaving the field to more popular writers, such as Anthony Sampson (1987).

## Paying the Piper: The Commissioned-History Genre

A significant limiting influence on discussions of this nature has been the commissioning of house histories by major corporations, beginning with Charles Wilson's landmark study of Unilever (Wilson, 1954). For a time, it seems to have been *de rigueur* for every business historian to produce a doorstep-size house history. All the leading academic business historians in Britain active after the 1950s—Barker (Pilkington), Coleman (Courtaulds), Alford (W. D. & H. O. Wills), Supple (Royal Exchange Assurance), Church (Kenricks), Ashworth (British Coal)—wrote commissioned histories (Barker, 1977; Coleman, 1969–80; Alford, 1973; Supple, 1970; Church, 1969; Ashworth, 1986). The number of such histories—written either by academics or in-house—is enormous (Goodall et al., 1997). The genre provided a steady income for some freelance business historians, such as W. J. Reader, author of several house histories, beginning with his two-volume study of ICI (Reader, 1970–75). In the 1990s, the number of commissions hardly slackened, with major histories published on British Petroleum, GKN (a UK-based automotive and aerospace engineering group) and the Hong Kong & Shanghai Bank. Presently, the leading academic centers for business history at the LSE, Glasgow and Reading remain closely involved in the production of company histories, with sponsored volumes planned on Unilever (Geoffrey Jones), British Rail (Terry Gourvish), and Wellcome (Roy Church). This trend has had its counterpart in America, where the Harvard Business School, Yale, the Massachusetts Institute of Technology, and Columbia University have helped produce major authorized histories of companies such as Standard Oil, Ford and IBM.

Thus business history has fulfilled what some of its practitioners have seen as one its objectives: to be the handmaid of industry. The nature of the relationship can be shown by quoting from a primer, co-authored by one of the leading business historians of his day (Barker et al., 1971: 5–6):

> The success of any business history depends on . . . access to all the company's records . . . and freedom to comment upon them as he may choose. Of course, this freedom of search and comment may not extend to the present time . . . [as] . . . it is difficult to divulge anything which might embarrass the company in its present business affairs. A terminal date . . . should be agreed upon between those commissioning the history and the historian himself. Beyond that date . . . what the historian proposes to publish should be submitted for approval and amendment by the Board . . . Business history is not peculiar in this respect.

Obviously the chances of publishing anything critical under these deferential arrangements are slim. But, even today, this is the way many company histories are planned and written.

This is not entirely to denigrate commercial patronage: indeed, I have written a short commissioned history myself and, for a time, I was attracted to the genre. A commission gives an entrée to sources and key individuals; raises the profile of a university; enlarges a historian's income; often provides handsome funding for expenses; and offsets publication costs. A big company name and sponsorship can help smooth the path towards publication with the most prestigious presses (the current catalogues of both Oxford University Press and Cambridge University Press carry a sprinkling of commissioned histories). It might also be argued, paradoxically, that business support offers the scholar a chance to enjoy a measure of independence as a freelancer. Sometimes the formula has produced some outstanding work, such as Coleman's acerbic portrait of Courtaulds and Reader's magisterial two-volume history of ICI. However, there are many potential pitfalls, which are usually glossed over by the practitioners of business history. A classic example of these drawbacks is the commissioned history of Morgan Grenfell by Kathleen Burk (1989). This contains an intriguing preface, in which the author first expresses doubts about the wisdom of corporate histories and then credits Morgan Grenfell with giving her unrestricted access. It was said that only one actionable sentence in the book needed excision, but both the author and the company agreed that the period since 1981 was "of a different order" than the rest. This period proved so "different" that it is covered in an epilogue of about two pages. The reason: Burk's book was being completed as the Distillers-Saunders share-dealing scandal broke—a scandal in which Morgan Grenfell was implicated and related to which its staff were later convicted. To add spice to the tale, as the Burk study was being completed a former employee of Morgan Grenfell, Dominic Hobson, was writing an independent and far less flattering account (Hobson, 1990). The bank started legal proceedings to kill off the Hobson book, but failed.

They also considered shelving the Burk study, but eventually decided to publish it as the lesser of two evils.

Perhaps one should be grateful that the Burk history was published at all. Or should one? It seems that the bank was able to use the study as a counterweight to Hobson—with Burk in effect helping the company, as she herself put it, "to claim the ground." Hobson described this as a spoiling tactic (Kransdorff, 1998: 160–62). One business historian later dismissed Hobson's book as ephemeral and not history, believing that the Distillers-Saunders affair would only be "worthy of a full study when all the evidence has been reviewed and the courts have made their final judgements" (Chapman 1991: 126–27). On the other hand, the same criticisms could as easily be levelled at Burk's epilogue. One is hardly likely to consult it for insights into how Morgan Grenfell became involved with Ernest Saunders. One needs to turn to other sources for a perspective on Morgan Grenfell's business methods which offer as an alternative to that presented in its official history (Punch, 1996: 164–80).

The difference between the authorized history of a company and one penned by an outsider can be glaring. Allan Nevins, an American business historian, was responsible for multi-volume histories of Standard Oil and the Ford Motor Company. A conservative and an admirer of big business, Nevins, writing in the 1940s and 1950s, emphasized the constructive features and business genius of men such as Henry Ford and J. D. Rockefeller. Nevins described the latter as an industrial hero and philanthropist and was critical of the muckrakers of the Progressive era and writers such as Ida Tarbell (the scourge of Standard Oil) (Nevins, 1940, 1953). Among Rockefeller's papers, Nevins found only one case of Standard Oil bribery. Yet a more recent and widely-praised independent biography found that Rockefeller and his company "entered willingly into a staggering amount of corruption" (Chernow, 1998: 209). To cite another example, in 1987, Paul Johnson, a former left-wing editor of the weekly *New Statesman,* wrote an official "centenary portrait" of the South African mining company, Gold Fields. In his glossy book, Johnson had nothing but praise for the company, comparing its creative and morally elevating activities in South Africa to a work of art (Johnson, 1987). A somewhat different view of Gold Fields is presented by Laurie Flynn, who links the company with the brutalities of apartheid (Flynn, 1992).

Some company histories are simply suppressed. Mostly, this is because of the whim of the company, rather than the fact that anything untoward has been uncovered: however, it does underline the vulnerable position of commissioned histories. Most writers of such histories are familiar with that uneasy period after the final manuscript is deposited on the desks of the directors or the corporate communications staff. It is rare for drafts to avoid various suggestions for improvement, or even cuts. Sometimes historians collude with this process by voluntarily agreeing to a kind of historical elision (apparently acceptable to historians such as

Barker), in which anything that is too contemporary and controversial somehow never gets covered. This is perhaps the major weakness of company histories. It is not the fact that they are censored (though this does happen), but that they are usually profoundly formulaic. Such was my own history of Allen & Hanburys: it emanated—as do many such histories—from the public relations arm of the company. The historian does a chronological job that skates across the events of the immediate past and he/she (and the company) tacitly agree that such events are too recent to be placed in historical perspective or must wait for a later volume. Distillers (Weir, 1995), BAT (Cox, 2000), and Glaxo (Jones, 2001) have all been the subject of recent academic monographs which do not provide detailed accounts of recent and more controversial decades.

*The Global Cigarette,* the study of BAT by Howard Cox, illustrates this syndrome. The author has argued that his book is not a conventional corporate history, but this is somewhat belied by its company photographs, its foreword by BAT chairman Sir Duncan Oppenheim and its mostly favorable view of BAT's management. *The Global Cigarette* was especially lenient towards BAT's "unorthodox" chairman, Sir Hugo Cunliffe-Owen (who was involved in a number of financial scandals in the inter-war period). In his preface, Cox struck a sympathetic note when crediting an industry that he said had been obliged to become instinctively suspicious and defensive, arguing that BAT's support for his book (through its public relations department) represented an "extraordinary act of faith." BAT, of course, is well known for its largesse to worthy academic causes, but it is easy to see why it would be pleased with this effort: the book did not discuss anything controversial. As one reviewer noted, it was the first history of tobacco that he had read that did not mention cancer (Hilton, 2001). Nor would one guess from the text that BAT is the subject of intense interest at present, both for its activities in China (the country at the center of allegations of company involvement in cigarette smuggling), the nature of its relationship with its American subsidiary Brown & Williamson, and the status of its archive at Guildford, where lawyers and historians are afforded only the most carefully controlled access. For a more critical angle on BAT, one needs, again, to look at a non-academic study (Pringle, 1998).

Commissioned histories can exert a subtle influence on the way we view an industry. For example, most of what we know about the history of the pharmaceutical industry stems from a series of commissioned histories on Glaxo, May & Baker, Wellcome, and Smith & Nephew (Cantor, 1992). *No* business historian has yet written an independent monograph on the British pharmaceutical industry. Glaxo alone has commissioned three histories within the last decade or so (Tweedale, 1990; Davenport-Hines and Slinn, 1992; Jones, 2001). One might expect that the wealth of information in these meticulously researched and highly detailed books would be required reading for anyone interested in the turbulent environment in which the pharmaceutical industry now operates. Yet none of them look at the more controversial aspects of the drug industry. Business historians who had eagerly awaited Jones's volume (which was eight years in the making and was intended to bring the Glaxo story up to date) were no doubt disappointed to find that the cut-off date was 1985 (with the customary brief final chapter for more recent events). This was particularly frustrating, because Jones's book had been launched against the backdrop of a highly critical study of Glaxo by financial journalist Matthew Lynn (1991). Indeed, the savaging that the Lynn book gave Glaxo may have partly prompted the company's support for Jones. Lynn had pilloried chairman Sir Paul Girolami and Glaxo for raising drug prices and had compared the company unfavorably with its rival, Merck. Glaxo's "main impact on the world," wrote Lynn, "has been only negative" (Lynn, 1991: 235).

Lynn's grasp of history is not always as accurate or convincing as that contained in the more detailed Glaxo house histories. Nevertheless, he does raise key issues—pricing policies, uncompetitive practices, the subjective nature of drug trials and the nature of government regulation—that are mostly absent from the "history" funded by the company. Lynn's depiction of ferocious commercial rivalry and infighting between the top Glaxo directors is probably closer to the truth than the commissioned accounts. We know that drugs can cause horrendous human disasters, such as those associated with thalidomide (a drug marketed in Britain by Distillers). We know that the drug "industry" involves a huge illicit trade in narcotics, aside from a vast legitimate trade in tranquillizers and other mind-altering substances (Davenport-Hines, 2001). We know that the industry can be vindictive to whistleblowers, such as Hoffmann-La Roche's Stanley Adams, whose attempt to expose illegality in the Swiss drug company led to the suicide of his wife and his own financial ruin (Adams, 1984). And we are aware that some of the business practices of even the biggest firms can be unethical (involving bribery, fraud in drug testing, unsafe marketing practices, violations of antitrust laws, and exploitation in the Third World). But we have usually not learned this from the work of academic business historians, who depict the industry almost entirely in terms of its huge commercial successes and benefits to the community. It has been left to others to chart the more controversial reaches of the pharmaceutical industry (Braithwaite, 1984; Robinson, 2001).

I have been looking recently at industrial health and safety, where the cost in human life is staggering. The current death rate is still hundreds of fatalities a year through accidents and literally thousands a year through occupational health diseases (such as those caused by asbestos). Many, perhaps most, of these deaths involve *criminality*—in other words, breaches of health and safety laws. Despite its evident importance, occupational health as yet has no place in the business history literature (indeed, it is rarely encountered in medical history). The coal industry is as good as an example as any. It reveals some disturbing holes in our knowledge. The death toll from pneumoconiosis (black lung disease) has been enormous, with well over 1,500 a year dying from the disease in the 1960s—and that figure itself is a gross underestimate. Both exposure to coal dust and "accidents" in coal-mining have each been the cause of thousands of deaths. No coal historian has ever looked specifically at health and safety and for enlightenment I turned to the multi-volume official history of the National Coal Board (NCB), published by Oxford University Press. The modern period is covered by William Ashworth in a book of about 700 pages, in which about eight fairly pedestrian pages discuss dust diseases and generally provide a reassuring picture of NCB policies (Ashworth, 1986: 564–72). A very different picture has emerged in recent litigation against the NCB, in which the industry has been found liable for a whole range of criminal offences relating to failures to control dust and protect the workforce (British Coal Respiratory Disease Litigation, 1998). The failure to compensate injured coal miners adequately (a subject on which Ashworth is silent) has belatedly and predictably emerged as another scandal. Perhaps even more striking is the authorized account of the Aberfan coal tip disaster, with its sympathetic portrayal of the actions of the NCB and its chairman Lord Robens (Ashworth, 1986, 285–99). Robens is largely absolved of responsibility for Aberfan and particularly for the episode when he fought doggedly to prevent the NCB having to pay for the tip removal (eventually the government raided the Aberfan Disaster Fund for £150,000—a scandalous decision that was reversed only in 1997). However, a project on Aberfan at Nuffield College, funded by the Economic and Social Research Council (ESRC), describes the disaster in completely different terms—as an example of corporate criminality, with Robens at its center (McLean and Johnes, 2000).

## The Historical-Industrial Complex

Business history, of course, is no better or worse than any other academic discipline. It responds to the subtle pressures and constraints imposed by higher education, alongside external problems relating to funding, access to documents and publication. Financing specialist historical projects in any subject area is always difficult and the number of funding councils that offer substantial support to business history is small: the ESRC, the Wellcome Trust and the Leverhulme Trust. In addition, business historians have been plagued more than most academics by the uncertainties created by short-term university contracts. As regards archives, public records are subject to the 30-year rule, which hinders access to contemporary events. Not all public records are released after this period and, as historians know only too well, many records are found to have been arbitrarily destroyed by the Public Record Office. Zealous government officials destroyed large amounts of material relating to the government and the arms manufacturers (most of it covering the period between 1900 and 1939), not because of censorship, but merely because officialdom decided that the documents were of no further interest. Another obstacle to reconstructing the past is the protection given to litigation records produced in trials. Unless documents are read into the court record, then in the UK they are given absolute protection. This is typical British secretiveness and I have never seen any reasonable explanation of why in criminal trials records should not be made public. It is in complete contrast to the USA, where trials are public events and, unless there is a protective order in place, the documents can be obtained and used freely.

Company records—those produced and held by a business that is still operating—are usually private property and made available only with the consent of the owners. Business historians often forget that company documents are almost invariably the records that industry is making available, subject to all kinds of corporate control and filtering. Corporate documents will often subtly present an official view of the industry—surely an important consideration in the case of the pharmaceutical industry. Yet for most business historians, these records remain the primary source material for their research. The number of formal company archives has been increasing: the UK had less than 10 company archives in 1970, but the number probably now surpasses a hundred. In the USA, the number of such archives had reached 200 by 1980 and today most of the major US corporations have established their own corporate archives (E. Green, 2001). Not all of these archives were founded for the benefit of historians (who remain minor users of them), but some are intertwined with academic business history and the commissioning of house histories. The BP archive at Warwick University (and the resulting multi-volume history by Ferrier, 1982 and Bamberg, 1994, 2000) is an example of such a development. Another is the Hagley Library in Delaware (funded by Du-Pont), which has close links with the University of Delaware (also endowed by the state's chemical industry). The use of company archives as a basis for academic work raises a number of key issues. Although there are plenty of guides to corporate archives, no one, it appears, has yet examined the terms of access to these archives. Nevertheless, it is clear that some conditions of use (such as those imposed by Boots, a major UK drugstore chain) are highly restrictive. The BP archive at Warwick University imposes a 40-year closure rule. Whatever the terms, no one is in any doubt that permissions are needed for publication and that this depends on building a satisfactory relationship with the company and its archivist.

This has had the effect of creating a kind of historical-industrial complex, in which companies, their archivists, and historians rub shoulders and agree on common agendas. The manifestation of this entente cordiale is the Business Archives Council (BAC, registered in 1934), on which academics, business leaders and archivists intermingle to encourage the worthy aim of preserving and listing corporate records. Based in London, the BAC has strong banking and City connections and draws on corporate funding.

Of course, linkages between big business and historians are much more far-reaching than this. Corporate funding and influence can penetrate museums and the burgeoning heritage industry (both occasionally employers of business historians). The result is often a sanitized version of events. Museum displays of the history of technology and the publications that accompany them have been criticized for their "progressive" depiction of events. For example, an American diamonds exhibit (funded by the Diamond Information Center, the propaganda arm of the De Beers Corporation) and an accompanying book published by Cambridge University Press were roundly attacked by one scholar. Neither the exhibit nor the book had mentioned the social impact of South African apartheid, the environmental damage caused by the diamond companies, or the questionable business methods and cartels that allowed them to maintain a monopoly (Proctor, 2000).

## Perils of "Rocking the Boat"

Historians who nevertheless insist on pursuing contentious themes may discover other problems. Bad news is never kindly received, especially in institutions that increasingly draw on corporate goodwill and funding. Universities and industry have become more interlocked than ever (Monbiot, 2000b). It is salutary to know that Sutherland's pathbreaking work on white-collar crime was censored by his university (Yale), so that the corporations guilty of criminal behavior were never named until an "uncut" version of Sutherland's book was published over 30 years later (Sutherland, 1983). More subtle are the pressures exerted by publishers, lawyers and insurers through copyright and especially libel law. Copyright law can make it difficult (and at times impossible) to quote freely from records without permission; libel law can ensnare an author in a web of litigation.

English libel law is notoriously favorable to plaintiffs. Any unduly critical statement can be interpreted as defamatory, and that is all that is required to start a legal action. At this point the burden is entirely on the defendant to prove the truth of the comments. There is neither a right to free speech nor any public interest defense (as in America); the plaintiff does not even need to be named (provided he can be identified from the text); and there is no legal aid. Libel law is tailored for business people and for companies, which can also sue for their injured reputation. Criticizing a company or an executive for criminal activity can therefore be a risky affair—even for a lawbreaker like John Poulson (who had to withdraw his autobiography, *The Price*, in 1981). The McLibel trial has shown that companies can sue for libel over even the mildest criticism (Vidal, 1997). The Japanese company Nomura sued an American author, Albert Alletzhauser (1990), and the English publisher Bloomsbury, when they published a history of the company that emphasized its links with organized crime. This was described as "a particularly outrageous example of a powerful company trying to use the law of libel to muzzle its critics" (Hooper, 2000: 175). Robert Maxwell and Armand Hammer were experts in exploiting British libel laws and notorious suers. For years, both men waged wars of attrition against their unauthorized biographers, Tom Bower (1991, 1996) and Steve Weinberg (1989) respectively. None of these companies or businessmen were successful in their actions (though the McDonald's case might be seen as a split decision), but the litigation resulted in enormous trouble and costs to the defendants.

Authors often naively assume that by ensuring that their statements are true they can avoid problems with libel. Often, however—as the Maxwell case showed—it is the fact that statements *are* true that causes the problem. Moreover, as I found when writing *Magic Mineral to Killer Dust* (Tweedale, 2000), the threat of libel can trigger difficulties even before a book is published. Authors need publishers; contracts have to be formulated and signed; universities may want to protect their reputation; publishers have their own commercial interests; insurers may be involved; and legal counsel are sometimes retained. My asbestos book soon acquired a whole raft of interested parties, all intent on avoiding legal action from T&N—a company that was still operating (and defending multimillion dollar lawsuits) as I completed my book. One might imagine that legal action from a discredited industry would be a negligible consideration: however, Cape Asbestos had been swift in the 1970s to use the libel laws to suppress an amateur theater production criticizing its treatment of workers; and in the 1980s one of the most outspoken critics of the asbestos industry, Alan Dalton, was bankrupted by a libel trial after he had accurately portrayed a physician, Dr. Robert Murray, as a supporter of the asbestos industry (Dalton, 1979). In 1993 and 1994, T&N had attempted to intimidate the media by issuing formal complaints against the BBC for radio and television programs that had criticized the company.

My own university was uneasy about a project as controversial as the asbestos industry, especially since it was based on T&N documents that had been produced by legal discovery in America. The manuscript was therefore carefully vetted by a lawyer in London. He believed that the bulk of the book could be published as it stood: however, he recommended a number of cuts, among other suggestions. All prejudicial language would have to be removed. This meant deleting any reference to corporate *crime* (the preferred word was "misconduct"), even though Turner & Newall had been convicted and fined for health and safety violations. A reference to corporate "murder" was also marked for deletion, even though this word appeared in a quotation from someone else. All defamatory references to living individuals were earmarked for emendation or deletion, even though the statements could be supported. The libel lawyer was particularly punctilious about any criticisms of the medical fraternity. Any suggestion that doctors were complicit in the asbestos tragedy, or had any financial or legal relationship with the leading companies, was described as too risky for publication.

Most of these emendations I regarded as unnecessary or repugnant, but if they had not been made, then the university, its insurers and the publishers would have withdrawn their support. Eventually, after a year's delay, the book was published, but libel law had had its predictably chilling effect. Ironically, the trepidation proved to be misplaced: in a spectacular commercial blunder, T&N was bought by an American company, Federal-Mogul, which by 2001 was in Chapter 11 bankruptcy under the weight of its acquired asbestos liabilities.

## Conclusion

*Magic Mineral to Killer Dust* thus takes its place on a very limited bookshelf of business history books that have been critical of industry. These studies have shown that not all companies are respectable organizations and that there are darker aspects to industrialization—abuse of power, contempt for the law, unfair trade practices and fraud. Will there be many more books on these themes? Given the constraints noted above, it seems unlikely. Nevertheless, there is clearly great potential for alternative views of British industrialization, but only if academic business history adopts a wholly new mentality and approach—almost a new direction and range of source materials. Admittedly, it is not an easy route and this chapter has highlighted some of the problems. Nevertheless, I am convinced that this is an area that business historians should engage with more often. The problems are not entirely insurmountable and the results can be very worthwhile.

In his study of the South African mining industry, Laurie Flynn has argued that,

> Nowadays few popular newspapers bother to investigate the complexities of modern business life with any degree of scepticism or persistence, excusing their lack of vigilance in the public interest with explanations about the appetites of their audience, their readers' difficulty or disinterest in understanding the world of economic production. But investigative television can still lay that world bare and set out the intricacies of malpractice or intrigue in such a way that any citizen can comprehend the arcane processes by which people can be robbed with a fountain pen. (1992: 75)

Business history also has this capacity to lay the world bare. The subject matter is extraordinarily wide. We still have no major biographies of business rogues (despite the work of Richard Davenport-Hines); there is no monograph on the UK arms industry; the literature is almost devoid of studies on business and the environment (though Clapp, 1994 has made a start); and the history of law and business—even aside from criminal aspects—is badly in need of research. Company fraud remains a fertile area for study. So too does occupational health, and there are many contemporary issues upon which historians could shed light, such as the influence of lobby groups and the impact of business on science. The other side of the coin—ethical companies—also deserves more attention from business historians. In particular, Sutherland's work needs to be repeated for British industry. I am not urging that business historians should become muckrakers or that current concerns with strategy and structure should be discarded—merely that historians should adopt a much more sceptical and objective approach. Along with all the management-oriented work that passes for business history at the turn of the millennium, business historians should also include corporate criminality in the equation. Only then will they be able to hold up a mirror to the business world.

## Acknowledgments

I am grateful to my colleague David Jeremy for his comments on a draft of this chapter.

# CCTV Surveillance, Power, and Social Order

## *The State of Contemporary Social Control*

## Introduction

Research into the development of closed circuit television (CCTV) schemes in the towns and cities of the UK offers critical criminologists a gateway through which to develop an analytical focus on questions of power and its effects in reproducing particular social relations. Key questions raised by any analysis of the nature and role of CCTV should include the following: What does the growth of CCTV tell us about the nature of contemporary state power and the possibilities for scrutinizing that power? And how is the development of CCTV networks related to the establishment and maintenance of definitions of crime by those who have spearheaded surveillance networks? These are definitions which, incidentally, further obscure from political and academic agendas the harm generated by powerful agencies.

From a critical vantage point, CCTV can and must be understood less as a crime prevention technology and more as a social field of power that has denoted shifts in state organizational capacity and strategies of legitimacy. While the growth of visual surveillance has been bound up with these wider processes, it has been uncritically endorsed by academic criminologists whose limited research questions in this area have been largely concerned with whether CCTV can work as a tool for reducing both crime and the fear of crime. Of course, this work may serve to challenge the official rhetoric behind CCTV—specifically, that it can reduce crime—but it must be supplemented by critical qualitative investigations that examine more fundamental *political* questions of camera networks and the social relations they inhabit. Overall, and to date, camera networks have been less understood for the frameworks of material and ideological power out of which they have developed and more for their contribution to fostering very limited notions of "public safety" and crime reduction in urban settings.

This chapter explores briefly the dominant ways in which CCTV has been viewed by academic researchers. Notwithstanding significant differences between these, a common theme is their failure to attend to questions of power and "the powerful," specifically through a methodological, epistemological and theoretical myopia regarding the "state" and emergent state forms. The implications of bringing the state back in are discussed within the context of my own research, and the chapter also sets out the methodological consequences of acting upon this prescription: thus, I document the ways in which the locally powerful might be subjected to critical research. The chapter concludes with a general discussion of the implications for the research process of bringing the state back into understandings of contemporary social control.

## Contemporary Myths: CCTV, Social Control, and the Neo-Liberal State

Like all criminological research, the research process around CCTV has taken place within a politicized environment. According to Groombridge and Murji (1994: 283), CCTV has been viewed in government circles as unproblematic and has also become "big business" so that it "now seems set to achieve the status of an article of faith in popular crime prevention discourse."[1] At times the debate around CCTV has been sharply polarized among researchers. Some have argued *for* CCTV as a necessary and straightforward policy response to increasing crime and incivility, and as a tool in reviving the public realm (Home Office, 1994; Oc and Tiesdell, 1997; Tilley, 1998; Brown, 1995). These "mainstream" accounts have encouraged a discourse of administration and efficiency, a concern with "what works" that has helped marginalize wider questions and arguments and any deeper theoretical analysis concerned with the conditions of emergence of CCTV networks. Other researchers have noted the problematic nature of research in this area and produced findings questioning the value of CCTV; and they have "often [been] portrayed as enemies of the public interest" (S. Davies, 1996a: 328). These accounts—as "alternatives" to mainstream versions—have questioned CCTV for its detrimental impact upon civil liberties (Davies, 1996b; Fyfe, 1995; Fay, 1998), its limited value regarding women's safety (S. Brown, 1997) and its role in encouraging private sector involvement in circumscribing the legitimate uses of urban public centers (Fyfe and Bannister, 1996; Reeve, 1998).

In broad terms, along with the expansion of camera networks we have witnessed the growth of a technical and pragmatic knowledge. This has been based on a methodological approach informed by the mind-set of public/private security partnerships and their concern with efficient administration, rather than with any questioning of the domain assumptions and rationales that underpin this market/state nexus.[2] In expanding the research process to include questions of social theory, a number of researchers have started to develop more critical, theoretical accounts, raising issues connecting CCTV to processes concerning an intensification in the exclusionary potential of contemporary social control (Norris and Armstrong, 1998), in terms of the privatization of public space (Fyfe and Bannister, 1996), and as indicative of an emerging "new penology" concerned to manage "the dangerous" (McCahill, 1998). Yet although this work raises issues concerning the social aspects of CCTV surveillance, a central argument of my chapter is that this work remains remarkably under-theorized with reference to the wider shifts in state formation that have underpinned the findings from these studies. Furthermore, it often draws a false and hasty distinction between public and private domains of power and expertise concerned with the management and control of urban spaces. Thus, any historical continuities in the power to apply social censure to particular groups as ideological signifiers of urban decay have been lost along with the role of militarized state practices that coexist with camera networks in contemporary urban settings (Davis, 1990). More broadly there has been a turn away from state theory in social science generally and criminology in particular. This turn has had serious implications for understanding the operation and trajectory of power in contemporary societies and in downplaying any intellectual role in challenging that power. Thus, across an apparently broad spectrum of academic research on CCTV—from "mainstream" and alternatives to mainstream through to more critical, "theoretical" accounts—there is an almost complete failure to address the state, "power" and "the powerful" in any meaningful fashion.

The diminution of intellectual scrutiny of state power, along with a deemphasis on its theorization, has been supported, first, by globalization theses and, second, by neo-Foucauldian approaches to understanding power. Instrumental in the former has been the work of Castells (1997) who stressed a decline in "the institutional capacity" of the nation state, "undermined by globalization of core economic activities . . . media and electronic communication, and by globalization of crime" (ibid: 244) underpinned by the increasing role of corporations in political decision-making and policing and surveillance activities. Thus, Castells has argued that the state "in the information age is a network state," born of a complex set of transactions engaged in the sharing of power and decision-making between and within local, regional, national and international quasi-political institutions (Castells, 2000: 14). As noted elsewhere this line of analysis has underplayed the extent to which state and market forms of surveillance are interrelated (Fitzpatrick, 2001). Furthermore, globalization theses tend to omit sustained analysis of the characteristics and nature of the circuits of power that permeate the neo-liberal state form and of how that form is central to the ideological and material organization of surveillance practices. Neo-Foucauldian approaches have shared some of the implications of the above analysis in that power has become diversified and decentered through multiple logics and sites of exercise (Barry et al., 1996). This work has presented a form of pluralistic analysis and downplayed the possibilities for singular and unitary social ordering practices along with the possibilities for identifying, in ideological terms, centers of power. Furthermore, "public authorities" have sought to employ "forms of expertise in order to govern society at a distance without recourse to direct forms of repression and intervention" (ibid.: 14). Aligned to this understanding of contemporary power has been the concern to analyze this power in terms of managing social orders through the construct of dangerousness and techniques of risk assessment (Feeley and Simon, 1994). Writers in this field have characterized the development of a "new penology" that is actuarial in nature, less concerned with questions of morality and motivation in managing criminal behavior and more with managing border controls and the use of containment and exclusion practices under an expert panoply of preventative risk. The emphasis here also has been on the growth of corporate instrumentalism, driving social control practices and undermining the unitary order of sovereign states in depositing "not one conception of order but many" (Shearing and Stenning, 1996: 417).

Recent strands in the theorization of social control have brought forth a number of assumptions that have too readily distinguished between state and corporate forms of control, often viewing states as less powerful, and indeed often irrelevant in the formulation of control strategies. Sovereign control has been displaced by multiple orders.[3] Forms of ideological power and moral censure have been displaced by the cold, calculated gaze of "autonomous" experts reliant upon their statistical grids of risk assessment. Social control has become diffuse and filtered through a widening network of responsible parties who oversee and administer disaggregated parts of fragmentary social relations. Or so the story goes.

## Urban Power Blocs and the Role of CCTV

The camera network in Liverpool, the impetus for which emerged within the private sector, was established in July 1994 with £400,000 from European, central government, and private sector sources; in August 2001, a £4 million expansion was announced which will enable 240 cameras and 20 loud hailers to be monitored and controlled from a central control room and to cover an area bigger than 20 football pitches. The city center manager and Merseyside Police manage the system, which is operated by private security personnel who work closely with an intelligence-gathering forum, Crime Alert (Coleman and Sim, 1998). At the time the camera network was launched, a Home Office minister evoked the murder of a local child to stress the need for CCTV, and this was elaborated in local and national reports (Ibid). Those interviewed for this research[4] identified a range of other factors that led to the introduction of the cameras and their subsequent role in the city center and, for them, underpinned what was deemed to be in the interests of "the city as a whole." The notion of regeneration as articulated by senior urban managers aided the unification of an ideological framework that promoted particular visions for the city while identifying problems deemed to hinder these visions. The discourse of "regeneration"—"a powerful and particularly encompassing metaphor" (Furbey, 1999: 420)—provided the driving force for neo-liberal state strategies of political rule within which CCTV was rationalized. Under the banner of regeneration, the urban order and its rule were constructed by coalitions of established, locally powerful actors who were able to articulate and define a politics of responsibilization concerning the authorization of "credible" organizations marshalled in this process. Drawing the boundaries of state power and action involved "the focusing of minds and the negotiation of sensible terms of reference" (research interview). Another interviewee referred to "the transparency of the process," in that "when you are setting something up you go and talk to somebody who will respond to your need" (research interview). Police involvement "lends legitimacy to what they [partnerships] do" in handling recourses "and making partnerships do the right thing rather than what suits their own agenda" (research interview). In this sense, partnership has been constituted by a vernacular of power that has been emblematic of a "correspondence of interests" (Hall and Scraton, 1981: 474) between ruling fractions within the local power bloc.

In this context, the camera network expressed the "confidence" of urban managers in attracting businesses, consumers and tourists to the city: "CCTV has so many uses. It's fantastic. It helps us build the right image to make a world class city" (research interview). Sending out a message to "capital and people of the right sort" underpinned the establishment and promotion of surveillance in the city. At the same time, constructing a reinvigorated urban aesthetic involved sending out a message to those targeted by the system: "[T]hey know that we are watching" (research interview). Groups and individuals were identified as unfitting and unwelcome in the city's renaissance. Those interviewed expressed negative sentiments towards street traders, the homeless, shoplifters and young people. These observations were not based upon any abstract risk calculus but upon normative judgements as to the proper uses of city space and power-laden discourses of what constituted public safety and, therein, the role of surveillance cameras.[5] Licensed street traders were monitored since they contributed to the image of "a low grade economy." As part of this targeting, urban managers played upon and contributed to the construction of urban rumors regarding the street traders. They were described as benefit cheats and nuisances involved in the handling of stolen goods.[6] Young people and suspected school truants were also unwelcome in the city center: "The fact that they aren't doing anything intimidates people, and, it seems almost pointless to ask where are their parents in all of this?" (research interview). Under the Crime and Disorder Act, partnerships in Liverpool have utilized sophisticated geographical information systems to create so-called "yob maps" that have detailed the "top 130 yob zones" with one estimated youth disorder incident for every 40 people (*Liverpool Echo*, 16 March, 2001). There is nothing particularly new about the targeting of low-income groups within the capitalist urban form. Researchers may only be beginning to recognize that the power to marginalize and criminalize such groups has, however, been channelled more widely across the institutional components of the contemporary state/market nexus. A hegemony of crime prevention has been constructed through this institutional form which has prioritized public over private risk, pursuing petty violations over a range of powerful public and private actions that have deleterious effects on society in general and on the relatively powerless in particular. If CCTV networks are understood as neo-liberal state strategies of control, then we are in a better position to see how they have helped marginalize even further from public and intellectual scrutiny the socially harmful activities of corporations and public authorities. The marketization of the city center provided the context for the veneration and promotion of pro-business and entrepreneurial values in the name of the public interest. A reinforcement of the symbolic and moral capital of corporations, developers and businesses in the partnership network had occurred. Indeed, the involvement of private consortia within the trajectory of crime prevention and "community safety" has elevated private and unaccountable authorities to the status of guardians of the public good. Thus, it is less likely that these powerful coalitions will be scrutinized and considered as harm producers within academic and media circles.

The empirical and theoretical dimensions of my own work are not intended to suggest a monolithic state form that has been unravelling via a dispersal of discipline across the cityscape. Rather, my argument is for the need to "bring the state back in" as a contingent site for the organization and implementation of social control strategies. The forms of political rationale and domination with which these strategies have been conterminous must also be recognized. However, these processes have not been without contradictions and tensions between components of the state form. These extended to questions of who should fund the camera network,[7] and how it should be promoted and managed. Tensions existed over the deployment of armed officers in the streets of Liverpool in terms of image management.[8] Thus, although the police "are now part of the investment machinery" (research interview) in Liverpool, the tactic of visible shows of force on the streets was deemed, by other key players, to be harming the careful image management of the regeneration process, by portraying Liverpool as a dangerous city. Further tensions were born of the neo-liberal strategy of regeneration that prioritized expansion in the service industries, part of which included the objective of introducing a "bars" and "European-style café" culture in the city, which it was thought would lead to more crime.[9] What was deemed as "good" (or "bad") for the city's image constituted benchmark questions that guided senior managerial approaches and their ideological positioning to order maintenance practices. Other tensions arose not out of opposition to particular order maintenance practices but in their management and funding. In short, the *problems for order* were not deemed problematic, but the means to achieving order were.

It should also be emphasized here that the likelihood of the infliction of state harm and violence as a consequence of the measures outlined above has increased. Merseyside Police armed response units attend more incidents than anywhere else in the UK outside London. For example, the use of riot-trained officers in the city center resulted in out of court settlements costing £100,000 for one incident alone in September 1999; no criminal charges were brought against officers (*Liverpool Echo*, 5 July 2001). In the aftermath of this latter incident it was the image of regeneration that was seen as harmed: "Any disturbance causes me concern because of the wrong impression it can create of the city center" (Liverpool City Council Leader, quoted in Coleman et al., 2002). In July 2001, a mentally ill man was shot dead by police (*Liverpool Echo*, 6 August 2001).

## Power, CCTV, and Social Order: Researching the Emergent City-States

> Research is . . . beginning to examine the way that entrepreneurial landscapes—both real and imaginary—are ideologically charged and, moreover, to consider how urban regimes are capable of organising space and mobilising its meaning so as to give a semblance of democratic legitimacy to their activities. (Hall and Hubbard, 1996: 163)

What much of the social control literature and research into CCTV has omitted is any qualitative investigation of the agents and agencies involved in contemporary social control. Officially sponsored social control rhetoric has been taken as given, assumed rather than critically deconstructed. My own research has been concerned to explore contemporary social control through an examination of the development of camera surveillance within the processes of urban and state restructuring in the city of Liverpool in the UK. The material and ideological aspects of this restructuring are foregrounded in the analysis with particular emphasis upon the strategic visions for order articulated by senior personnel within coalitions of locally powerful interests and the neo-liberal state. Thus, underlying the promotion of CCTV networks have been powerful interests, organized through public-private coalitions, whose position of material and ideological power has been central to orchestrating local social ordering strategies (Coleman and Sim, 2000).[10]

Urban and political geographers more than criminologists have maintained an analytical scrutiny of the state, which can be understood as "a rapidly moving target" (Hay, 1996: 3). Weiss (1997) has argued that although it has become less fashionable to theorize the state in an era of "globalization" it has remained a key actor in building collaborative power arrangements to meet challenges to economic stability and social security. The devolution of state power is rejected in favor of an active "catalytic state" (ibid: 26). This has raised the problem of the nature of state boundaries and the authorization of the power to act within a given territory and thereby manage and shape social relations. Thus the state has to be understood historically via specific political practices through which power is organized and activated (Jessop, 1990). More pointedly state power must be analyzed as "socio-spatial activity" that presents "a series of context specific—but actively constructed—processes" (MacLeod and Goodwin, 1999: 505). The urban and regional restructuring that was underway from the middle of the 1980s became the means by which state restructuring was implemented (Swyngedouw, 1996). Traditional welfarist state forms became deemed increasingly inadequate to make possible the creation of competitive and entrepreneurial cities and regions. This has been important for thinking about how space has been rendered meaningful for urban managers and how such space has been ordered. Since the mid-1990s, in Liverpool, local government departments, businesses, developers, and policing agencies have formed (with the aid of European financing, central government grants, and private sector monies), partnerships in a selective process of regeneration in the city.[11] The marketing and image management of "place" has driven the work of these partnerships. Thus, alongside investment, tourism, and consumer campaigns have been discourses of safety and security seeking to re-image the locality as "a safe place to do business" (Coleman and Sim, 2000).[12] The representative and responsible individuals whose expertise and professional status have been so important in instigating partnerships and in activating so-called "government at a distance" can in fact be understood as a body of organizers and persuaders, or, in Gramscian terms, intellectuals of a leading social group (Gramsci, 1971: 10). These "new primary definers" can be understood as participants in the building of a particular social bloc, itself contradictory and discordant, designed to forge a "hegemonic project" (Jessop, 1990: 260) between the institutional components of a neo-liberal state.

State sovereign control over territory has not diminished but has realigned its institutional form and deployed a series of novel technologies and discursive arguments for territorial dominance. "Social sovereignty" has historically been the outcome of interaction between state forces and economic forces working in contingent "term setting" alliances able to make claims for sovereignty over particular domains (Latham, 2000: 1). In building a "hegemony of vision" (Zukin, 1996: 233), forces within the neo-liberal state have facilitated the "channelling of capital into the built environment" while providing assistance in "producing, controlling and surveilling social and physical spaces" designed to create "a relative crisis-free and cohesive civic order" (Swyngedouw, 1996: 1504). The focus on the technical aspects of social control within neo-Foucauldian approaches has downplayed both the processes orchestrating political control within the state form and the normative and ideological aspects of social control. City center partnerships can be understood, following Lacey, as engaged in "social ordering practices," as normative decision-making "in the context of underlying features of the social order" which also contains "locally dominant ideologies" pertaining to the nature of that order (Lacey, 1994: 30–31). Therefore, CCTV—as a contemporary aspect of social control practice—can be grasped less as a piece of technology involved in the control of crime, and more for its mediation by, and dialectical relationship to, wider social relations.

### Who Are the Powerful? Identifying and Accessing the Agents of the Neo-Liberal State

According to Crewe (1974: 17), one problem with British "elite studies" has been that they most commonly only recognize "'obvious' elites made visible by their concrete social organization"; thus "not all elites are embedded in tangible organizations with identifiable staffs, functions, buildings, etc.." This observation is particularly relevant in the era of *entrepreneurialism* referred to variously as "partnership" (J. Edwards, 1997), *local elite* (I. Taylor, 1997) or the *networked state* (Collinge and Hall, 1997). The mushrooming of partnerships has highlighted the problem of locating "elites" and powerful individuals within often dense, informal and sometimes *ad hoc* alliances which—in the case of the camera network in the city center—are relatively closed off from public access and scrutiny, and involve complex lines of delegation between public and private authorities. A starting point for my own research was, therefore, to recognize the changing material and ideological nature of "the powerful," and to identify those whose institutional status and informal connections made them key "primary definers" involved in sets of negotiations over defining and responding to local problems (Schlesinger and Tumber, 1995: 17). The imprecise institutional boundaries, relative invisibility and operational flexibility implied in the processes of "partnership" formation in the city center meant that a precise sample "hit list" of research subjects was not available at the outset. The research had three target groups as pools from which to select interviewees: public and private police, the retail sector, and public and private agencies concerned with regeneration in the city.

Initial contacts were made with obvious subjects, made publicly visible by their prominence in local media reports. These key players were the city center manager, the chair of the Stores' Committee and senior representatives of the Government Office for Merseyside. From these initial contacts, other contacts were offered to the researcher after informal requests for eligible interviewees. Thus a strategy of "network" or "snowball" sampling proved useful. Network sampling is often used for identifying people and agencies suitable for study when no obvious list exists from which to select them. This method of sampling is used when "the target sample members are involved in some kind of network with others who share the same characteristic of interest" (Arber, 1993: 74). However,

> This is both a strength and a potential weakness of the method. An advantage of snowball sampling is that it reveals a network of contacts which can itself be studied. A potential problem is that it only includes those within a connected network of individuals. (Ibid.: 74)

Any possible sampling bias was mitigated by the employment of a range of interdependent research methods towards a process of data triangulation. Thus, alongside interviewing, I obtained data from regular attendance at meetings and conferences organized by regeneration managers and by recording information through field notes. Official publications, pamphlets and press releases emanating from the subject population were gathered. The production of these materials and texts can themselves be understood as contemporary "state discourses" (Jessop, 1990: 347–50), indicative of entrepreneurial strategies of rule and indexes of self-promotion and representation. Thus the concepts and themes to emerge from the interviews could be checked against these other forms of data collection and vice versa.

Cultivating interest among the subject population for this research involved scanning local media, partnership brochures and newsletters to determine the concerns of key players and the language they employed in speaking about "regeneration," "order" and "safety" in the city center.

Building a strategy to access key players involved gathering and reading the various glossy brochures mentioned above and local press cuttings. It was important to digest these in order to become familiar with the powerful vernacular of regeneration and to comprehend the ideological mind-set of partnership players. In this way I was able to grasp the signifiers of regeneration for urban elites, for example, "talking up" the city as a "forward looking" entrepreneurial city—economically competitive, "politically stable" and security conscious. These locally powerful promotional discourses provided me with a linguistic map with which to explore the "common sense" of partnership players and provided a linguistic glossary to help in the process of approaching subjects.

This tactic was useful in structuring the letter to potential interviewees, as well as in structuring the interview. It meant that I did not approach subjects "blind," and did not appear to be potentially "irrelevant" to the concerns of regeneration agencies. Following this initial process, a standard letter was drawn up for distribution. All agencies were initially contacted by a letter addressed to the senior management or director level requesting a formal interview that covered three key areas: (1) perceptions of security and insecurity in the city center; (2) the level of involvement in security and policing initiatives and the rationale for these initiatives; and (3) general views on the meaning of a "secure," "orderly," and "regenerated" city center. In all, 28 agencies were contacted by letter, explaining the research and requesting participation by way of interview: eight refused to participate, including three who refused on the grounds that they thought discussing aspects of security was too sensitive.

Access to the security network involved gaining entry into the networks of the locally powerful by interviewing senior representatives and attending formal meetings to which "the public" would not normally have access. No major obstructions to gaining entry were experienced. Thus, representatives of the police, private security companies, local government, local business and city developers participated in the research by giving me formal access to meetings and by granting interviews.

Access was also granted to the monthly meetings of "Crime Alert," based in the suite of a major city center retailer. These meetings provided a forum for private security and police to collate information and intelligence from the CCTV network and discuss strategies for the coming month. By "sitting in" on these meetings, I was able not only to observe their course, but also to talk informally to security and policing personnel (each meeting was attended by 25 to 35 people) and to establish further lines of contact. After introducing myself to the meeting at my first attendance I established a pattern at later meetings whereby I would sit at the back to observe and take notes. In this context my role as researcher cohered with what Gold (1969: 35–36) refers to as "participant-as-observer." As with other researcher roles adopted in the field, the role of "participant-as-observer" brings with it problems. In this case, "the field worker is often defined by informants as more of a colleague than he [sic] feels capable of being" (ibid.: 36). This problem tends to compromise self-conceptions and role-conceptions and manifested itself during one meeting of "Crime Alert" when I was asked by the chairperson if I would "update the group" on my research and, in particular, whether I could "shed any light" on the "problem" they were discussing, namely, identifying homeless people and keeping them out of the stores! I answered that I was still interviewing and that no firm findings had emerged as yet. In my field notes I recorded that I was taken aback by this, uncomfortable in being asked to contribute "positively" to solving a "problem" the terms of reference of which I fundamentally disputed. My answer was couched in a way that allowed my researcher "role" to act as protection (Gold, 1969: 31). This helped me to balance the tensions between irreconcilable perceptions: on the one hand, I identified my research role as one that was not in collaboration with the security network but, on the other hand, subjects within the network identified me as a "colleague" and "collaborator" in aspects of their work.

In general, then, access to the senior echelons of partnership power was not a problem. A number of points can be made regarding this relative ease of access. Hughes (G. Hughes, 1996: 67) notes a shift in the 1990s towards "a grudging 'perestroika'" regarding criminal justice research, leading to a more open system of access for researchers. This in part is fuelled by the rise of auditing in criminal justice, which has fostered increased concern about the legitimacy of criminal justice practices. More pointedly, the relative ease of access can be explained by the fact that the university that funded the research was also a key player at corporate level in the partnership forums and therefore engaged in strategies of local state activity concerned with regenerating the city center. Liverpool John Moores University has been a key representative within Liverpool Vision, a major regeneration agency, through which the university has been involved in bringing derelict land and buildings back into use as well as part-sponsoring city center projects. Academics within the University have been involved in partnership work, acting as research advisors in the implementation of security and policing initiatives in the city (for example, the "City Safe" initiative). The status of the university as a recognized ideological player was illustrated by the appointment of its ex–vice chancellor to the position of chairman of the Liverpool Culture Company.[13] These wider symbiotic relations formed the backdrop against which the research fieldwork took place. The time period (1996–1998) was characterized by intense debates that were reflected in local media and local conferences on the strategic direction and governance of the city center. Consequently, I often felt that I was being welcomed into partnership circles both as someone coming from an institution recognized as a partnership player and as an academic who might be "useful" in some way. For example, one interviewee spoke of the problems he saw in instigating partnerships and managing them towards "security minded" regeneration initiatives:

> "Winning hearts and minds can't be done in a day, it's a cultural thing. You coming in here is part of the trust. Your paper and research will be read by people and there may be some fairly powerful messages in it—so the truth needs to come out. It will be interesting . . . to see how other organizations perceive this—whether they align or not with what we've said. (research interview)

Indeed, openness and candor particularly from the private sector marked the responses of partnership players once the interviews were underway. For this group, "red-tape" and bureaucracy—associated with formally accountable political decision-making arenas—were non-issues, certainly not impediments. The confidence of the "new primary definers" was a reflection of their enhanced political power and clout in the city center, unrestricted by what they described as "old style" politics. CCTV was expressive of that confidence in its role in reclaiming, both physically and discursively, city center space.

## Conclusions: Authoritarianism, the Neo-Liberal State and Critical Research

Some writers have argued that surveillance technologies can be understood not as instruments of state surveillance but as *technologies of freedom* (Barry et al., 1996). Within this analysis, camera networks can be understood as helping to create public spaces for "free" and "responsible" consumer-orientated individuals who independently choose their autonomous role in the life of the city. Such an analysis can be placed alongside official discourses around CCTV as an "empowering" technology that has enabled "the freedom and safety to shop" (Home Office, 1994: 9). These discourses have not only sought to promote and redefine a responsible citizenry but are themselves indicators of a new politics of legitimacy being constructed within, and aiding the reproduction of, a neo-liberal state form. The salience of prevailing discourses around crime has been central to the spatial strategies of local power blocs whose entrepreneurial spirit and self-promotion have provided the ideological building material with which to forge a hegemonic project organized around the operation and trajectory of urban political rule. CCTV was described in the following way: "the city center is a people's place first and foremost and CCTV is a people's system. It's got to be, otherwise it could not be successful in terms of what we are trying to do" (research interview). Keeping "Mr and Mrs Bloggs on board" (research interview) with entrepreneurial initiatives was undertaken through a re-channelled decision-making process, beyond the local democratic structures established in the postwar period. Articulating "public needs" has increasingly been managed through consultative frameworks. Thus, Fairclough (2000: 127) has observed not only that "most of what now passes as public debate takes place in the mass media . . . constrained by market factors," but that "The argument over what constitutes 'real' dialogue is a central part of the political struggle over the public sphere." Thus, a form of "consultation as promotion" has emerged (ibid.). For example, a Community Safety Survey, using a regularly consulted "Citizens Panel" numbering 2,500, recently reported that 85% responded positively when asked "would you feel safer with CCTV"? Only 6% thought it might constitute "an invasion of privacy" (City Safe, 2000). Neither the constitution of the panel nor the means by which its members were selected has been made known. The phrasing of just three questions on the subject of CCTV was problematic, and these questions reflected the methodological flaws indicative of surveys in this area (see Short and Ditton, 1995).

Thus the parameters of the public interest have become increasingly aligned to powerful visions of urban renaissance that have involved "a rhetorical appeal to an essential community of 'the city' or 'the people'" in a manner that has sought to promote a form of "urban patriotism" (Goss, 1996: 288). The ideological and material contours of these developments are only just being recognized as presenting broader questions and problems for research. Confronting the power of neo-liberal state forms will be difficult given the entrepreneurial pursuit of external research funding that has been consolidated with the involvement of universities within urban growth machines. As two commentators have indicated,

> As all institutions of higher education seek to forge ever more symbiotic relations with local and regional, public and private sector interests it is pertinent to wonder to what extent debate in certain media will be circumscribed by these evolving dependencies. (Hall and Hubbard, 1998: 318)

This state form needs to be theorized as part of a critical research process. Thinking about shifts in the organization and rationale of contemporary power flows in the urban setting, and about the processes through which the proper objects of that power have emerged, will necessitate an understanding of more than abstracted risk systems; it requires an understanding of how the logic and uses of these systems are entwined ideologically with "'unscientific' impulses such as racism, heterosexism, classism" (Rigakos, 1999: 146).

Authoritarian tendencies within states cannot be assumed to exist in a pure or abstract form. Contemporary processes of state formation, in which CCTV networks play a role, are in the process of redefining citizenship and the relationship between "citizens" and state/market forces. A danger within this realignment has been in the concentration of public and private funds, state and social capital, within a small, locally powerful network of interests that has shaped the urban fabric in its own image. Mapping the organizational and ideological contours of state formation points to a moment of authoritarianism that is in the process of generating its legitimacy for a form of "low intensity democracy supported by elite management of popular pressures within civil society" (Zuege, 1999: 105). Camera networks are being developed at a time when advanced capitalist states have denied their political agency in regulating markets in the face of global economic conditions (Crowther, 2000; Weiss, 1997). Representing the contemporary form of sovereign command over the urban territory, camera surveillance has been characteristic of an intensification in the monitoring and codification of social inequalities alongside a deepening marginalization of "democracy in the sense of majority control" over the direction of local economic and social development (Eisenschitz and Gough, 1998: 766).[14]

The reluctance of intellectuals to think through these developments as powerful state projects rooted in material and an ideological struggle has signified a pessimism in dealing critically with, and then challenging, processes of social change. Indeed, the supportive alignment of the academy with these management processes often, at best, results in merely describing the rationales that underpin mechanisms of rule without developing a reflexive critical distance that is rooted outside of strategic official discourses. Further, while academics fail to question fundamentally what the locally powerful have defined *into* research agendas, they at the same time reproduce the absence from such agendas of crimes by corporations and local states themselves. Of course, neither CCTV nor the strategies of rule within which they are located are turned towards corporations and states. Contemporary strategies of rule in Liverpool and other UK cities and the role of CCTV therein are emblematic of a society that has downsized the importance of ideological struggle in favor of technical fixes. Of course, CCTV is more than a piece of technology—it is underpinned by frameworks of human agency with ideological preferences and vested interests, often outside of public debate and scrutiny. If we are increasingly "governed through crime" it will be important for research to move beyond the crime-preventive capacity of initiatives such as CCTV and explore, as well as deconstruct, state power and ideological reasoning as processes that organize the materiality of contemporary political rule. In my own research, it was possible to gain access to and challenge some of these processes of urban rule while working within an institutional framework responsible for aspects of that rule. This research has not aided that rule and my status was, and still is, that of an "insider-outsider" within the local contours of the neo-liberal state form. It is unlikely I would be able to repeat this process given my lack of any "positive" contribution to pro-entrepreneurial strategies and values. However, the research, and the issues raised by it, has not remained "useless" or marginal in terms of informing wider public debates. Between April and December 2001, I was interviewed for three local, one national and five international media outlets. Utilizing the media has not been unproblematic for reasons of time, space and the ideological spin characteristic of that domain, and demands for "horror-comedic" tales of the uses of CCTV have not been uncommon. These factors, coupled with the local media's own involvement in the "politics of growth" (Molotch and Logan, 1985), make the media an unlikely source of serious debate. However, issues that have previously been missing from the local media have been raised. This in turn has raised the profile of issues surrounding the politics of surveillance and has helped to change the parameters of debate. For example, this has been done in forcing debate around issues of presumed community involvement and support for CCTV schemes, and the undemocratic nature of these schemes, and through challenges to the hegemonic meaning of a "safer city." In this sense critical research can appeal to and defend a construction of the "public interest" that is at odds with the valorized notion of this concept held by neo-liberal state architects. This defense or re-articulation of the public interest will be crucial within the context of the increasing extensions of state/market territorial dominance and the increasing forms of social and economic injury that this form of territorial logic has both intensified and dissipated.

## Notes

1. The business community has been encouraged to develop, build and maintain CCTV systems so that by 1999 the largest market in Europe for CCTV was established in Britain. It was worth over £385 million (Graham, 2000: 45).

2. Between 1994 and 1999 a total of £38.5 million was allocated by the Home Office along with an estimated £51 million in matching private sector funding to establish CCTV schemes (*Hansard,* Written Answers, Col. 112, 2 November 1999). New Labour's flagship announcement was made in March 1999 under the Crime Reduction Programme for the allocation of £170 million for a three-year competitive bidding process to extend national CCTV coverage by 40,000 extra cameras (*Independent,* 23 June 1999) — far outstripping previous government efforts both financially and numerically.

3. Stenson (1998) has pointed to an "impoverished theorization of sovereignty" in neo-Foucauldian studies. For him sovereignty, particularly over "disorderly" areas, has remained "at the very cutting edge of liberal political rationalities within the nation state" (ibid.: 343).

4. Twenty semi-structured interviews with such individuals were undertaken to ascertain their "visions" for the city, and the meaning attributed to order and security therein, before exploring their rationale for camera networks in the city. My methodology is discussed in more detail later in this chapter.

5. As one interviewee said about the homeless selling the magazine *Big Issue:* "Oh yes! There is a 'big issue.' When people come out of Lime Street . . . they've passed seven or eight Big Issue vendors and it really pisses them off. You then think this city is seedy and full of beggars . . . like something you stand on." *Big Issue* sellers were surveilled by cameras in order to "check their validity" (research interview).

6. Though no criminal charges were brought in this area, traders, as an unwelcome group, were subject to a form of disciplinary surveillance through intimidation — "they know we are watching." Traders organized their own campaign against this.

7. One urban manager stated of CCTV financing: "It is no good having to go cap in hand [for resourses]. This is no way to run a business."

8. Scholars of urban surveillance have been "strangely silent about the militarization of city life so grimly visible at street level" (Davis, 1990: 223) that has formed a key aspect of contemporary social ordering. In Liverpool this form of policing included armed patrols and the use of the Operational Support Division. The latter received a record number of complaints in 1998, and the use of CS gas received more complaints in Liverpool than anywhere else in England and Wales for 1998 (*Liverpool Echo,* 5 March 1999).

9. Conflict also rose between the idea of the café culture and order in the streets. On the one hand, the café culture was thought to bring economic benefits to investors in the service sector while, on the other hand, simultaneously generating disorder in the form of, for example, drunkenness. Thus the extension of legitimate business interests central to the regeneration process was also seen to promote sites of potential street disorder. This factor was highlighted most forcefully by the police for whom "regeneration" brought with it potentially negative aspects. As one interviewee put it: "We've got to manage it [. . .]. We recognize that we might actually see a rise in levels of recorded crime if the renaissance is

successful [. . .]. It is part of a trade off. The benefits of the vibrant twenty-four hour economy on the one hand balanced against the downside of more crime, more drug abuse and drunkenness."

10. The discourses emanating from these partnerships are seldom subject to deconstruction or scrutiny by researchers. Importantly these discourses "are not neutral" in the sense "that they construct problems, solutions and actions in particular ways that are congruent with existing relations of power, domination and distribution of resources" (Atkinson, 1999: 70).

11. These bodies include Liverpool Vision (with an over £1 million annual budget to fund, among other things, the office of city center manager), the Mersey Partnership and the Safer Merseyside Partnership (see Coleman et al., 2002). These bodies have a role in local decision-making and in managing property-led regeneration schemes. They are unelected and unaccountable to the wider public and have pursued an "enterprise"-based strategy of regeneration as established under the Thatcherite Urban Development Corporations. Importantly these forms of partnership rule in urban centers "do not need to exert total power *over* the city's population to act effectively (i.e.: whether through the ballot box or other means), but rather they merely need the power to act" (Hall and Hubbard, 1996: 156 *emphasis in original*).

12. Such marketing strategies have diverted "the attention of local residents, as well as potential investors, away from the city's real social and economic problems, by fostering cohesion and local pride; and by generating support for entrepreneurial projects" (Griffiths, 1998: 54).

13. A body concerned with the city's Capital of Culture Campaign for 2008.

14. Some have noted the "democratic deficit" in the development of CCTV networks (Fyfe and Bannister, 1996), in contemporary crime prevention partnerships (Crawford, 1997) and in the partnership form of state management generally (Hutton, 1995). Calling for a re-democratization of these areas through greater public participation and accountability may, however, mean that camera networks will be normalized as an acceptable "governing through crime" strategy as long as the "quangoization effect" can be checked. Ideological processes involved in the construction of risk and local indices of "quality of life" will still need to be addressed and involve challenging strategically organized discourses within a powerful regenerative state (Atkinson, 1999).

# In the Valley of the Blind the One-Eyed Man Is King

## Corporate Crime and the Myopia of Financial Regulation

### Introduction: The Power of Definition and the Barriers of Commercial Exclusion

On 7 July 2001 the *Financial Times* reported the findings of a then-unpublished Financial Services Authority (FSA) consumer survey. The survey had found that 60 percent of the six million households with endowment-linked mortgages had potentially been mis-sold[1] endowment policies, having been told that their policy was guaranteed to pay off their mortgage (Jenkins, 2001; FSA, 2001b). The same survey also revealed that 90 per cent of existing policyholders believed they had received poor advice (Inman, 2001). Endowment-linked mortgages had once been a core component of the life assurance industry's profits (see, for example, Bolger and Croft, 2001). In 1983, they had outstripped the repayment method as the most common type of mortgage. It was endowments that had made mortgages accessible to people who had never previously owned a house and, therefore, endowments that had underwritten the great property-owning democracy that had once been claimed to characterize modern conservatism. The suggestion that nearly two-thirds of all policyholders, over three and a half million, had purchased an endowment policy on the basis of manifestly incorrect and materially misleading advice seemed to finally validate the misgivings of financial journalists and consumer groups over this mass experiment in endowment-linked mortgages. Other figures, published earlier in the year by the Association of British Insurers (ABI), had revealed that an estimated 4.4 million endowment policies, or 43 per cent, would not produce sufficient funds to pay off the mortgage at the recommended projected rates of growth (E. Jones, 2001). Not only, therefore, had people been misled but, as financial journalists and consumer groups had also warned, there was also the possibility that they had been financially disadvantaged—two of the basic components of criminal fraud.

To date there has been one major criminal investigation into mis-sold endowment policies in England and Wales and no criminal prosecution. This is despite the fact that less than a decade earlier the same companies had been involved in the mis-selling of pensions scandal which in terms of financial loss to consumers and investors was even more spectacular than the collapse of Maxwell Communications Corporations, Barings Bank and the Bank of Credit and Commerce International combined (Clarke, 1998). What the absence of criminal prosecution asks us to believe is that although the insurance industry is riddled with incompetence, poor training and inadequate systems of quality control, it is, nonetheless, honest or at the very least, free from crime.

This chapter explores some of the problems involved in objectively testing this interpretation. The chapter will demonstrate the methodological and practical barriers to research that attempts to establish whether or not consumers may have been the victims of widespread criminal selling practices. It will also demonstrate that these barriers are located in and arise out of the specific regulatory environment within which the financial services industry is situated. To this end, it examines the interdependence and interaction between three basic processes: the control that companies exercise over information about their operation, the system of financial regulation, and the production of public knowledge concerning the legal status of potentially mis-sold financial products. The organizing principle of the discussion is the idea that corporations have a decisive, if mediated, influence on the form, content, and extent of publicly held and available information about their business. One consequence of this influence is that companies are granted an extraordinary power of definition over how the nature, purpose, and impact of their operation can and should be understood. The basic conclusion is that both past and present regimes of financial regulation, first under the auspices of the Securities and Investment Board (SIB) and now under the direct control of the FSA, do little to mitigate this exercise of control. On the contrary, the system of financial regulation (and, therefore, commercial fraud control) allows itself to be excluded from selecting, assimilating, and ultimately generating information which can form the basis of a criminal investigation, leaving the question of criminal liability unexplored.

This, of course, has fundamental epistemological implications for what we know about financial crime, what is capable of being known about financial crime, and what claims can be made about the social and geographical distribution of crime and offending (what types of offences are committed, in what context, and by whom). Unlike the formal recording of conventional crime in the official statistics and the British Crime Survey, which depends on the experiences and claims of victims, the formal recording of financial crime is ultimately dependent on the process of financial regulation and criminal prosecution. One reason for this is that victims of criminal mis-selling are almost disregarded as a potential source of criminal intelligence, but a further reason is that evidence of commercial fraud is seldom either self-evident or in the public domain. In fact, the contrary seems to be the case. Evidence of fraudulent patterns of behavior usually comes in the form of commercial documents, bank accounts and, in the case of prosecutions against senior company officers, the testimony of more junior employees—information over which the company involved in the fraud, and, therefore, its company officers, exercises almost complete control. Commercial control of commercial information, of course, is not total. But public and, therefore, criminological access to that information tends to occur only when there is a change in the control or ownership of a company (when the company merges, is taken over, or goes into liquidation or administration, for example), or as a consequence of regulation. If regulation, as I argue in this discussion, is not structured towards producing information that can form the basis of a fraud allegation, the commercial monopoly over the production of information necessary to detect fraud is left untouched, and commercial fraud is left undiscovered. The potential implications for the production of criminological knowledge are quite spectacular, not least in terms of how the concept of the high crime area should be calculated and how the individual at high risk of offending should be assessed. The noncriminal emphasis of financial regulation, in other words, corrupts the very empirical foundations of the criminological enterprise, which is built on a particular understanding of the nature, extent, and distribution of crime.

The extent to which the apparatus of commercial regulation has challenged the power of companies to define endowment mis-selling, by default, as noncriminal is considered in the second part of the discussion when the focus of the analysis shifts to exploring how the functions of the Financial Services Authority (FSA), the Financial Ombudsman Service (FOS) and, to a lesser extent, the police overlap to further limit the way in which mis-selling is represented in the public domain. Before embarking upon this discussion, the analysis begins with a brief chronology of trends in the endowment mortgage market.

## The Rise and Fall of the Endowment Mortgage

### Risk, Reward, and Misrepresentation

An endowment mortgage is, put at its simplest, a form of life assurance used to pay off a mortgage loan extended to buy a house. It is a form of geared investment in which money is borrowed and invested in the financial markets in the expectation that the returns will outstrip the interest paid and amass sufficient funds to discharge the capital value of the loan. This generally makes such mortgages an attractive option when inflation and real investment returns are high, but unattractive when inflation and real investment returns are low. High inflation ensures that the real value of the mortgage debt is eroded over the term of the endowment policy, while high real investment returns ensure that the premiums invested produce sufficient returns not only to pay off the mortgage, but also to provide the policyholder with a cash surplus. When inflation is low, on the other hand, the real value of the mortgage debt is not eroded over time. This can cause serious problems when real investment returns are low, since, as the growth of the sums invested is dependent on fluctuations in the financial markets, there is no guarantee that an endowment policy will make enough to pay off the mortgage even when regular payments are maintained.

### No Guarantee, No Problem?

The absence of any guarantee that an endowment policy, unlike the repayment method, will discharge the mortgage debt even if regular payments under the policy are maintained is absolutely central to making sense of endowment mortgage selling as well as highly relevant to the possibility that endowment mis-selling may have been criminal. A good way of illustrating this point is to begin by looking at trends in the endowment mortgage market.

What the table clearly shows is that endowments were traditionally a niche product that only a minority of people relied on. Not only, however, had endowment mortgages outstripped the repayment method as the most common means of financing the purchase of property by the early 1980s, but, by the end of the decade, endowments accounted for four out of every five new mortgage contracts. The obvious question, of course, is why so many people came to rely upon this method of financing their home—something fundamental to their security—when there was no guarantee that their endowment policy would produce enough money for them to own their home at the end of the mortgage period. The obvious answer, implied in the introduction, is that people were simply not informed of the risks involved,[2] but instead were given verbal guarantees that their policy

Table 5.1  Repayment Method by Type of Advance, Percentage of
Loans (All Buyers)

| Year | Repayment % | Endowment % | Combination or other % |
|------|-------------|-------------|------------------------|
| 1969 | 88 | 9 | 3 |
| 1970 | 88 | 7 | 5 |
| 1971 | 86 | 8 | 6 |
| 1972 | 80 | 12 | 8 |
| 1973 | 72 | 17 | 11 |
| 1974 | 73 | 16 | 11 |
| 1975 | 74 | 16 | 10 |
| 1976 | 72 | 18 | 10 |
| 1977 | 71 | 21 | 8 |
| 1978 | 67 | 25 | 8 |
| 1979 | 64 | 27 | 10 |
| 1980 | 69 | 23 | 9 |
| 1981 | 74 | 20 | 6 |
| 1982 | 73 | 20 | 7 |
| 1983 | 41 | 54 | 5 |
| 1984 | 38 | 61 | 1 |
| 1985 | 42 | 57 | 1 |
| 1986 | 28 | 70 | 2 |
| 1987 | 18 | 80 | 2 |
| 1988 | 14 | 83 | 3 |
| 1989 | 18 | 79 | 3 |
| 1990 | 20 | 76 | 4 |
| 1991 | 18 | 77 | 5 |
| 1992 | 21 | 68 | 12 |
| 1993 | 26 | 59 | 15 |
| 1994 | 30 | 56 | 14 |
| 1995 | 35 | 46 | 16 |
| 1996 | 38 | 32 | 24 |
| 1997 | 41 | 34 | 26 |
| 1998 | 43 | 34 | 25 |
| 1999 | 47 | 28 | 25 |
| 2000 | 58 | 21 | 21 |
| first quarter 2001 | 63 | 17 | 20 |

*Source:* Council of Mortgage Lenders and the Office for National Statistics
*Note:* The sharp change in the endowment percentage between 1991 and 1992 is apparently due to interest only mortgages previously being recorded by some building societies as endowment products.

would generate sufficient funds to discharge their mortgage debt. This can be seen most clearly in the fact that in 1998 endowment mortgages continued to represent a third of the market in new mortgage business—nearly three times the percentage in 1972—despite a growing public acknowledgment that they were a poor value product for many consumers. What is important, in the context of this discussion, however, is not simply whether mis-selling was widespread, but whether the criminal law was violated as a matter of routine.

On first examination, the systemic nature of mis-selling may seem to suggest routine violation of the criminal law. This, however, is not something that can simply be inferred. Mis-selling can take a number of non-criminal forms. Moreover, some of the growth in endowment mortgages, particularly in the early 1980s, reflected the convergence of a range of economic and fiscal circumstances which, for some consumers, made endowments a valuable product—a fact suggesting that not all the growth in endowment mortgage business should be attributed to mis-selling, but also raising the possibility that senior management may have believed that the spectacular growth in endowments was a genuine result of the value that the product offered to consumers, rather than a result of widespread bad advice.

This last possibility requires serious consideration. The following section, therefore, attempts to unscramble the possible explanations for endowment mortgage sales with a view to clarifying what senior management could reasonably have been expected to know about the market in endowments and the extent of mis-selling.

### The Economic Context of the Endowment Mortgage Market

The spectacular growth in endowment mortgages coincided with the provision of tax relief which either (in the case of Life Assurance Premium Relief which was abolished in 1984) applied exclusively to endowment mortgages or (in the case of Mortgage Interest Relief at Source [MIRAS]) which was introduced in 1983) favored them over the repayment method.[3] This was central to realizing the key selling point of the endowment-linked mortgage—the offer of a lump sum over and above the amount required to pay the mortgage loan (for a relatively low premium over the term of the endowment policy). Moreover, for policies contracted into before 1984, when the most generous concessions offered under Life Assurance Premium Relief were still available, high long-term rates of inflation as well as high real investment returns made an investment surplus a very real possibility (Institute of Actuaries, 1999; OFT, 1995b). Some of the growth in endowment mortgages in the 1980s, therefore, does seem to be explicable in terms other than rampant mis-selling—a possibility that derives more force from the fact that the decline in endowment mortgages coincided with changes in precisely those economic and fiscal conditions that had originally made a surplus a possibility and high-risk endowments, therefore, a viable mortgage product. Tax relief under MIRAS, for example, was steadily reduced from 1991 onwards, before being abolished outright in April 2000. This, in conjunction with the end of the long bull run on the stock market in the 1980s and sustained low inflation from 1991 onwards, not only made endowments seem more expensive, but massively reduced the likelihood of a surplus at the end of the mortgage period. The impact that these trends in themselves had on the endowment mortgage market is questionable. Most consumers would have been unlikely to appreciate the implications of sustained low inflation on the relative value of endowment mortgages. Fewer still would have been aware of the fact that real investment returns were falling. Perceptions changed not so much because of the stock market crash in 1987, but because of the recession that it anticipated.

This would have had a far more powerful effect on the perception of endowment mortgages as a poor value product because of the spectacular impact that the recession, with its attendant growth in unemployment and employment stability, had on the early surrender of endowment mortgages. Early surrender was invariably financially disadvantageous. The surrender value of policies cashed in after only a few years was, as a matter of routine, even lower than the full value of the sums invested (OFT, 1995b; PIA, 1999; Collinson, 1999. See also PIA 2000a). Significantly, in the early 1990s more than three quarters of all endowment mortgages were surrendered early (OFT, 1995a). The effect on people's perceptions of the true value of endowment mortgages in the context of the negative equity crisis of the early 1990s was dramatic (Cowie, 1995). The true value of endowment mortgages in a low-inflation environment—stripped of significant tax relief and underpinned by a system of market distorting commissions—was conclusively revealed. As a Consumers' Association report later recorded, endowments had become a "risky, inflexible and more expensive" way of discharging a mortgage debt than a repayment mortgage (Consumers' Association, 1999).

By 1999, it was not surprising that the proportion of all new mortgage business made up by endowment mortgages was just over a third what it had been at the height of the endowment mortgage market in 1988. But what is important to recognize is that, despite this vague correspondence between trends in the endowment mortgage market and economic and fiscal fundamentals, the correlation was an imperfect one. Life Assurance Premium Relief, which had given endowment mortgages a real competitive advantage over the repayment method, was abolished in 1984, but still the growth of endowment mortgages relative to the repayment method persisted. More important perhaps is that even once endowment mortgage sales began to decline in the face of less favorable economic and fiscal conditions they held up remarkably well despite the emergence of a fragile consensus among regulators, financial journalists, and consumer groups, as well as some life assurance companies which not only questioned the financial value of endowment mortgages for the mass market, but also raised a number of uncomfortable questions about the continued strength of the market in endowments (see OFT, 1995b and FSA, 2000a). The exact origins of this consensus are unclear, but, as early as September 1991, the Securities and Investment Board (SIB), the forerunner of the FSA, had demanded that building societies stop the practice of forcing home-buyers to take out endowment mortgages. David Walker, then head of the Board, added that up to eight out of ten homeowners might have been sold the wrong mortgage by lenders who stood to gain from the insurance commission (Hunter, 1991a). Walker's comments were echoed by his successor, Andrew Large, and consumer protection groups who publicly denounced the misleading advice that some mortgage lenders gave, indicating that the economic and fiscal fundamentals did not justify the share of the mortgage market occupied by endowments (Hunter, 1991b; Whitebloom and Atkinson, 1993).

Walker's and Large's warnings were steadily reinforced as a succession of major life assurance companies declared their withdrawal from endowment business, significantly reduced annual bonuses (see Wright, 1995; *Daily Telegraph*, 1995b), or conceded the possibility that the investment growth of endowment policies might not be sufficient to pay off the mortgage debt linked to them (Boliver, 1993; see also Hunter and Pandya, 1993, and *Daily Telegraph*, 1995a). The broader implications of these announcements seemed to be underlined by an Office of Fair Trading (OFT) report, published in 1995, which questioned the continued status of endowment mortgages as a mass-market product (OFT, 1995b). Criticism from the OFT continued throughout 1995. When its director of consumer affairs claimed that most ordinary borrowers had been sold endowments without much option, even though in many cases these were more expensive than simple repayment mortgages (Cowie, 1995; Hunter, 1995), the outlook for the endowment mortgage market not only looked bleak, but the imminent collapse of endowment mortgage sales looked likely.

This prospect was raised in an article in the *Daily Telegraph* which, in the aftermath of Norwich Union's announcement of its intention to stop selling endowments, declared that the "game is up at last" (*Daily Telegraph*, 1995a). The *Telegraph's* prediction appeared prophetic when, in the following year, endowment business suffered its biggest single fall as new regulations forcing sales advisors to disclose their commission came into force (see below). Thereafter, however, sales of endowment mortgages held up. In both 1997 and 1998, endowment mortgages constituted 34 percent of new mortgage business—up 2 percent on 1996. Thus, after almost a decade of sustained criticism from regulators, consumer protection groups, and financial journalists, reports of companies withdrawing from the market and stories confirming the risks inherent in endowment mortgages, as well as economic and fiscal changes which made endowments less financially attractive, endowment mortgages still constituted a third of the mortgage market. The important question, of course, is why?

## The Economics of the Market: Mis-Selling and Commissions

The most convincing answer, indicated in the introduction, is that trends in the endowment mortgage market must also be understood in terms of the techniques used to convince consumers to chose high-risk, poor value endowment mortgages over low-risk, better value repayment mortgages. Put simply, mis-selling—in which the financial advantages of endowment mortgages were overstated, while the risks associated with them were understated—may have driven the market in endowment mortgages as much as the economic and fiscal context in which endowments were sold. This, at least, is the irresistible inference from the available evidence. The FSA's own consumer surveys, the ombudsman's complaints statistics, and mystery buying exercises carried out under the direction of the Consumers' Association all suggest not only that mis-selling took place on a massive scale, but also that the form the mis-selling took was designed to stimulate demand for the product by overstating their advantages of endowment mortgages and understating their disadvantages (Consumers' Association, 1998, and see below). Thus, the methods used to mis-sell endowments might not only account for the imperfect correlation between market trends and economic context, but may also serve to implicate sales advisors and senior management in the commission of criminal offences.

This last possibility is not immediately apparent from the explanations that have typically been advanced to account for endowment mis-selling. These explanations have predominantly conceived the cause of mis-selling in terms of a number of mutually interlocking interpretations implying negligence, incompetence, and poor training, rather than criminal liability (Consumers' Association, 1998, 1999; PIA 2000b; and Wright, 1995). This emphasis on negligence, incompetence, and so forth is, in some respects, a simple recognition of the capacity (or rather lack of it) of primary commercial regulation to unearth fraud. Nonetheless, there are fundamental problems in prejudging the form of mis-selling as a simple consequence of negligence or poor training. Negligence suggests that poor advice was an inadvertent consequence of poor training or administrative incompetence. There is a strong possibility, however, that the commission structure of the industry performed an important role in driving the speculative rise in endowments and arresting the rate of their decline (when economic and fiscal changes had eroded the financial advantages associated with them) by promoting mis-selling. There are no conclusive data to this effect—an interesting omission from the FSA's research and supervisory program—but there is a measure of agreement. Endowments generated large commissions for those responsible for advising potential homeowners. Repayment mortgages did not. The effect, according to the Consumers' Association, was to create what it later described as a "bias" in favor of endowments (Consumers' Association, 1998 and 1999; see also Hunter, 1991b; Cowie, 1995; and Hughes, 1995).

Significantly, although the suggestion that mis-selling was commission-driven may not discount the effects of poor training, individual incompetence and so forth, it does raise a number of pertinent questions concerning the motivation and level of knowledge that can be imputed to endowment sellers and, also, the knowledge that can be imputed to senior management within the life assurance industry. More specifically, it raises the possibility that misrepresentation was deliberate—consciously directed towards personal enrichment—rather than an inadvertent consequence of ignorance, and, at the very least, raises a presumption that sales advisors suspected, or even knew, that their selling techniques amounted to mis-selling and, therefore, that they might have committed criminal offences under either the Financial Services Act of 1986 or even the Theft Acts. More significantly, the effect of the industry's commission structure on sales techniques and endowment mortgages sales might even implicate senior management in the commission of criminal offences. If, as it seems reasonable to assume, senior management suspected that the market performance of endowment mortgages was not always justified by the value of the product to consumers, the evidence concerning the effect of commissions seems paramount. More specifically, the suggestion that commission-driven mis-selling was widely acknowledged outside of the industry not only suggests that senior management might have been aware of this risk but also suggests that senior management would have been aware of a plausible explanation for the imperfect correlation between the demand for endowments, on the one hand, and the basic value of the product to most consumers on the other. The effect, in other words, is to at least raise the possibility of a link between mis-selling methods, decisions taken at board level (that is, not to alter the commission structure), and what senior management might have suspected about the scale and form of mis-selling.

What is significant in the context of this discussion is that the possibility of people at board level suspecting that the spectacular rise in endowment mortgages was a product of commission-driven mis-selling is, in the absence of sustained evidence, only speculation, albeit speculation that seems to correspond with the facts as summarized above. It is significant, because, in all probability, it will remain speculation, not necessarily because of an absence of crime, but rather because of how the available information concerning mis-selling has been selected, and how it has since been contextualized and reworked. This is the issue that the discussion will now explore.

## Financial Regulation and the Barriers to the Discovery of Crime: The Financial Services Act, the Police, and the Serious Fraud Office

The best available evidence indicates that there has only been one major criminal investigation into mis-selling and that there have still been no prosecutions. This dearth of criminal investigation seems to apply as much to sales advisors who sold endowment products as it does to managers who managed the sales process, as well as to senior executives, who, it is reasonable to expect, would have known the real benefits of the product to consumers, the commission structure, and its effects on the sales process and, ultimately, endowment mortgage sales. One explanation for the absence of criminal investigation, of course, is that it reflects a corresponding absence of criminal activity. However, the following analysis suggests that despite the numerous investigations into endowment mis-selling undertaken by the regulators, the absence of crime was never established. This was for the simple reason that the organizations of financial regulation—the FSA, the old SIB and the Personal Investment Authority (PIA)—are not concerned with detecting, selecting and assembling evidence of recklessness or dishonesty from the information that large corporations generate and supply to them (either as a matter of routine or in the course of exceptional or "targeted" regulatory action). Nor is the wider system of financial regulation structured or organized to elicit evidence of this kind. In other words, the apparent absence of crime may be an organizational and procedural construct—a product of a regulatory system in which crime is subordinated to other concerns.

This proposition is easily stated, but less easily established and even less easily explained. It is also incomplete. The police, for example, can investigate cases of mis-selling without the authority of the FSA but, as the lone police investigation into mis-selling suggests, this is rare. Noncriminalization, it seems, therefore, cannot be traced solely to the organizational imperatives of the FSA, the legal constraints that it operates under, or the occupational culture of its staff—although these are all important. Instead, the absence of criminal justice intervention seems to be better understood as part of a process in which organizational imperatives, occupational culture, and legal constraints shape and dictate decisions and possibilities in other parts of the process that may themselves have other, independent, determinants. Policing priorities, the resource constraints that these require the police to observe, and the police's traditional focus on criminal offences under the Theft Acts, for instance, are also a cause of noncriminalization, as are the Serious Fraud Office's organizational structure, the legal framework in which it operates and its historically contingent strategic aims (see Fooks, 1997). In short, to understand the inertia that characterizes the formulation of criminal suspicion, to understand how attempts to initiate criminal investigation are neutralized and deflected, to understand how the momentum of criminal investigation is dismantled, to understand, in other words, the immediate reason why these offences are not prosecuted (other than in terms of the simple and simplistic contention that there is no crime), we need to focus on the accumulation and interaction of organizational practices, imperatives and procedures, legal constraints, professional concerns, and cultural assumptions involved in and relevant to the regulation and control of mis-sold endowment mortgages. This analysis does not, however, explore all of these interactions, but rather focuses on those organizations responsible for regulating endowment mortgage and responding to consumer complaints concerning endowment mortgages—the Financial Services Authority and the FOS.

The FSA (and before it the SIB and self-regulatory organizations recognized under the Financial Services Act of 1986) has primary responsibility for the regulation of endowment mortgages. From the outset, the effect of the FSA's response to endowment mis-selling has been to stifle awareness of the potential criminal dimension of mis-selling and, more generally, to direct and redirect public unease about mis-selling away from the police and the prospect of criminal investigation towards the possibility of compensation, the FOS and the life assurance companies themselves. Put more directly, the FSA has sustained confidence in the life assurance industry by facilitating the capacity of life assurance companies and other financial institutions to maintain control over disputes with consumers concerning possible mis-selling, by channelling problems over endowment mortgages towards regulatory outcomes and generally navigating the problem of mis-selling away from the criminal courts.

### Managing Dissent

The FSA's first public response to the problem of mis-sold endowment mortgages was not made until August 1999—eight years after Andrew Large had first expressed reservations about the indiscriminate sale of endowment mortgages. Both the timing of the response and the form that it took exemplify perfectly the FSA's concern to eliminate the language of crime from the public lexicon used to make sense of mis-selling. The FSA's response, a press release and a published Factsheet, followed the publication of an article in *The Times,* and two earlier less substantial articles in *The Independent* and *The Sunday Express,* which reported that two Guardian Royal Exchange directors had been arrested in connection with endowment mortgages. The article summarized the contents of a Scotland Yard report which asserted that endowment mortgages had been "mis-sold on a 'colossal' scale" and recommended the possible prosecution of some insurance companies (Leppard et al., 1999). The effect of the report on consumers' perceptions of their endowment mortgages was dramatic. Both the FSA and the Metropolitan Police fraud squad were inundated with calls from anxious consumers asking whether their policies were at risk because of fraud, mis-selling or both.[4] Confidence in existing endowment mortgage products and, therefore, the life assurance industry was fast disappearing as a significant minority of consumers not only began to question the techniques used to sell them their endowment mortgage, but also began to make sense of their experience in terms of the language of fraud and criminal liability. The problem warranted a response. The FSA's statutory objective to maintain market confidence meant that some form of reassurance was necessary. The means the FSA used to achieve this were twofold: to restate the life assurance industry's assertion of the good value endowment mortgages still offered to existing policyholders and to represent the police investigation as irrelevant to the sale of domestic endowment mortgages. The press release, in short, was aimed at redirecting emerging consumer anxiety over endowment mortgages away from concerns over crime and criminal justice intervention, towards the question of the financial value (and even potential advantages) of their policies. Specifically, the press release stressed the negative effect of inflation on expected future returns while informing consumers that "most people" with an endowment mortgage "should find that it is doing the job perfectly well" (FSA, 1999a). This implied that economic conditions, rather than widespread mis-selling, were responsible for any potential disadvantage suffered by endowment mortgage holders (compared to those with repayment mortgages), although no such widespread disadvantage was, as yet, evident.

The part of the press release explaining the criminal investigation was equally designed to discount the widespread existence of past, potentially criminal, mis-selling. The press release recorded that the "small number of allegations regarding mis-selling endowment contracts . . . relate primarily to endowments connected with commercial financing arrangements and not the household mortgage endowment held by millions of ordinary homeowners" (FSA, 1999a). To some extent this was correct. The investigation concerned three life assurance companies, Guardian Royal Exchange, Sun Life of Canada, and Legal and General. Only the Legal and General case involved a specific case of domestic endowment mortgage selling. On closer inspection, however, the implication that domestic endowment mortgages were only a peripheral part of the criminal investigation and, therefore, that crime was not generally suspected in the sale of endowment mortgages was misleading. The directors of Guardian Royal Exchange who had been taken into custody had been arrested in relation to accounts missing from the company. These related to domestic endowment policies as well as other products. Moreover, the focus on only a selection of commercial endowment mortgages was not for the lack of other allegations concerning commercial or domestic endowment mortgages. Alleged fraud involving domestic endowment mortgages had been reported to the Metropolitan Police before, the police having declined to pursue these cases not on merit, but because of chronic shortages of personnel, resources, and, initially at least, expertise in the area of the Financial Services Act.[5] More significantly, the complainant who had originally reported to the police the cluster of cases that were now being investigated, the head of an *ad hoc* action group, was also acting for people with domestic endowment mortgages. These had been excluded from the investigation because of a concern to first test the amount and quality of evidence required to underpin a prosecution and because the need to use limited resources sparingly meant that only the most serious cases, in which the most money had been lost, precisely those cases involving commercial endowment mortgages, could be investigated. The same considerations led the police to decline to investigate the large number of complaints that were made following the publication of a *Sunday Times* report.[6] Moreover, the issues raised in relation to the commercial endowment mortgages were exactly the same as the issues involved in domestic endowment mortgages, notwithstanding the fact that the products were marginally different. The sales personnel and companies at the center of the investigation were also involved in the sale of domestic endowment mortgages.[7] The commission structure was the same and the legal issues similar. In short, the police investigations did involve endowment mortgage mis-selling and, if the focus of the investigation was not on domestic endowment mortgages, this was a product of police operational priorities and resources rather than confirmation that the sale of endowment mortgages had not involved the widespread commission of criminal offences.

The factsheet made available to consumers seemed to be designed to achieve the same ends. Although it claimed to set out the "options" for consumers, the options specified were limited to the factors that prospective homebuyers should take into account when deciding between an endowment mortgage and the repayment option, rather than the options available to existing policyholders who had bought potentially poor-performing endowments on the basis of misleading advice. Neither existing nor prospective consumers were offered advice on the circumstances in which a complaint was legitimate, the circumstances in which mis-selling might amount to a criminal offence, or the ways in which either a criminal complaint or a claim for compensation could be made. Instead, two check lists were provided: the first provided a comparison of the advantages and disadvantages of endowment mortgages, while the second was a list of points sales advisors should explain to consumers, presumably to remind sales advisors of their obligations under the Financial Services Act and its attendant regulations if evidence of noncompliance emerged. No instructions were given as to how, or even where, consumers should complain if sales advisors fell short of the standard of advice required.

The presumption that underpinned the focus of the factsheet seemed to be that mis-selling was exceptional, undertaken in good faith where it had occurred and, therefore, easily and appropriately rectified between seller and consumer—a policy that revealed a whole range of assumptions the FSA had made about the degree of trust that could be extended to the life assurance industry, its perception of the extent and form of mis-selling, and its understanding of the appropriate balance to be struck between sustaining confidence and enabling consumer restitution. Significantly, however, even though the factsheet seemed, by omission, to delegate the role of securing "best advice" to the consumer, consumers were nevertheless assured that "[t]he regulators check[ed] firms to make sure they [were] meeting these standards" (FSA, 1999c) This assurance completed the puzzle of the FSA's initial strategy. Not only had it placed initial responsibility for resolving contractual disputes on the consumer, but—by restating its overarching responsibility for quality control while, at the same time, failing to explore the full range of options open to consumers—it had also reserved its right to direct the course of action consumers should take by reaffirming its ultimate authority over the management of the selling process. This approach, involving the management of consumer expectation and choice, as much as the operation of life assurance companies, to avoid both the question of criminal liability and its detection, has, in one form or another, characterized the FSA's actions ever since.

### The FSA's Action Plan: "Targeted Regulatory Visits"

The package of measures announced by the FSA in December 1999 as its "action plan" for endowment mortgages illustrates this perfectly. The components of the plan and the advice given to consumers were identical to previous action and advice by the FSA in all but three important respects—the promise of better consumer information, the extension of "targeted regulatory visits" and, for the first time, the provision of clear guidance on how to complain. Conceivably all three might have facilitated the discovery of crime, if the form that the FSA's intervention took, and the practice of its implementation, had not been designed to achieve ends other than criminal justice intervention (FSA, 1999c).

The contrast between the potential inherent in the FSA's targeted regulatory visits to uncover crime and the extent to which targeted action has, in practice, been exploited for this purpose illustrates this point well. Targeted action, in contrast to routine supervisory visits, concentrated (and continues to concentrate) primarily on mis-selling and, therefore, seemed (and continues to seem) concerned with a range of questions relevant to the question of criminal liability. Among other things, it explored the circumstances in which mis-selling took place, the systems in position to prevent endowments from being mis-sold and the procedures in place to correct any errors in the selling process. However, apart from this basic focus on the process and context of mis-selling, targeted regulatory visits were not organized to uncover evidence of crime. This is best exemplified by the fact that, as with later targeted visits in 2001, their focus was on current selling practice, well after the industry had been alerted and, therefore, allowed to adapt, to the emergence of endowment mis-selling as a social and regulatory problem (Consumers' Association, 1998).

Even if companies had failed to adapt their practices over the medium to long term, however, the practice of giving three weeks' advance notice of an impending visit[8] ensured that the life assurance industry had, if necessary, ample opportunity to modify any documentation that might suggest the commission of criminal offences and to rehearse answers to questions that might otherwise be incriminating. Significantly, the fact that interviews were arranged on a top-down basis—with an emphasis on senior management and other senior employees responsible for training and compliance, rather than on sales advisors—greatly enhanced the latter possibility. The effect was that few sales advisors—who might not only give less-rehearsed answers, but would also be in the best position to explain the reason why erroneous advice was given—were interviewed. Even more significant, however, was the fact that few victims were interviewed, on the basis that it was unclear how they could help—a direct repudiation of the principles of criminal investigation.[9]

In practice, however, it is unlikely that either focusing on management, as opposed to sales advisors, or giving advance notice prejudiced the detection of criminal offences. This is because FSA personnel seem to be either unaware of the importance (to the question of criminal liability or to the question of regulatory breach) of, or unconcerned with, asking sales advisors why particular advice was given. Moreover, even in 2001, when the FSA had become aware of the full scale of mis-selling, some visits were still "desk-based" and all were aimed at achieving "an understanding of the effectiveness of systems and procedures across a range of customer groups," not at uncovering criminal offences under the Financial Services or Theft Acts.[10] Corrective action could, therefore, be left to line supervision managers at companies providing endowments and, exceptionally, the enforcement division of the FSA. Police investigation was not only unnecessary, it was not even a consideration.

### The FSA's Action Plan: Consumer Information, Consumer Complaints, and the FOS

The other major feature of the FSA's action plan, its guidance to consumers on how to complain, showed signs of the same preoccupation with avoiding criminal investigation. Consumer complaints, at least at a level of abstraction, offer a rich seam of intelligence, which if properly recorded, collated, and interpreted can supply important information about the pattern of mis-selling undertaken on behalf of a particular firm.[11] On first examination, a commitment, contained with the action plan, by ABI member firms to informing consumers, for the first time, of the performance and projected value of their policies (a process which became known as the premium review) seemed to open up the possibility of complaints data being exploited for the purpose of criminal intelligence. By forewarning policyholders that their policy might not discharge their mortgage debt, the provision of this information had the important effect of revealing the general risks involved in endowment mortgages to those who, thus far, were not aware of them, as well as the fact that endowment policies were neither guaranteed to produce an investment surplus nor even guaranteed to clear the mortgage debt (FSA, 2000b). Consumers were, therefore, not only given a motivation to complain in the form of an unexpected financial outlay; the premium review also revealed that there might be good grounds for a complaint as well.

Consumer complaints, helped by the publication of information on how to complain, multiplied. By February 2001, 50 per cent of all complaints to the FOS related to mortgage endowments (FOS, 2001b) By August the proportion had risen to 60 per cent (FOS, 2001c).[12] But, in striking contrast to the publication of the investigation in *The Sunday Times,* this time consumer anxiety failed to translate into widespread suspicion of crime.

Thus, the ombudsman was presented with a deluge of complaints from thousands of concerned consumers. Many of them claimed that the terms of their endowment mortgage had been fundamentally misrepresented to them, but few, despite the high level of anxiety that they must have been experiencing, sensed the need to claim that their sales advisor or endowment provider had acted criminally. The obvious question is why? Some important clues, which may partially explain this apparent disjunction, are to be found in the FSA's guidance on how to complain, which, in privileging consumer compensation over and above the detection of crime, tends to direct consumer decisions away from allegations of fraud. Significantly, for example, consumers are still not informed of the alternative of criminal investigation, nor the circumstances in which a criminal offence may have been committed (FSA, 2001a). The effect is that consumers are not encouraged to understand the mis-selling process in terms of the language of criminal liability and retribution (in which compensation, as well as fines and confiscation, was still obtainable), leaving them to fall back on the default interpretations of poor training or sharp practice and the default remedy of compensation. More important still is the fact that the FSA's guidance directs consumers to take their complaint, in the first instance, to the firm that originally sold them the endowment policy, and only then to the ombudsman if satisfaction is not forthcoming.[13] This "firms first policy" is predicated on the assumption that the "main priority" of dissatisfied consumers is compensation (FSA, 1997: 9). The effect, however, is to allow firms considerable control over how complaints are processed and, therefore, recorded. Instead of disrupting the monopoly of information that firms exercise over their operation, in other words, the regulatory response tends to reinforce it. It does not necessarily follow from this, of course, that firms' complaints procedures militate against the production of information that may form the basis of criminal suspicion. The available evidence, however, not only tends to suggest this, but also indicates that the FSA and FOS play a vital role in the process. The containment of criminal suspicion, it seems, is incorporated into every aspect of the process.

Thus, the reports of endowment mortgage complaints that firms are required to supply to the FSA under the new financial regime do not require potential violations of the criminal law in the context of the selling process to be listed. In fact, there is only one category that relates to sales advice and this is so broadly defined as to provide no immediate indication of the basis of the complaint (see FSA, 2001c: Annex A at 16). Not only, in other words, are firms not forced to consider the question of their criminal liability, but the one category capable of providing the FSA with some indication of the basis of complaints is insufficiently nuanced to provide further leads through which crime might be uncovered and constructed. This pattern of neglect is reinforced by the FOS's "Endowment Mortgage Questionnaire" which the ombudsman uses to resolve complaints, and is also made available to the life assurance industry as a guide to assist them with their complaints procedures. The questionnaire contains over 30 questions, not one of which refers to the possibility of criminal liability (FOS, 2001a). And finally, although there is no direct evidence of how firms resolve their complaints, the ombudsman's requirement of documentary evidence of misrepresentation and that the fact each case is considered on its own facts tend to promote the resolution of cases on the basis that insufficient account was taken of the consumer's attitude to risk, rather than on the basis that the advisor misrepresented the risk involved in an endowment mortgage. The result is that the pattern of misrepresentation—specifically the claim of a guarantee—is at once understated and distorted, excluding any possibility of uncovering why a particular pattern of misrepresentation may persist—a question that goes to the essence of criminal liability.

Thus, even though the FSA's agreement with the life assurance industry to provide consumers with better information promised to unlock the considerable potential of complaints to facilitate the discovery of fraud, the value of complaints to the detection of criminal offences still remains unrealized. The available evidence not only suggests that consumer complaints are not exploited as a potential resource of criminal intelligence, but also indicates that the complaints process is structured to extinguish the formation of criminal suspicion. This is, in part, because of the form in which most consumers make complaints. It is also, in part, because the principle of determining each case on its own facts means the process of resolving and, therefore, recording complaints is predisposed towards emphasizing concerns around imperfect risk assessment, as opposed to the less ambiguous issue of misrepresentation. Collating and recording practices at worst seem to reconstruct a distorted picture of the nature of mis-selling, and at best a vague and imprecise picture from which the true pattern of mis-selling cannot be reconstituted. This, in itself, represents a decisive limitation on the systematic discovery of criminal offences, but there is also evidence to suggest that direction, advice and guidance from the FSA and FOS to both consumers and the life assurance industry at once devalue, neglect and demote the relevance to the public interest of uncovering recklessness and dishonesty. Consumers' concerns and needs are generally diverted from the possibility of criminal justice intervention and maneuvered towards the circumstances in which compensation is payable and the amount that can be expected. What seems of equal importance, however, is that the experience of the few consumers who have ignored these directions, or, for one reason or another been unable to obtain satisfactory redress through the complaints process, and have called, instead, for criminal justice intervention, seems to be one of opposition and obstruction.[14]

This is not to claim that deliberate opposition—in which the neutralization of criminal complaints is an unambiguous expression of FSA policy—is routine. Consumers alleging recklessness or dishonesty may be rebuffed because staff with limited training—given no express instructions as to which organizations such allegations should be referred—administer initial complaints. Obstruction seems to be an oblique effect of emphasis, as opposed to an intended outcome. Nevertheless, there is also limited, as yet uncorroborated, evidence to suggest that the FSA, its forerunner the SIB, and the forerunner to the present FOS have refused, without any clear justification, to refer cases to the police when specifically requested to do so. Moreover, according to one victim of mis-selling, officials from the Treasury (which has overall political responsibility for financial regulation) even attempted to dissuade police officers from accepting cases for investigation—an objective later pursued in the same case by the PIA, which requested the police to discontinue their investigation once it had commenced. Significantly, the available evidence suggests that neither the Treasury nor the PIA had undertaken sufficient inquiries to allow themselves to conclude with confidence that the criminal law had not been breached.[15]

## Conclusion

Not only are consumers diverted from making a criminal complaint, but also, in the unlikely circumstances that a criminal complaint is persisted with, the evidence suggests that the organizations of primary commercial regulation are prepared to withhold their support from the police as well as to exploit their influence by requesting that investigations are abandoned. More generally, all investigations undertaken by financial regulators have worked to divert, neutralize and suppress information about the commission of possible criminal offences, rather than to generate or discover that information. This is in spite of the fact that the available evidence suggests that there have been credible grounds for exploring the question of criminal liability. The implications for social scientific research, and for what we know about crime in general and in the financial service industry in particular, are fundamental. Hundreds of thousands, perhaps even millions, of potential offences in this small area alone do not seem to register on official records. Significantly, these are conventional offences of fraud committed by unconventional defendants—professionals, the middle classes, suspects, in short, from populations whom the police generally service as opposed to those from populations whom the police have generally regarded as their property. The effect, if not to invalidate the Home Office evidence that has been drawn upon to justify the concentration of criminal justice resources onto, for example, problem schools or persistent young offenders (Travis, 2001; Wintour, 2002), is at least to suggest strongly that we revisit such evidence. Perhaps even more interesting is what the above observations suggest about the control that criminology cedes by default to corporations over the production of knowledge within the discipline. Corporations, rather than the institutions of primary commercial regulation, control the form and content of corporate-related information that enters the public domain. The reason for this is simply that the access the FSA has to information is not generally used to explore the question of criminal liability. Rather than confront this, however, the criminological enterprise seems to acknowledge the possibility and then discount it as having a significant bearing on what we already "know" about crime and the crime problem. Criminology's claim to expertise beyond the confines of the discipline is preserved. The fact, however, remains. Our understanding of the form and scope of crime within the commercial world seems ultimately to be defined by the companies themselves.

## Notes

1. Few words are used so frequently with so little apparent need to reflect on their meaning as "mis-selling." There is no formal definition of mis-selling, although the context of its use implies that a product is mis-sold if it is not sold in accordance with the relevant regulations. What also seems clear is that, in most circumstances, inaccurate information material to the prospective policyholder's decision will amount to mis-selling (although mis-selling is not dependent upon proof of a misrepresentation) (see FSA, 2000a).

2. Any mortgage arrangement involves a risk. Under the repayment method, interest rates fluctuate. If interest rates rise, or household income declines, or both occur, there is a risk that a homeowner may not be able to keep up payments. There is, however, no additional risk that the capital may not be repaid at the end of the mortgage term.

3. For a full discussion on the impact of tax relief see OFT, 1995.

4. Correspondence with FSA manager, 17 August 2001. All correspondents and interviewees gave permission to use information and responses provided.

5. Interview with victim, 8 October, 2001, interview with police officers from the Metropolitan Police fraud squad, 2 September 2001.

6. Interview with officers from the Metropolitan Police fraud squad, 2 September 2001.

7. Interview with a victim, 8 October 2001.

8. Correspondence with FSA manager, 17 August 2001.

9. Interview with FSA manager, 7 November 2001; interview with officers from the Metropolitan Police fraud squad, 2 September 2001.

10. Correspondence with FSA manager, 17 August 2001.
11. Complaints data, for example, can indicate that the risks involved in endowment policies were systematically misrepresented.
12. There is no conclusive evidence confirming the link between complaints and the provision of information concerning the projected investment growth of endowment-linked mortgages. The evidence that does exist, however, points to a strong correlation (see, for example, the case studies contained in FOS, 2001b).
13. This is a requirement under the Financial Services Ombudsman Scheme.
14. Interview with head of *ad hoc* action group, 7 October 2001.
15. Interview with head of *ad hoc* action group, 14 October 2001.

# Confronting Power:
# Scrutiny
# Within Limits

6    EILEEN BERRINGTON,
ANN JEMPHREY, AND
PHIL SCRATON

# Silencing the View from Below

## *The Institutional Regulation of Critical Research*

## Introduction

In the development and consolidation of critical analysis within criminology the priority has been a systematic examination of the structural relations which not only exploit but subordinate and diminish human potential. Essentially these are relations of power—economic, political, ideological—which form the determining contexts for personal action and social interaction. While all actions are invested with meaning, they can be fully understood and represented only in their historical and material contexts. As Messerschmidt (1997: 6) states, "structured action" is "what people do under specific structural constraints." Critical analysis, whatever its precise focus, emphasizes the determining contexts of production and distribution (class), reproduction, gender and sexuality (patriarchy), "race" and "ethnicity" (neo-colonialism), and childhood (age) (Scraton and Chadwick, 1991). Each determining context is exemplified, maintained, and reproduced via the relations of power and hegemony. Central to both representation and reproduction are the means through which knowledge is constructed and legitimated. Yet knowledge, as critical analysis demonstrates, also has the potential to contest dominant ideologies, academic traditions and official discourses. Determining contexts can be overwhelming in setting formidable boundaries to life chances and opportunities, but they are rarely total or absolute in their determination.

Advanced capitalism, even in its most predatory global manifestations, patriarchies, and neocolonialism are contested terrains. While many people experience the subjugation of these interlocking determining contexts simultaneously, the administration of power within state bodies and corporate institutions is invariably met with individual acts and social movements of resistance. These both inform and are informed by alternative, oppositional discourses which identify, name, and organize against oppression. Yet the material and political power inherent within advanced capitalist state institutions and multinational corporations, as chapters in this text demonstrate, underwrites and delivers life-changing, occasionally fatal, and destabilizing political-economic interventions. From the unacceptable levels of risk—such as Union Carbide's Bhopal plant—in economic free zones and the permanency of economic destitution established by the dynamics of "Third World" debt, to the endemic poverty and social exclusion which prevail in established industrial democracies, the social and cultural consequences of structural relations based on material inequalities are profound. Power, however, does not stand apart from the processes of legitimacy that deliver power relations their formal mechanisms of authority.

This chapter, while not concerned specifically with the macro dynamics and institutional arrangements of political-economic power, takes the critical analytical context as a backdrop against which the local state prioritizes, negotiates and legitimates certain discourses on crime and policing while disqualifying and ignoring alternative accounts. It examines how a local authority, in collaboration with its key professional agencies, commissioned a significant piece of research into crime, fear of crime, and police effectiveness only to mobilize its executive power first to modify and then to withhold the findings and recommendations of the project.

## The Challenge of Critical Social Research

> Critical social research begins with the premise that "knowledge," including the formalized "domain assumptions" and boundaries of academic disciplines is neither value-free nor value-neutral. Rather, knowledge is derived and reproduced, historically and contemporaneously, in the structural relations of inequality and oppression that characterize established social orders. (Chadwick and Scraton, 2001: 72)

Harvey (1990: 4) argues that critical social research "delve[s] beneath ostensive and dominant conceptual frames, in order to reveal their underlying practices, their historical specificity and structural manifestations." This is not simply a theoretical exercise because critical analysis "does not take the apparent social structure, social processes, or accepted history for granted." Rather, it examines "how social systems really work, how ideology or history conceals the processes which oppress and control people . . . direct[ing] attention to the processes and institutes which legitimate knowledge . . ." (ibid.: 6). Critical research is concerned with both the workings and consequences of structural inequalities and with the forms of official discourse which seek to justify, rationalize and reproduce inequalities through "acceptable" knowledge.

Criminal justice institutions, their policies and their practices are bound inextricably to the reproduction of the established social, political and economic order through processes which regulate individuals and groups differentially. Jupp (1989: 13) argues that critical analysis "seeks to understand the functioning of the criminal justice system in terms of the role of the state in maintaining social order" while addressing "questions about the nature of crime and about what, at any given time, is treated as criminal, and why." Through state interventions, structural determining contexts become tangible. Conflicts and struggles around the rule of law, its enforcement and its administration are the visible manifestation of political-economic marginalization and social exclusion. In delving beneath the surface, critical research has the potential and purpose of discovering and exposing the realities and myths of social conflict (Sarantakos, 1998: 3). This includes disclosure of the "means by which existing structures and social arrangements are legitimized and maintained," through research methods that "help uncover the structural and ideological bases of phenomena" (Jupp et al., 2000: 173–74).

Inevitably, critical criminological analysis provides an alternative discourse, arising out of an oppositional agenda, to that proffered by government-funded and policy-oriented "administrative criminology" and much so-called "independent" research. The critical "project," albeit diverse and far from unidimensional, recognizes that mainstream criminology, in its traditions, domain assumptions and state sponsorship, "has the most dangerous relationship to power: the categories and classifications, the labels and diagnoses and the images of the criminal being both stigmatizing and pejorative" (Hudson, 2000: 177). In contrast, critical academics "have challenged state practices, provided support for the powerless, influenced, to a limited extent, the introduction of more humane legislation and provided considerable opposition to the encroachment of state institutions into the lives of the powerless" (Sim et al., 1987: 37). Central to its challenge to mainstream analysis is an emphasis on the "view from below." This ensures that the voices and experiences of those marginalized by institutionalized state practices are heard and represented (Alasuutari, 1998). What follows is a systematic review of cases and, as Sivanandan (1990) proposes, the transition of such cases into issues.

As Jupp and Norris (1993: 46) note, critical social research is concerned particularly with producing alternatives to official discourses embodied in what Foucault (1980) describes as societal "regimes of truth." Such discourses formalize language, often using academic and professional conventions, to legitimate "knowledge," forming the parameters within which issues can be discussed, explained and understood. Official discourses are fluid over time and space, "ruling in" and "ruling out" particular views or ways of communicating, promoting some as acceptable while disqualifying others. Certain discursive formations become institutionalized as "knowledge" which, through this process, becomes authoritative: "constituting the 'truth of the matter,' at a historical moment" (Hall, 1997: 45).

Regulation and control of information directly impact on researching powerful corporations and state institutions. As Becker (1967) established, political and economic institutions are powerful definers, their influence extending well beyond the boundaries of their immediate operations. Spokespeople for state institutions and corporate bodies comment first and most prominently on key issues and the circumstances which contextualize them. They stand highest in the hierarchies of credibility (Becker, 1967; see also Hall et al., 1978). Through facilitating, limiting or suppressing the release of information, theirs become the versions of "truth" which are established and promoted. As Foucault (1980: 131) concludes, in establishing a "general politics of truth," disclosure is managed and manipulated through "techniques and procedures accorded value in the acquisition of truth" and status is ascribed to "those who are charged with saying what counts as true."

Alternative accounts, then, are oppositional not only to the purveyors of "official" discourse or truth, but also to the techniques and procedures they employ. Critical research is geared to redefining the constituents of problems and, accordingly, to seeking out quite different solutions. Significant here is the promotion of radical agendas and ideas "of how human relationships might be alternatively organized so that conflicts are resolved in new and socially acceptable ways . . . developing the conditions fostering and nurturing the anti-authoritarian features of human relationships" (Mathiesen, 1986: 86–87). Essential to these critical and reconstitutive objectives is a broad inclusivity of participants in the construction and realization of critical social research.

## Case Study of a Crime Audit: Management and Manipulation

In the mid-1990s the Centre for Studies in Crime and Social Justice (CSCSJ)[1] was approached by a local authority to conduct a crime audit as part of its development of a safe communities strategy. This work was intended to anticipate and inform a locally based "partnership against crime" involving all relevant interventionist agencies (Social Services; Youth and Community Services; Probation

Service; Enterprise; Health Authority; Community Voluntary Service). From the outset, in initial meetings and in the research proposal, CSCSJ was clear that the research would require a "thorough critical evaluation" of the central issues within the Conservative Government's "Safe Cities" program. Further, an audit would establish the relationship between community "needs," community "demands," and service provision relating to actual crime, recorded crime, "fear of crime," and the responses of the criminal justice agencies, particularly the police.

A research proposal went forward following meetings between local authority representatives and the CSCSJ research team. Given that the commissioned project was to provide a "snapshot" of crime, fear of crime, and police effectiveness, that the time-frame for completion, analysis, and publication of findings was less than six months and that the budget was conservative, the demands on the research team were significant. Six research elements were included in the audit, combining quantitative and qualitative methods. These elements were: a thorough and detailed analysis of recorded crime statistics for the area in the context of regional and national trends; a survey of the extent of crime within the area, including unrecorded crimes and the reasons for non-reporting; the significance of the fear of crime for "quality of life"; the views of lead agencies on criminal justice, particularly police policies and responses; the views of non-statutory community agencies on crime, the fear of crime, and law enforcement; and the views of small business proprietors and shop owners.

The proposal went before the authority's Policy Committee and was accepted as the "first step" in the development of an inter-agency partnership providing the foundation for a safe communities strategy. It would provide a comprehensive analysis of crime, fear of crime, and the responses to crime for the area (Policy Committee, 31 October 1995, minute of meeting). All local agencies approached, statutory and non-statutory, unreservedly endorsed the proposal. Within weeks the local authority chief executive, the head of planning, the divisional police superintendent, and the project director met to discuss and agree on the program. Much of this meeting was "off the record" and, among other more practical issues, concern was expressed that the research should not be seen as an opportunity to criticize policing unfairly. While the meeting was justified as "familiarization" and informal planning, it was exclusive insofar as other agencies in the safe communities working group were not invited.

Several months later, in March 1996, a meeting between the safe communities working group and the research team was held at which the former was informed of the main research objectives and progress. Apart from the "extent of crime" and fear and perception of crime, the "effectiveness of police strategy" was established as a key research focus. The street survey, involving four distinctive and significant areas within the local authority, was outlined and agreed. The areas were "New Town," "Old Town," "Traditional Rural," and "Growth Rural." Qualitative interviews had been arranged with the police (including community police officers), the probation service, social services, the youth and community service, estate management boards, non-statutory agencies including Women's Aid and the credit union, the local media and tenants' associations. Focus groups had been initiated within youth centers and arrangements were in place to survey senior citizens' clubs and other organizations. At the meeting the research team requested specific policy, documentary and statistical material held by the agencies and considered essential to the audit.

A further meeting of the working group and the research team was held in May 1996 to discuss preliminary findings. This included discussion of the early indications from the street survey and focus groups. Issues were raised by the research team concerning delays in accessing information including official crime statistics, a local youth survey, the anti-poverty strategy, information on people with learning difficulties, and information on local businesses. While the active research had progressed, the audit schedule was delayed by inhibited access to documents and statistics held by agencies. Despite these delays, within two months (in July 1996) two copies of the draft report were deposited with the local authority. A meeting to discuss the draft was cancelled without explanation, although the local authority's head of planning considered it "extremely interesting" and "well-written . . . which will be of significant help to the Council in the formulation of its Safe Communities Strategy" (personal correspondence, 8 August 1996).[2]

The cancelled meeting was never rescheduled. Police opposition to the preliminary report was rumored via leaks from within the local authority and the police although, at that point, no copies had been authorized for distribution to any of the participating agencies. The police, however, undertook to supply further information on crime both nationally and regionally. This information had been promised early in the project but had not been provided in full. Inquiries to local councillors on the Policy Committee indicated that no elected members had seen the preliminary report, and they had not been briefed on its contents. Following further equivocation and delays the final report was presented nine months after the cancelled meeting, eighteen months after it had been commissioned. It was over 35,000 words in length and detailed 82 major findings. These included: perceptions of crime and causation; the extent and experience of crime; key issues (drugs, young people, neighborhood nuisance, domestic violence, disability-related issues, business and commercial, fear of crime; media representations of crime and community; policing crime; and poverty, unemployment, and crime. The complexity of the research carried the potential for multiple, diverse recommendations. Yet the priority was to present a series of broad recommendations which would contribute to the development and agenda-setting of the safe communities strategy. Accordingly, the report highlighted 20 key recommendations.

The final report was never put to the Policy Committee and was never discussed by the safe communities working group. An informal meeting between the newly appointed Chief Executive of the Local Authority and the project director was held several months after the report was delivered. The chief executive posed questions over methodology, focusing particularly on the reliability of the street survey. He stated that "behind-the-scenes" concerns had been raised about the more controversial findings, particularly issues around police effectiveness, discriminatory policing, and police intimidation of young people. The CSCSJ research team had worked for over a year on the project and its in-depth and far-reaching work had been censored. The sequence of events from commission to completion demonstrates the ability and capacity of powerful definers, at the level of the local state, to withhold and manage information, disqualify alternative and independent accounts, and reinforce and sustain official discourse. Ironically, some of the significant negative practices regarding reputation, labelling and marginalization identified by the research as serious inhibitors in dealing with crime and antisocial behavior were subsequently employed to shelve the report, its findings and its recommendations.

## The Audit and Its "Controversial" Findings

As indicated above, the local authority area is a mix of new urban, semirural, and rural communities. It includes a second-generation "New Town" which never reached its planned potential due to under-investment in the region and the 1970s recession. New Town estates have high levels of poverty, disadvantage, and structural unemployment across all generations. Most "incomers" have roots in the inner city and, throughout the area, these families endure a negative reputation and discrimination. The prevalence of this negative reputation and its consequences in the region have been well documented (Scraton et al., 1995; Jemphrey and Berrington, 2000; Berrington, 2001). Its impact and consequences were significant elements of the context and experiences of people reported in the research. It provided the background to the three initial foci: crime (recognizing the complexity of classification); fear (popular assumptions and media representations); and policing (policies, priorities, practices, and community perceptions). A fourth focus, poverty and unemployment, was added as it emerged that both were significant in reality and perception.

It was also clear that while the local authority and other agencies readily talked of "the community," the local authority area was deeply divided in terms of location (the "indigenous" population versus "incomers"; "urban" versus "rural"; "Old Town" versus "New Town"), class and age. While the area has some of the most expensive accommodation in North West England it also has some of the most economically deprived estates. Even among those generally viewed as powerless there are hier-archies of access and influence. Young people in particular are socially, politically, and economically excluded, their views not sought and their voices silenced. This was evident in the community forums and in the decision-making processes ob-served early in the research. It was further evidenced in the focus groups with young people and in the interviews carried out with youth workers.

As noted earlier, the research utilized both qualitative and quantitative meth-ods. Perceptions of the "scientific" construction and "reliability" of official statistics as neutral and "value-free" indicators of crime and its prevalence remain dominant despite strong critiques (see Coleman and Moynihan, 1996). It was important to analyze officially recorded police crime figures (Hough and Mayhew, 1983) and to conduct random street surveys in four distinctive areas within the local authority. Local residents over 18 were age-banded and selected to provide a gender balance. The questions were extensive, mixing single-choice, multiple-choice, and open-ended questions. Further, an abbreviated questionnaire was used in a postal survey to involve local groups and organizations. Structured and semi-structured inter-views were conducted with "key informants" from community-based agencies, participating organizations, and the police. The involvement of the working group minimized problems of access to key informants, and all requests for interviews met with a positive response. Interviews with police officers, particularly commu-nity beat officers, were agreed upon, but the selection of interviewees was at the discretion of the police. Where it was necessary to interview a named officer, our requests were granted.

As the research progressed the team became aware of the emergence of poten-tially controversial findings. These arose primarily from questions relating to com-munity perceptions of policing. Allegations of inappropriate police behavior and practice were evident from the street surveys and from discussions with young peo-ple. They ranged from being "wound up" by officers "looking for trouble," being "moved on" for no good reason, to receiving "verbal abuse" and "minor injuries." As mentioned previously, the local authority area has one of the largest concentra-tions of New Town dwellers in the region, combining an established semirural population with urban "incomers." New Town is perceived as an "extension" of the inner city with all its attendant negative imagery, and from interviews, including those conducted with the police, it was evident that stereotyped assumptions had been absorbed into police attitudes towards inner-city "incomers." This was endorsed by a New Town senior police officer who acknowledged historical factors such as the decline of traditional industries, rising unemployment, and a poorly implemented redevelopment plan, but identified a "rogue population" with "no sense of direction, no community spirit, no loyalties." These people had been "dumped" in a rural area. It was clear from the interviews that the police regarded the majority of those they dealt with as "first or second generation" inner-city people.

This formed a perceived link with criminality, manifested in a confrontational style of policing in New Town. There was considerable evidence from a range of young people, and those working with them, of unfair and aggressive treatment by the police that, in their view, was unprovoked. Young middle-class people in the area reported very different experiences of contact with the police. On the whole they enjoyed relatively positive, friendly relations with police officers, unlike the more hostile, condemnatory and often physical interventions reported by their peers in New Town. The influence of stereotypes and assumptions is important in this context, with the presence, absence, or degree of inner-city accent a key determining factor, alongside place of residence and perceived class location.

The street surveys conducted with local residents and the interviews with young people revealed strong anti-police sentiments. While people in rural areas were generally satisfied with police performance in terms of crime prevention, there was marked dissatisfaction in both New Town and Old Town. A significant minority (19%) rated their performance as poor, and the group least impressed by police "performance" was young men. Nearly 70% of respondents considered police provision within their neighborhood inadequate, with women expressing slightly more concern than men. A high percentage of men and women interviewed considered that a greater police presence on the streets would improve neighborhood security and reduce personal concern. This reflects a national trend in public opinion, evident in the British Crime Surveys, and is not indicative of a police failing unique to the local authority area. Other findings, however, reflected specific concerns within communities. When asked if the police treated people "fairly and equally," 42.5% of people's responses were negative. Although concern was concentrated among young men and women living in the towns, a disturbing level of concern was evident across all age ranges. Respondents believed that the police targeted specific groups, according to age/youth (82.4%), gender/being male (68.4%), appearance (68.4%), "race" (51.8%) and accent (49.1%). The last mentioned referred to alleged victimization of young people who spoke with inner-city accents. Of those surveyed, 17% "personally knew" of police officers who were regularly ill-mannered when dealing with the public. A similar proportion had witnessed or experienced situations in which the police had used more force than was considered necessary, amounting to minor assault (pushing or punching). These responses revealed a poor record of police-community relations within specific areas. They are indicative of prejudicial police attitudes and consequent differential treatment of identified "communities" or neighborhoods.

To combat the exclusion of young people evident in other crime audits, a series of in-depth interviews was carried out, individually and in focus groups, in which young people were encouraged to talk about their views of and experiences regarding the police. Some accounts were highly critical of police behavior, reinforcing the street survey findings. Criticisms centered on the police practice of "moving on" groups of young people from public spaces. Often this related to underage drinking, but regularly it was simply a case that young people had nowhere else to go. Young people's use of public space is construed as problematic, as both a "nuisance" and a source of anxiety, by the police and local adults (Loader, 1996). The contemporary police response of "moving on" groups of young people irrespective of their behavior has a detrimental effect. Young people increasingly see the police in a negative light. Assumptions that groups of young people in public might be involved in illegal activities are used by the police as an excuse for over-policing. Groups of young people are seen as a "symbolic threat" to law enforcement, local regulation, and control (ibid.: 78), resulting in criminalization through visibility.

Young people living in the towns were more vocal in criticizing police behavior than those living in rural areas. They felt that police officers were verbally aggressive and confrontational in dealing with young men and young women. For example, in relation to police activity on certain estates within New Town, many young people felt they were pressured unfairly by police "stop and searches." They suggested that "stop and search" was a tactic designed to intimidate them into supplying information about drug dealing. If the police genuinely believed they were drug dealers, they were looking at the wrong generation. Payment for drugs is frequently "on tick" and, as one young person explained, they did not have the necessary "hard reputation" to ensure debt settlement. Yet drugs and drug-related problems were a significant cause of concern within the communities. There was a widespread perception that burglary, theft, and shoplifting were directly drug-related. Yet, there was no evidence to suggest that young people were regularly involved in the use of illegal drugs. Perceptions were based on stereotyped assumptions, hearsay, and an over-emphasis on the issue in the local press.

Young people's accounts of their experiences were balanced against the views of a number of residents' groups drawn from estates in New Town. Typically, residents' contact with the police was dominated by "neighborhood or juvenile nuisance." Examples given included noise, gangs, children and teenagers playing soccer near houses and fear of damage to property. Reference was also made to "gangs of youths" congregating around shopping precincts. Many residents feared going out, particularly in the evening. On certain estates a significant minority feared and/or experienced intimidation by young people and this anxiety impacted on their lives. They considered that limited police powers, poor parental discipline, and a general lack of authority influenced youth crime and antisocial behavior. Overall, a complex picture of community relations emerged, with considerable evidence of tensions between young people and the police, and young people and other residents.

In an attempt to improve police-community relations, operational police policy and practice initiatives included a renewed commitment to strengthening community and rural beats through the assignment of known, named officers to certain areas. Community and rural beat officers were interviewed to assess the effectiveness of their role. It was clear that the work of these officers challenged some of the barriers between residents and the police. Officers felt that people were more willing to talk to a community officer, identifying them as less confrontational. Inter-agency collaboration, as a means of breaking down preconceptions about the police and developing a more coordinated approach to problems, was stressed. Community-based officers also acknowledged that poverty and unemployment contributed to some residents' problems, including feelings of apathy. There was evidence of tension between community officers and other sections of the police (for example, CID and traffic). Community officers were aware of conflicting policing styles within their areas. Due to limitations on their availability to deal with persistent problems, particularly those occurring at night, situations arose where a community officer had formed a good relationship with local residents, only to have that undermined by the negative attitudes and dismissive behavior of other officers. Consequently, community officers experienced a backlash of community resentment and hostility.

A further "conflict of interest" manifested itself through community officers' dual role to "combat crime" and to "'provide public reassurance." Community officers had responsibilities to construct profiles of known "troublemakers" and to pass information to other police departments. This "softly, softly" approach within communities often leads to more subtle forms of surveillance (Scraton, 1985). It can also be counterproductive to "trust-building," adding to the alienation of those whose relationship with the police is already rooted in suspicion and hostility. Finally, there was a general awareness among community officers of the "low status" attached to their job. Colleagues regarded their work as a "soft option" rather than "real police work." Yet, despite these internal tensions, the positive achievements of community policing were reflected in the research findings.

The audit recommended a full review of police-community relations addressing the range of issues raised in the research, particularly concerning young people. It proposed the prioritization and extension of effective community policing as the primary context of police work, with care taken to establish clear parameters in gathering and using information within local communities. Having identified differential and discriminatory policing as a major problem throughout the area, the audit recommended that such policing be ended. It called for effective, independent community consultation forums, representative of all age groups, to develop inclusive local initiatives dealing with crime, fear of crime, and policing strategies. Drop-in information centers for young people, providing independent advice and access to facilities concerning the law and rights, benefits, general health, and sexual health matters were advocated, alongside further investment in outreach youth work. A key objective was a fully integrated local policy for the provision of comprehensive information and support on drugs and drug-related issues. Each of these recommendations, derived from the audit and from wider national research, was perceived as controversial, not only in its direction but also because the recommendations had emerged from a critique of existing policy and practice (personal meeting with the local authority chief executive, October 1997).

Of all the findings and associated recommendations the issue of violence against women appeared to cause the most controversy in terms of the audit's reliability. Research into violence against women has been consistently controversial in its findings. As with child sexual, emotional, and physical abuse, there is a reluctance to accept the prevalence of male violence within communities. The local authority and the police together had adopted the zero tolerance strategy imported by Lothian (Scotland) from Canada. The scheme was publicized in libraries and health centers and on police vehicles and buses throughout the area. A woman police officer was dedicated to working with non-statutory agencies to develop policies and strategies for effective intervention. The audit found that, in keeping with research nationally, there was evidence of high levels of domestic violence across age and class boundaries. Of the women surveyed, for example, 29% stated that they feared assault in the home by a man known to them. While this figure is not exceptional, it was treated with some scepticism—including serious doubts that it could be so high—by those who read the draft report. Yet the audit noted the positive and supportive local initiatives, the adoption of the zero tolerance campaign, and the work of the police. More negatively, it found that statutory agencies, as a matter of procedure, did not provide consistent advice or referral opportunities to all women who suffered male violence. Nor was there regular or informed independent rape crisis support in the area. The recommendations included long-term strategic planning and inter-agency provision for tackling male violence, new school-based initiatives as part of personal and social education provision, and the resourcing of a rape crisis center for the area.

The survey and interviews established strong perceptions throughout the area of links between unemployment, poverty, property crime, and benefit fraud. There was recognition at all levels of the debilitating effects of poor capital and industrial investment over the previous 20 years. This had led to marginalization, criminalization, and, particularly among young people, homelessness. Despite evidence of progressive inter-agency working parties combatting poverty and unemployment, key voluntary agencies suffered from under-resourcing and insecure futures. In particular, the credit union was identified as making a positive contribution to the prevention of material crime yet its initiatives, together with those of the trade union resource center, provoked controversy within the local authority. While the research exposed conflict between New Town community agencies and the local authority, it was not possible to uncover the source of this conflict. Within the context of local politics it appears that the recommendation that the local authority should be proactive in the development and consolidation of the credit union's anti-poverty strategies was not well received.

The level and extent of crime was not as pronounced as many people in the area believed. The relatively low level of crime compared favorably to other areas in the region and was confirmed by official statistics. One explanation for the discrepancy between perception and "reality" concerns local press coverage of crime-related issues. Crime news is given prominence and this contributes to exaggerated fears and perceptions of crime (see Williams and Dickinson, 1993). Content analysis of local media coverage found that the relatively low crime rates in the area were rarely reported. Official sources, particularly the police and "respected" community leaders, were over-represented in providing and commenting on stories. There was, however, some evidence of discretion in crime reporting and the use of the local media to provide important information to the public. The editor of the main local newspaper confirmed that local crime coverage was dependent on the police as a primary source of information. "Off the record" briefings played an important part in this process. The editor acknowledged that the police effectively "control the flow of information" (research interview with AJ and PS, June 1996). Police-led definitions of crime, its causes and its effects contributed to an emphasis on violent crime and "youth crime" in reporting. Further, portrayals of particular estates as crime-ridden reinforced their negative reputation. This created additional problems for community activists and workers struggling to tackle inherent problems, while further strengthening distorted perceptions of the incidence of crime in certain areas. The newspaper had limited resources for alternative or investigative crime reporting, resulting in only partial coverage of complex issues and an overly narrow definition of "community."

## Silencing the "View from Below"

> Sponsors of research include government departments [local and central], especially the Home Office, institutions of criminal justice, such as the police and legal profession, and pressure groups . . . Each of these stakeholders has interests to promote and interests to protect . . . each has differential levels of power with which to promote and protect such interests. The exercise of such power is ingrained in the research process from the formulation of problems through to the publication of results. (Jupp et al., 2000: 170)

The process through which the audit was managed and manipulated to prevent the disclosure of its findings and recommendations provides clear evidence of the "co-incidence of interests" and political mutuality that prevail between local authorities and the relatively autonomous institutions and professional organizations which, in part, they finance. While the research confirmed *pockets* of good practice within local authority service provision, community intervention, and policing (rural communities and domestic violence), the critique of policy and practice was received as unfair and embarrassing criticism. Rather than supporting the commonly held view, regularly promoted in the local media, of increasingly violent crime and worsening antisocial behavior among young people in New Town, the research indicated the demonization and vilification of children and young people. It also found reliable evidence of unprovoked attacks and institutionalized intimidation by the police. Hostility towards New Town "incomers" was evident in the semi-structured interviews with police officers and other professionals. What began as an audit of crime and the fear of crime also became an analysis of the dynamics of police effectiveness and intervention. Instructively, the findings of the street survey, which suggested that the area ranked low in the region regarding crimes of violence, theft (including burglary) and car crime, matched police statistics. As with the issue of young people, this profile did not suit the official discourse or media portrayal of escalating crime. While the audit delivered "good news" concerning the reality of crime and the likelihood of local people becoming victims, the vested interests appeared more concerned with talking up crime, particularly emphasizing antisocial behavior.

Placing the research in the wider context, in 1996 the national Audit Commission (1996: 3) had argued for a systematic overhaul of youth justice, directed at "inadequate parenting; aggressive and hyperactive behavior in early childhood; truancy and exclusion from school; peer group pressure . . . unstable living conditions; lack of training and employment; drug and alcohol abuse." Within a year the new Labour Government's Home Secretary, Jack Straw, condemned the "excuse culture" he claimed had consolidated around young offenders. Following a public outcry, provoked and fuelled by tabloid newspapers, over the killing of James Bulger by two ten-year-olds (see Scraton, 1997; Haydon and Scraton, 2000; Goldson, 2001), together with exaggerated concern over "persistent young offenders," the Labour Party had already established its position on youth justice reform (Labour Party, 1996). Within three months of the 1997 General Election the new government published consultation papers in preparation for its Crime and Disorder Bill.

In New Town, in October 1997, the local MP held an evening seminar on the range of proposals put forward for consultation. The Crime and Disorder Bill was presented as more far-reaching than a revision of youth justice. Crime strategies would be developed for each area, with local authorities, the police, and all other public authorities obliged to participate. The strategies would be based on key issues identified locally and audited on a three-year cycle. Civil injunctions—agreed by local authorities and the police in joint consultation—would be introduced. These would comprise parenting orders, child safety orders, child curfews, and antisocial behavior orders (ASBOs). As civil injunctions, they would be made "on the balance of probabilities" by magistrates, using professional witnesses. A breach of orders would constitute a crime. The extension of the law beyond established protocols for law enforcement and prosecution was greeted with overwhelming enthusiasm by delegates attending the evening seminar. Young people had not been invited to the seminar, while those, such as youth workers, who raised important questions of civil liberties or children's rights were derided by many of the community "representatives," councillors and professionals present. This was the climate in which the audit was delivered. It not only caused embarrassment for the police and raised questions over the appropriateness of existing policies and practices within the local authority, but also bucked the national shift towards draconian new legislation which culminated in the authoritarian 1998 Crime and Disorder Act. This has led, inevitably, to criminalization via net-widening. ASBOs, for example, are imposed for "sub-criminal behavior" which "for one reason or another cannot be proven to the criminal standard" (Home Office, 2000b).

Under the new Act, local crime strategies have to be based on locally identified needs derived from "independent" research. Not only are strategies monitored, but they also require evaluation. Unprecedented funding has been set aside locally and nationally to carry out "evidence-based" evaluations of strategies and projects, with crime audits central to decision making (see Leishman et al., 2000). What this form of policy-strategy-practice evaluation amounts to is a renewal of positivism under the guise of "best value," "best practice" and public accountability. For university departments eager to increase their diminishing budgets, "evaluation" is an attractive proposition. As Jupp (1989: 175) argues, "the balance of power between different parties (subjects, researchers, gatekeepers, sponsors) and the way in which it is exercised, determines what gets studied, by whom and with what outcome."

Whyte (2000: 420), reflecting on a discussion with a senior civil servant at the Health and Safety Executive (HSE) while researching safety in the offshore oil industry, was instructed that "government funding would be forthcoming only for research . . . constructed around the HSE's agenda." Wider access and funding would come at a price: substantial restrictions on the "freedom to publish and disseminate findings." As Whyte concludes, once researchers accept a "grant-holding relationship with either government or corporate funders," their "research activities will, to some extent, be structured by those who hold the purse strings" (ibid.: 421). There is no question that the audit was circumscribed, inhibited, and eventually silenced by a coincidence of interests at the heart of local government and policing.

Jupp (1989: 158) makes the point that when sponsors commission research on their policies and practices, or those of institutions for which they are responsible, "they will be concerned with the way in which they are portrayed, with the way in which their management and control of institutions is portrayed, and with the way in which conclusions might be used by others." The most "serious threats" to the publication of research findings come from sponsors and influential gatekeepers "who have the power to protect their interests." It is in this community or neighborhood context of local government, reproduced many times over within the national context, that official discourses are reinforced, alternative accounts disqualified, and local "regimes of truth" validated.

In the aftermath of the audit, the research team considered that its personal and professional integrity had been compromised. The audit report, particularly the final version, was self-censored. The dual concerns of protecting respondents' identities and safeguarding against possible reprisals necessitated the revision or omission of interview content (see Kvale, 1996). Since the research team was acutely aware of the trust placed in it, particularly by young people who had reported graphic experiences of harsh treatment by the police, certain events were omitted or downplayed. The levels of prejudice and discrimination against inner-city incomers reported by some police officers were also toned down. Had these comments been published in their entirety a more serious picture of police-community relations would have materialized.

The irony of the self-censorship and the modification of the text to guarantee publication was that such issues had been to the fore in the research team's initial deliberations over accepting the commission. Throughout the preliminary meetings between the research team and local authority representatives the tension that could arise, should findings over agency intervention and policy implementation prove controversial, was emphasized. Expanding the audit from a survey of crime to include the context of fear and the effectiveness of policing signalled that the audit would not be bound by quantitative indicators of crime and its commission. As the discussion of the early management and progress of the audit shows, the research team felt the pressure of agency defensiveness, particularly from the police, from the outset. Yet it was a pressure the team considered it could manage, given that elected representatives rather than local authority officers would eventually receive the report.

The decision to abandon the publication and distribution of the audit report was taken behind closed doors and without any political debate within local authority committees or among their elected members. Yet people had participated in the research on the understanding that their views and experiences would be incorporated into an official report commissioned to influence policies relating to crime and safety in their localities. The research team had no opportunity to provide feedback to participants concerning the reasons why the report was not publicized. Given the sequence of events described earlier, it can be concluded that the scale and complexity of the problems relating to the perceptions and causation of crime and fear of crime were neither expected nor desired by those who commissioned and agreed to contribute to the research. The findings and recommendations challenged those in positions of responsibility and power within the local authority and the police. The issues could not be addressed via "quick-fix" solutions. They required both political will and financial investment. The former was within the powers of the local authority and the latter necessitated substantially increased central government funding and private investment to tackle structural inequalities.

Clearly, the police were unhappy with the findings of the audit, yet it represented the views, experiences and concerns of local people to whom the police have a duty and are, theoretically, accountable. In a climate of discourses that are increasingly articulated around consumer satisfaction, participatory democracy and local consultation, criticism should be expected and considered constructive. Yet it became evident during the course of the research that neither the local authority nor the police were willing to accept or respond to criticism. The audit provided a sound basis on which to build more inclusive strategies to combat crime-related issues in the area. Given that police forces and local authorities are impelled into "partnership" initiatives as a means of tackling crime-related problems within communities, it is essential that prevention initiatives ensure the representation of all—including the politically marginalized and socially disadvantaged or dissenting voices. Suppression of their views cannot lead to improved intercommunity relations or to safer environments. If commissioning bodies, or their powerful representatives, are concerned over research findings, it is important to initiate further consultation and discussion rather than to reject or suppress these findings in their entirety.

More broadly, this chapter exposes how vested interests can be mobilized to inhibit and suppress critical social research into powerful organizations and institutions whose daily operation carries major consequences for those living in local communities. Given the major investment in the evaluation of local crime strategies, the experiences of the research team prior to the current political pressures over crime reduction targets do not inspire confidence in the independence and thoroughness of future evaluations. Those undertaking research, evaluation, or consultancies commissioned by local state institutions must recognize that with sponsorship comes gatekeeping, selective disclosure of information, and possible manipulation and control over dissemination and publication of findings. Yet access is often impossible without sponsorship. The research team experienced the neutralization and disqualification of "knowledge" and the processes through which those in powerful positions imposed their authority to legitimate official discourse while dismissing critical analysis. Effectively, the research findings, and the views and opinions they represented, were negated while the local authority and the police persisted with a rhetoric of participation, consultation, and public accountability. This episode should sound a clear warning about the reliability of crime audits which underpin local crime strategies, particularly regarding silencing the "view from below."

## Notes

1. CSCSJ is located within Edge Hill University College, Ormskirk, Lancashire.
2. All correspondents and interviewees were aware that there would be a written report. No requests for anonymity were made.

# "Telling It Like It Is"?

*Power, Prejudice, Politics, and People in the Qualitative Process*

## Introduction

This chapter is based upon the author's research into antiterrorist policing and its legal context in Northern Ireland (NI), the Republic of Ireland (RoI) and the Basque Autonomous Region (BAR) in Spain during the 1990s. The initial section examines some epistemological and ontological aspects of knowledge and perception relating to research processes. This leads into a general discussion of knowledge production and reproduction in academic institutions and by social researchers in particular, and a discussion of some academic contributions to debates on location, perspective, subjectivity, and the veracity of elite respondents. The chapter then identifies some particular problems with regard to researching state security and power, and points to means by which these problems may be overcome. The discussion then moves to how inter-personal perceptions and dynamics (including political/cultural/personal prejudices) impact upon the nature and quality of information exchanges produced in the qualitative research process.

The research in which these issues were explored involved a series of interviews with selected police, government, political, and community representatives.[1] The interviews began with appropriate subject areas (determined by the respondent's expertise and location). Interviews were semi-structured: key areas were covered, but with intuitive deviation where appropriate and varying from one to three hours in length. This research attempted to examine the provenance, nature, and development of antiterrorist cross-border operational collaboration, and its legal grounding in a European Union (EU) context. In particular, the research explored how as internal crises within particular states deepen, elements of the permanent "security layer" of government and police collude against resistance groups and suspect populations. Constrained in their response by law, local opposition, and international monitoring, state security agencies resort to clandestine extra-judicial operations by "special forces" and/or proxy "death squads" and extraordinary legislation that often becomes normalized over time. The strategies used to contain populations characterized as threatening state power, often involving covert action and illegal methods, were investigated. The interviews also examined the adaptation of national antiterrorist cross-border strategies for securing the EU's "continental sovereignty" and borders (Power, forthcoming).

## Knowledge Production and Critical Social Research

Wright Mills (1967: 405–406; see also Turk, 1982) identifies the complex nexus of societal power centers that contribute to the production of a common assumed social knowledge and construct of reality:

> For most of what he calls solid fact, sound interpretation, suitable presentation, every man is increasingly dependent upon the observation posts, the interpretation centers, the presentation depots, which in contemporary society are established by means of what I am going to call the cultural apparatus.

To critically analyze any social power base, the epistemological and ontological assumptions of an objective positivist extant reality must be ditched. Power produces "reality" by the mediation of specific knowledge forms through ideologically framed discourses that are inculcated through various regimes as Foucault (1979: 194) explains:

> The individual is no doubt the fictitious atom of an ideological representation of society; but he is also a reality fabricated by this specific technology of power that I have called "discipline."

Academe and its constituent disciplines play a central role in reproducing these realities (Christie, 1997). From a methodological and practical investigative perspective, some particular power concentration reproduces the relative reality and "rituals of truth" of all research participants. So the socially constructed products of Wright Mills "cultural apparatus" have effects similar to Foucault's "reality" of power production.

But Foucault (179: 194) continues:

> We must cease once and for all to describe the effects of power in negative terms: it "excludes," it "represses," it "censors," it "abstracts," it "masks," it "conceals." In fact, power produces; it produces reality; it produces domains of objects and rituals of truth. The individual and knowledge that may be gained from him belong to this production.

Foucault's dismissal of the negative effects of power aggregate, in any lived extant reality, as academic sophistry and conceit. The effects of power are to exclude, repress, censor, abstract, mask, and conceal. So Foucault's influential analysis (cited in Gold-Biss, 1994: 48) of the insidious and symbiotic nature of the power/knowledge relationship is often interpreted as either a despondent existentialist or a relativist postmodernist critique of proactive political engagement for social change:

> The historical analysis of this rancorous will to knowledge reveals that all knowledge rests upon injustice (that there is no right, not even in the act of knowing, to truth or a foundation for truth) and that the instinct for knowledge is malicious (something murderous, opposed to the happiness of mankind).

Norris (1996: xv) counters rhetorically: "Can truth-claims be reduced, as Foucault would have it, to transient effects of the epistemic will-to-power within discourse. . . ?" Many academics seem to think so. A feigned detachment and/or positional duplicity characterizes much contemporary academic writing in the social sciences. Postmodern interpretations obfuscate the fearful and selfish withdrawal from active politics by the tenured cap 'n' gown hamlets of academe. This trend is rooted in the accelerating marketization of campus environments by the state and private corporations (Jacoby, 1999, 2000; Ricci: 1984).

Social power and authority are founded on the accumulation of information and its exclusive interpretation through ideological discourse into knowledge (Turk, 1982; Foucault, 1979, 1980). The power/knowledge bond has specific implications for critical research. The "critical" element deconstructs dominant ideological discourses and related policies and practices. The complex interaction of myriad societal power centers produces "lived" realities that are structured and real from macroscopic to microscopic social situations. Critical research defines itself relative to the power centers it critiques (for example, state institutions, patriarchy) and is by implication in opposition to them. Truly critical research should produce Said's (1981: 149; see also Christie, 1997; Jacoby, 2000) idea of antithetical knowledge "produced by people who quite consciously consider themselves to be writing in opposition to the prevailing orthodoxy." The social "reality" of the West is constructed and reproduced by the complex and contradictory socio-economic dictates of the major stakeholders in the capitalist system. Regional variants of this reality are mediated through local hegemonic institutions creating a vaguely coherent Western ideological discourse.

Critical social research connects personal, social, and structural relations. It attempts to deconstruct, analyze, and critique all structures of power in their horizontal, vertical, and shifting temporal indices from a perspective rooted somewhere towards the bases of the myriad pyramids of social power deposits (Haraway, 1988). Its political remit is to positively influence policy initiatives while simultaneously exposing state, institutional and corporate crimes, and abuses of power. So it is, paradoxically, both reformist and potentially revolutionary in its goals. The central difficulty, therefore, for the critical researcher is one of positioning in relation to the power structures being studied while struggling with the paradox previously suggested. At what point, for instance, if ever, does a critique of state actions become an overt apology for sustained resistance by insurgent groups? How can the critical approach to research articulate a coherent view from the margins of complex power structures that go far beyond the state's confines?

## Critical Principles or Prejudices

In a recent journal article, Liebling (2001) challenges Becker's (1967: 241) hierarchy of credibility thesis. Becker argues that powerful people have the ability to "shape" the truth in professional or institutional situations and are prone to prevarication when they fail to perform adequately. Dismissing this argument Liebling (2001: 476) counters that

> To take this for granted is sociologically naive. . . . Some powerful officials lie, play games, fool themselves and others, or defend the indefensible. . . . Most (in my experience) simply want to participate in the account: "This is my world and I will share it with you. But you must treat it kindly."

Liebling peculiarly invokes Gouldner's constructive critique of Becker's thesis by appealing for a "human sociology" that appreciates the "suffering of 'superiors'" (1975: 36). Gouldner criticizes Becker for dismissing the powerful as lacking "a sense of common humanity" (ibid.: 36). Gouldner's reflexivity recognizes élite perspectives, while accepting the general veracity of the "view from below" (Finlay, 1999). However, this approach obfuscates the arrogance of the dominant and their tendency to displace blame downwards within and across institutions. Power, paranoia, and self-preservation coalesce to suborn "a sense of common humanity."

Objectivity and its presumed opposite, subjectivity, are both functions of social power relations, as Haraway (1988: 583–584) observes:

> All western cultural narratives about objectivity are allegories of the ideologies governing the relations of what we call mind and body, distance and responsibility. . . The 'equality' of positioning is a denial of responsibility and critical inquiry. Relativism is the

perfect mirror twin of totalization in the ideologies of objectivity; both deny the stakes in location, embodiment, and partial perspective; both make it impossible to see well.

Renouncing structural and ideological power relationships (as Liebling does) negates crucial contexts for the extrapolation of research data. However, the prevalent academic misuse of the excluded sociological perspective is devastatingly critiqued by Gouldner (1970: 500–501; see also Jacoby, 1999, 2000):

> Under the banner of sympathy for the underdog, the liberal technologues of sociology have become the market researchers of the Welfare State, and the agents of a new managerial sociology.

Haraway (1988: 590) accepts the dangers of academic appropriation of the view from below but counters Gouldner's negativity with her preference for a view from somewhere "real" in a lived sense:

> The only way to find a larger vision is to be somewhere in particular. The science question in feminism is about objectivity as positioned rationality. Its images are not the products of escape and transcendence of limits (the view from above) but the joining of partial views and halting voices into a collective subject position that promises a vision of . . . living within limits and contradictions—of views from somewhere.

Historically the rich and powerful have preferred hagiographic enquiry. Feminist methodology emphasizes the establishment of non-hierarchical relationships between researcher and respondent (Oakley, 1981). This is hardly possible when researching the powerful from a critical standpoint. There is an elite preference for the "blessing" of academics and a commonly held belief in the general efficacy of empirical methods (Lee, 1993). Scientific empiricism dominates almost exclusively in social science data collection and knowledge production (McKendy, 1992; Pickering, 2001). Moreover, Christie (1997: 14; see also Jacoby, 1999, 2000) asserts that academics are "oversocialized" through submersion in an educational orthodoxy that can suborn the researcher, the researched, the process and its results:

> First, in the process of giving room to the authorized perceptions, a depreciation of the importance of one's own personal experiences will take place. Second, deviant findings, that is results not expected according to theory, will have difficulty in surviving.

Here Christie refers specifically to criminology, but this point is relevant throughout the social sciences. Authorities interpret and validate research findings primarily in relation to an author's reputed ideological stance (Rolston, 1998). Research funding and institutional imprimatur are increasingly dependent on market forces (Christie, 1997; BBC Radio 4, 2001).

Too often academic discipline and detachment ignores those processes and poses as the epitome of objective enquiry, but results in a form of equivalence that fails to highlight the structural roots of conflict, or fails to challenge corrupted authority and abusive power. In order to challenge these dominant regimes of truth, academic researchers must subjectively engage with their own emotional and ideological baggage—the most common being their presumed political and ideological detachment and impartiality. This means, in effect, actively engaging emotionally where necessary and eschewing the empirical notion of impartial, rational, objective enquiry (Pickering, 2001).

Leibling's over-socialized assumption that personal power transcends institutional prerogatives represents an arrogant dismissal of the significance of power structures in the research process. This isolated and elitist position can, to some extent, be redressed by consciously positioning oneself within the social power matrix. At the very least, the researcher must have a reflexive approach to negotiating power.

## Qualitative Approaches to Researching the Security State

Critical studies of research into the Irish conflict point to a marked lack of reflexivity on the part of many individual researchers through their own pre-conceived prejudices. More insidiously, these studies point to constraints imposed on researchers by academies when projects risk the possibility of confrontation with state institutions (Finlay, 1999; Smyth and Moore, 1996; O'Dowd, 1990; Rolston, 1998). Moreover, criticism of the state and its coercive elements is often read by the powerful as either implicit or explicit support for anti-state activity and insurgency. US President Bush's global dictum on dissidents frankly reflects these brutal times: "either you are with us, or you are with the terrorists" (*Irish Times,* 22 September 2001). Security forces in liberal democracies are always extremely sensitive to how they are portrayed publicly and may therefore hinder or control attempts at research. Researching areas connected with state security—in particular, scrutiny that seeks to describe or explain state illegalities—can become a nether world where lying is the operative principle and everything is deniable.

Epistemology, the nature, origin, foundations, limits, and validity of knowledge, is particularly complex in research focused on the societal impact of coercive legislation through policing (Cayne, 1991). Procedures and policies can be recorded and dissected. But to reach an appreciation of the human cost of state-administered policies, investigations must go beyond the plethora of facts and statistics produced by state-related research institutions and by their critics, whose interpretations are also largely based on officially sanctioned and digested data (Christie, 1997).

Smyth and Moore (1996: 17–18) claim academic social research in NI "largely unreflexively mirrors and re-enacts the divisions occurring in the society it is observing and writing about." Researchers often have a limited appreciation of the "lived" perspective due to the compartmentalization and rigorously empirical requirements of academic disciplines. In 1995 a respected professor gesturing towards nationalist West Belfast from his university office tower commented to me: "You know, there are mothers up there who glory in the deaths of their sons." Yes, social scientists are often elitist, even overtly prejudiced. The mythical academic high ground (in its moral, ethical and intellectual guises) can diminish both understanding of, and sympathy from respondents, be they marginalized or elite (Christie, 1997). Which is more real: the rough and tumble of lived and experienced realities, or the modular, sanitized, codified, compartmentalized, focused, and tightly disciplined academic gaze that affects distance, balance and objectivity? But which perspective has, or should possess, the most influence and legitimacy?

Miller and Glassner (1997: 105) claim that "social distance" can be an advantage when interviewing and that deliberately putting respondents in a powerful position by affirming their particular expertise encourages them to reciprocate by "rewarding" the researcher with relevant material. However, this approach could reinforce official discourse and afford tacit approval to the actions of elites. Contrary to Miller and Glassner's assumptions, Collins (1990: 232; also Smyth and Moore, 1996) argues that legitimate knowledge can be created only if the researcher has "lived or experienced their material in some fashion." This insistence on direct experiential knowledge is too didactic and ill defined—especially in relation to researching state security issues. It is arguable that the security sphere of the state impacts on everyone in some form or other—but what constitutes lived experience in this context?

In mass Western societies most people are hegemonized through broadly similar orthodox socialization processes of which education is a crucial component. Eagleton (1996: 175) argues that

> becoming certified by the state as proficient in literary studies [as in all academic study] is a matter of being able to talk and write in certain ways. It is this which is being taught, examined and certificated, not what you personally think or believe . . .

This experience intrinsically deskills people socially through encouraging an over-reliance on impersonal methods of validation. The certificate, title, rank, and uniform impress. The validated professional personality dominates one's own inner identity, resulting in compartmentalization, duplicity, confused perspective. Foucault (quoted in Poster 1997: 152) outlines the ambiguous character of the public and private persona in this context:

> Do not ask who I am and do not ask me to remain the same: leave it to our bureaucrats and our police [and academies] to see that our papers are in order.

Doing qualitative reflexive research is essentially about possessing the confidence to understand and appreciate the sociopolitical dynamics of one's own particular life situation including the structural processes that underpin it, and extrapolating this to people's diverse experiences through the investigative process (Christie, 1997).

## Political Context and the Research Process

An obvious problem in researching state security and power involves the availability and quality of access to official information sources and personnel such as police forces, security organizations, and government representatives. With the requisite credentials access to the powerful is reasonably easy except where "undercover-work and state secrets" are concerned (Christie, 1997: 19). In one instance Garda[2] Headquarters in Dublin requested from the author detailed question areas, which were duly dispatched, resulting in an arranged interview with a supposed expert on security issues. When I checked the day before the interview the respondent was identified as the head of the Garda Drug Squad. Reminded of my written request to meet a security expert, the press officer retorted that this could not be helped—otherwise the interview "would have to be rearranged at some future date."

Investigations carried out at the interface between the security forces and communities in NI can be difficult and sometimes traumatic for those involved. Lee (1993: 7; see also Taylor, 1988) states that "some researchers were forced into hiding or had to leave Northern Ireland altogether as fears arose in some communities that research materials were finding their way to the security forces." The defensive, secretive, and sometimes obstructive culture that permeates all levels of security in NI (as in all liberal democracies) was palpable when I attempted to research security and antiterrorist issues (Agee, 1983: 5–11; Stalker, 1988; McNamee and Ruane, 1991: 73–80). My field research in NI began in February 1996. The NIO[3], the RUC[4] and the Police Authority of NI (PANI) were approached. When initially contacted from Britain, the secretary to PANI stated: "I'll consider setting up an interview after you've spoken to the RUC." It felt like an informal vetting operation by the RUC and NIO's performing poodles.[5] While I was in Belfast the same secretary again promised during a number of telephone conversations to set up interviews with the PANI chair and other members giving (and regularly changing) dates—but providing no definite appointment. In the end time ran out.

The RUC engaged in a protracted telephone, fax, and letter exchange during which they demanded detailed information on the nature of the research including the proposed question areas and the intended use of the results. An interview with an RUC security spokesperson was eventually arranged—but again with the proviso that the agreed date be confirmed on arrival in NI. When I had sent personal and institutional details along with a description of the research and a list of detailed question areas, the RUC seemed reasonably amenable and set up an interview with a named detective inspector. His competence in the realm of security policing was not disclosed. My field research in NI coincided exactly with the end of the Irish Republican Army (IRA)—the main insurgent group in NI—cease-fire on the 16 February 1996. The interview was never consummated. When contacted, RUC headquarters instigated a total shut-down of communication: "no briefings at the present until the situation stabilises. . . . maybe an interview sometime in the future." The RUC detective inspector contacted me after the IRA bomb in Canary Wharf that ended the cease-fire. He was not very encouraging but did not dismiss prospects of a meeting. After some days he contacted me again to cancel any prospective interview.

Neither the RUC nor the Garda Special Branch section has a reputation for openness to outside enquiries. However, the Garda Press Office promised an interview with "someone" with expertise in security affairs during the February 1996 research visit. When I contacted the press office on 20 February, I found that the Garda on duty was aware of the previous request but said that research "bona fides had to be checked before confirmation of an interview." He suggested telephoning the following day, notwithstanding the detailed research and background information I had sent to the Garda before my departure for Ireland. Security services in both the north and south of Ireland seemed to close ranks after the end of the IRA cease-fire in 1996. After I had been told that final arrangements for interviews could be completed on arrival in Ireland, access was completely refused, or subjected to constant rearrangement and/or cancellation, or seemingly "inappropriate" respondents[6] were assigned.

The Departments of Justice and Foreign Affairs in Dublin were positive and, before the fieldwork began, virtually assured me that interviews would be arranged. On my arrival, however, previous contacts were unavailable—they were "all away at this time." An internal contact in the Justice department later informed me that the contacts were in Belfast and London due to the end of the cease-fire. The NIO did provide a pretty innocuous "security expert" during this visit, his stock response to questions being, "I haven't got any particular detail on that area of operations at present." Overall, this research trip did produce excellent data from community and resistance groups, but the response from the powerful was generally poor, partly because of the cease-fire's ending. One particularly interesting interview did occur, however, with a powerful inappropriate respondent.

## Inappropriate Respondents

Where apparently inappropriate respondents for the research were assigned by security institutions, deft improvisational questioning was often required (McGrath and NIO interviews, 1996). Holstein and Gubrium (1997: 115) refer to this semi-improvised research as "a highly sophisticated technology." Douglas (1985: 25) reiterates that creative interviewing requires "the use of many strategies and tactics of interaction . . . to optimize cooperative, mutual disclosure and a creative search for mutual understanding." Terkel's (1972: xxv) method epitomizes this reflexive conversational method of enquiry: "In short, it was conversation. In time the sluice gates of dammed up hurts and dreams were opened." The humanity of this approach belies the complexity of interactive and interpretative skills required by the interviewer. Good social skills are essential: the ability to listen intently and intuitively lock on to subtle nuances in the respondent's discourse and demeanor—while constantly deciphering and contextualizing these complex data sets by being well briefed and reflexively responsive.

Winckler (1987: 137) argues that the manipulation of elite psychology can be helpful in accessing information—the desire of the powerful to know "how one stands in relation to others" can help motivate responses. This can occur where respondents identify with certain presumed characteristics of the interviewer such as university-level education, ethnicity, social or class status, and presumed prejudices based on "common sense" truths. The head of the Garda Drug Squad, Chief Superintendent McGrath (interview, 1996), commented on his extensive experience of the tensions between individual initiative, professionalism, and police institutional culture:

> In my own career going back over the years I'm fond of saying that the only thing that ever got me into trouble internally in the Force was telling it like it is. It's not always a good thing. The fact is that sometimes it would be better to say nothing.

In a personal and structural sense McGrath's remarks betray the underlying epistemological difficulties, distortions, weaknesses, and complexities of institutionally based communications, resultant actions and knowledge production/reproduction. Those in powerful positions often present themselves as reasonable, civilized, and educated human beings in an institutional situation out of their control, but one that they grapple with "heroically" to the best of their "professional" ability. Telling it like it is—but only within a particular institutional economy of truth. "Don't rock the boat too much or we'll throw you overboard" is the salutary lesson for those pursuing "truth" within institutions. McGrath's comment indicates how bureaucratic imprimatur overrides personal interest.

Though a powerful policeman, McGrath was friendly. He was welcoming, gave me ample time and delivered an interesting, often candid, and insightful interview. He tried to be as honest as his position would allow. He nostalgically recalled studying for his masters degree in criminology, having ascertained my academic background. He treated academic space (including the interview) as a relatively free (and innocuous?) forum for discussion of ideas and practices—somewhere to elucidate and expiate his practical policing experience. He broadly agreed with the relatively liberal Dutch approach to narcotics, believing "decriminalization and medicalisation was the way forward in dealing with the drugs problem" (ibid., 1996). Academic space and discourse seemed to afford a safe forum to positively articulate his experience—and project himself as a "decent" and educated human being. But McGrath seemed to believe that there was a huge gulf between elite ideas (including academic theory) and the reality of institutional practice, political expedience, and the main social catalyst—public opinion. The McGrath interview became a form of free-flowing informational exchange. An ostensibly inappropriate interview became an interesting and candid discussion covering cross-border operational co-operation in the narcotics and other fields; attitudes displayed at EU-wide policing conferences, academic criminology, Garda management practice, and a unique insight into Europol operations.

When discussing his view of co-operation with the RUC he outlined in some detail the nature and extent of cross-border links and operations concerning illegal narcotics. When the discussion broadened to the RUC's role in the management of social conflict McGrath struggled for a definitive purchase on the subject and defaulted to a narrow affirmation of the RUC's anti-narcotics work:

> Researcher: There's no political context to the fact that they are involved in policing a political conflict?
> McGrath: No, that wouldn't . . . I have never a . . .
> Researcher: You see them as pigs in the middle—basically?
> McGrath: Yes, they are caught in a particular situation. Certainly, unless you could say that they. . . . We would be quite impressed with the work that they are doing: in our field, we would be.

Here McGrath affirms the professionalism of the RUC's drug squad; but there is an implicit distancing from other RUC operational functions in his addendum: "in our field, we would be." His admonition that "they are caught in a particular situation," recognizes the extraordinary policing situation in NI while ignoring the RUC's role as the main coercive arm of a sectarian statelet that reproduced that "particular situation." But there is also uneasiness here about engaging in politics beyond the institutional/state matrix: perhaps it's better to say nothing again.

The Garda themselves are rooted in an ideology of civil policing that draws on the British model of unarmed "citizens in uniform" (Shiells, 1991: 151). The reality, however, is that the Irish state has always relied on special coercive legislation (including the use of armed Special Branch police) to maintain order. Townshend (1983: 412) argues for the legitimacy of the RoI's security policy in the light of its need to stabilize a newly emerging democratic polity:

> The cohabitation of authoritarian and democratic norms within the Irish state, offers a paradox, but one which can be resolved as a fruitful symbiosis wherein stern government

has helped to defend and nurture Parliamentary democracy against the threat of violent subversion. There has been an acceptance, throughout the short life of the new state, that it needed to take extraordinary judicial and security measures against those who questioned its legitimacy.

Townshend exceptionalizes the RoI's security needs as particular to newly developing states—instead of conceding that this "cohabitation" exists in all democratic and populist majoritarian states. McGrath and his educated liberal ilk know there are more efficient, alternative, and humane methods of social control, both from personal experiences and from recorded knowledge sources. But they ultimately embrace their professional role (like Christie's over-socialized academics) and suborn better human judgment and experience within hierarchical security institutions that reward compliance with career advancement and a state pension. This reverses Townshend's thesis: increased government authority and stability enhance the paranoia that feeds state security concerns.

## Negotiating Power and Status

Everywhere I encountered the paramilitary Guardia Civil in the BAR they seemed a socially separate, heavily armed, and threatening paramilitary presence. Even the peculiar headgear they wear stands out as antiquated, anachronistic, but decidedly militaristic. They wear paramilitary uniform and to all intents and purposes act as an occupying army. Their collective attitude distinctly reminded me of the atmosphere created by the RUC and the British Army in nationalist areas of Northern Ireland. In both jurisdictions these forces behaved aggressively through their attitude, demeanor, uniform, and offensive equipment. While I was doing research in Bilbao a member of a Guardia Civil unit pointed an automatic weapon at me as I was trying to photograph a street patrol from a car. I dropped the camera on the seat and achieved hasty acceleration as the traffic lights changed to green. The only time I experienced a similar threat, one more unsettling at the time, was when stopped while driving (a British registered car), then searched and questioned by the locally recruited Royal Irish Regiment (RIR) outside Portadown (NI) in 1996. Though British Army foot patrols are legally required to have at least one accompanying RUC officer, this one did not. The atmosphere during the five-minute stop and search was very intimidating and seemed to intensify when the RIR recognized my southern Irish accent. RIR members have been convicted for collusion with Loyalist death squads and a good deal of cross-membership is suspected.

Spanish security organizations, the RUC, and the former Police Authority in NI (PANI) were both highly suspect of my inquiries and repeatedly requested detailed information about the nature and use of my research. However, the possibility of access to highly secretive institutions may even be possible for researchers perceived as the dangerous "other." Lee's (1993: 11) contention that in violent situations "the researcher provides an audience and a voice for the factions involved" seemed to be borne out by my Basque experience. In the BAR all respondents seemed to have at least a working knowledge of the Irish peace process and a positive interest in Irish affairs. This affinity helped to lower barriers. Moreover, regular British Army and RUC reaction to a southern Irish accent, in my own personal experience, was cautious to begin with, but a deferential regard grew when my university identification was presented. Native, yes, but neither "Taig" nor "Prod," educated, safe, and from the "soft" distant south it seemed (Brewer and Magee, 1991: 25).

During my research in the BAR a heavily armed Guardia Civil unit on sentry duty at the fortified entrance stymied my initial appointment with the Spanish Government Deputation to the BAR Government (September 1997). This unit refused to grant me access, even when the respondent's name (Sr. Ortega) and full details of the previously arranged official appointment at the Spanish Deputation were explained. Following some furtive phone calls from the guardhouse, the sentries stated curtly in a mixture of Spanish and broken English that they had no knowledge of this man, his official status or any appointment and brusquely dismissed my request for access. This reaction was perplexing, as Sr. Ortega had given assurances by telephone and fax that everything had been agreed and arranged.

When I contacted Sr. Ortega later, he was initially peeved by the missed appointment, complaining about his valuable time being wasted. But when he was given an explanation, including the Guardia Civil's aggressive attitude, he apologized citing (but not explaining) a "misunderstanding" and rescheduled the meeting for the following afternoon. When approached the following day, the Guardia Civil sentries were most civil and an immediate escort was provided through the guardroom to the main building. Sr. Ortega was waiting there and seemed at pains to compensate for the previous day's "misunderstanding." He smiled and announced that he had checked the College website, presumably in order to prove its existence—and my credentials as a researcher.

While researching security issues, my background as perceived by respondents sometimes created an "objective" distance (constructed by the respondent's subjective presumptions) that opened up discursive corridors that may not otherwise have appeared. This echoes Harding's (1991: 124) views on the efficacy of women researchers operating in the public realm:

> The stranger brings to her research just the combination of nearness and remoteness, concern and indifference, that are central to maximizing objectivity. Moreover, the "natives" tend to tell a stranger some kinds of things they would never tell each other; further, the stranger can see patterns of belief or behavior that are hard for those in the culture to detect.

Educated Irish southerners in NI are perceived as familiar, but often not close enough to be directly sectarianized by the conflict. Respondents tend to want to educate southeners about their own particular "realities" and presume an ignorance of lived NI realities.

I supervised an Irish Studies field trip to NI for British degree students in 1996, including a visit to the NIO at Stormont. Some research-related interviews were carried out during this visit. Through personal contacts and interventions in the NIO an interview was arranged with two senior officials. These officials (interviews: Gates, Tab, 1996) emphasized that since the Anglo-Irish Agreement (AIA) in 1985 massive changes had been engineered on both sides of the Irish border to enhance security co-operation operationally, but also through synchronization of discourse.

> Researcher: These [special cross-border powers] were negotiated in meetings from the late eighties onwards?
> Gates: Yes, that's right—yes—from the late eighties onwards we've been getting better and better . . . I think actually it's even better to say really late eighties onwards . . . the whole change in things, the AIA, yes, quite—since eighty-five.
> Researcher: These agreements have been made on an *ad hoc* basis?
> Gates: Well, they are not within the course of law or anything like that, yes, on an *ad hoc* basis, but statutory provisions they can't really be, but . . . Obviously a lot of it was getting better—the whole business of. . . . overflights to look at . . . aaaah at explosive devices . . . being able to sort of chase people up on hot pursuit . . . all of that, these are the things which have developed over the years and are now of a state where we would say that they were satisfactory.
> Researcher: So there are provisions for hot pursuit and over-flights—these are actually agreed?
> Gates: These are agreed with the Irish—we don't give details of them out—as to what they are.

In effect Britain and RoI were operating their own mini-Schengen[7] system on the Irish border with the crucial difference that over-flights and hot-pursuit were a one-way agreement—from north to south. This interview was revealing and unexpectedly candid. Hot pursuit—although an open secret to local people on the border—is an issue that has never been discussed or recognized in official sources and could be found unlawful if ever tested in the courts. Gates talked loosely in a manner that his employers would hardly have sanctioned. He (having operated in NI security since the 1970s) continued chatting amiably—as if he knew the endgame was being played out in NI. Gates was clearly relaxed in the company of a presumed professional academic ally from the south and his extension of the "cameraderie" between Britain and the RoI that followed the AIA to this interview opened up new discursive corridors.

Sometimes a less sophisticated approach tainted with arrogance rather than reticence is adopted by powerful respondents who admit to mistakes and problems in the past (usually someone else's responsibility). They then claim that the adoption of British standards of governance in NI, burgeoning Spanish or Basque democracy, or Garda professionalisation in the RoI has resolved any substantive problems. The "you know as well as I do" approach admits that there may be residual problems with the rank and file, but "that's all being dealt with now" through new legal and policy developments and practices (interviews: Ortega 1997, Gates 1996; McGrath, 1996; NIO presentation). The mistakes of history and the policy initiatives of the present are spun to legitimize the state and obscure the unchanging remit of the permanent security and coercive layers that underpin all liberal-democratic forms of governance. Thus, the message is plain: resistance is now unnecessary, regressive, futile, and essentially criminal by nature—"come join us." It is an inclusive process that also obscures ongoing state illegalities.

## Exploiting Internal Conflict

Competing international claims to sovereignty can be exploited to advance research (Lee, 1993). Differences of opinion in relation to the interpretation of internal Spanish law and international treaty agreements occur regularly between the BAR and Spanish governments as they jostle over any issue related to sovereignty. Competing institutional discourses can therefore be exploited during interviews by emphasizing the (sometimes starkly) different interpretations of events, legislation, and competencies in order to encourage more pointed and engaged discussion. This was more difficult to achieve in NI. Though there is intense rivalry between the various security agencies operating there, my research access was restricted to a number of senior NIO security officials, due partly to the end of the IRA's cease-fire in 1996. Cross-border security disputes in Ireland are also difficult to exploit in light of enhanced inter-state and inter-agency co-operation as Gates (interview, 1996) observed, "certainly all stemming from the cameraderie—the arms around one another's shoulders . . . of the first Anglo-Irish Agreement." Security co-operation between the RoI and Britain has increased greatly since the 1985 agreement.

Distinct and frequently contradictory political, institutional and professional prerogatives and loyalties among the powerful can also be exploited to the researcher's gain. While I was leading an organized student visit to the NIO, one of the civil servants that briefed our group on recent political developments alleged strong links between the Irish language movement in NI and militant republicanism. I drew his attention to a large financial grant just donated by the NIO to the Irish language movement, announced in the previous day's newspapers. He was completely thrown by this and finished his talk abruptly. This civil servant approached me later at the lunch reception (he was a native from a nationalist background) where he confided in a somewhat embarrassed fashion that, "It's just a job, you know [he smiled thinly]. These talks are aimed at business people and prospective investors in the Province [NI]." He was implying that a different version of the truth was peddled to more informed visitors (or should have been).

The space between the operational practice and the discursive modes of the powerful can be exploited to expedite critical enquiry. The paranoid morass evident in security networks is further complicated in both Spain and Ireland (indeed, in the whole EU) "by a history of fierce rivalries between different branches of the security forces" (*The Guardian,* 20 February 1999). It is difficult to take advantage of this internecine strife as external researchers can be perceived as disruptive uncontrolled interlopers in security and police institutions, especially if considered unsympathetic. However, Spain has a number of independent police trade unions, and these afforded relatively open access. Members of the BAR Ertzaintza police and the Spanish National Police active in independent trade unions feel their constructive criticism of internal police organization and external Parti Nacionalisti de Vasco (PNV)—the main Basque nationalist political party in the BAR—and Madrid Government interference is perceived by their management as undermining their respective governments' security remit. Their ability to speak openly about their concerns is related to independent trade union protection. For example, interviews with one officer (Retta, 1997) illustrate the complex overlapping of loyalties and positions that he grapples with as a socialist, a union activist, a member of the Ertzaintza police, and a Basque-speaking native with a Spanish grandfather married to a black Englishwoman.[8] In contrast to some respondents, Retta expressed and dealt with complex sets of loyalties and perspectives, eschewing simplistic explanations and solutions (Power, 2003).

One research experience illustrates the often contradictory and conflicting political dynamics involved in researching the security state. Sr. Ortega was interviewed (initially alone) and then with Captain Trevo present in September 1997 at the Spanish Government Delegation (SGD) to the BAR headquarters in the Basque political capital, Vitoria/Gasteiz.[9] Ortega's interview (1997) stuck rigidly to the official Spanish Government line on law, policing and the autonomous regions. Any challenge to the official discourse of the Spanish government he dismissed confidently as Basque terrorist propaganda or wishful thinking by the BAR government. Ortega vehemently insisted that the Spanish Government could never consider any extension of Basque powers or sovereignty beyond the limitations of the Statutes of Autonomy passed in 1979. He insisted that the Ertzaintza (BAR's own police force) was no more or less independent than any other local autonomous police force in Spain.[10]

The second interview with Sr. Ortega was more revealing, as it meant that a confident and candid (almost cavalier) senior police officer was being interpreted and translated by the urbane, careful, and avowedly centralist bureaucrat Ortega.

Captain Trevo could speak no English (and I, no Spanish), so Ortega interpreted for us. No tape recording was permitted. The subject matter of the interview concerned the development of co-operation and information sharing between the National Police, the Ertzaintza and the Guardia Civil. I took notes throughout while Ortega sometimes resorted to a dictionary to support his translation. When asked about Basque armed resistance, Trevo crudely explained that Euzkadi Ta Askatasuna (ETA)—the main armed militant Basque insurgent group in Spain—had only patchy support among some sections of the youth and that an outright ETA victory would be like a Maoist take-over (gesturing that this would be disastrous). Ortega seemed content with this reply.

The BAR Ministry of the Interior spokesperson Coilea (interview, 1997; also, interview, Retta, 1997) had boasted in a previous interview that "his" Ertzaintza police force regularly crossed the French border on Schengen-inspired "hot-pursuit" missions with the collusion of the local French police. The word "boasted" is used advisedly because when requested to expand on his initial statement through an interpreter, Coilea did exactly that. He was proud of the Ertzaintza's "international" role and encouraged this extension of their power as proof of the BAR's own burgeoning sovereignty in the context of European Union subsidiarity and regionalism. But only the National Police and the Guardia Civil have the legal sanction as "national" forces to operate the transnational provisions of the Schengen accord (Agreement, 1990). Trevo (interview, 1997) was somewhat ambiguous when asked about the role of the Ertzaintza apropos Schengen: "They will be involved in border policing—they may be! But Schengen says no—they cannot!" Trevo seemed to sympathize with the professionalized Ertzaintza in contrast with the paramilitary Guardia Civil. Other evidence in this and other interviews indicated that good relations existed between the two "civil" police forces at many levels—while poor relations existed between both forces and the Guardia Civil (interviews, Retta, Zaba and Natpol, 1997).

Ortega had dismissed Coilea's claim that the Ertzaintza regularly used "hot pursuit" (as in Schengen) into France during his personal interview. However, he was visibly taken aback when he heard and translated Trevo's reply to the same question later. He asked Trevo to repeat what he had said, and he did translate though he seemed very surprised (even shocked) by this revelation. There was noticeable tension in the room after that. Trevo shrugged and declared: "Well, it's not allowed by Schengen rules, but it happens." Competing and contradictory official discourses which often occur between the Euzkadi (BAR) and Spanish governments and their competing agencies—can "force" opinions beyond the usual mundane nature of governmental polemic and official discourse. Ortega was confronted by evidence from his own police force that the Ertzaintza was already doing what he had earlier dismissed as the BAR Government's baseless propaganda. The Ertzaintza were involved in illegal international operations with the knowledge of the Spanish National Police. The Spanish and French have since successfully challenged the right of the BAR Ertzaintza to prosecute "hot pursuit" in the French courts thus reasserting Spanish internal sovereignty (Statewatch, 1999).

From his journalistic experience interviewing leaders and decision makers, Hobsbawm (1994: x) maintains somewhat diplomatically that "most of what such people say is for the public record." Trevo had previously proudly displayed his official badge of office like a freshly doctored academic. Fired by arrogance, honesty, ambition, and rapid promotion, Trevo was "telling it like it is." He lacked the reticence imbued by prolonged institutional over-socialization (Christie, 1997; interview, McGrath, 1996). He did not as yet subscribe to the elite's "economy of truth." He (as a National Police member) also seemed to accept and respect the professional credentials of the Ertzaintza police, while Ortega stuck rigidly to the centralist view that sovereignty resided in Madrid, while autonomy and autonomous policing were largely symbolic gestures. Both men reflected their different institutional and professional backgrounds and ages—one a cautious, solicitous civil servant, the other a dynamic, precipitate policeman.

## Conclusion

The research experiences outlined above testify to some of the dilemmas and challenges that confront the qualitative researcher when recording and critically interpreting deeply contested versions of the truth in particular situations. Who can be believed? How can interview testimonies be corroborated and verified to any degree, if at all? Can the subjective views of powerful respondents be critically located and assessed by recourse to theoretical paradigms? How valid are the particular perspectives and investigative techniques adopted by the researcher when trying to interpret the disparate views and experiences of individuals (powerful and otherwise) in relation to the relevant structures and economies of coercive power? How does state security impact on researchers and their work? What constitutes resistance, acquiescence or support (whether conscious or internalized) in relation to institutionalized forms of power and control? How do the complex prejudices of researched and researcher impact on the conduct and interpretation of qualitative field research? The avalanche of questions in the research process is endless, but the ultimate query involves the endgame: how is the data to be interpreted and used?

Good interactive and intuitive social skills are crucial tools when attempting to access and elicit data from the powerful. These skills are also essential in volatile, obstructive, and difficult political contexts where serendipity and contingency can play a major part in determining the extent and quality of the research access and the data collected. In my research, the exploitation of tensions within state apparatuses created spaces that I utilized to collect more accurate data by challenging powerful respondents' evidence where appropriate through reference to conflicting evidence from other authoritative institutional allies or "legitimate" competitors. The conflicting agendas of elite fractions (particularly useful in NI and the BAR) often lead to contradictory interpretations of particular legal and political contexts and operational happenings that can be exploited to increase the depth of enquiry. Tensions are created by legally sanctioned rivalry over that most basic and crucial of state concerns—sovereignty—as illustrated by the security strains stemming from the BAR Statutes of Autonomy. New concepts and forms of sovereignty are opening up investigative vistas where constitutional law and related discourses and practices can be juxtaposed in order to challenge bland institutional interpretations. This context of competing or overlapping sovereignties is now beginning to present opportunities for critical research on powerful elites as international treaties in Ireland (Belfast Agreement, 1998) and the EU obfuscate simple territorial supremacy.

Powerful operatives within the state apparatus are not homogenous personalities and can be skilfully manipulated in interviews to improve data collection. Respondents' personal prejudices in relation to their perception of the researcher can be utilized to improve their responses. Some individuals can also be encouraged subtly to go beyond their strict professional remit, played off against each other during group interviews, or challenged by using testimony from other powerful sources that conflicts with their particular account. The existence of independent police trade unions in Spain also facilitated openness in some cases. Academic interest itself can massage elite respondents' sense of self-importance, as can their craving for legitimacy and status through recognition in scholarly discourse. Academic credentials also mollify respondents by creating elite common ground between professionals (habitually academically trained) where research data is presumed to remain in exalted isolation (unlike journalism) and/or used to bolster the ascendant system. The danger that researchers must avoid when engaging with the powerful is the conscious or subliminal professional collusion that can develop between the institutionally over-socialized in interview situations.

## Notes

1. Personal interviews and presentations are referenced in the text as follows (names are fictionalized; for a comprehensive discussion of the interviews, see Power, forthcoming): Coilea (1997), Press Secretary for the BAR Ministry of the Interior; Gates (1996), Northern Ireland Office (NIO) civil servant responsible for border security and arms decommissioning; McGrath (1996), Head of the Garda Drug Squad; Natpol (1997), Spanish National Police Corps member and union activist translated by Retta; NIO, various presentations and interviews at Stormont (1996–1997); Ortega (1997), Spokesman for the SGD to the BAR; Retta (1997), Member of Ertzaintza police and organizer for police trade union; Tab

(1996), Northern Ireland Office lawyer responsible for drawing up special legislation; Trevo (1997), National Police, advisor to Spanish Government Delegation (SGD) to BAR and Police Liaison Officer for BAR; Zaba (1997), Human rights lawyer and former Herri Batasuna MEP. Interviewees agreed to be quoted subject to their real names not being used.

2. Garda Síochána (guardians of the peace) — the RoI's police force.
3. Northern Ireland Office — the British state institution that, at the time of writing this chapter, exercises direct rule in NI.
4. Royal Ulster Constabulary — NI's former armed police force — now Police Force of NI.
5. A description of PANI given by member of the committee after he resigned in February 1996 and widely reported in the press at the time. The phrase 'performing poodles' refers to PANI's lack of independence from RUC and NIO influence.
6. An inappropriate respondent is defined as a research subject who does not have professional competence or expertise in the specific research area. During the course of this research, several "inappropriate respondents" were allocated the role of interviewee by state institutions after the researcher had requested interviews with relevant "appropriate" personnel.
7. The Schengen Agreement is the key treaty which provides for the abolition of border controls in European Union countries. The Agreement covers a series of protocols for cooperation in policing and security matters.
8. His own description.
9. Respectively, spokesman for the SGD to the BAR; and senior National Police officer advising the SGD.
10. Local police are concerned with traffic control, policing local statutes, and petty crime.

# Researching the Turkish State

T his chapter draws upon two empirical investigations conducted in Turkey during the past decade. The first (and the principal study for the purposes of this essay) is an examination of criminal justice in an authoritarian regime struggling with democracy and the impact of democratization on the development of state strategies of containment and crime control. The second study, currently in progress, concerns the Turkish state's level of criminal culpability in relation to the scale of catastrophe that followed the earthquakes in north-western Turkey in late 1999.[1] This research is concerned with the enforcement of earthquake codes, the regulation of the construction industry, the relations between business and government, corruption, and criminal negligence. Here, as in the previous work, issues of political economy, social structure, and nationalist ideology (in Turkey's case, Kemalism) must be in the foreground of any research methodology which has as its primary subject the Turkish state. Kemalism defines the ideology underpinning the foundation of the Turkish Republic in 1923 and continues to represent the ruling ideology of the modern Turkish state. It is fundamentally secular *(laiklik),* and it speaks of the indivisibility of Turkish national unity and of a "Turkish" ethnic ideal (into which Kurds, Armenians, Laz and other minorities must assimilate). To challenge these fundamental principles of Kemalism is to invite a vicious state response.[2] Since the inception of the Republic the military have assumed the role of protector of the Kemalist state and on three occasions since 1960 have seized power in order to defend the "integrity" of the Turkish state.[3]

One of my principal concerns in researching the Turkish state has been to explore and analyze the impact of both authoritarianism *and* processes of democratization on the policy and practice of criminal justice. What happens to criminal justice and the regulation of public safety in a democratizing state where human rights violations and state repression remain commonplace? What do the findings tell us about state practices in our own liberal democracy? It will be helpful in this discussion of research methodology to first outline the nature of my criminal justice research findings, which are more fully documented elsewhere.[4] The research suggested that strategies of crime control and the practice of criminal justice tended to exist independently of any formal policy-making process by the Turkish state and most significantly that this absence of formal policy appeared to have a *benign* impact on certain stages of the criminal justice process. I followed up this finding by arguing that:

> To imagine that criminal policy in Turkey can be isolated from wider political processes, and reformed along western lines, is to ignore the centrality of the political dynamic currently shaping Turkish criminal justice. Until that dynamic is addressed, until a political solution is found for the Kurdish crisis and the authoritarian responses it elicits, criminal policy reform will remain marginal to the actual practice of criminal justice. (Green, 2000: 220)

This chapter first outlines the wider political framework that has informed the development of social science in Turkey. The complex and unstable character of Turkish democracy is discussed only briefly while greater attention is paid to the impact of Turkey's authoritarian structures on government "policy" with respect to my research issues (criminal justice and earthquake mitigation), and, more specifically, to the practice of conducting research on those issues in Turkey. Issues of personal safety, fear, and the potential compromising of personal integrity are explored as very real concerns of the research process in, and on, a state renowned for repression and rights violations. This is followed by a discussion of what I have called the "organic" nature of research in Turkey, by which I mean the importance of one's place in the social world and the interaction of that place with chance and coincidence. I then examine the impact of "otherness" in my own experience and explore the extent to which the cultural distance between myself as outsider and those I have interviewed is significant to research outcomes.

What seems evident from the research I have conducted in Turkey is that assumptions about progress and democracy and the "superiority" of democratized criminal justice are often misplaced and this paradox must stand as a cautionary tale. To this end I explore the role of the Council of Europe's Committee for the Prevention of Torture in encouraging the Turkish government's disastrous reforms of prison accommodation. And finally, I remark on a number of cultural factors which in the clinical world of research design would seem to have little place but in the reality of researching the Turkish state are fundamental—the influence of "influence" or *torpil* and the often complex and frustrating issues of communication, language and culture are all discussed as barriers to, or facilitators of, truth and knowledge.

## Coups and Their Epistemological Consequences

Researching the Turkish state (and criminological issues more generally), one is faced with a major epistemological problem. Following the 1981 military coup, in a climate of brutal repression of dissidents, left-wing academics (along with right-wing and religious extremists) were expelled from universities throughout the country and they remained in the intellectual (or better institutional) hinterland until they were re-instated towards the end of the decade. It is difficult to assess the precise impact the expulsions have had on the development of an indigenous critical social science, but it must be considerable. The discipline of criminology has remained underdeveloped in Turkish universities, a small field dominated by biological determinists, empiricists, and administrative criminal lawyers. The work of nineteenth-century phrenologist Cesare Lombroso is afforded considerable credibility and crime causation is understood in the crudest terms. Neither criminology nor criminal justice are taught in law faculties and criminology does not have the status of a discipline.

> The experience of decades of acute political repression and severe violations of human rights has not inspired the development of a highly critical discipline of criminology as seen for example in the Latin American academy (see Bergalli, 1997: 36–37) and the subject has not been adopted by critical sociology, which has itself, in recent years, steered the safer, politically unchallenging course of post-modernism.

This absence or diminution of a critical criminological tradition in the Turkish academy has certainly influenced the course of my research. In some ways it has left a free field, a rich arena of research opportunities into which no critical criminologist has yet entered. I have been able to create my own research agenda, and approach the questions I am interested in without the interference or influence of extant work. But my research is necessarily the poorer for this lack of critical epistemology. When even basic data in relation to prison statistics and criminal statistics are non-existent or so unreliable as to be rendered useless for research purposes, it would be enormously helpful to have existing critiques of those official sources. Even general overviews of the criminal justice process (of which we in the UK suffer an abundance) are absent from the Turkish literature. Thus my analysis, my critique, must always be on the basis of primary empirical research; certainly interesting but also demanding. There is no criminology on which to build this research.

As with research on the state more generally, however, the corpus of criminological literature is found wanting and it is to other disciplines that researchers must turn to assist in the analysis and explanation of the phenomena under study. In Turkey political scientists have explored the crucial political issues of the strong state (see Heper, 1985, 1992), clientelism, and patrimonialism (see for example, Sayarı 1977; Ayata, 1996; Roniger and Gűneş-Ayata, 1994). Human rights defenders have exposed, documented, and described the range and extent of rights violation, the conditions inside prisons and police stations and the institutional structures (see Amnesty International, 2001; Human Rights Watch, 2000), while seismologists, urban planners, and earthquake engineers have provided detailed analyses of earthquake and earthquake damage causality. This work has been essential in providing me with the substantive and analytical tools necessary for my research.

## Danger, Fear, and Personal Integrity

To conduct research on a state notorious for its human rights violations presents a range of methodological issues for the researcher, some expected and others quite unexpected. Here, I am largely referring to foreign academics such as myself. Turkish academics have, understandably, been inhibited by the repressive control over freedom of expression and exercise their own form of self-censorship; and as such academic critiques of the state are relatively rare. As with much research conducted into the practices of states and their agencies, a certain element of personal danger underpins the process. Turkey has at various times blacklisted Amnesty International researchers, imprisoned with impunity many of its critics, silenced its journalists, shut down its newspapers, and generally made clear it brooks no dissidence.[5] Researching the state as subject from the perspective of critical criminology, therefore, requires a certain caution, restraint, and at all times political sensitivity. In some ways the insignificance of foreign academia is itself a protective device. The articles we write tend to be published in journals or books beyond the reach or interest of the Turkish security services. Our work is published in English and is, in real terms, accessible only outside Turkey's borders. It has no immediate influence on the Turkish population, unlike the reports of Amnesty International that have an automatic international as well as a hungry domestic audience. Journalists Nicole and Hugh Pope (1997) captured the Turkish state's attitude in the following anecdote. They recount how in the early 1990s, a delegation from the short-lived Foreign Press Association paid a courtesy visit to the then-governor of Istanbul province, Hayri Kozakçioğlu. This took place a few days after Turkish television journalists had been dragged in front of a military court for a documentary on conscientious objectors that had offended the army. "Don't worry," Mr Kozakçioğlu said, "You can write what you want, because your articles are published abroad. But you must understand," he added, "that our people in Turkey are not equipped to cope with certain ideas. This is the reason why we have to impose limits."

Our work does not, indeed cannot, have the same impact as the work of Amnesty International in exposing state abusive practices. Rather our task is more to make sense of those practices, to analyze, interpret, and theorize them. In the process of data gathering this sometimes requires a careful balancing act by the researcher between the desire to extract information and the need to retain a personal sense of political integrity.

Researching in Turkey can be an immensely frustrating and distressing experience. The issues are harrowing and impact on the researcher in ways not easily quantifiable. Negotiating a repressive state means never fully relaxing. Moving between state and state victim creates potential for dissonance. There is a constant and nagging anxiety as one travels between victim and oppressor. Interviewing victims of torture, prisoners, and earthquake survivors confronts the researcher with the raw consequences of state crime. It makes it more difficult (but in some respects more urgent) to speak with the agents of repression and violence.

Adopting a modicum of charm and polite inquiry when interviewing men responsible for wide-scale brutality and repression is extremely unpalatable and unnerving but it is sometimes necessary in securing both access and information, and later, in order to understand the justifications and rationales behind the repression. This is especially so in a country like Turkey where documentary evidence detailing "policy" development is wholly absent. It does not implicate the researcher in the activities of the regime nor does it represent complicity or sympathy with those being interviewed. It is merely a strategy to secure information. Our discomfort tends to center on the impression that our rapport-building devices would give to an external observer. While smiling at a prison governor or exchanging pleasantries with the Minister for Justice we imagine being observed by a critic of the state, particularly one who has been a victim of state violence. We feel uncomfortable and unclean colluding, at least, in the charade of polite social discourse with these architects of repression, but how could it be otherwise? There is no escape from the discomfort that this kind of fieldwork entails. Researchers, therefore, need to be very clear at the outset about the purpose of every interview, its contribution to the wider research agenda, and the potential impact that the knowledge acquired may have on the process of reform. Here, adopting Marx's famous maxim that "The philosophers have only interpreted the world. The point is to change it," is, I believe, crucial. For the critical criminologist, understanding and exposing the dynamics involved in state repression must be seen as part of a process of change, of contributing to a body of knowledge which in some way, however small, contributes to that change.

In many respects this presents problems not dissimilar to those involved in researching the British or American state and its agencies. Being polite to overtly racist or sexist prison guards or governors in order to secure access to inmates or criminal justice personnel is part of the process and sometimes it is awkward and unpleasant. Of course we don't have to be too nice!

My first visits to Istanbul's Bayrampaşa Prison were frightening and confusing and illustrate the complex personal/political dynamics which the researcher must negotiate. My relationship with the governor, Veli Bey (and therefore my ease of access within the prison), was to some extent predicated on his expectation that we would enter into a relationship outside the prison walls. Our few meetings, therefore, became, for me, fraught exercises in conscious "misunderstanding." I had first visited his very large office alone and had been warmly welcomed. We chatted informally and he offered the services of his staff and himself. At the end of the meeting he intimated he wished to take me out. I feigned incomprehension and during the following visit I made sure I was accompanied by my great friend, "Aylin." At this meeting the atmosphere soured considerably. Notes from my research journal capture my predicament:

> Veli Bey's change of mood is both surprising and very unhelpful. He became very aggressive with "Aylin," told me "no more interviews" and refused further access. With persuasion he finally changed his mind and said I should phone tomorrow saying, however, that there would be problems—the atmosphere very unpleasant. We left his office and went to see the prosecutor who also has an office in the prison. We wanted permission from him to return to the prison housing foreign inmates, Özel Tip. He was friendly and helpful and returned with us to Veli Bey's office. Now the mood changed dramatically. Veli Bey, in the presence of the Prosecutor, became helpful and joking—a mood which was dropped automatically when the prosecutor left the room.[6]

And what of feelings of "betrayal"—a potential consequence of my representation of the voices of the Turkish state within a political framework I failed to reveal during interviews? I confess to none. Nor do I imagine that the Turkish Minister for Justice, or the Chief Prosecutor, or the prison governors or government officials I interviewed would expect any such emotional commitment on my part.

There is now a considerable literature on the question of emotionality in the research process.[7] Most of this work, however, deals specifically with issues arising in research undertaken by feminists and it is a literature which while raising some interesting issues also reveals an unhelpful degree of self-absorption. Maureen Cain, however, in her application of standpoint theory, usefully argues that not all those interviewed in the course of fieldwork should have their subjectivity acknowledged. Those in politically dominant positions, because they do not share the standpoint of the research "subjects," should be denied a subjectivity (Cain, 1986). This is in contrast to the powerless, the sometimes voiceless, the victims and the subjected. I am content with this.

## An Organic Process

My research has taken me into some of Turkey's most notorious prisons, into the Stalinist-styled offices of Istanbul's Chief Prosecutor and into the marble-floored corridors of power in Ankara to interview an erstwhile Minister of Justice and his advisors. I have talked with human rights defenders, victims of torture, Presidents of the country's most influential bar associations, criminal lawyers, prisoners and ex-prisoners, prison governors and guards, journalists, law professors and criminal justice reformers, seismologists, architects, engineers, mayors, and urban planners of the earthquake-damaged zone—all with relative ease, though at the time the bureaucracy seemed unnecessarily Byzantine.

Methodologically this research has by necessity developed "organically." The complex of cultural, political, and economic conditions which characterize modern Turkey play a significant if unpredictable role in determining the research process. A chance meeting in an Istanbul antique store may lead to a decade of research opportunities; an attack by Kurdish opposition forces on a state target may close crucial doors of inquiry that previously had been open; a new economic crisis (in the context of perpetual crisis) may so disrupt the lives of those you wish to interview that research opportunities diminish with the value of the Turkish lira.

And it is not always the hoped-for and pre-arranged interviews with key opinion leaders or subject experts that yield the richest data. Rather it is the incidental discussion at a party or over lunch with new acquaintances that may throw up whole new directions for thinking about an issue that more frequently energizes the research. My co-researcher on the Kocaeli earthquake project attended an interview with an important government official who provided information that was no more illuminating than that available in popular daily newspapers. Following the interview, and while she waited in his secretary's office for her transport to arrive, the secretary revealed that she lived in the earthquake–damaged region and that her own home had been destroyed. She provided a first-hand account of the procedure of classification for damaged buildings—a procedure her employer had failed to reveal. Despite direct questioning of the relevant local government officials, this information had not previously been forthcoming and it provided a solid set of details that could then be reliably checked against a range of other sources.[8]

Cultural factors mean that the process of researching in Turkey is greatly assisted by the generosity and friendliness of ordinary people. Interviews arise in surprising places as a result. In the early 1990s, while waiting for permission to visit Bayrampaşa Cezavi (Prison), I took a few days out to explore the country. On a beach in southern Turkey I was chatting in my then rudimentary Turkish to the cleaner of the little hotel in which I was staying. This man was a fisherman in the winter but picked up odd jobs in the summer months. I noticed ugly scars on his arms. He noticed my noticing. He told me he had been imprisoned and tortured for the alleged killing of a policeman in Eastern Turkey. His scars were testimony of the truth of his claims. Reported experiences like this were not uncommon and while they could not, by themselves, be viewed as substantial criminological evidence, they nonetheless suggested the extent and degree of state abuse in the everyday lives of Turks. In some ways this also illustrates the importance of engaging with the community in which you are researching. Most Turks I have spoken to have themselves been imprisoned, arrested, or tortured at some time in their lives, or they have close friends or relatives who have been imprisoned, arrested, or tortured. This lived experience of repression is very much a part of the cultural and political landscape in which ordinary Turks navigate their lives. Their accommodations and resistances to this repression reveal much about the ways in which civil society is developing in Turkey.

## The Outsider and the Other

As a foreign researcher one is acutely aware of the possibility of cultural oversights and obfuscations that might influence the course of the research, of nuances misunderstood or overlooked that might be significant to the outcome of the inquiry. Given my status as an outsider who will never be fully engaged in life in Turkey, this is a problem that is unlikely ever to fully disappear. In order to control for its effects I therefore rely on my Turkish friends to moderate its impact on my work. However, because most of the issues related to the practice of state crime transcend culture,[9] I suspect the overall impact of the cultural distance between researcher and subject, while not to be ignored, is smaller than might otherwise be expected.

Luisa Passerini (1986: 190–1) has explored the issue of "otherness" not only in the more obvious sense of the distinction between researcher and subject but also in terms of the relationship between "those aspects of one's culture that are taken for granted," i.e. *self,* and "other aspects discovered in what had been taken for granted," i.e., *other.*

Being foreign, always to some extent on the outside looking in, is probably more of a help than a hindrance. Being an Australian is also, paradoxically, helpful. In the first instance I am not seen as a European anxious to instruct the Turks on how they should reform their penal system for entry into the club of Europe. Here being a "double" outsider, in part, negates my "otherness." My identity lies outside the European zone of inclusivity,—we share that exclusion from Europe, that "otherness." In Passerini's terms, by exploring my own cultural location I discover a level of commonality with my subject, in that part of myself is in fact *other* in this particular context.

The Turks have long been puzzled by Australia's ANZAC Day celebration of the World War One Gallipoli (Gelibolu) defeat at the hands of Turkey's General

Mustafa Kemal Ataturk. Ironically the tragedy of Gallipoli is celebrated by Australians and Turks in the small Turkish village of Gelibolu each year and provides a sympathetic point of connection between the two nations. It creates a discourse of understanding, a certain empathy, a sense of equality, at least at the superficial level of formal encounters such as those between the researcher and Turkish officials.

State officials are also keen to persuade outsiders of the justification for their practices and to demonstrate their "democratic" credentials to the international community. Outsiders, particularly independent outsiders, are largely perceived as less politically threatening, as the words of from Hayri Kozakçioğlu, quoted above, suggest. As such our requests tend to cost little and may be met without much fear of consequence.

## Paradox and the Democratic Ideal

One methodological lesson that I learned early on in my research in Turkey is to "be prepared for paradoxes." Democratization may lead to elements of increased repression and coercion; prison dormitories are a more humane form of accommodation than single cells; political enemies may open doors for each other to assist one's research; releasing thousands of prisoners on conditional discharge may improve a ruling party's electoral advantage as well as deal with a crisis of over-crowding.[10] Fixed criminal justice notions borne out of years of research in liberal democratic jurisdictions may no longer hold true and the researcher must acquire an openness of mind capable of questioning the validity of firmly held suppositions.

Researching in Turkey is quite unlike researching in the UK, Australia, or the United States. Official statistics are unreliable (well beyond the unreliability of the official data available in our own jurisdictions) and access to reliable documentary evidence is limited, largely because the kind of documentary evidence which we normally rely on such as Green Papers, White Papers, specialized government reports and so on are simply not produced in Turkey. Documentation from international and domestic NGOs such as Human Rights Watch, Amnesty International, The Medical Foundation for the Victims of Torture, and the Human Rights Foundation of Turkey thus become crucial sources. Turkey's European ambitions have led to the close monitoring of a range of political, economic, and social issues by the European Union, in particular by the Council of Europe and its Committee for the Prevention of Torture and Inhuman or Degrading Treatment or Punishment (CPT). Regular reports on rates of imprisonment, the conditions inside prisons, the extent of the practice of torture, and other human rights violations across the country and so on provide not only a sense of the scale of the issues in Turkey, but very importantly a guide to the relationship between Europe and Turkey and the role of Europe in influencing the development of its own brand of criminal justice policy outside its borders.

As Marx observed in *Capital,* the colonies reflect what the metropole cannot or will not see in itself (1979: 765–766). He, of course, was writing in relation to the concept of private property which, while assumed in the Western capitalist states to be natural and inevitable, was, when transferred to the developing colonial world, both alien and culturally inapplicable, so much so that colonial powers frequently employed violence to destroy the cultural obstacles to the incorporation of private property. This is in many ways analogous to the process of democratization in Turkey and was particularly brought out in research I conducted on the 2000–01 prison protests against the introduction of F-Type prisons for political prisoners (Green, 2002). While Turkish prisoners on death fasts and hunger strikes died (and continue to do so at the time of writing) in scores, Europe and Turkey found fundamental agreement on the desirability of the single-cell occupancy afforded by the F-Type prisons. For the Council of Europe the F-Type prisons represent a more "civilized" means of incarcerating inmates; for the Turkish government single cells represent a way of breaking the organizational strength of "terrorists" and political prisoners currently afforded by the traditional ward or dormitory system. Following a visit to Turkey in August 1996 the CPT reported:

> In fact, large-capacity dormitories are for various reasons not a satisfactory means of accommodating inmates. They inevitably imply a lack of privacy for prisoners in their everyday lives. Further the risk of intimidation and violence is very high, particularly in dormitories such as those in Turkey which have no means of direct supervision from outside. Such accommodation arrangements can facilitate the maintenance of the cohesion of criminal organizations—whether terrorist or non-terrorist in nature. They can also render all the more difficult the task of security forces called upon to deal with prison disturbances. . . . there is little to be said in favor of—and a lot to be said against—arrangements under which scores of prisoners live and sleep together in the same dormitory. (CPT, 2001)

For the more than 10,000 political prisoners in Turkey's jails, single-cell prison accommodation means an end to the solidarity, humanity and community nature of traditional Turkish imprisonment and exposure to the dangers that isolation from other inmates can bring in a country where state officials have a reputation for torture and brutality.

This example cautions against an uncritical acceptance of what might in other circumstances be considered objective reporting by a progressive human rights body. It is also an illustration of the hegemonic power of European cultural institutions. The CPT here demonstrates a disregard for the political realities of imprisonment in Turkey (namely, the existence of a very large body of political prisoners steadfastly opposed to the introduction of single-cell prisons) and a dogmatic commitment to a Euro-centric and culturally exclusive belief in the virtue of single cell occupancy. The CPT's interest in Turkish prisons and human rights is myopic, and in consequence fundamental issues related to justice and humanity are disregarded in favor of what is seen as the over-riding issue of democratic-style practices. The methodological implications of this example suggest that there are dangers in uncritically accepting the evidence of bodies such as the CPT or the Council of Europe because of the hegemonic role they necessarily play in the development of penal and criminal justice policy in democratizing states. This example also makes clear the need for a thorough knowledge of a country's political economy before making claims about its penal policy and more dangerously making demands for reforms that in practice collude with strategies of repression.

The example is equally illuminating in what it reveals about the practice of criminal justice in Europe and Britain in particular. It reveals the unwillingness of Western states to learn from the developing world in arenas where their own track records (on issues such as prison over-crowding) leave much to be desired.

## Friends in All Places

The question of access is often a crucial one when the state is the subject of criminological inquiry, particularly in a state dominated by the military. Turkey, with its international reputation for gross human rights violations, its "Midnight Express" prison imagery, its history of military coups, and its undercurrent of Islamic fundamentalism suggests a possibly frightening and dangerous research landscape for the critical criminologist. Researching the Turkish state, however, was to be in many respects a surprisingly rewarding and accessible experience. Routes to the voices of power in Turkey are different from those in the UK and the USA. They are more haphazard and sometimes unnecessarily bureaucratic, yet they are also far more open and in a sense more reliable in terms of positive outcomes. A relatively limited amount of bureaucracy (requests and faxed permissions from the Ministries of Foreign Affairs and the Interior) afforded me access to interview prisoners in Istanbul prisons, and a phone call from the president of the Istanbul Bar Association secured me an hour-long interview with the Minister of Justice and his deputy. There are "correct channels" and for me it was essential to proceed through these, particularly when I was first establishing myself as a researcher in Turkey. My research into the Turkish state began through an accident of opportunity—lawyers and academics I befriended while on holiday shared my intellectual interests and a concern (much more pressing for them) about issues of justice, human rights, and politics in Turkey. More importantly they could provide me with resources, advice and introductions to opinion leaders, criminal justice professionals and relevant intellectuals—in other words they provided me with shortcuts to my subject.

In Turkey, *torpil* is the oil which facilitates the wheels of possibility. *Torpil*, a colloquial expression for "influence" or "pull" is a way of life for Turks who frequently need to negotiate and, where possible, bypass the barriers of a burdensome bureau-cracy. My great good fortune was to befriend influential left-wing lawyers and uni-versity professors who could use *torpil* to great effect.

There is also a snowballing effect, however, which comes into play almost as soon as one begins the research process in Turkey. Contacts suggest a range of other contacts who in turn open new doors and raise new directions. The research pro-cess grows like topsy. My interview in 1997 with Minister for Justice, Oltan Sun-gurlu, was the product of a chance journey my Istanbul host was making to Ankara the following morning. "I could arrange a meeting with the Minister if you wish." And so he did. Such offers are not refused lightly and so it was that in a matter of hours I re-scheduled my return to London, booked a flight to Ankara, and found myself the following morning in the office of the Minister. Paradoxically my host who had arranged the interview (and who sat in to assist with translation) is a left-wing lawyer who had in the past been threatened with imprisonment by this very minister. None the less, as President of the Istanbul Bar Association, my host still represented an authority to be reckoned with and mutual distaste proved no bar-rier to my research opportunity. These kinds of research conditions require a con-stant state of preparedness, a spirit of adventure and a considerable degree of stam-ina. On another more recent occasion, when my own attempts to secure interviews with mayors of the earthquake-devastated municipalities were floundering, an-other miracle of access was presented to me. With three brief phone calls, and the exercise of *torpil,* I had arranged meetings with 3 mayors—all in different towns along the Northern Anatolian Fault Zone—and all in a single afternoon! A state of constant readiness is, therefore, essential.

These kinds of entrées would be unimaginable in Britain or the United States. At some level then state power in Turkey may be paradoxically considered as less hidden and less inaccessible (certainly to the outsider) than western democratic states.

## Frustrations and the Wisdom of Not Planning

In the first instance the attitudes that, at times, make for much of the spontane-ously rich data that I have had the opportunity to gather, also contribute to create situations of prolonged inactivity, frustration, or a paralysis of direction. The re-laxed nature of Turkish civil life does not always complement the deadlines and time constraints imposed by short field trips and British academic demands.

My co-researcher investigating state responsibility and the construction in-dustry in the Northern Anatolian Fault Zone describes her efforts there "as bouncing from catastrophe to catastrophe," all the while accumulating data of a powerful and insightful kind. One cannot have too fixed a program. The idea of a regularized research methodology pre-ordained and executed to the letter is in the realms of fantasy when tackling research in Turkey.

There is, for example, very little value in attempting to arrange interviews in advance. Before a field trip, in the early days of my research interest in Turkey, I would studiously phone or email key figures I wished to interview. None would commit to a specified time but "please call when you arrive in Istanbul and I should be available any time." Turks are certainly more relaxed about notions of time. I have spent many anxious weeks in Turkey attempting to schedule interviews only to find that I see everyone on the final day of my visit. I have also arrived, having attempted to pre-arrange interviews from England, only to find that most of the people I wished to interview were in Germany or the United States attending conferences for the whole period of my visit.

## Language and Communication

Many research opportunities arise spontaneously in Turkey and, given the level of English proficiency among certain sections of the population, this usually means that with a combination of my own conversational Turkish and the respondents' English, communication is relatively straightforward. When I first began researching in Turkey I knew very little of this difficult, beautiful language. In normal circumstances this might have put paid to my endeavors. I was, however, overwhelmed by the research possibilities that were being placed before me. In these early days friends made research possible by identifying key players, offering their translating services, accompanying me on visits to prisons, prosecutors' offices, making awkward phone calls, and so on. In many instances respondents spoke excellent English and in those situations where I was interviewing a professional who spoke only Turkish they would, almost inevitably, have arranged a translator for our meeting. When interviewing academics, graduate students invariably played this role. Keen to both improve their English and assist their professors, they also provided valuable insights into the research process. Rudimentary Turkish was important as an ice-breaker in the early days and I struggled to acquaint myself with the basics as a small courtesy to those I interviewed. I have since enrolled in Turkish language courses and programs whenever it is possible and now approach the research process with a small degree of linguistic confidence.

Cultural and political factors do, however, intervene to impede the process of communication once an interview has been secured. There is reluctance on the part of Turkish officials and other respondents to use the word "no" in response to questions or requests. And a tension between the natural hospitality of Turks and this reluctance inevitably surfaces in some interview situations. Interviews can become very convoluted as a result. Agreeing to an interview, it quickly transpires, is not the same as agreeing to answer questions, so interviews often end up in pages and pages of tangential discourse. As was evident in my dealings with Bayrampaşa's governor, inexplicable unavailability at particularly crucial or convenient times in the research process must be read as a "no," but will never be verbally articulated as such. Much of this is a product of culturally required and delineated forms of hospitality. In order to secure useful data, the researcher must learn to anticipate or at least recognize these obfuscations, move with them, and then challenge them as firmly as possible.

## Conclusion

Researching the Turkish state has been something of a labor of love. I am a self-confessed Turkophile. I am enchanted by the radiance of Turkey's cultures, towns, ancient sites, and extraordinary countryside. But I am more drawn by its people. They display a resilience and generosity which overwhelms the spirit. In the midst of state violence and corruption, systematic denials of human rights, appalling tragedy and widespread poverty, ordinary Turks continue to resist incursions by their state, to build political opposition, and to create a vibrant intellectual and cultural world. But, it is not easy.

Turkey is a land of parallels in which the repressive state apparatus seemingly exists on one plane while the population exists on another—meeting only in the harrowing clashes around which I base my research. I am constantly challenged by the chaos and difficulty of life in Turkey but I am also inspired and if my research makes some small contribution to understanding the relationship between state crime, criminal justice, and civil society then I am satisfied. My own reading of this work, however, suggests that researching the Turkish state may have greater value in illuminating our own Anglo/European criminal justice practices and challenging the superiority of the Anglo/European hegemonic standpoint.

## Acknowledgment

I would like to acknowledge the support of the Economic and Social Science Research Council (Award Reference Number R000223401) in funding part of the research on which this article is based.

## Notes

1. The author gratefully acknowledges the valuable and insightful comments of my co-researcher, Christina Curry.

2. In March 1994 eight Kurdish Deputies (Members of the Turkish parliament from the now disbanded DEP), including Leyla Zana, were sentenced to terms of imprisonment of up to fifteen years for making declarations of Kurdish independence in parliament, in interviews and in conversations.

3. The Turkish state is effectively comprised of three tiers: the national state (elected representatives); the military, which in effect oversees the political practice of the state; the Valilik (regional administration, unelected); the Kaymakamlik (provincial administration, unelected) and at municipal level the Belediye (elected officials).

4. See Green, 2000, 2002.

5. For example, the recent trial of Fatih Taş, of Aram Publishing, for publishing Noam Chomsky's *American Interventionism*, which includes a highly critical account of Turkey's treatment of the Kurds is a case in point.

6. Research journal notes, Istanbul. August 26th 1992. Quotations are with the permission of interviewees.

7. See Pickering, 2001 for a particularly interesting account in relation to her work on Northern Ireland.

8. Anecdote supplied by Christina Curry, School of Law, University of Westminster.

9. Claims of cultural relativism are frequently employed by offending states as "techniques of neutralization" (see Risse et al., 1999). In developing a theoretical framework for understanding state crime, Tony Ward and I have drawn a distinction between human rights violations (transcending culture) and perceptions of deviance (culturally bound) (Green and Ward, 2000).

10. See Green, 2000.

9    ANNE ALVESALO AND
ERJA VIRTA

# Researching Regulators and the Paradoxes of Access

*. . . the government will make the control and the tracing of the proceeds of economic crime more effective . . .* (Excerpt from the Finnish Government's 1995 program)

*. . . the trends and development of economic crime and the grey economy are subject to continuous research work.* (Excerpt from the Finnish Government's 1996 action plan against economic crime and the gray economy)

## Introduction

In this chapter we draw upon the experiences of two large research projects examining economic crime in Finland. We describe the data, methods and main results of the projects, and place them in the context of the widespread political and popular support for the control of economic crime, which led to a governmental action plan to combat it. Through drawing upon experiences in researching both the crimes of the powerful and their control, we focus particularly upon questions of access and funding in researching economic crime, and address the obstacles to disseminating our findings. Furthermore, we show that the strong governmental support and a social "mood" conducive to combating economic crime in Finland made it possible to conduct extensive studies on relevant research questions. Governmental support created the possibility of accessing data which we probably would never have gained had we conducted our research as total "outsiders." On the other hand, there were some limits on how far some of the funders were prepared to accept and publish critiques of their functioning as control agencies, and we address the differential responses of some state officials and academics to the findings of the projects. There were both positive and negative aspects in conducting research for funders, who had a clear agenda on how they wanted to use our results. An important general lesson of our experience is that we cannot treat states as homogenous or monolithic, to be opposed in every circumstance. Both research projects indicate that there are circumstances in which it is possible to use the state and to work from within the state to challenge the state's own agendas and confront the abuse of power by other (economic) elites.

## Economic Crime and the Political Agenda

Since the 1970s, in many Western industrialized countries, there has been some recognition and discussion of economic crime, a rubric covering a broad range of business illegalities.[1] In Finland, the debates were characterized by a particular kind of attitude: economic crime was defined early as a social problem. Various *ad hoc* committees and working parties were appointed as early as the 1970s to investigate the problems related to specific fields of economic crime. There was another period of public concern at the beginning of the eighties when several important cases came to light and a boom in prosecuting appeared to emerge. Despite the public pressure to intensify economic crime control, little or nothing happened following the publication of the report of the "Pasanen Committee" in 1983. The "Pasanen Committee" had been established in 1982 to examine the extent of economic crime and the possibilities for its prevention. In addition to an extensive list of recommendations, including suggestions for strengthening control, a statement was also made on the need for long-term research. However, no such program was launched or financed at that time. All in all, the public discourse became gradually weaker towards the end of the 1980s. This political turn away from considerations of economic crime also had an economic basis—the 1980s were a period of economic boom in which business and entrepreneurship achieved an elevated status and were seen to be delivering the goods (see Alvesalo and Tombs, 2001b).

After the long period of economic growth and excessive consumption in the 1980s, a period of depression began in Finland at the beginning of the 1990s. Finland's economic recession of the early 1990s is often referred to by economists as "The Great Depression" (Kiander and Vartia, 1996). The scale of this depression was made worse by bank failures, and there emerged perceptions that illegality was linked to or even caused some of these bank failures (see Huhtamäki, 1994; Alvesalo and Tombs, 2001a). Despite the failure of the Pasanen report to prompt any large-scale program against economic crime, there had emerged during the 1980s a series of *ad hoc,* on-the-ground initiatives developed in various "low-level" efforts to intensify control. The role of a small number of individuals was clearly crucial in keeping economic crime on the law enforcement agenda and developing forms of co-operation. By the beginning of the 1990s, the decision makers' and the public's attention was once again drawn to economic crime, and the possibility of developing and intensifying control emerged. The emergence of the economic crime control program can be understood as due to a combination of two sets of factors: on the one hand, a political and social "moment" at which economic crime became a potential target for control; on the other hand, measures for—and experience of— the control mechanisms already in existence. This combination of factors meant that there emerged widespread political and popular support for the control of economic crimes (Alvesalo and Tombs, 2001a, 2001b).

## Launching the Research Projects

One of the key goals within the result-orientated plan of the police in 1993–96 was the prevention of economic crime (Ministry of Interior, 1992: 8). In order to achieve the objectives set out in the plan, a project was launched in the Supreme Police Command—which together with the tax-authorities was an active developer of economic crime control methods—to draw up a concrete strategy on the measures required for the effective prevention of economic crime. One area of concern among those working in the various committees and working groups was that there was not enough knowledge on the extent of economic crime and the modus operandi of offenders. At that time, there already existed large-scale popular support for economic crime control (Korander, 1994; Alvesalo and Tombs, 2001b). Yet, to achieve a stronger basis for the demand to intensify control, there was a need for "scientific" facts to point out the scale of the damage that this type of criminality does to society. Some research projects[2] were launched earlier, but the particular "theme" of the year 1993 in the developing projects for economic crime control within the police was "getting knowledge" of the phenomenon. Hence, the initiation of research was relevant to the policy under construction.

In 1993, after an initial approach by the Supreme Police Command in the Ministry of the Interior to Ahti Laitinen, her professor in the sociology of law, Anne began to participate with Ahti in a project examining the extent of monetary losses in cases of economic crime. After some preliminary work, which included an analysis of a survey of economic crime investigators to establish the problems of investigation and the estimated amounts of economic interests in cases under investigation (see Alvesalo- Laitinen, 1993), the project on economic crime cases in courts, which was to be titled "The Dark Side of the Economy," was launched in autumn 1993. Anne was hired as a project researcher. Erja was employed first as a research assistant, and later as a researcher in the project.

Apart from our master's theses, neither of us had much practical experience in research work. In addition, the universal absence of statistics, the scarcity of research on economic crime and the complete lack of methodology texts in the area made the task difficult. In the beginning the research was funded for four months only, after which the Ministry of Interior would decide—depending on the progress of the project—whether they wanted to continue with funding. However, the authorities' craving for "knowledge" did not end with this project. Apart from continuing the "The Dark Side of Economy" project, another research project was to be launched immediately after its publication. In 1994 there would arise a need to learn about the misuse of state subsidies by enterprises. This was another area that had not previously been researched empirically in Finland.

## Governmental Support and Access

### Agendas of the Research Projects

Our perception as researchers was that both research projects, one on the damage caused by economic crime, and the other on misusing state subsidies, included unambiguous goals on the part of the funders. In order to gain even stronger popular and political support, the authorities involved in preparing the action plan against economic crime needed "facts," *scientific, academic, autonomous* facts, to support their demands to justify proposals which had already been accepted, and to justify providing the resources needed to fund the new measures. Based on the everyday knowledge of practitioners in the field of economic crime control, the reality of the situation regarding the scope of losses and the problems of control was evident. However, the apparent power of quantification and measurement was recognized by those who wanted to keep economic crime on the political agenda (see Maguire, 1997: 139, Slapper and Tombs, 1999: 55). Neither one of us knew at that time exactly what was going on within the authorities, but what we understood was the explicit desire of the funder for empirical research attesting to the fact that economic crime caused extensive social and economic damage. Even though the prospect of extensive damage in cases of economic crime was almost axiomatic for us, the fact that the funder was, if not demanding, at least expecting predetermined results was naturally disturbing. It was constantly pointed out to the funder that the research should be conducted in order to *find out* the extent of damages assessed by the courts, not to "show" something that might or might not exist. While the funder accepted the autonomy of the research, its preference was clearly for particular kinds of findings.[3]

Since the research data in "The Dark Side of the Economy" consisted of those cases which actually reached the courts, we knew that the total of *adjudged damages* would be incomplete and therefore probably not be so "scandalous." Cases that had been filtered through the criminal justice system would not really tell much about the totality of harms caused by economic crime, but would reveal more about the ability—or inability—of the criminal justice system to deal with these types of offences. Our aim—as much as the tight time schedule allowed—was to collect other data from the cases as well, especially data that would reveal something about the functioning of the criminal justice system. Thus there was the possibility of mapping different indicators of the amount of economic damage in the earlier stage of the process, for example, those suspected by the police and those estimated by the prosecutors.

The initiative to develop the second research project on the misuse of state subsidies was taken by the tax authorities and the Ministry of the Interior. The Ministry of Employment, the Ministry of Agriculture and the Ministry of Trade and Industry, which grant and regulate the vast majority of state subsidies to enterprises, were also asked to participate in the financing of the research. After various negotiations, the parties, with the exception of the Ministry of Agriculture, agreed to take part in the project, albeit some more enthusiastically than others. Evidently the political context, the fact that at that time there existed "a mood," a "social demand," a "popular desire" that "something be done" about the problem of economic crime (see Alvesalo and Tombs, 2001b), made it difficult for the authorities to refuse to sponsor research on such crime. The importance of getting the officials who granted subsidies to finance the research was not simply monetary, but also facilitated our gaining access to their data on subsidies. These two aspects of the research process were inextricably linked: even if we had had university funding for the research, it would most likely not have been possible to access the data we needed without the support of the agencies in question.

The aims set out by the funders in the second research project were first, to map the problems in granting and supervising the use of subsidies; second, to get some idea of the extent of the misuse of subsidies; third, to estimate how many of the enterprises which are actively engaged in the illegal economy[4] are supported by the state. The third aim was included in our research because it was a part of a larger ongoing project in the tax-administration: a general mapping of the illegal economy.[5] Another, more pragmatic aim specified by the funders for us was to develop and propose control measures, as well as to map the accumulation of different state subsidies. The latter activity was connected to an attempt to amend the supervision of the accumulation of different subsidies, a duty imposed on member states of the European Union, which Finland was in the process of joining.

At the beginning of the projects it was not necessarily clear to the funder that one inevitable result of the research projects was that they would reveal something of the functioning or, more importantly, the non-functioning of the control that the agencies in question attempted to practice. In addition, it might not have been fully realized by the sponsors that, since the projects were conducted by academics, the results would be published, meaning that the sponsors would become vulnerable and open to criticism. After all, the projects were research projects, not internal development projects.[6] Our perception that there were limits on how far some of the funders and other control agencies were prepared to accept and publish critiques of their functioning as control agencies was confirmed when it became time to publish the results of the research.

## Research Methods and Access to Data

Both research projects yielded extensive empirical data. Some of the data and, more importantly, the databases that contained the required information were not public, and to access them required patient navigation of bureaucratic procedures. The fact that governmental authorities financed the research made access to sources of information hardly easy, but at least *possible* (and, of course, inexpensive).

The first step of the research project on the damage caused by economic crime included the mapping of economic crime cases in courts. Even with access to a data base including all court decisions in the whole country, collecting "economic crime" cases was not simple. Anyone involved in researching economic, white-collar, or corporate crimes is familiar with the problems regarding statistics: there are hardly any (see, for example, Friedrichs, 1996). When one looks at crime statistics, one has to hunt for economic crimes in different places, under the headings "crimes against property," "crimes against life and health," "crimes in business," or "other offences." Moreover, many economic crimes are left out of the penal code. Most importantly, in crime statistics no differentiation is made between offences committed in a purely individual capacity and those committed in an organizational context.

An attempt was made to accumulate as comprehensive a selection of crimes as possible, and the number of different crime categories included was 167. The most essential criterion in selecting relevant cases was that the crime had been possible only in connection with or using a company or other analogous organization. The first stage was to make a list of those court decisions that might include "real" economic crimes, and to separate the cases that were purely individual acts with no connection to business activity.[7] On the basis of an agreement with Statistics Finland, a list of 14,000 identification numbers of possible economic crime cases was received.

The Data Administration Office of the Ministry of Justice was asked for permission to use the database on judicial decisions. Court decisions *per se* are naturally public, but the electronic *database* is not accessible to everybody, and to obtain the permit was not a simple matter; it took several months and required negotiations between our professor, representatives of the Ministry of Justice and representatives of the police. To manually go over 14,000 case files—located all around the country—would have been an impossible task. During autumn 1993, Anne went through those 14,000 cases, and collected the relevant ones. This could not be done at the university, however. Due to considerations of data security, the Ministry of Justice did not allow the researchers to have an on-line connection to the database from the university, where they feared that "anyone" could walk into the researchers' room and access the database! In the end, after negotiating the matter, Anne was able to collect the cases in the local Court of Appeal, where an on-line connection already existed.

An unforeseen problem arose from the fact that the information obtained from the case studies in the database was more limited than had been expected. Because the descriptions of criminal activities were very brief, it was difficult to deduce whether the crime in question was an actual economic crime or a purely individual one. Therefore, to test the selected cases, a sample was taken from the lowest courts. The original court records, which included the records of the preliminary investigation on each case, were gone through. This was done in order to test whether we had selected actual economic crimes on the basis of the truncated case studies. In addition, we wanted to collect information other than what appeared in the judicial decisions, for example, how the crime had come to the knowledge of the police and *the amounts of financial losses in the reports of offences.* After the analyses, 927 cases were selected to be included in the research.

The research on the success of collecting damages (Virta and Laitinen, 1996) was conducted a couple of years later since there was no point in looking at the collection of monies immediately after the court decisions. The purpose of the study was to find out how far the authorities had succeeded in collecting the assessed damages, that is, the compensation on the basis of an offence, from the 927 economic crime cases. This part of the project seemed at first to be fairly simple. The task was to contact different authorities and ask for information about these cases and the sums that they had managed to get back. Although the authorities were very helpful, obtaining the necessary information demanded a great deal of work on their part as well. In addition to the practical obstacles, it soon became evident that this kind of sensitive data would not be obtained unless we got permission from the Data Protection Board, which makes decisions falling within the scope of data protection and has the right to grant special permissions to process personal data, provided that certain prerequisites are fulfilled. Furthermore, it was necessary to apply for licences from every authority in order to get access to their information sources. All in all, it took half a year before the actual collection of data could be started.

The practical obstacles varied depending on the different authorities. For example, in dealing with the tax authorities the main question was how to locate the right cases. The debts to tax authorities were handled as debts of companies, not as debts of the people against whom damages had been adjudged when they had committed a crime using a company.[8] There was no common reference point between the information from the trial (person) and the information tax authorities had (company), and this simple fact made it difficult for us to assess the success of collection. What we had was the name and the social security number of the offender, but *not* the registration number of the company which the offender had used to commit the crime. The only way to connect the data was to go through all of the offenders one by one to see in which part of the country they were registered as taxpayers and then send a list to the appropriate county tax office. In the county offices, all the companies these persons were involved in were checked to find the relevant one. In addition to the success of the collection processes, very specific information about these practices was received. The information delivered by the authorities was manually connected to the database that was used in the first phase of "The Dark Side of the Economy."

In the research project "Depending on Subsidies" (Alvesalo et al., 1994), in addition to mapping possibly fraudulent enterprises, one aim was to discover the methods and problems involved in granting subsidies on the local level. A survey was conducted among the provincial authorities granting subsidies. In the survey, the measures for controlling the applicants for subsidies were studied in the different phases of subsidizing: when the decision to give such financial support was made; when the subsidy was paid and finally, after it was paid. The more difficult aim of the project was to discover "suspicious enterprises," those that had given misleading information, either to the tax authorities or to the officials that grant subsidies. The empirical data consisted of information on about 26,000 enterprises, which had been granted subsidies in 1993. The study was conducted by comparing the databases of the tax authorities to the databases of the branches of administration which grant subsidies. This was the first study in which a cross-checking of such material had been done. Due to both technical obstacles and legal restrictions concerning the exchange of information between authorities, even the regulators themselves had not been able to combine their databases in the way that we did in the research. The data was highly sensitive because it included information that could be classified as commercial secrets, including new investments, product development or export marketing projects carried out by the subsidized businesses. Each of the authorities had to make an explicit decision to allow the delivery of the data to us, and we had agreed to secrecy regarding specific facts about individual enterprises. In addition, the results of the cross-checking were to be reported in such a way that the names of the individual, possibly fraudulent, enterprises, would not be revealed.[9]

What happened in practice was that the different authorities sent us files including information which the enterprises had given about themselves when they had applied for a state subsidy. The information included, for example, their turnover, balance sheet, staff numbers, and labor costs. All the files were combined electronically with the more comprehensive files of the tax authorities. This was done with the aim of comparing the information that the tax authorities had on the subsidized enterprises with the information the companies had given to other authorities which grant subsidies. It was sometimes extremely difficult to combine the files for many technical reasons, and also because, despite the fact that enterprises have their own special ID numbers, these were not always included in the files. When this was the case, other identifiers had to be used, such as the address or telephone number of the company. Finally, it should be noted that the different technical structures of the databases proved to be an obstacle to analyzing the material.

The difficulties concerning both the identification of enterprises and the linking of them to individuals who held responsible positions in them, in the second stage of "The Dark Side of the Economy," constituted much more than technical obstacles. They also indicated the problems a society has in controlling enterprises and the resources the state is channelling to them. To access all the data in both projects would not have been possible without the support, contacts and authority enjoyed by the representatives of our funders. These advantages were used in every possible way. For example, in applications to attain data from other officials, the funders were always mentioned. Numerous visits were paid to various authorities to negotiate the technicalities and practicalities of using and understanding the data we had obtained from them. All doors seemed to be open to us. Generally there was a very positive attitude and the officials were very communicative. The costs relating to the data files were minimal for the project, probably because the data was received from the authorities that financed the research or because their representatives endorsed the requests.

In retrospect, it might not be far-fetched to speculate that one of the reasons for the openness of the authorities could have been that the research projects, at least the efforts of Anne and Erja who were relatively young at that time, were not taken very seriously. Even though there were no explicit doubts expressed as to our capabilities, "Here come Ahti and his angels" was a comment not much more flattering than being constantly referred as "Ahti's girls."[10] It might have been that, at the end of the day, no one believed in the ability of two women, inexperienced as researchers, even with the supervision of a (male) professor, to be able to assess the scope of subsidy fraud—particularly when the authorities themselves had for some time been trying to establish a uniform register on state subsidies. Due to technical difficulties in combining the different databases, an intended accumulation register had not been built. Unsurprisingly neither Ahti's nor his angels' technical capabilities were sufficient to combine the masses of data: it was obvious from the beginning that technical assistance was imperative. Consequently, the tax authorities had provided extra resources for the hiring of IT-experts to make special computer programs that made the combination of the files possible. After several months of hard work, telephone calls, and meetings between the computer experts and researchers, the database was finally complete, and it was time to start the cross-checking.

## Results: Their Construction and Reactions

### "The Dark Side of the Economy"

During the first phase of the research process on the extent of economic crime and damages caused by economic crime, it became apparent that the amount of adjudged damages was not that extensive. This meant that the funder would not —on the basis of *adjudged* damages—receive some enormous figure that would then appear in tabloids in order to show how much harm is caused by economic crime. As with all data relating to "crime," the figures in the court decisions of course did not reveal anything of the actual numbers of losses caused by economic crime, but revealed more about the functioning of the criminal justice system. Be that as it may, the project included also data from various sources on how much the estimated damage caused by economic crimes were in the *earlier stages of the process.* Hence, it was possible to present estimates of the *yearly losses known to the police,* and compare them with the *adjudged yearly losses.* The total losses per year caused by economic crime known to the police was about 2.5 billion marks. In the court data the total sum of yearly losses presented to the court was about 0.5 billion marks. Finally, the amount of adjudged damages found in the 927 cases in courts was only about 0.25 billion marks (see Laitinen and Alvesalo, 1994: 115).

The final report included a massive amount of data on different aspects of economic crime cases in the courts.[11] The *main* result of the first research was in the press release presented in a way that was satisfactory to us, but also was useful for the sponsor. "Only a fraction of known losses caused by economic crimes are adjudged as damages" (Sisäasiainministeriö tiedottaa, 1994). Also, an estimation was presented of the annual *total amount*—the amount including hidden criminality—of damages caused by economic crime. This sum was 14 billion marks (about

2.4 billion euros, the annual Finnish Government budget being about 33 billion Euros). Despite the careful presentation and the fact that the amount of hidden criminality was underestimated rather than overestimated, many people held this amount to be highly inflated. Most notably, Pasanen, the chairperson of the "Pasanen Committee," who was the deputy chancellor of justice at that time, challenged the estimates presented. This was a response given to the critique that was presented by the Minister of Justice, Anneli Jäätteenmäki, just after "The Dark Side of the Economy" was published. She claimed that the criminal justice system is too soft with economic criminals, and that the threshold for prosecution is too high. In an extensive interview, titled "Jäätteenmäki is talking through her hat," Pasanen, together with Chancellor of Justice, Jorma S. Aalto, responded defensively to the accusations made by the minister, and to the estimates presented in our research, stating for example, that ". . . we have to remember that the damages can be linked to either criminal or civil actions . . . our job is to concentrate only on criminal activities" (*Iltalehti,* 31 August, 1994). On the other hand the figure of 14 billion marks came to be used generally as the "true" amount of annual losses caused by economic crime. It was, and still is, referred to in numerous publications, and also in the introductory part of the Finnish Government's 1996 action plan against economic crime and the gray economy.

Moreover, a finding that raised attention in the media was that punishments for economic crimes were lenient. Of all sanctions adjudged, 58.1% were fines, while 32.2% were conditional and 9.7% unconditional prison sentences. These results, which indicated lenient judicial practice in cases of economic crime, created scepticism among some academics. Lawyers particularly seemed to have problems with the results, and since the research project was based in a law faculty, we recieved our share of criticism. For example, the fact that our definition of economic crime was not one based solely on legal categories was regarded as a deficiency which made our results non-comparable to other punishment practices. Of course, criticism and critique is something a researcher has to accept, but some of the reactions seemed to be partly caused by a negative attitude often held by legal scholars towards any "mushy and inaccurate" sociological studies on *their* terrain, the functioning of the justice system. The other reason for the critical reactions was that in Finland, there has been a strong tradition of lenient criminal policy. It has remained characterized by a social liberalism that is being abandoned in the majority of other industrialized nations (Christie, 1993: 46–50; Lappi-Seppälä 1998, Korander, 1998, 1999). The motto of those academics striving for a lenient criminal policy was (and is) "the less talk about crime, the better"; and so it was not a habit—at least among academics that belonged to this school of thought—to publish research results with the explicit or implicit message that there should be harsher punishments. This was, of course, not our intention. Our intention was to emphasize first, that the criminal justice system systematically fails to concentrate on the crimes that are the most costly to society, and second, that punishments are not commensurate with the harmfulness of the crimes.

One of the more "media-sexy" findings in the first stage of "The Dark Side of the Economy" was that in cases of economic crime, a free trial, a trial paid by the state because of the impecuniousness of the defendant, was granted to 27% of defendants; yet the corresponding percentage in all crime cases was only 12. In other words, economic criminals got a free trial more often than other criminals did. This made the second stage of the research, looking at the collection of damages, quite interesting. The results indicated that people convicted of economic crime are either actually or formally impecunious.[12] Consequently, what the second stage of the "Dark Side of the Economy" revealed was that it was very difficult to recover the damages that had been adjudged in cases of economic crime. The amount of money recovered in the collection processes was only 5.7% of the value of the original amounts under collection (see Virta, 1999). The lack of success in retrieving the assets of economic criminals was not totally a surprise. Most of the problems were naturally known within the authorities and a reform of the recovery proceedings was just about to take place.[13] The research was conducted just in time to confirm the problems and inefficiency of the control process and the need for reform.

In general, the results were well taken by the authorities. According to one official within the tax administration, it was common knowledge that nobody wanted to work with economic crime cases, because one could hardly ever recover anything from them. But even though the problems in the field had been recognized, the depth of the problem in the sphere of economic crime cases still came as a surprise to some people, even to those who had been planning the reform of the recovery proceedings. This revealed the authorities' difficulties in grasping the total picture of "success" in collecting the damages adjudged in cases of economic crime. These difficulties were caused mainly by the numerous legal and practical obstacles to accessing reliable information. On the other hand, it was felt that the failure in recovery proceedings (calculated in monetary value, only 3.4% had succeeded) was also due to the fact that it represents the second stage in the process of collection: the amounts of adjudged damages that the creditors have not succeeded in collecting are transmitted to the execution authorities/bailiffs who continue the recovery proceedings; in other words, they get "bones" that have already been "chewed." Living proof of the amazement expressed at the results was given in an economic crime seminar for the police and some other authorities, where Erja presented the findings: this prompted an aggressive outburst from one of the participants, who claimed that the results could not be true. The disbeliever was working on the reform of the recovery proceedings. Erja suggested sitting down with him after the seminar and explaining the methods and results of the study in detail. And, indeed, he kept Erja on the rack for several hours afterwards. After the seminar he promised to check on the situation at his workplace, and a couple of weeks later he called and admitted that the results were correct, but he still couldn't really believe that the success in recovery was so low.

## *"Depending on Subsidies"*

As a part of the research project "Depending on Subsidies," a questionnaire was mailed to the different authorities responsible for granting subsidies. One of the main findings was that the intensity of control dropped rather heavily after the decision to subsidize. Especially, controlling *how* the enterprise had used a subsidy was very weak. It was clear that the authorities were not interested in the ways the subsidized enterprises used the money and the purposes for which they used it seemed to be very clear. "Oh my god, the control goes down like a cow's tail!" was a comment made on the revelation of the lack of control. When the results of the survey were reported to the funders, they responded with telephone calls and demands for checking the reliability of the results and the relevance of the questionnaire. The sponsors wanted to find some "rational" culprits to explain away the bad results: for example, there was speculation that the results were distorted by the fact that officials in the field were not satisfied with their working conditions; indeed when an anonymous survey was conducted, most of them used this only as a opportunity to protest about their work situation, rather than to talk about the reality of the effectiveness of control. Anyway, everything was checked many times before the results were accepted for dissemination. The reactions indicated the concern that some of the sponsors seemed to have about the publication of the results; despite their knowledge of some of the inefficiencies of control, they didn't seem to feel comfortable when someone else was about to point them out in public.

The databases of the 26,000 enterprises contained several features that may have indicated a certain risk or possibility of fraud. These we called risk indicators, revealing a kind of contradiction that may have indicated fraud. For example, the subsidized enterprise had not given notification of registered employees, although some salaries had been registered in the files of the tax authority; the enterprise had gone bankrupt or an action for bankruptcy had been started the same year or even before they had applied for or been granted the subsidy; the enterprise had announced that there had been no business activity that year, and yet applied for or received a subsidy; or the enterprise had not submitted any tax return for the year it applied for or received the subsidy. The cross-checking showed that at least one risk indicator proved accurate for almost 9% of the subsidized enterprises. Without any doubt, the most problematic enterprises were those possessing more than one risk indicator (18.2% of all risk enterprises, or 1.6% of all the enterprises in the study). One remarkable feature among subsidized enterprises was the extent of taxes owed: both the monetary value of back taxes and the number of firms owing these taxes increased greatly from February 1993 to January 1995, while all of these enterprises also received subsidies from the state in 1993. To owe back taxes is not against the law, but it is against the "spirit" of subsidies for the state to support companies that have not paid their taxes, that is, companies that are in debt to the state.

Despite some interesting results, the reporting by the media of the study "Depending on Subsidies" was rather insignificant, at least compared to the massive media attention the first study received. Several reasons might explain the lack of reporting. It might have been that the research simply was not media-attractive, or that the general interest in economic crime had diminished. But from our perspective as researchers, there seemed to be other reasons for the scarce reporting.

To begin with, the construction of the press release was not very smooth. One understandable reason was that there were four funders who all had views on how the results should be presented. The most careful of the commentators on our press release seemed to be the Ministry of Trade and Industry which had granted the most money in subsidies. Several times suggestions for improvement were made to our draft press release, to avoid "misunderstandings." Our perception as researchers was that the rhetoric was toned down so that no single sentence in the press release would enable the media to make the authorities look bad.

Concern about the results could also be seen in other ways. Two months before the results were published, a press release on another inquiry conducted in the Ministry of Trade and Industry appeared. In the Finnish news agency's release on the research it was stated that ". . . in opposition to what may have been thought [. . .] there is no evidence to show that criminal activity is common in the field of subsidies to enterprises [. . .] this is because the subsidies are paid according to very tight instructions . . ." The result of the inquiry was that there had been very few, if any, misuses of state subsidies admitted by the Ministry of Trade and Industry. It was also emphasized that the Ministry of Trade and Industry has instructions on how to avoid subsidy fraud, and that those instructions would be further improved (Suomen Tietotoimisto, 1995). Finally, our perception of the sensitiveness of the subject was augmented by the fact that, despite a tentative decision to continue the study in order to look at the suspicious cases more carefully, the funding of the project was ended.

## Summary and Discussion

The existence of a political and social mood to combat economic crime at the beginning of the 1990s was crucial for the launching of extensive studies on such matters. To provide a stronger basis for the demand to intensify control, there was a need for research to point out the scale of damages that economic crime causes to society. The importance of having control agencies financing our research was not only monetary, but also a question of accessing different sources of information. Some of the data and, more importantly, the databases that contained the required information, were not public, and to access them required support from governmental agencies. These two aspects of the research processes were inextricably linked: even if we had had university funding for the research, it would most likely not have been possible to access the data we needed without the support of the agencies in question.

The dissemination of findings was for the most part without problems, since the results were relevant to the policy under construction. Some of the problems that were raised in the research projects had been recognized within the control agencies before the reports were published, and the research confirmed the inefficiencies in controlling economic crime. But there were also limits on how far some of the funders were prepared either to accept or to publish criticism of their functioning as control agencies. The reactions indicated the concerns that some sponsors seemed to have about the publishing of the results; despite their knowledge of the inefficiencies of control, they did not seem to feel comfortable when someone else was about to point them out in public.

On the practical level, there were some clear examples of changes on the level of everyday regulation based on the findings of the research projects. For example, the procedures for granting subsidies were reformed within various authorities. In addition, the tax authorities built a system similar to the one that was used in the research on state subsidies, of cross-checking companies on the basis of the information they held *ex officio*. Furthermore, based on our initiative, an important improvement was made within the police: through cooperation between the police and ourselves, a uniform definition of economic crime was constructed.[14] The investigators in the field have now been instructed to use this definition when they register crimes, so that comprehensive statistics on economic crime could be made available, and since 1996 rather extensive statistics have been gathered by the police.

In 1996, the Finnish Government passed a decision of principle to combat economic crime and the gray economy.[15] A formal Action Plan set out a three-year program based upon a series of proposals for reforms in the control of economic crime and the gray economy. This initiative raised economic crime as an economic, social, and crime problem that causes damage to the material and moral fabric of Finnish society. From this starting point, the action plan both consolidated and also initiated a series of reforms in legislation, regulatory agencies, enforcement practice, and research activities. The action plans were continued with governmental support in 1998 and 2001.[16] The reasons for the emergence and realization of the action plans are manifold (see Alvesalo and Tombs, 2001b). The role of research in those processes was for the most part confirmatory, since the initiatives for intensifying control existed even before the studies were launched.

A part of the funds that the government committed to "fight economic crime" was invested in academic research. Some of the resources have been granted to research projects in universities, and Erja is continuing her work in the University of Turku. One position of senior researcher was created in the Police College of Finland in 1996. Anne was hired in that position, and in addition to conducting research, her task is to maintain a database on Finnish publications and research projects and to contribute to the promotion of coordinated, extensive, and long-term research in the field of economic crime. Thanks to the continuation of the action plans, the financing of research has at this date become quite regularized. But some years ago, when the political interest turned more to drug-related crimes, Erja's professor suggested that she should start thinking about changing her focus and make a research plan about drug matters to ensure financing in the long run. This is a clear example of one of the dangers in being dependent on outside financing: the pressures both to change research focus according to policy needs, and to conduct research as a means of securing further funding.

It is essential to recognize the dangers of conducting research for sponsors who have a clear agenda—even if one agrees with it. The numerous concerns and dilemmas cannot be considered exhaustively here, but some points need to be made on the dangers associated with advocating greater criminalization (see Alvesalo and Tombs, 2001c). In the case of both "The Dark Side of the Economy" and "Depending on Subsidies," the research projects were sponsored in order to obtain a stronger basis for the demand to intensify control. And this is what happened subsequently: economic crime was subjected to harsher control. In demonstrating the criminal justice system's failure with regard to economic crime, there lies the pitfall of advancing—at least implicitly—*more repressive measures as the only solution to control crime*. There is a risk of research being used for the expansion of the repressive armory of the state in general. One should always bear in mind the risk of conventional crime control efforts fuelling the engine of crime, and the fact that modernist criminological research, with its production of "scientific results" plays its part in this by concretizing and affirming reality (see Henry and Milovanovic, 1996:196). There is a risk of economic crime crusades and research being used as "Trojan horses" to expand the totality of the repressive armory of the state (Alvesalo, 1999).

On the other hand, given the scale and consequences of economic crime, and the persistent problems in addressing it, it needs to be raised as an issue in research (see Alvesalo and Tombs, 2001b). The place of "conventional" crime on law and order agendas is secure. If one argues for equality in criminal policy—which entails the need for a balance in the treatment of different forms of crime—economic crime and the harms it causes need to be raised in research. If we accept that certain forms of "conventional" crimes are subject to criminalization, we should point out that less "conventional" offences which on many criteria are more serious in terms of level of economic, physical and social harm are also subject to such processes. In this sense, research on economic or other crimes of the powerful does not affirm existing realities; on the contrary it may have a role in changing popular, political *and* individual perceptions of "crime" problems. As one police investigator—now working in the field of economic crime—told Anne, "reading the 'Dark Side of the Economy' changed my view of the world . . . it changed my life."

In terms of the relationship between the state, the social mood and the construction and control of research agendas there are lessons to be learned from our experiences. First, it was the political and social mood that made it possible to conduct extensive studies on economic crime. Second, the fact that the studies were relevant to the policy under construction not only facilitated the research projects but also contributed to their recognition, and thus to the fact that some of the results and suggestions for reform directly informed the practices of authorities combating economic crime. Third, the continuation of the social mood against economic crime and the formulation of the action plans made economic crime research regularized and hence more independent of immediate political and bureaucratic pressures. Finally, it is important to realize that negotiating power in the research process is not just about choosing whether or not to "engage" with the state. In fact, the important aspect of conducting research may be not whether it is conducted inside or outside the state, but how it seeks to engage in the struggle over the social mood.

## Acknowledgments

We would like to acknowledge the support Professor Ahti Laitinen gave to us through the years we worked with him. We would also like to thank the Ministries of the Interior, Trade and Affairs, and Employment as well as the tax authorities for their support in the research projects we have described in this chapter. Particular thanks are due to Steve Tombs and Dave Whyte, for their advice, assistance and comments in the course of writing this article. We remain, of course, solely responsible for the contents.

## Notes

1. The term "economic crime" encompasses elements of what have been referred to elsewhere as corporate and white-collar crimes. It is used throughout this chapter, since it is the term that is used by the police of Finland for the purposes of reporting and classifying. It is defined as follows: "a criminalized act or neglect which is committed in the framework of, or

using, a corporation or other organization. The act is done with the aim of attaining unlawful direct or indirect benefit. A criminalized, systematic act that is analogous to entrepreneurship and has the aim of considerable benefit is also defined as economic crime" (Sisäasiainministeriö, 1997: 6).

2. For example, Hakman (1993) and Huhtamäki (1994).

3. No explicit pressure for particular results was ever placed upon us, but the fact that the funder wanted reports on the progress of the project every couple of months, and might have broken off the financing, constantly reminded us of their expectations.

4. Illegal or "gray" economy is the term used to describe activities for which the statutory taxes and payments have not been paid because the activities have taken place in secrecy; or incorrect, misleading, or insufficient information has been given about the activities.

5. The working group on the illegal economy was established by the Ministry of the Treasury 22 March 1994. The illegal economy, as far as it concerned enterprises, was perceived as one element of economic crime.

6. Despite the trend toward increasing outsider funding, the vast majority of university research is funded by the state and the tradition of its academic freedom and scientific results being public domain has remained strong in Finland. The text written on the main building of the University of Turku characterizes this ethos: "A gift from an independent nation to independent science." On the ownership and secrecy of research results, see Niiniluoto, 2001; and Bruun, 2001.

7. In Finnish criminal law, the one who bears criminal liability is always an actual person, not a legal person. Even if, according to the law on corporate liability, it has been possible to fine a corporation since 1995, corporations cannot be formulated as offenders.

8. For example, an owner-director can commit a bookkeeping crime, fraud, or tax evasion using his or her company. In the case of company tax evasion, the person is convicted, but the one in debt to the tax authorities is the company.

9. In general, various secrecy regulations in Finland include exceptions to protect the freedom of research.

10. Later on, we were also referred to as "The Spice Girls" by some colleagues in the law faculty.

11. In addition to what is mentioned here, there were data on the offenders' age, sex and profession, plaintiffs, types of enterprises, modus operandi, length of time of judicial processes, and so on.

12. We mean here that economic offenders are either factually without means, or as often is the case, they have arranged the formal ownership of their property in ways that make them seem indigent in the face of tax-authorities or other creditors. See also Virta, 1998, 1999, 2000; Hansen 1995; Suontausta and Hämäläinen 2000; Mäkelä, 2001.

13. The reform was a proposal for new legislation concerning more effective execution proceedings. See Oikeusministeriö, 1996.

14. See note 1.

15. Government's Decision of Principle, 1 February, 1996.

16. The government's decisions to combat economic crime on 22 October, 1998 and 20 June, 2001. Both decisions also included new resources.

# Exposing Power: Scrutinizing the Crimes of the Powerful

# Imaginative Crimes or Crimes of the Imagination

## Researching the Secret State

## Introduction

State crime, defined by Chambliss (1995:256) as "acts defined by law as criminal and committed by state officials in the pursuit of their job as representatives of the state"[1] has received very little attention in British, or indeed, North American, criminology. In contrast to the many studies of different types of street crime, for example, homicide, rape, burglary, robbery, or fencing, it is necessary to trawl the textbooks to find any reference to major state crimes such as state-directed violence or terrorism, espionage, drugs or arms trafficking, or other illegal activities. What research has been done into these types of crimes has been carried out by journalists as immortalized in the Bernstein and Woodward investigation into Watergate.[2] Criminology, for its part, has remained distinctly disinterested in the topic.[3]

Yet in Britain, and even more so in Northern Ireland, there have been numerous allegations of state servants carrying out illegal activities during the course of their work. The allegations cover a range of criminal activity including an attempt to undermine a Labour prime minister, assaults, theft, burglary, fraud, smear tactics and defamation, perverting the course of justice, attempted murder, conspiracies to murder, and murder. It has been left to two journalists, Stephen Dorril and

Robin Ramsey, rather than criminologists, to research and document these allegations. In 1983, they set up a magazine called *Lobster,* which has published critical commentaries and systematic analyses of the activities of mainly, but not exclusively, the British security agencies ever since.

In Northern Ireland, allegations of state conspiracies have been commonplace, hardly surprising in the context of 30 years of a bitter and bloody struggle between the security services, the Irish Republican Army (IRA) and loyalist paramilitaries. A wider range of people have taken an interest in the allegations including journalists, political activists, and academics in the fields of law, criminology, and sociology. One of the first books alleging a serious crime by state servants was written by Kennedy Lindsay (1979), based around the shooting of a man by a special army unit. Lindsay claimed that the man was shot because he had unwittingly stumbled on events that could have seriously embarrassed the authorities. Since Lindsay's book there have been many others dealing with events which are captured by the definition of state crimes. The allegations over the years have included concerns over numerous state killings (Asmal, 1985; Murray, 1997, 1998; Ní Aoláin 2000; Rolston, 2000); paramilitary-security forces, collusion in murders, and even allegations that the lives of security personnel and citizens have sometimes been sacrificed in order to protect the identify of a key informer (N. Davies, 1999); the use of "black" propaganda and dirty tricks (Faligot, 1983; Holroyd and Burbridge, 1989; Moore, 1966); the widespread use of informers as *agents provocateurs* (Dillon, 1988; Urban, 1992); the abuse of people during interrogation (McGuffin, 1974; P. Taylor, 1980); the widespread use of supergrasses (Boyd, 1984; Greer, 1995); and threats to lawyers and the fitting-up of innocent people (Dickson, 1999). According to one journalist, a dirty undercover war existed for many years "in the shadowy world of agents, double agents and informers; the world in which intelligence agencies and terrorists seek to outwit and kill each other and different rules can be applied, and often are, without the consent or approval of government" (Dillon, 1988: xix). Mark Urban deals with similar themes in his appropriately titled book *Big Boys' Rules.* He argues that short-term gains and political expediency, rather than the rule of law, have characterized the war.

Within Northern Ireland, intelligence has been at the heart of the struggle against both republican and loyalist paramilitaries. All the agencies have developed their own systems for collecting it, and the recruitment and retention of informers has been central. Because of the level and nature of the conflict, the best placed and most trusted informers were those that had taken part in bombings, murders, and other acts of political violence. There are now numerous incidents in which it has been suggested that the protection of an informer's identity was considered by the security services to be more important than the arrest of suspects. These include the murders of Pat Finucane and another lawyer, Rosemary Nelson, the journalist Martin O'Hagan (McDonald, 2001) and the bombings of Manchester city center

(Carter, 2002) and Omagh. It has also been alleged that in many instances, members of the security services have ignored warnings about murder bids in order to protect well-placed informers. Some of the more high-profile cases include the murder of Francisco Notorantonio in 1987 (Mullin, 2000); the attack by Michael Stone on Milltown Cemetery during an IRA funeral in March 1988 which led to the death of three people and injuries to many more (Harkin, 2000); the murder of John McMichael, Ulster Defence Association (UDA) commander, in 1987 (*Sunday People*, October 15), and the murders of Pat Finucane and Rosemary Nelson.

Such allegations and events form the background and context to the study of one alleged state crime which is the focus of this chapter—the removal of John Stalker, then Deputy Chief Constable of Greater Manchester,[4] from an investigation into the death of six young men shot dead by the Royal Ulster Constabulary (RUC) in three separate incidents in Northern Ireland in 1982. At the time of his removal, the press and media almost unanimously suggested that there must have been a conspiracy. Despite intensive investigation by journalists at the time, there has been no further investigation into the allegations. This chapter is based on a long-term research project revisiting the case.[5] The aim here is to describe some of the problems of conducting research into an alleged conspiracy by unspecified state servants. The first section looks at some of the general problems facing a researcher of alleged state conspiracy: the view that conspiracies are mainly figments of overactive imaginations; the problem of truth and method in a poststructuralist environment; and the lack of comparative research material. The second section gives a brief overview of Stalker's removal. The central allegation against him was that during the 1970s and 1980s he "associated with Kevin Taylor and known criminals in a manner likely to bring discredit upon the Greater Manchester Police" (Sampson Report, 1986: 1).[6] The third section of the chapter examines some of the specific research problems of researching the alleged conspiracy to remove Stalker.

## Researching State Crime: Some Contextual Issues

### Imagining Conspiracies

The first problem any researcher into this type of state crime must confront is the slippery nature of the notion of a conspiracy. Conspiracies present a paradox. On the one hand, it is taken for granted that many crimes are committed by groups of people who conspire together to commit some act. It be may a group of men who plan to rob the local bank or supermarket, a bevy of schoolgirls who encourage each other to carry out a little shoplifting at the end of a lack-luster day at school, or a group of company directors who decide that the cost of withdrawing a faulty car to replace a fuel tank, which has the propensity to explode when hit by another vehicle, is too high. None of these particular examples stretch the imagination. None will lead to accusations that the person who describes these criminal acts is being conspiratorial. The events are common-place and readily believable, and the criminal law makes plenty of provision for these types of conspiracies. These are crimes, some of which are more imaginative than others.

On the other hand, if it is suggested that a group of state servants or politicians have conspired together for political reasons to commit illegal acts, such as conspiring to pervert the course of justice, exploding bombs in foreign states to guarantee the introduction of repressive anti-terror legislation, collusion with paramilitary death squads, attempting to rid the country of a democratically elected left-wing prime minister, or smearing the head of a trade union or, for that matter, anyone who has suggested that some group of state servants had committed crimes, most people would respond with incredulity and propose that the person who suggested such possibilities is far too conspiratorial, or perhaps obsessed with conspiracy. These are crimes of the imagination.

While it is accepted that people do conspire together to commit illegal acts for personal or other reasons, certain conspiracies are considered too far-fetched, not on the basis of any careful assessment of the evidence but on the basis of some gut reaction. Milne (1994: 38), in his analysis of the 1984–85 coal dispute, has put it this way:

> it is hardly surprising perhaps that many people feel unhappy with any suggestion of behind-the scenes collusion and manipulation of events. To suggest anything else is regarded as somehow naïve and insufficiently worldly. Among journalists in particular, it is an article of faith to insist on the "cock-up theory" rather than the "conspiracy theory" of history.

Robin Ramsey, a former editor of *Lobster,* has made a similar point about academics. He has asked the question, "why is it that, for so long, apparently intelligent people—mostly Anglo-American political scientists—have failed to notice that conspiracy is an everyday and rather important part of the phenomenon they purport to be studying?" (1996: 8). He cited the example of the Economic League, which operated for over 60 years working against the British left, yet he could find no academic article about the organization. Conspiracies, he argues, in contrast to conspiracy theories, are a very common form of political behavior. Criminologists, as well as political scientists, need to grasp this obvious point and accept the popular view that conspiracies are imaginative crimes and not crimes of the imagination.

### Truth and Methods

The second problem which any researcher of an alleged conspiracy must confront is what is meant by "truth." This is a general issue which faces all researchers in the context of post-structuralism where it is argued that there is no such thing as "truth" but there are many truths which are products of their own discursive regimes (Smart, 1995). In addition, a more specific issue arises from the nature of the material being studied. In the Stalker/Taylor affair it is how to assess the genuineness of different parts of the official story from the outside, without access to either the official documentation or the key people involved. In this context "truth" is partly speculative.

I will begin with the more general problem of multiple truths. There is no doubt that social scientists have moved from the certainties of positivism to postmodernism via hermeneutics and social constructionism and arrived at a position where everything can be seen as a product of some discursive apparatus, whether it is the notion of the state, of power, or of the "social" itself (Rose, 1996). The current dogma on truth also suggests that even if we believe in some truth there are no methods to produce it—both quantitative and qualitative methods are suspect, and all that we can do is to resort to triangulation. Knowledge is simply relativist. There are no universal steps to knowing. This critique, in my view, is wrong. While there may be many imperfections in the methods that are used to understand social reality, it is wrong to suggest that everything is relativist.

I would argue that this state of affairs has arisen from a misreading of Foucault, who provided some of the ideas on which poststructuralism has been built. While he presented many insights into the role of the normalizing disciplines of criminology, psychiatry, psychology and sociology, and the way the social is constructed, he emphasized the importance of the materiality of life, institutions and, importantly, discourses. He did not deny the reality of a range of objects and circumstances about which everyone would agree. There are many material facts, social circumstances, and social categories over which there is a broad, if not universal, acceptance. Few, for example, would argue with the notion of age and the fact that we will all die sometime. Similarly, most people held against their will and locked up in a building with bars on the windows and locks on all the doors and gates at the end of every corridor accept that the building is a prison. While there may be arguments about whether a certain building fits this description, there is a wide consensus about what prisons are, and few would disagree that the number of people locked up in them can be counted and the trends in numbers shown over time. In short, there are broad universal social categories and circumstances which we can identify and comment upon. Crucially, if we accept the relativist position that there are only multiple truths then we have to accept that one truth is just as valid as another—and there can be no injustice.

The second issue concerning "truth" stems from the nature of the material being studied. The central question in the Stalker/Taylor affair is whether or not there was a conspiracy to remove Stalker. To prove or refute such an allegation requires a systematic analysis of every detail in the official story and a "cross-examination" of all the people who gave what appeared to be inconsistent, contradictory or otherwise problematic information. With only limited resources and no cooperation from many of the officials—points which are discussed more fully below—any analysis from the outside is, therefore, likely to be incomplete. Although it is possible to draw attention to the gaps and the contradictions, it is hard to avoid speculation. As a consequence, the stories which are told by those investigating state crimes in general, or conspiracies in particular, will be to some degree an imaginative exercises in themselves—partially imaginative/partially factual accounts. And, of course, although the need to speculate is a direct result of the power, privacy and secrecy of those being researched, the first line of attack against this type of research is that *it is* speculative.[7]

### *Lack of a Subject*

The third problem which confronts the researcher of state conspiracies is the dearth of a coherent and systematic body of research on which to draw or, perhaps more importantly, the dearth of any detailed overview of some of the patterns, trends and characteristics of state crime. It has been pointed out at the beginning of this chapter that criminology, particularly, in Britain, has long ignored the topic and most textbooks have no section on the subject. Green and Ward (2000) have drawn attention to the neglect of state crime in the bestselling textbook, the *Oxford Handbook on Criminology*, where they could find only one sentence on the topic. The author, Nelken (1997:907), notes simply that "the army, police, or government bureaucracies" are among those who generate crime and corruption. There is not a single bibliographical reference to state crime and no mention of key texts such as *Spycatcher* or *The Enemy Within*. More importantly, the tome, which is 1267 pages long, is totally silent on state crime in Northern Ireland. For the thousands of students who use this book as their principal source of reading, state crime does not exist.

Typically, activities which clearly fall within a definition of state crime are conceptualized under some other topic. For example, one of the most pervasive and well-documented types of state crime—illegal behavior by those working within the criminal justice system—is conceptualized under the quaint expression "miscarriages of justice," and discussed in a section on criminal justice. Similarly, racist behavior or criminal assaults by police or prison officers are discussed in sections on policing or prisons. Not only, therefore, is state crime deconstructed but also its extensiveness is underplayed. Moreover, when considered under these other topics the behavior can easily be explained as an aberration or an idiosyncrasy of some "bad apple" rather than the product of the routine structures and effects of power.

This is not to say that the work on miscarriages of justice is unhelpful—in fact, it is of particular relevance here because it provides valuable insights into some of the methods of police deviance and therefore could be important in broadening our understanding of alleged conspiracies in general and the Stalker/Taylor affair in particular. Miscarriages of justice have occurred for many different reasons and not all of them, of course, involve criminal acts; many, however, do. These include: the fabrication of evidence, including the construction or doctoring of key documents; the production of unreliable statements or confessions as a result of police pressure; the non-disclosure of evidence; and the presentation of people in a prejudicial manner (Justice, 1989; Walker and Starmer, 1999).

Another area which might provide valuable insights into the Stalker/Taylor affair concerns the use of smear tactics or rumor. There are numerous incidents, both historical and contemporary, where smear or rumor has allegedly been used to discredit particular individuals. Gill (1994), in one of the few academic books on the security services, provides an analysis of some of the more important allegations. There is, however, no systematic discussion in British criminology literature on the use of rumor and smears to discredit and defame.[8] Ramsey (2000) considers that attempts to smear people are part of the state's armory, and are often used against whistleblowers, such as Wallace and Holroyd (see above). The substance of what they were saying was ignored, and the secret services did everything in their power to discredit them and ruin their lives. Wallace was sacked from his job and was subsequently successfully prosecuted on a manslaughter charge, which he strenuously denied. It is alleged he was framed (Foot, 1989). An official enquiry into his sacking concluded that he was unfairly dismissed and wrongly denied his right of appeal by the Ministry of Defence. Holroyd was "shuffled away," certified as mentally unstable (Hainsworth, 1994).

There have been numerous other alleged smears of people who have been critical of the security services in Northern Ireland. In 1979 there were widespread allegations that the RUC were assaulting people during interrogation. Dr. Irwin, a police surgeon, after expressing his concerns in private for over two years, then went public in March 1979. He said in London Weekend Television's *Weekend World* program that he had seen roughly 150 to 160 cases in which he was not satisfied that the injuries he examined were self-inflicted. Shortly after the interview, the *Daily Telegraph* was fed a story by a confidential source in Whitehall. The paper reported that Dr. Irwin's wife had been raped in 1976, and the doctor had harbored a grudge against the RUC ever since for failing to catch the assailant. The details were true but the spin false. Mrs Irwin had been held at gunpoint and raped by someone with an "English" accent; however, Irwin had nothing but praise for the way the RUC handled the case (P. Taylor, 1980: 319–20).

Smears have also been used to discredit those involved in some aspect of the criminal justice process. A month before the murder of Pat Finucane, Douglas

Hogg, an Under-Secretary at the Home Office, following an RUC briefing in Belfast, told the House of Commons: "I have to state as a fact, but with great regret, that there are in Northern Ireland a number of solicitors who are unduly sympathetic to the cause of the IRA" (Hogg, 1989). He did not name anyone. Following the shooting of the three IRA people by the British Army Special Air Service (SAS) in Gibraltar, one of the key witnesses to the shootings was defamed in the press: it was suggested that Carmen Proetta was a local prostitute. She subsequently brought a number of successful libel actions against various newspapers. Another witness retracted a serious allegation concerning one of the SAS soldiers that he had made to the makers of the Thames Television documentary, *Death on the Rock* (Bolton, 1988).

Finally, it is alleged that smears have been used in the turf war in Northern Ireland between MI5 and the Secret Intelligence Service (SIS). It has been suggested that MI5 orchestrated an attack on Maurice Oldfield, who became intelligence coordinator in Northern Ireland in 1979, because it was concerned that some of its power might be lost (Gill, 1994). Anthony Cavendish (1990) later wrote a book defending Oldfield against the "smear" that he had been a practicing homosexual.

What this brief analysis suggests is that the researcher of an alleged state crime is confronted not only with a lack of systematic research, description, and analysis of the topic, but also with the fact that the issue has either been ignored in mainstream criminology or reconstructed as part of some other areas of criminology. This is not accidental. There are powerful forces at work to deny and disguise the nature of state crime.[9]

## A Synopsis of the Stalker/Taylor Affair

In May 1986, John Stalker, Deputy Chief Constable of the Greater Manchester Police (GMP), was removed from heading the Northern Ireland enquiry into the killing of six men. All six men had been killed by members of the RUC's Headquarters Mobile Support Units (HMSUs). A number of politicians, church leaders, and many people in the Nationalist and Republican communities argued that the shootings had all the hallmarks of a shoot-to-kill policy. In response to this widespread concern, the Chief Constable of the RUC, John Hermon, agreed to an enquiry. Stalker began his work in May 1984. In September 1985 he submitted an interim report to the chief constable. His team intended to complete the final report after they had gained access to a number of items of evidence, to which, it was claimed subsequently, they had been denied access. Before the final report was completed, however, Stalker was removed from the enquiry for a number of alleged breaches of the Police Discipline Code.

The government announced that Colin Sampson, Chief Constable of the West

Yorkshire Police, would complete the investigation in Northern Ireland and also investigate the allegations made against Stalker. Sampson began his investigation into Stalker in May 1986. It was supervized by the Right Honourable Roland Moyle, Deputy Chairman of the Police Authority. During the investigation further breaches of discipline were discovered. These included the allegation that as a member of the GMP, Stalker "acted in a manner which is likely to give rise to the impression amongst members of the public that he may not be impartial in the discharge of his duties," and that he made unauthorized use of a police vehicle on a number of occasions (Sampson Report, 1986: z). Sampson completed his report on 6 August 1986 and made the recommendation that "the evidence supports, *indeed demands*, that it be ventilated before an independent Tribunal" (ibid.: 144, italics and underlining in the original). The Greater Manchester Police Authority, however, rejected this recommendation and reinstated Stalker. He subsequently resigned from the force in December 1986.

After intensive investigation of his removal, the British press concluded that Stalker may have been naive, but was innocent of the charges, and had been the subject of a conspiracy at the hands of a number of possible organizations. Those suggested included the Masonic Order in Manchester, a section of the GMP, the RUC, the RUC Special Branch, MI5, MI6, and last, but by no means least, the prime minister herself.[10] The first extended analysis in book form was written by Frank Doherty (1986), a Dublin journalist who, at the time, was the Dublin correspondent for the *Sunday News*. He had followed affairs in Northern Ireland for many years and was extremely well informed about security matters, a subject on which he had written extensively in Irish, British, American, and Australian publications. He argued that Stalker was getting to know too much about the presence of a British security mole in the Irish police, the Garda Siochana, and about the numerous illegal operations by British intelligence and security services in cross-border activities. According to Doherty, Stalker had to be removed before his investigation did irreparable damage to these activities, and MI5 played a key role in Stalker's removal.

The official line, however, has always been that there was no conspiracy, simply a set of events that occurred in parallel. The Chief Constable of the GMP, Sir James Anderton, issued a statement on 1 September 1986 in which he said:

> I wish to make it absolutely clear that there was no conspiracy attached to the case. As far as I am concerned the investigation into John Stalker was justified, necessary and properly conducted. I am also satisfied that all the action was taken in good faith according to the authorised procedures. I did no more, nor less than my duty. (quoted in Davenport, 1986: 3)

Peter Taylor, a highly respected BBC journalist and reporter on Northern Ireland supported this view of events in a *Panorama* program—"Conspiracy or Coincidence?"—which was broadcast within weeks of Stalker's removal. He subsequently wrote a book on the subject stating his position at greater length (P. Taylor, 1987). Crucially, however, he admits that it was not easy to find out what actually happened in the period in which he considered that the seeds of John Stalker's downfall were sown—the period from June 1984 to February 1985. "The main difficulty," he wrote, "has been to tie down the precise nature of the intelligence, the channels through which it came—and whether there has been any corroboration of it, without which Chief Constable James Anderton ought not to have taken such an extraordinary course of action which led to the investigation of the Deputy Chief Constable by his own men." He also emphasized that "The timing of the events is critical" (ibid.: 1987: 136).

Peter Taylor (1987: 123) does not deny that "all the *circumstantial* [italics added] evidence seemed to point to a conspiracy at the hand of MI5." He acknowledges that if there was any conspiracy, there were certainly a number of very good political reasons for it: the revelation of MI5's activities would cause a major political scandal, and the airing of Stalker's findings through the courts would send shock waves through the RUC at the very moment when their morale needed to be preserved in the context of the Anglo-Irish agreement. However, notwithstanding the fact that he never did manage to tie down "the precise nature of the intelligence" or "the channels through which it came" (ibid., 136) in the crucial six-month period, he argues that "there was no conspiracy—at least not involving Northern Ireland" (ibid: 190). Instead he suggests that there were "two largely unconnected chains of events" in the period between May 1984 and May 1986 (ibid.: 128). One set of events involved Stalker running into problems in Northern Ireland. The other set of events took place in Manchester and involved the investigation and prosecution of Kevin Taylor.[11]

Since the publication of the two competing and contradictory positions, three important developments have made it possible to examine again many of the key elements of this "case." The first was the criminal trial of Stalker's friend, Kevin Taylor, in 1989–90. It had been widely rumored that Taylor had been involved in the financing and importation of illegal drugs, though he was not charged with any drug offense. On the contrary, he and three others—Britton, his accountant, Bowley, a Co-operative Bank official, who had granted him loans, and McCann, a quantity surveyor, were all charged with conspiring to defraud the Co-operative Bank of £240,000—a relatively small amount as far as serious fraud cases go. They came to trial in December 1989 but the Crown threw in the towel after the police committed perjury and admitted not knowing what had happened to key documents. The jury on the instructions of the judge acquitted Taylor and his co-defendants. By this stage, Taylor had been declared bankrupt as a result of the police investigation into his affairs, and Bowley had killed a pedestrian while driving to court on the first day of the trial (K. Taylor, 1990: 169).

The second development occurred in 1993 when Kevin Taylor began proceedings against the GMP for malicious prosecution. The civil action began in the High Court in Liverpool in June 1995. After 21 days the authorities offered Taylor a settlement of over £2 million, which he reluctantly accepted because he feared that otherwise his legal aid would be withdrawn. The third development was the signing of the Good Friday/Belfast Agreement[12] in 1998 and the calling of the cease-fires by the IRA and loyalist paramilitaries. The first two developments provided over 1,000 pages of court transcripts and other documents detailing various aspects of the story, while the third development provided the opportunity for people in Northern Ireland to talk more openly about events in the 1980s.

## Researching the Stalker/Taylor Affair

This third and final part of the chapter examines some of the difficulties experienced in attempting to ascertain whether or not Stalker's removal was a conspiracy or simply, as the official version has always suggested, a coincidence of two parallel set of events. Much of the research was based on a detailed analysis of the court transcripts of the criminal action brought against Taylor and his co-defendants in 1989–90 and the civil action by Taylor against the chief constable of the GMP in 1995. Information provided in the transcripts was supplemented by other sources, principally investigative journalists' reports and articles. Some of the more important detail was then filled in through interviews, where possible, with key people. Each source of information presented its own problems.

Court transcripts generally provide a rich resource for the researcher but they are becoming prohibitively expensive for academics to access without a research grant. They provide a verbatim and accurate account of everything which is said in open court and contain references to the numerous statements and exhibits produced by either side. Typically, sections of a particular document are read out in open court and reproduced verbatim in the transcripts. It would greatly enhance this form of research if access was granted to the documents themselves. There is, however, what is known as an "implied undertaking" by both parties in a civil action that the documents may only be used by the recipient for the purpose of the particular proceedings. Any abuse of the implied undertaking is contempt of court which can carry a sentence of imprisonment.

There is a public interest defense to an infringement of the discovery rule. But no individuals can afford the risk of being taken to court to argue that their use of the documents is in the public interest because, for example, it reveals extensive police malpractice and conspiracy at the highest level. They would not only face the risk of imprisonment but also substantial legal costs if they lost the argument. An injunction for contempt of court could be sought by the police or some other organization in the knowledge that while the monetary risks to the individual could be considerable, their own costs would be paid from the public purse—an ironic situation given that the public have the most to gain from knowing the truth. Thus any attempt by an individual researcher to try to argue a public interest defense to breaking the "implied undertaking" rule would be a battle between David and Goliath. Whatever the law's rhetoric about "parity of arms" or "equal before the law," in the context of the investigation of alleged corruption and malpractice the law protects the powerful institutions of the state.

Another problem associated with the civil action brought by Taylor was the widespread use of public interest immunity certificates (PIICs). These are now popularly called "gagging orders" and prevent disclosure of key documents, either because of national security or because of the need to preserve the integrity of criminal justice investigations. The transcripts, therefore, record only part of the story. A detailed classification system was devised and documents were graded with a letter indicating the extent to which they should remain confidential. In some cases documents were considered by the judge, who was then required to exercise a balancing act between the interests of preserving the integrity of the criminal justice system and the interests of either the plaintiff or the defendant in seeking justice. Ironically, in some instances it is clear that both plaintiff and defendant wanted disclosure. The state, however, was opposed on grounds of "national security."

The most blatant use of a PIIC concerned Stalker's evidence. The Northern Ireland Secretary, Sir Patrick Mayhew, signed an order banning him giving evidence relating to his Northern Ireland enquiry. It was maintained that any discussion of the RUC's alleged "shoot-to-kill" policy could affect the peace process.

> It remains very much in the public interest that all terrorist violence be permanently ended and that nothing should be done which would prejudice or impede the efforts of Her Majesty's Government to that end or which would be of assistance to terrorists now or in the future. (Mayhew, quoted in Lashmar, 2001: 1)

As Lashmar (2001: 1), a freelance journalist and TV producer who did more than any other journalist to unearth the truth about the Stalker/Taylor affair, commented: "This is a stunning assertion." He went on to point out that the immunity was clearly in the government's rather than the public's interest.

The extensive use of PIICs, mainly on grounds of national security, took place against the backdrop of the Matrix Churchill scandal, in which PIICs were used to cover up the Department of Trade's issue of export licenses in apparent contravention of government guidelines. Two directors of Matrix Churchill were set up to take the blame and were charged with exporting goods with intent to evade export restrictions. But during the trial the judge ordered the disclosure of the official documents, which were subject to PIICs, and the defense lawyers obtained an admission from the former minister responsible, Alan Clark, that there had been a cover-up (Robertson, 1999). The trial collapsed and Lord Scott was asked to carry out an official inquiry (Scott Report, 1996).

Once a document is read out in open court it is considered to be in the public domain. Few documents, however, are ever read out in full. It is common practice to read the first and the last few words of the relevant pieces of text to identify the relevant passage. As both sides and the judge have copies of the document, it is not necessary to read out the whole section. The only people who do not have access to the documents are members of the public, which, of course, undermines the very notion of justice being open and transparent. However, in both the criminal and the civil proceedings, sufficient elements of some of the key documents were read out at different stages to make it possible to reconstruct a large part of their content.

The criminological literature is replete with descriptions of criminogenic situations. In relation to state crime, the most obvious situations are those in which some group of state servants has acted contrary to the law, or government guidelines as in the Matrix Churchill case, and wishes not to be exposed. In other cases public pressure to produce results may lead to suspects being assaulted or documents being fabricated, as in the Birmingham Six or Guildford Four cases. Following Stalker's removal, the GMP received widespread bad publicity and were under considerable pressure to show the public that there were genuine reasons for pursuing the inquiries into Stalker and his friend Taylor. This, then, was a potentially criminogenic situation and in such a context it is possible that some crucial documents were withheld and, more importantly, some documents may have been fabricated to support the official line that there was no conspiracy.

The issue of the authenticity of the documentation arose most starkly in relation to three key events, which, according to the police, all took place on 11 June 1984. These were the reporting of a conversation on a golf course alleging that Stalker attended parties at which criminals were present; a telephone conversation from an informer to the police reporting that someone had told him that Stalker was "bent"; and the arrival of a boat full of wanted British criminals in Gibraltar. Dates are of crucial importance in the Stalker/Taylor affair. The GMP have always argued that there was no conspiracy because they had important intelligence in early June 1984 that gave rise to genuine suspicions about Stalker's associates which were then subsequently investigated. As Stalker had been appointed to the enquiry only a month earlier, the wider implications of his investigations would not have been apparent at this point. There was, therefore, no conspiracy but simply two parallel sets of unconnected events in Northern Ireland and Greater Manchester. In such a context, the occurrence of three very different events, which all took place on the same day and hundreds of miles apart, does suggest that the researcher should look beyond an astrological explanation of an odd configuration of the position of the planets to a careful scrutiny of the documentation and a search for some corroboration of the events recorded.

Interviews were conducted with a wide range of people, but again a number of problems were encountered. First, there was the problem of access, particularly to the police and other personnel in the security services. A number of the police who had played a central role in some aspect of the Stalker/Taylor affair took early retirement on health grounds and others resigned and moved into other occupations. While this exodus from the GMP is a major story in its own right, it did make it difficult to make contact with the officers. One attempt was made to interview a key police officer by sending a letter to him at police headquarters with a request that it be forwarded. It was forwarded and a reply was received. But although he would have liked to tell his side of the story, he pointed out that he could not cooperate because he was subject to the Official Secrets Act. More direct methods of contacting officers were tried and, in some cases, were successful. One approach, to the immigration service in Gibraltar, had a surprising outcome: the security section of the university was contacted by Customs and Excise, who then contacted the department to ascertain the nature of the research and my position.

The key issue in this type of research is the extraordinarily powerless position, however senior he or she may be, of the academic researcher. An important consideration here is that there are numerous unseen relationships between various elements of both public and private security establishments. Many of the security officers in both sectors are ex-police officers. It is not surprising that Customs and Excise first approached the Security Department in the university rather than the head of my academic department to check out the nature of the research. Notwithstanding the rhetoric about academic independence and support for the quest for the truth, in material terms there are very real barriers to conducting research outside of the conventional boundaries of the discipline.

By contrast, journalists are in a different position. The police and other sectors of the security services need them to disseminate their stories and the press need them for their copy. This explains how they were able to obtain so much detail immediately after Stalker was removed. They had established relationships with the police, developed over many years, and they were able to use their contacts and, of course, the police were only too willing to release confidential information in order to support their line. Peter Taylor, the BBC journalist, appears to have had access in 1986 to much confidential police information about certain criminals and key aspects of the investigation into Kevin Taylor—information which was only revealed publicly during the civil action in 1995. It is not known, of course, if other confidential information was released to him but was then subject to PIICs, never to emerge in the public domain. In any event, the police willingness to provide journalists with confidential information, for whatever reasons, contrasts with the authorities reluctance through the extensive use of PIICs, to allow the same or similar confidential information getting into the public domain for the purposes of justice.

Access to members of the public was much easier and interviews were conducted with a range of people from all walks of life in Manchester and Northern Ireland, including alleged members of the so-called Quality Street Gang[13] in Manchester, and also former members of the Provisional IRA. The people interviewed, however, formed a very small proportion of the total number of people who were connected with the affair in some way and subject to police attention. The GMP in their investigation into Kevin Taylor searched far and wide for information from his relatives, friends, enemies and associates. Anyone who might help them with their inquiries was interviewed. They even checked out the guest lists of four major social events held in Manchester at which Stalker and Taylor were present.

Moreover, they mounted a very long surveillance operation keeping watch on Kevin Taylor's office in the middle of Manchester for 118 days. Taylor has never disguised his passion for gambling and would often gamble during the quieter moments when little was happening in his property development business. Numerous people from all walks of life visited his office for a game. The police, therefore, recorded the movements of a significant cross-section of Manchester during this period. Everyone who entered his office was photographed, and attempts were made to identify them. It is not known how many of the great and the good—and not so good—were investigated by the police, but the number at the four social events alone exceeded a thousand. As a researcher, however, with limited financial resources, it was possible to interview only a very small selection of this number.

The interviews, whether with the police, members of the public or people with some past in political violence or the criminal underworld posed problems of interpretation. Few people associated with the Stalker/Taylor affair were neutral players. Some were on one side or the other in the affair and they wanted to tell their side of the story. Others were on the wrong side of British law and therefore may have had particular reasons for being "economical with the truth." The principal difficulty for any researcher in this context is how to validate what is being said. The difficulty is further compounded by differential power relations. In some situations the academic researcher is in a more powerful position than the interviewee, particularly in terms of how much may be known about a situation, and thus can challenge what is being said. In other interview situations, principally with members of the police, the immigration service and the security service, the interviewee is in a much less-powerful position and it is more difficult to challenge and query what is being said and what is left unsaid. How does a researcher respond to, say, a police officer or immigration official whom the researcher suspects is not telling the truth? How does one read potential clues? Does, for example, an emerging ball of sweat on the brow indicate a lie or simply the heat of the day? Criminologists of the powerful have little or no training in these critical circumstances.

The newspaper coverage of the affair provided a rich source of information to supplement the details from the transcripts and the interviews but this source, too, has its limitations. Murphy (1991), in an excellent but regrettably largely ignored book on the affair, analyses the way the press reported the story and shows how sections of the British press, left, right and center, all expressed the view that John Stalker had been the victim of a cover-up or conspiracy. As an ex-journalist and now as an academic, Murphy provides fascinating detail on how the stories were constructed in the "limbo of state secrets and allegations of conspiracy" (Murphy, 1991: 50) and the constant threat of libel. One consequence for journalists was that sources always had to be "moles," or nameless officials. This, of course, makes it impossible for others—including researchers—to identify or to track down any of these people to re-interview.

The threat of libel is not only a problem for the journalist but also for the researcher of crimes of the powerful. A number of critical criminologists over the years have fallen foul of the laws of libel in their analysis of the behavior of police and prison officers and people working in a range of other state institutions from social work to mental health. Libel law in this context provides powerful protection for those who, at best, may be simply unprofessional or incompetent or, at worst, may be criminal in their behavior. The Police Federation and the Prison Officers' Association have used the libel laws extensively to challenge any adverse criticisms of their members. In relation to the Stalker/Taylor affair, it is known that a number of libel actions have been brought by police officers from Northern Ireland and GMP. With such powerful and litigious organizations lined up against them, the researcher of state crime must tread very carefully.

Every public body, including the secret services, in a democratic society should be open to fair public criticism. The current libel laws make a mockery of this principle as the very secrecy of these bodies makes it almost impossible to prove the truth of the facts which emerge in serious investigations. In *Reynolds v. Times Newspapers*,[14] the Law Lords have recently considered whether there should be restrictions on the right of state servants to sue—and accepted that the media should be free to publish inaccurate information on matters of public interest provided it acts fairly and reasonably and follows professional journalistic standards. The court will take account of such factors as the level of seriousness of the allegations; the type of information; the source; verification attempts; the status of the information; the urgency; whether any attempt to obtain comment from the claimant has been made; whether both sides of the story were included in the publication; the tone of the published material; and the background to, and timing of, the publication (Whitty et al., 2001: 289). Although this ruling is clearly an advance, it relates to journalists who have the support of their powerful organizations. The lone academic has no such support. In addition, the ruling still leaves the academic in difficulty because she or he does not know, prior to any court action, how each of these factors will be interpreted. It is not a situation that is likely to encourage criminologists to explore the murky waters of allegations against state servants.

## Conclusions

In broad terms, a number of conclusions can be drawn about researching this type of alleged state crime. Notwithstanding all the inherent problems, it is possible to research the secret state by using a number of different methods: analyses of official records, such as the documentation which emerges in the course of inquiries and court cases, reviews of journalists' accounts of events, and via interviews with state officials, informers and others associated with some aspect of the case. Academics tend to privilege official documentation as being the most reliable source, but when investigating crimes of the powerful the accounts of informers may be more reliable than the accounts of officials and it is often necessary to reverse assumptions about credibility. Research of this type is a long and time-consuming process but it provides information on the patterns of activities and forms of deception which take place, and the elusive piece of material evidence which will prove categorically that there was a conspiracy may occasionally emerge as a result of carelessness—for example, in forging documents, or through failure to deal with the contradictions which emerge in the official narrative.

Criminologists need to pay more attention to alleged conspiracies in order to build up a substantial body of scholarship. This, however, is unlikely to occur because of numerous structural, cultural, and personal factors. There have long been powerful forces at work to deny and disguise the nature of state crime. British criminology, in particular, has been unable, despite its rapid expansion in recent years, to break loose from its origins as a state-sponsored subject. Its orientation has been sustained by millions of pounds of state-funded research. Over the last few years there has been a revolving door, in part a product of the Research Assessment Exercise (RAE), between the Home Office and universities with academics moving into the Home Office and Home Office staff moving into universities. Moreover, numerous close personal relationships exist between senior civil servants, law enforcement personnel, and academics in high-graded research universities, which have been built up over many years. And underpinning these relationships is an ideological affinity, which not only reproduces notions of "crime" that ignore state crimes, but which also embraces an establishment notion of social order. In such a context, it is not particularly surprising that few criminologists have examined the illegal activities of state officials either in Britain or, perhaps more importantly, in Northern Ireland. Those who have the courage to suggest that some imaginative crime has been carried out by a group of state servants will be informed that it is, in truth, only a crime of the imagination.

# Notes

1. This definition focuses on acts of commission and leaves out acts of omission such as the denial of basic human rights.
2. Milne (1994: 38) has argued that there is not the same tradition among British journalists and there has been a "chronic refusal by the mainstream media in Britain—and most opposition politicians—to probe or question the hidden agendas and unaccountable, secret power structures at the heart of government."
3. There are, of course, a number of important exceptions. See, for example, Croall, 1998, Muncie and McLaughlin, 1996.
4. At the time considerable controversy surrounded the GMP concerning the policing of a student demonstration and subsequent alleged harassment and assault of some of the students involved. See Walker (1986).
5. A book is in preparation and will, it is hoped, be published in 2003.
6. The Sampson Report was leaked to the press. The lack of evidence in the report to support the allegations against Stalker further added to the conspiracy theory. Another police enquiry was set up to investigate who leaked the report. It was the second of six known police enquiries into various aspects of the Stalker/Taylor affair. None of these have been published.
7. Interestingly, research into "ordinary" crime is often speculative, but it is seldom criticized on these grounds.
8. The best known Irish historical example concerns the allegation that Roger Casement's "Black Diaries" were forged by the British Secret Service in order to discredit the man before his trial for treason. Angus Mitchell (2001) is convinced that they are forgeries, while Sawyer (1997) is not. The diaries have recently been subject to a scientific analysis of the hand-writing and found to be genuine (Donnelly, 2002). This, however, is unlikely to be the end of the matter as the tests are not foolproof.
9. For an analysis of the way states deny their criminal activities, see Cohen, 2000.
10. For a Masonic conspiracy, see Wigmore, 1986. For the involvement of MI5, see Wallis, 1986. Prince, a freelance writer for the *Daily Express*, argues that within weeks of setting up the Northern Ireland Inquiry, members of the Special Branch, MI5 and MI6 met in a Liverpool hotel to consider the implications of Stalker's appointment and how he could be framed (see Prince, 1988: 129–37).
11. Stalker himself never used the word conspiracy, yet anyone reading his description of what happened to him would conclude that there was a conspiracy. See Stalker (1988: 263–65).
12. There is no consensus on what the agreement should be called.
13. A *so-called* group of "criminal associates," because there is little or no evidence that any such "gang" existed. Taylor knew some of the alleged "members" from the days when he had worked in the motor trade.
14. [1999] 4 All ER 609 (HL).

# Researching and Redefining State Crime

## *Feminism and the Capital Punishment of Women*

*One of the key ideological functions of the rule of law is to represent the criminal process, and in particular the trial process, as a politically neutral one which generates "objective" determinations of fact and law.* (Lacey et al., 1990: 152)

*The authority to identify "empirical truths" and to interpret observable, testable "facts" is dependent on existing power relations within given social contexts. But as new materials are produced, ideas can be reconstructed in new configurations of "truth" which allow for previously silenced groups to name themselves and to describe their own experiences.* (Faith 1993:9)

Due process, the rule of law, and presumption of innocence form the foundations of the British criminal justice system and play a crucial role in maintaining the legitimacy of the state and its ability to deliver justice. Employing a feminist epistemology and adopting a historical perspective by utilizing case studies about women who were executed during the twentieth century, this chapter argues that the state frequently failed to live up to these rules and procedures which it itself took credit for having established. As such, the state violated the very principles which it claimed to be founded on; hence it is argued that it committed "state crime" against its citizens. In that sense the chapter argues for a redefinition of state crime—an argument which is sustained by employing a feminist epistemology during the research process. Feminist epistemology generally— and standpoint feminism in particular—reject the notion of objectivity, neutrality and value-freedom in the research process and instead emphasize the production of knowledge from "below." In doing this, feminism is able to create a new site on which the voices of the powerless can be heard and thus construct an alternative "truth" about specific trials and executions of women, and about the state's role in those events. In that sense this analytical process also allows feminist epistemology to challenge the social construction of state-defined "truth."

To demonstrate how this may be achieved I shall apply feminist theory, method, and epistemology to state documents concerning women who were executed in England and Wales during the twentieth century. In turn, I shall indicate how this epistemological challenge has implications for definitions of state crime. Moreover, it is appropriate to note that the state documents examined are the original ones available at the time of the trials; the author does not claim to have discovered new evidence since the trials took place. Instead a new analysis of existing evidence is presented—an analysis made possible as a direct result of the utilization of feminist epistemology.

## The Feminist Challenge to Legal Truth Claims

In 1885 the jurist A. V. Dicey outlined what he saw as the three defining elements of the rule of law. First, "the absolute supremacy of law over arbitrary power including wide discretionary powers of government." Second, "every citizen is subject to the ordinary law of the nation administered in the ordinary courts." Third, "rights are based not upon abstract constitutional statements but upon the actual decisions of courts" (quoted in Cotterrell 1984: 168). From these three elements, it follows that the rule of law must be predictable, consistent, egalitarian, and applied with equanimity. Due process, equality before the law, the right to a fair trial, legal representation, presumption of innocence, and "burden of proof beyond all reasonable doubt" are the main discourses which ensure legitimacy for the criminal justice system, together with the ideology of neutrality, objectivity, and fairness, symbolized by the blindfolded Justicia (Lacey et al. 1990: 147).

Law claims to be based on rationality and objectivity, with its legal procedures and methods guaranteed to result in the correct interpretation—"or even a direct access to the truth which avoids the problem of human interpretation" (Smart,

1995:74). Legal procedures thus successfully disguise the mediation of defendants' own accounts of the crime of which they stand accused. By contrast, lay-persons' commonsense knowledge, biographical claims, and experiential truth claims are easily undermined by experts' version of events—which ironically—came about as a result of applying legal formulation to lay-persons' accounts in the first place. In sifting through original accounts, legal representatives decide which aspects are relevant and which should be ignored, a process which serves to disqualify, limit, and silence the defendant's version of the truth (Smart, 1995: 74; Worrall, 1990: 20–21). In the words of Smart,

> the legal process translates everyday experiences into legal relevances, it excludes a great deal that might be relevant to the parties, and it makes its judgements on the scripted or tailored account . . . parties are not always silenced, but . . . how they are allowed to speak, and how their experience is turned into something the law can digest and process, is a demonstration of the power of law to disqualify alternative accounts. (Smart, 1989: 11)

Smart subsequently developed her challenge to law's truth claims into a gendered critique, and following this and other early works which identified androcentrism and sexism within established research (Stanley and Wise, 1983), several important works have been produced, designed to justify the use of feminist methods and methodologies which in turn are tied to epistemological and ontological issues. The work of Maureen Cain provides an important example. In order to establish what is *not* feminist method, methodology, and epistemology, Cain refers to Hartsock's traditional "straw-man" researcher who is concerned with establishing himself as a "scientific expert" and strives to achieve and maintain the most highly prized goals and values within the knowledge-seeking scientific community: neutrality, objectivity, dispassion, and value-freedom. These aims are justified on the grounds that research must be separated and protected from the political interests of society and the social values of researchers (Harding, 1987: 182).

Such aims stand in sharp contrast to those of the feminist researcher. Feminism is an overtly political movement which exists to generate social change, and feminist researchers openly proclaim our political and social interests. Yet this highly politicized form of inquiry claims to produce better quality research precisely because the values held by the researcher are acknowledged. There is no attempt or desire to strive for so-called objective and neutral knowledge—instead, knowledge arises from the deliberate and direct engagement with feminist politics and values (Smart, 1990: 80).

These features ensure that the feminist standpoint is particularly well suited to giving voice to the oppressed—it is a method of creating knowledge from "below," and thus establishing an alternative truth to that expounded by those in authority. In particular, Cain has outlined how such a "transgressive criminology" can be achieved through a three-stage strategy—deconstruction, reconstruction, and re-flexivity (Cain, 1990b: 6). First we deconstruct the official, state-defined "truth"; second we reconstruct our own "truth." Lastly, we "reflect," that is, theorize about the difference between the state-defined truth and our alternative truth generated by feminist epistemology. Thus, "theoretical reflexivity" forms a crucial part of the process of identifying a standpoint and producing feminist knowledge.

Even after taking all of the above into account, standpoint feminists still ac-knowledge that the knowledge produced will be influenced by the "relational and historical site in the social world" which the researcher occupies—hence research will always be a socially constructed product. This is unavoidable and applies to all forms of research whether in natural science or social science. As "the presence of the researcher as an ordinary human being with the usual complement of human attributes, cannot be avoided" it is better to devise a research method which utilizes this presence, than to pretend it does not exist (Stanley and Wise, 1983: 150). Thus, standpoint feminism is particularly well suited to make the researcher's conscious-ness explicit; moreover, it is precisely this feature which ensures the production of more accurate and hence better quality knowledge.

Stanley and Wise note that "it is around the constitution of feminist epistemol-ogy that feminism can most directly and far-reachingly challenge non-feminist frameworks and ways of working" (1993: 189). In particular, standpoint feminists can "evade dominant knowledges" and "generate new knowledges from repressed common senses" (Cain, 1990b: 134–35). For the purposes of this chapter, this ana-lytical process allows feminist epistemology to challenge the social construction of state-defined "truth," thereby producing an alternative truth which challenges the state's claim to deliver justice for all. In the following section I apply feminist standpoint epistemology to statistics concerning capital punishment in the twenti-eth century before moving on to an analysis of specific casestudies in the remainder of the chapter.

## Official Statistics and Capital Punishment

In order to continue my demonstration of why feminists object so strongly to "ob-jective" research I shall apply Cain's prescription "deconstruct, reconstruct and re-flect" to statistics concerning executed women during the twentieth century. Between 1900 and 1950, 130 women were sentenced to death in England and Wales, yet only 12 were executed. Therefore 91% were reprieved. Examining the corresponding figures for men during that period, 1,080 were sentenced to death, 621 of whom were executed. Thus, only 39% of men had their sentences com-muted—a substantially lower figure than that for women. According to the *Royal Commission on Capital Punishment 1949–1953 Report,* such statistics demonstrated a "'natural reluctance' to carry out the death sentence on a woman" (RCCP, 1953: 12). In other words, this is evidence of the "chivalry" that women supposedly benefit from, which ensures they are treated more leniently than men by the criminal justice system (Pollak, 1950).

The application of feminist epistemology to such statistics offers a strong challenge to this official discourse. Deconstructing the statistics according to the *type* of murder committed, we find that 102 of the 130 women had killed a child, nearly always their own, most of them under one year old. This type of crime inevitably resulted in a reprieve, even before the introduction of the Infanticide Act in 1922.[1] Moving on to *reconstruct* these statistics, we discover that when a woman killed an *adult,* she was *more* likely to be executed than a man found guilty of a similar crime. The large proportion of female murderers who killed their own children therefore created a false impression about other women's treatment by the criminal justice system. In short, differences between women were ignored.

Following Cain's third step in her prescription for a transgressive criminology and feminist epistemology, we need to reflect on what this deconstruction and reconstruction means theoretically. During the previous three decades feminist theorists have carried out substantial research projects in all the major areas of the criminal justice system. This research has repeatedly demonstrated the centrality and importance of women's conduct and behavior within our culture, and the particular consequences of this for criminal women and their punishment (Heidensohn, 1986; Carlen, 1985; Jones, 1991). Women who transgress patriarchal definitions of acceptable and appropriate femininity are regarded as dangerous and unruly. In particular, the discourses around sexuality, domesticity, respectability, and motherhood have been shown to play an important role in the final outcome of criminal women's punishment. I have documented the importance of these discourses in relation to executed women elsewhere (Ballinger, 2000). It will suffice, therefore, to reiterate that the mere fact a woman has broken the law ensures her identification as deviant and unruly, someone who has transgressed acceptable female conduct. If her crime takes the form of extreme violence and murder against another adult, that transgression is magnified many times over. If that violence is overlaid by a lack of commitment to appropriate gender role conduct—especially in the areas of sexuality, respectability, domesticity, and motherhood—her status as unruly becomes maximized—symbolizing dangerous womanhood posing a threat to the social order.

The above analysis is an example of how a reflexive feminist epistemology can theorize its findings. Unlike "objective" statistics such as those provided by the *Royal Commission for Capital Punishment,* a feminist epistemology problematizes gender, whereas a simple measuring of women against men leaves the subject under discussion—in this case punishment—unanalyzed. Moreover, this form of comparison cannot be trusted as an indicator that *men* receive justice within the criminal justice system, because it accepts the number and nature of male executions as unproblematic—the norm from which women's punishment can be measured (Cain, 1990b: 2–3). In other words, this feminist deconstruction is an example of how "objective" research and "hard facts"—that is statistics—"are androcentric in their premise" (Cain 1990b:2). In turn, this explains why traditional epistemology has little or no theoretical value—its gender-blindness ensures it cannot analyze its own data. Instead it simply asks "how are women different to men?" In contrast, feminist epistemology asks "who are women?" To answer this, it is necessary to develop "women only" studies:

> Studying women as women, and comparing different groups of women, rather than women and men, takes off the blinkers of the male-as-yardstick and male common sense, so that *new* thoughts can come into the social and criminological worlds. (Cain 1990b: 9)

After all, it seems inconceivable that issues such as sexual harassment and domestic violence could have entered discourse without "women only" studies. This does not mean a descent into essentialism; on the contrary, the social construction of both genders only ever takes place in *relation* to each other. Herein lies the key difference between traditional and feminist epistemology—the latter would also support the study of masculinity but in relation to the social construction of gender, rather than simply measuring how men and women differ.

So already feminist epistemology has demonstrated its ability to challenge a state-defined truth about executed women in the twentieth century, as well as the ability to construct its own alternative truth: that statistics about such executions do *not* indicate greater leniency in women's punishment compared to men's; rather what is at issue is the *type of woman* the offender is: has she conducted herself appropriately, according to dominant discourses around femininity, or was she unruly and devious, representing dangerous womanhood?

The *type of crime* is also important—did she commit the feminine crime of infanticide or did she kill in cold blood and/or for personal gain? In other words, the threat she poses to the social order is reflected in the severity of her punishment. Already therefore, state allocation of punishment appears to be closely connected to issues around gender conduct with potential implications for due process and the rule of law. And already we can begin to observe the processes involved in creating a new site for generating new gender-specific knowledge. I shall now demonstrate how these processes operated in relation to individual cases of executed women.

### The Case of Louise Masset

Closely related to the discourses surrounding female conduct and behavior is law's construction of the "natural" woman who possesses a maternal instinct, longs to have children, and actively embraces the role of carer within the domestic setting.

She is emotional, irrational, and passive by nature in contrast to the natural male who is rational, objective, and active. Because of law's alignment to scientific discourses it speaks the voice of reason and rationality; hence its construction of femininity becomes self-evident—it is *obvious* what a woman is:

> No matter how you may dispute and argue, you cannot alter the fact that women are quite different from men. The principal task in the life of women is to bear and rear children. . . . He is physically the stronger and she the weaker. He is temperamentally the more aggressive and she the more submissive. It is he who takes the initiative and she who responds. These diversities of function and temperament lead to differences of outlook which cannot be ignored. . . . (Lord Denning quoted in Smart, 1995: 83)

Implicit in the construction of the self-evidently natural woman is the construction of the "unnatural woman"—the characteristics of deviant and unruly femininity become equally obvious. Thus, far from being blind, the criminal justice system takes a great deal of notice of such constructions as I shall now demonstrate in relation to the case of Louise Masset, who was executed in 1900 after being found guilty of murdering her four-year-old son, Manfred. His body had been found in the women's toilet at Dalston Junction on the afternoon of 27 October—a time when Louise claimed to be on a train to Brighton.

The state defined the truth about Louise as cut-and-dried—she had killed her illegitimate son in cold blood because he was a hindrance to her relationship with her lover who was 17 years her junior. The murder had involved "premeditation and cruelty . . . far beyond the usual features in the ordinary cases of the murder of illegitimate children" (HO144/1540/A61535 Judge's Notes):

> Surely no more cruel or *unnatural* crime could have been conceived and perpetrated. The weight of circumstances forcibly compels us to regard her as a most wicked and calculating woman who, for selfish purposes, coldly planned this murder. . . . For a crime so shocking little or nothing can be pleaded in extenuation. (*Daily Telegraph* 19 December 1899; my emphasis)

A rather more complex analysis is arrived at when applying a feminist epistemology to Louise's case. There was no direct evidence against her and the circumstantial evidence available was highly problematic, contradictory, and inconclusive. For example, inaccuracies and serious doubts emerged about the validity of key pieces of evidence during the trial. Similarly, the testimony of witnesses who had initially identified Louise later proved to be inconclusive. Moreover, Louise's alibi was never fully investigated, nor was the prosecution ever able to establish a motive for Manfred's murder (Ballinger, 2000: 103–28).

However, there was plenty of evidence of the *type* of woman Louise was. She had failed to adhere to the rules of appropriate feminine conduct in relation to every one of the discourses discussed above: respectability, sexuality, motherhood, and domesticity. In what was still the Victorian era she was the mother of an illegitimate child, she was financially independent due to her career as a tutor, and she had taken the initiative in establishing a relationship with her 19-year-old lover despite being 36 years old herself. In every aspect of her conduct Louise therefore challenged the legal construction of a natural woman and appropriate femininity and instead represented dangerous woman/motherhood.

Precisely because of her unconventional lifestyle, Manfred presented no obstacle to Louise. Her financial independence allowed her to employ a nanny to look after her son while she went about her business, both professionally and privately. However, due to the law's inability to see beyond its own construction of femininity, repeated attempts were made to construct a motive based on that construction—for example, that Louise saw Manfred as a obstacle to marriage. Thus, both she and Eudore—her lover—were repeatedly pressed on the subject of marriage, Eudore no less than five times in the space of nine handwritten pages of testimony. When he insisted that Manfred was not an obstacle "in connection with the fact I was making love to her" (CRIM1/58/5) and that neither he nor Louise had considered marriage, the trial judge found it inconceivable that illegitimacy could be treated with such indifference, and concluded—without supporting evidence—that neither Louise nor Eudore had told the truth (HO144/1540/A61535).

On each occasion when Louise (and Eudore) attempted to tell an alternative truth about their domestic arrangements, the state—represented by the prosecution and the judge—reasserted the dominant state-defined truth—illegitimacy is wrong and the only appropriate conclusion to an intimate relationship is marriage. In challenging this "self-evident truth" Louise merely reinforced her image as deviant and unruly—she was now also a liar. Judge Fordham commented that "Miss Masset's word goes for nothing. The jury did not believe her. Nobody believes her" (*The Daily Chronicle* 4 January 1900).

Already therefore, Louise's failure to comply with dominant discourses around respectability, sexuality, motherhood, and marriage was interfering with the "objectivity" of the courtroom and hence had implications for the delivery of a fair trial. However, due process and the rule of law were to be breached in a far more direct manner when her *defense* barrister, Lord Coleridge, wrote to the Home Secretary *after* the trial:

> I see that a movement is on foot for a reprieve in this case, and as I was Counsel for the accused, I think I ought to communicate the fact that the prisoner had reason to think that she was abandoned by the father of the child + I believe she did think so. This state of things naturally I suppressed, as to disclose it would have been to supply a motive for the crime, + I argued that no sufficient motive was disclosed by the prosecution. I think that you should know this, before arriving at a final decision in the case. (HO144/1540/A61535)

The Home Office staff could not have wished for a more useful piece of information. Operating from preconceived ideas about women's "nature" they accepted uncritically that a woman abandoned by her child's father provided a motive for killing that child, despite the fact that it was known to the court that Louise was financially independent, had not seen Manfred's father in 18 months, and had been embroiled in a relationship with Eudore until the day of her arrest.

Whether Lord Coleridge, despite having been paid to act in Louise's interests, was incapable of separating himself from this case of severe judicial misogyny and therefore believed she ought to hang, or whether he acted from good intentions, assuming the Home Secretary would take a more lenient view of her case because of the supposed disappointment and hardship she had suffered, must remain an open question. Either way, the Home Office response was swift and to the point:

> This letter supplies the missing link of motive. . . . I fear that Lord Coleridge's letter while tending to clinch the prisoner's guilt by supplying the motive does not go further in favour of the prisoner. . . . (HO144/1540/A61535)

A second Home Office memo indicates that Coleridge's letter not only provided a motive for the murder, but also did irreparable harm to the credibility of the petition submitted on Louise's behalf:

> Lord Coleridge's letter seems to destroy any possible weight the solicitor's petition might possibly have had beforehand. (HO144/1540/A61535)

If the Home Secretary had any reservations about taking responsibility for Louise's execution, her *defense* counsel had laid them to rest.

In applying feminist epistemology to this evidence we find that due process and the rule of law were compromised at several levels. First, phallocentric assumptions about women's nature were presented as *evidence* of the defendant's guilt: that an unmarried mother *must* be ashamed of her illegitimate child; that a woman engaged in a sexual relationship *automatically* desires marriage; that the abandonment of a child's father provides its mother with a motive for killing her child. In other words, assumption and evidence became interchangeable.

Second, due to the alignment of legal discourses with scientific discourses as well as the gender-blindness which engulfs both, this interchangability was neither analyzed nor challenged, but instead was immediately accepted as *the* correct explanation, despite all the evidence to the contrary. As Smart commented in relation to Lord Denning's statement above, "[a]lternative accounts can hardly compete with such powerful and . . . commonsensical discursive statements" (Smart, 1995: 83).

Third, such phallocentric assumptions about women's nature would appear to have legitimized a blatant disregard for due process and the rule of law by allowing evidence not heard by the jury to be taken into consideration *after* the trial had been concluded. As is apparent from the quotations given above, Lord Coleridge's letter "clinched" the decision to let the execution go ahead.

Fourth, speculations and phallocentric assumptions about female behavior and desires in relation to motherhood, marriage, and illegitimacy are neither scientific nor objective or value-free. They are examples of masculine subjectivity, created from sexist ideology, which serve the interests of existing power relations through the state and ultimately help to maintain the social order.

Finally, as indicated above, women who kill their own children are usually reprieved, and if Louise really had been abandoned by Manfred's father we might assume this would be a mitigating circumstance, strengthening the case for a reprieve. Only a feminist epistemology can explain why her abandonment had exactly the opposite effect and strengthened the case for her execution. That is to say, Louise's punishment reflected not only the crime for which she stood accused, but also her numerous transgressions of acceptable female conduct within the areas of sexuality, respectability, motherhood, and domesticity. Whilst the criminal justice system reserved the right to judge her according to natural womanhood, it also placed her firmly within the discourse of unnatural mother. To do otherwise would pose a severe threat to the social order:

> What is . . . apparent is the extent to which marriage as a formal legal status, locates women inside or outside certain categories of dangerousness. The unmarried mother was the most dangerous of all, not only to her infant but also to the social order. (Smart, 1992: 24).

Rather than complying with the ideal image of woman as dependent, subordinate, passive and respectable, Louise was single, independent, sexually active, an unmarried mother who took pride in her illegitimate child. That Louise's truth about her life could not be heard—even by her own defense counsel—is a testimony to the success of the legal process's translation of everyday experiences into legal (ir)relevances, excluding much that might be relevant to the defendant, and "a demonstration of the power of law to disqualify alternative accounts" as discussed above. In applying the feminist standpoint to this case we are now able to theorize and problematize the very same data which passed through the criminal justice system as unproblematic a century ago. We are able to analyze the consequences for women's punishment when the means available to articulate their experiences is made *for* them and not *by* them; when the voice of those experiences is deprived of authority and instead women are made to live inside a discourse presented as "universal," "objective," and self-evidently "true." In a world where phallocentric beliefs about women are presented as scientific fact, such "objective," "value-free" data may tip the balance between life and death in terms of women's punishment.

### The Case of Ruth Ellis

From the point of view of the state, the case of Ruth Ellis was noteworthy mainly for its "stark simplicity" (DPP2/2430). The "facts" spoke for themselves. Ruth, a single-parent divorcee and working-class nightclub "hostess" had gunned down her upper-middle-class playboy lover in cold blood in an unprovoked attack in front of witnesses. As far as the Crown was concerned there were no mitigating circumstances. Ruth had played the part of the cool, rational, lethal, and jealous *femme fatale:*

> . . . she was having simultaneous love affairs with two men, one of whom was the deceased and the other man called Cussen . . . It would seem that Blakely . . . was trying to break off the connection. It would seem the accused woman was angry at the thought that he should leave her . . . although she had another lover at the time. She therefore took a gun which she knew to be fully loaded which she put in her bag. She says in a statement. . . : "When I put the gun in my bag I intended to find David and shoot him." She found David and she shot him then by emptying that revolver at him. . . . Members of the Jury, there in its *stark simplicity* is the case for the Crown, and whatever be the background and whatever may have been in her mind up to the time when she took that gun, if you have no doubt that she took the gun with the sole purpose of finding and shooting David Blakely and that she then shot him dead . . . the only verdict is wilful murder. (DPP2/2430; my emphasis)

When standpoint feminism is applied to this state-defined truth about Ruth Ellis we are overwhelmed with evidence of an alternative truth. The case has become a chilling example of the level of abuse, violence, exploitation, humiliation, and double standards tolerated against women in a world without feminist discourses. For example, there was plenty of trial evidence of David's violence:

> What did he do to you?
> *He used to hit me.*
> "David got very, very violent" and punched her in the stomach, an act which was "followed by a miscarriage."

> Have you ever seen any marks or bruises on her?
> *Yes.*
> How often?
> *On several occasions.*
>
> . . .
>
> Did you on one occasion take her to Middlesex Hospital?
> *Yes, I did.*
> Why was that?
> *She had . . . been very badly bruised all over the body.*
> And did she receive treatment for that condition at Middlesex Hospital?
> *Yes.* (DPP2/2430; Ballinger, 2000: 307–8)

There was also plenty of evidence of David's unfaithfulness, including one period when he was involved in three relationships simultaneously (Ballinger, 2000: 308–9). There was yet more evidence of what this combination of unfaithfulness, violence, and a resultant miscarriage was doing to Ruth's state of mind, for she had been receiving psychiatric treatment in the three months leading up to the shooting and was still being treated for "intense emotional distress" at the time of the shooting (Marks and Van den Bergh, 1990: 157).

Thus, the two most common causes of provocation—unfaithfulness and violence—were present in abundance in this case, yet carried no weight within the phallocentric courtroom. Even at the very end of the twentieth century women were not considered to have the same right to be provoked by their partners' unfaithfulness as men who found themselves in that situation (McNeill, 1996).[2] In 1955, however, the gendered nature of provocation had not even entered official discourse and phallocentric reasoning could pass through the courtroom virtually without challenge. Thus, Ruth's defense counsel demonstrated awareness of the difficulties facing him in having a defense of provocation accepted in this case of a *woman* defendant:

> We are all very, very familiar with . . . the degree of provocation which is required so far as a man is concerned . . . one finds . . . complete silence in the authorities as to the effect of jealous conduct on the average female's mind . . . . (DPP2/2430)

He also attempted to move away from phallocentric definitions of provocation—that the act took place in the "heat" of the moment, that there had been no "cooling off" period before the crime, that the crime was a knee-jerk reaction to extreme provocation such as adultery—and instead attempted to introduce the notion of cumulative provocation:

> Repeatedly during the time that she was in this state of emotional tension about him he went off and consorted with other women; marks upon his body which indicated a love affair with another woman were observed by her from time to time while he received financial support, clothes, food, and other advantages from her. (DPP2/2430)

Within this context, "provocation derived from jealousy . . . [and] emotional pressure . . . had caused her immense suffering over a long period of time." However, within the phallocentric hegemony of the 1950s, the term "provocation" was not only ungendered, it was also unproblematic; indeed the judge appeared to define the concept in factual "scientific" terms:

> The whole doctrine relating to provocation depends on the fact that it causes or may cause a sudden and temporary loss of self-control. (DPP2/2430)

In a world where neither "domestic violence" nor "double standards of morality" had yet entered official discourse in the epistemological sense we recognize today, it was an easy task for court personnel to maintain the phallocentric nature of legal procedures within the courtroom by undermining Ruth's defense (and evidence)—"excluding a great deal that might be relevant" as noted above—and disqualify alternative accounts, thus preserving the state's self-evident truth, that the main feature of this case was its "stark simplicity."

Central to this incontestable scientific "truth," was the emphasis the law places on the *type* of woman standing in the dock. Ruth had showed consistent disregard for appropriate feminine conduct in all the areas discussed earlier; she was a woman with "a reputation"—a single parent, a divorcee, a prostitute, and a drinker who engaged in relationships outside marriage—someone who was described as a "brassy . . . blonde tart" (Ballinger, 2000: 311). In short, a most "unnatural" woman. As a lower-class, immoral, deviant woman she was never considered entitled to be protected from moral scrutiny as David's other lovers had been, for even though Ruth was standing trial for her life, the defense counsel considered it more important to protect the identities of his other lovers who shared the social background of David and the court personnel (Ballinger, 2000: 309). Moreover, despite David's violence and because of the "double standard of morality" (Smart and Smart, 1978: 4–5), his victim status remained intact while Ruth's remained muted. Even when acknowledged, David's violence was never problematized because Ruth was the kind of woman who had "asked for it."

The creation of the discourses of "domestic violence" and "double standards of morality" as well as the scale and quality of new knowledge this creation has generated, remain two of feminist epistemology's greatest achievements. In 1955 Ruth had to articulate her experience of domestic violence through male discourses of this act. For example, "he *only* used to hit me with his fists and hands" and "I bruise very easily" (DPP2/2430; my emphasis). It is inconceivable that a case similar to Ruth Ellis's could take place today without the defendant being identified as a victim of domestic violence, or without vociferous resistance from feminist writers and activists. As such, the Ellis case reminds us of the level of success already achieved by feminist epistemology.

However, as in Louise Masset's case, it was not only dominant discourses around femininity and the law's construction of the natural woman which influenced the final outcome of Ruth's trial. Equally seriously, the criminal justice system breached the principles of due process, the rule of law, and the right to a fair trial by failing to act when new evidence was uncovered. Thus, 24 hours before the execution, police officers were made aware that far from this being an "open and shut" case, there was evidence that Ruth had an accomplice—Desmond Cussen—whose love for her provided the motive for his involvement. The day before her execution Ruth was persuaded by her solicitor, Mr. Mishcon, to elaborate on events leading up to the shooting. Consequently the police now became aware that Desmond had provided the murder weapon as well as lessons in how to use it. After a protracted drinking session together, Desmond gave Ruth the loaded gun and drove her to the murder scene (Ballinger, 2000: 320). Yet, such was the unwillingness to challenge the dominant truth that this was an "open and shut" case that no serious effort was made to act upon this latest evidence. The Home Secretary's claim that inquiries into Cussen's involvement had been "considerable" was challenged by journalists:

[A]t 4.30 on the day before the execution two detectives . . . were detailed to investigate Mr. X. The two detectives missed their quarry at his office by a narrow margin—he had left 20 minutes before they arrived. They rushed to his home—to find that he had been seen leaving with two suitcases. The detectives maintained their vigil until what they call "late in the evening," when they were instructed to withdraw by a Deputy Commander at Scotland Yard. Ruth Ellis was hanged the next morning. (*Sunday People*, 9 December, 1973)

Ruth's previous solicitor, John Bickford, to whom Cussen had confessed his part in the crime, added:

The Home Office did not contact me. The police did not come near me. Yet I possessed the evidence they were seeking. . . . I could have given the facts that would have saved Ruth Ellis. (*Sunday People*, 9 December, 1973)

This refusal to carry out a full and proper investigation into David Blakely's murder provides a clear demonstration of the state's power to construct and *maintain* a dominant truth, despite firm evidence of the existence of an alternative truth. Indeed the Home Secretary appeared acutely aware of the potential power of this alternative truth when he stated: "If she isn't hanged tomorrow, she never will be" (G. Lloyd George, quoted in Goodman and Pringle, 1974: 73). He further noted that "if a reprieve is granted in this case we should seriously have to consider whether capital punishment should be retained as a penalty." Thus, Lloyd George's political commitment to the retention of capital punishment conflicted with his belief that a reprieve for Ruth would cast the entire future of the death penalty into doubt. As was later observed:

The case for a reprieve was meant to be assessed on the facts of the case, but Lloyd George undermined the impartiality of this procedure with his political conviction that this hanging should happen. (Ruth Ellis: A Life for a Life BBC 1, 28 November, 1999)

In that sense the Ellis case provides a further challenge to the law's claim to objectivity, and the neutral, scientific interpretation of the "facts." Moreover, the case demonstrates how the law—like other state institutions—was deeply influenced by the specific social and moral climate of the 1950s. Within the context of an era stifled by snobbery and respectability and where increased surveillance and regulation of women was believed to be a key strategy in stemming the rising tide of moral decay, her *defense* QC called her story "sordid," and appeared more concerned with "unnecessary mudslinging" than with providing her with an adequate defense (Ballinger, 2000: 311). Once again, therefore, feminist epistemology has demonstrated that far from being the end product of due process and scientific rationality, women's punishment is intrinsically linked to dominant discourses around appropriate feminine conduct at specific historical moments.

## The Case of Ada Williams

Of the 15 women executed during the twentieth century, five went through double trials with their male partners. In three of these cases the couple were carers who stood trial for killing their charges, and in every one of them the men walked free, while their partners were executed. The focus on the women's character and reputation became particularly noticeable in these cases,[3] and the final trial outcomes did not come about as a result of juries finding the three men innocent, but as a result of a lack of evidence against them. Yet the evidence against both defendants was purely circumstantial in nature, hence the fact that the women were found guilty had more to do with preconceived ideas about their role as carers than actual evidence against them, as I shall now demonstrate.

Space does not permit an examination of all three cases. I shall therefore focus on the case of Ada and William Williams, a married couple who stood trial in 1900 for the murder of a toddler they had obtained through their activities as babyfarmers.

After the trial the Home Office personnel, whose task it was to consider a reprieve, showed extensive awareness of the fact that—despite the verdict—there was no proof Ada, rather than William, had carried out the murder; indeed they even suggested William had played the leading role in the crime:

> I am in doubt whether the hands were those of the husband or of the wife, and I confess it seems to me the more closely I examine the exhibits . . . *that the work is more probably that of the man than of the woman.*

> Can it be fairly said that it is more than a *probability* that this is the true explanation; and would it be safe to hang the woman when *we are absolutely in the dark* as to whether it was her hand that actually committed the murder, and when possibly at the last minute the husband might come forward and say "I did it" and it would be impossible to prove that he was not speaking the truth.

> It is difficult to believe that this was done by the prisoner unaided and alone. Taken in connection with their previous history it appears to me that there is a very grave case of suspicion . . . that the husband as well as the wife was concerned in this wicked work. Then there is the evidence connecting him with the murder. He makes the arrangement to revive the letters [responses to Ada's babyfarming advert] . . . and calls for them. He is present when the arrangements for the rooms . . . is made [where the victim's mother handed her over]. He is "about daily" at . . . [the Williams home]. . . . On the whole, except the instance of his interference when the woman was beating the child, there seems very little to distinguish between the two cases. The jury might in my opinion have nearly as much justification for drawing an unfavourable view in his case as in his wife's. (HO144/280/A61654; my emphasis)

Why, despite such obvious and clearly articulated doubts by those speaking on behalf of the state, was Ada executed while William was freed? A feminist epistemology reveals that within a phallocentric courtroom which cannot see gender, assumptions about Ada's character and conduct in relation to discourses of motherhood took the place of evidence against her, and crucially, this was not *problematized* due to "male occupancy of authoritative sites of discursive enunciation" (Cain, 1990b: 5). Thus, babyfarming was a despised activity because it illuminated the contradictions between the dominant image of idealized "natural" motherhood, and the reality of motherhood for those whose circumstances did not fit this image. Those with the authority to define the dominant truth ignored the fact that this activity could only exist within a culture that stigmatized illegitimate children and denied single mothers access to the means to support themselves. Instead, drawing on dominant discourses around motherhood, they focused on the "unnatural" behavior of women who took money for what they should give for free and by "instinct" (Smart, 1995: 227). Discourses around motherhood therefore ensured that while it was officially recognized the couple had played identical or equal parts in the crime—and that it might even have been William who committed the actual murder—Ada's behavior was nevertheless constructed as "worse" since she had also committed transgressions against the "natural" woman and her maternal instinct. Unlike William, Ada was on trial not only for murder, but also as a mother. Moreover, because of the strong tradition of associating both childcare and babyfarming with women, it *must* have been Ada who cared for the child and therefore also committed the murder. To emphasize this point, and despite the Home Office's recognition of evidence to the contrary[4] she was constructed as the dominant partner within the marriage, transgressing yet more discourses around feminine conduct:

> [I]t would appear that the woman is hot-tempered, violent and hysterical; the man meek and small and so the *probabilities* are in favour of the murder having been committed by the woman, while the tying of knots etc were *probably* done by the man. (HO144/280/A61654; my emphasis)

Probabilities are of course not evidence, yet discourses surrounding the "bad" mother and the unruly and manipulative wife became so dominant (yet invisible) that the fact there was not a shred of evidence suggesting Ada had been the dominant—or even an equal—partner in the crime could be ignored. Ultimately, therefore these discourses filled the void left by lack of evidence and allowed a conclusion "that the woman actually committed the murder and the man disposed or helped to dispose of the body" (HO144/280/A61654). That this verdict could be reached, despite the fact that even the prosecution could not differentiate between Ada's and William's involvement in the murder. The Home Secretary readily admitted that ". . . it is quite possible and even *probable* that the husband was jointly and equally guilty . . ." (HO144/280/A61654; my emphasis)—is a testimony to the power of ideologies around women's conduct and behavior generally as well as to the discourses around the "unruly" and "unnatural" woman within the courtroom in particular. Yet, this verdict was not problematized prior to the application of feminist epistemology. As in the Ellis case, applying standpoint feminism to the Williams case demonstrates that ideological beliefs—not scientific fact or due process—played a decisive role in the outcome of a capital trial.

## Conclusion

What do the cases examined in this chapter mean for the development of a critical research agenda concerning capital punishment? Several important elements can be identified. First, Maureen Cain's three-step plan for a transgressive criminology has been implicit throughout—evident in every one of the processes involved in researching the state. That is to say, initially, state-defined truths about women who were executed in the twentieth century were deconstructed to demonstrate the complexities which lie beneath so-called facts and statistics. Following this process, the application of standpoint feminism allowed a reconstruction of these cases: the formulation of an alternative truth which emphasized knowledge from "below," accounts which seek to understand events as experienced by the defendants themselves.

I then reflected upon the new knowledge and discourses generated by this re/-de-construction, by analyzing how they can add to our theoretical understanding of state power. This chapter has therefore not presented new evidence about the cases under examination; all the evidence analyzed here was available at the time of the trials. What *is* new, however, is the analysis of that evidence which has been generated solely as a result of feminist epistemology. Traditional researchers striving for objective data and value neutrality could not challenge, theorize, or even uncover the androcentric discourses documented here, because this process requires a political commitment to share the site of the researched and to generate knowledge from below which can be utilized to challenge the dominant truth generated by the powerful—in this case the state.

In sharp contrast, standpoint feminism is able to respond to traditional researchers on *their* terms and terrain by presenting statistics and "hard facts" in support of critical feminist theory. Thus, when analyzing the 15 women executed during the twentieth century, the following statistics apply:

> five had been prostitutes at some point in their lives; two had abortions; seven had illegitimate children; six had affairs while still married; five had lived with men who were not their husbands; six had children who were in care or otherwise not living with them; three had separated from their husbands when divorce was still extremely rare; five had affairs/relationships with men several years their junior; six were described as promiscuous or over-sexed; seven had previous criminal records (two more would have had records if their abortions had been discovered); four were repeatedly described as heavy

drinkers or alcoholics. Numbers in each category may have been higher since much of the data are unavailable. Thirteen of the 15 women had committed between two and seven of the above transgressions. One had committed all but one of them. (Ballinger, 2000: 329–30)

The full importance of these statistics however, only become apparent when we understand their *theoretical* roots—the social construction of femininity, the law's construction of the natural woman, the discourses mobilized around deviant women—and the differential punishment which flows from these roots.

This leads to a second and related point in our formulation of a critical research agenda, for the case studies also demonstrate that standpoint feminism is able to expose the gendered nature of both the courtroom and the legal processes, which in turn stands as a powerful challenge to the law's truth claims regarding the delivery of objective and neutral justice. Far from being based in rational, scientific procedures generating value-free "facts," the courtroom symbolizes the state's ability and power to mobilize and establish a dominant truth based on gender-specific ideologies and discourses. Only three cases have been presented here, yet they have demonstrated state violation of every one of the legitimizing principles of the criminal justice system—equality before the law, the right to a fair trial, the presumption of innocence, and the burden of proof beyond reasonable doubt. The Louise Masset case demonstrated not only how ideological assumptions about the natural woman and true femininity were allowed to replace evidence—but also how—as the *result* of such assumptions—a motive for Manfred's murder was created *after* the trial. The outcome was therefore based on evidence not tested in the courtroom, evidence which "clinched" her guilt and ensured her execution by the state.

The Ada Williams case demonstrated that while the state recognized the possibility that William had been the dominant partner in the crime, or at the very least that the two had been equal participants, that equality did not extend into the courtroom or onto the scaffold. Furthermore, Ada's journey to the scaffold was not based on evidence tested in front of a jury, but on probabilities and speculation. No evidence was presented which proved that Ada rather than William had committed the murder, yet William left court a free man while Ada was executed.

Even in the Ruth Ellis case, where a murder was committed before witnesses, the state-defined truth turned out to be problematic. From the moment of Ruth's arrest, when police officials failed to order a blood test to determine Ruth's alcohol and drug intake or to examine the murder weapon for fingerprints, through to her last 24 hours, there was a total failure by criminal justice personnel to question the "stark simplicity" of the case (Ballinger, 2000: 322). It is only with the application of standpoint feminism the punitive consequences of taken-for-granted ideologies about women and femininity are exposed.

Here a third point emerges in our construction of a critical research agenda, because the new knowledge generated about these cases demonstrates standpoint feminism's ability to challenge state power and lack of accountability, for example, by redefining these cases as examples of state negligence. In view of the state's well-documented eagerness to allocate culpability to female victims of rape and domestic violence according to their conduct, behavior, and appearance (Lees, 1996; Edwards, 1987, 1989), perhaps it is time for feminism to redefine the state as "culpable" in state executions where there is evidence of negligence on its part during the investigation, trial, or the period between sentencing and execution.

Here it is appropriate to return to Dicey's defining elements of the rule of law with which this chapter began. For example, this chapter has documented both arbitrary and discretionary state power *without accountability* in terms of allowing Ada Williams's execution to go ahead rather than granting a reprieve, in spite of the problematic nature of the evidence. Such arbitrary and discretionary powers can also be observed in the Ruth Ellis case in terms of calling off the investigation into Desmond Cussen's role in David Blakely's murder before Cussen was even located, let alone interviewed. In Louise Masset's case it has been demonstrated that rather than being "subject to the ordinary law . . . administered in the ordinary courts" her fate was sealed by a communication outside the courtroom *after* the trial, which—in a Home Office representative's own words—"clinched" the case. Indeed the same may be said of Ada Williams: her chances of receiving a reprieve were calculated according to "probabilities" if not sheer speculation following her trial. These are just a few examples generated from only three cases as to the problematic nature of "due process" and the "rule of law" and the state's omission to operate according to its own professed principles.

It is within this context that feminist theory and epistemology can participate in a redefinition of "crimes of omission" (McLaughlin, 1996: 286–87). That is to say, the state's failure to carry out an adequate investigation in capital cases and the subsequent loss of life is redefined as a "crime of omission," thus formalizing this failure as a state crime for which its servants should be held accountable. This analysis may be taken one step further whereby allowing an execution to proceed in the knowledge that the investigation was incomplete is understood as a crime of "commission." That is to say, instead of facilitating the procedures associated with "the rule of law" and "due process," state servants actively facilitated these women's executions by engaging in discretionary acts outside the courtroom following the conclusion of their trials.

It is by involving ourselves in such "redefinitions" of state activity that standpoint feminism creates a new terrain on which women's experiences of the criminal justice system can be heard, establishing new discourses through which an alternative truth emerges. Such activity has provided concrete examples of Stanley and Wise's theoretical contention that it is through feminist epistemology that feminism can most directly challenge non-feminist frameworks. For example, the appropriateness of that contention is evident in the current review by the Criminal

Cases Review Commission of the Ellis case, a clear demonstration of the ability of feminist epistemology to create new knowledge from below. In this case the subsequent alternative truth may be successful in overturning what has been the dominant truth about the Ellis case for nearly 50 years—that this was self-evidently an "open and shut case"—and instead demonstrate that far from being neutral or scientific, the state was *negligent* in its investigation of the case, and thus *culpable* in Ruth's death by actively facilitating her execution.

While the three women discussed in this chapter were never to experience the benefits that standpoint feminism brings in terms of evading dominant knowledge and creating new knowledge in its place, this type of analysis can nonetheless bring an end to their muted state and render them visible (Worrall, 1990). That is to say, their lives and deaths have become crucial, not only to the establishment of "a historical knowledge of resistance and struggle" (Sawicki 1991:57), but also to the creation of new discourses and hence new spaces on which state-defined truth and its claim to value-freedom can be challenged. In that sense the life-histories of executed women have made an important contribution to the principle of generating knowledge from "below" and as such they are entitled to be restored to their rightful place in history.

## Acknowledgments

My thanks to Dave Whyte and Steve Tombs who provided valuable suggestions on an earlier draft of this chapter.

## Notes

1. No woman has been executed for the murder of her own child under 12 months of age since 1849. Following the enactment of the Infanticide Act of 1922 such cases did not usually result in a murder charge; instead the charge was likely to be infanticide. No mother has been executed for the murder of her own child, regardless of age, since Louise Masset in 1900.
2. A situation which is far from resolved in the beginning of the twenty-first century as can be seen from the case of Zoora Shah, still imprisoned at the time of writing (*The Guardian*, 4 May 1998; Ballinger, 2000: 334–36).
3. As is still the case, Myra Hindley and Ian Brady and Rose and Fred West being cases in point.
4. For example, Home Office personnel showed awareness that William was the instigator of the letter written to the police by Ada which led to their arrest. For a full examination of the available evidence, see Ballinger, 2000.

# Whose Side Are We Not On?

## *Researching Medical Power in Prisons*

*One surgery ran from 9.15 to 10.00 am during which time the doctor saw around 15 prisoners. Before the surgery I observed one prisoner crying. The doctor's response was aggressive: "The trouble with you people is that you think that you know better than us . . . Don't make me angry, I don't want to shout at you." The prisoner left still in a distressed state. After the surgery, the doctor talked with two health care officers about the case. One commented he [the prisoner] was a troublemaker. All three laughed because the doctor had threatened to hit the prisoner. The doctor discussed how malingerers in the army were "sorted." "If they were threatened with a beating and took it they were not malingering; if they refused a beating then they were malingerers." On another occasion, he said [to me] that 95% of prisoners were "the scum of the earth" that "prisons should be a place of punishment and not enjoyable" and "these bloody people, what the hell do they want?" He justified his abrasive manner and cursory examinations thus: "They [the prisoners] don't understand medicine; what is the point of explaining it to them, they don't know anything, they have education in here but don't learn anything."* (Field Notes)

The scenario outlined above is taken from one of eleven fieldwork notebooks written in the first 10 months of 1999 during the 1,400 hours I spent conducting ethnographic research into the delivery of health care in three male prisons in England. It provides a stark and compelling illustration of the operationalization of Foucault's "micro physics of power" in that it captures a specific though not unusual penal moment in which a group of powerful men—a prison doctor and two health care officers—exercised their medical power over the body and mind of a powerless, individual man—a distressed prisoner. In the hidden, micro world of the prison surgery, the domination of the medical practitioners was reproduced and reinforced, ready to be mobilized again when they interacted with other prisoners who, despite being sick, were also normatively judged as numbered convicts whose ascribed status often denied them the care, attention, and support they needed and deserved as human beings. In this case the prisoner's subjugation was intensified and his acute distress remained untreated. Like a sore it was left to fester in the fetid atmosphere that dominates local prisons.

The notes also capture a specific, and again not unusual, moment during the research in that they describe events I witnessed as a researcher whose theoretical and methodological imperatives derive from the critical wing of criminology in general and the neo-abolitionist movement in prison studies in particular. Do they accurately reflect the reality of the interactions that took place? What did I feel about these events both as a critical academic and as a human being? How should I bear witness to them? Despite the recent welcome resurgence in debates around the methodology of prison research (Sparks et al., 1996; Liebling, 2001; Medlicott, 2001), these questions, which go to the heart of the event described above, intertwine with a number of issues that have remained unexplored with respect to researching penal institutions and in turn intertwine with this book's broader concern with the question of researching the powerful.

This chapter explores a number of these issues through discussing and dissecting the routinized and sometimes contradictory everyday exercise of medical power in prisons, where the imprimatur of enlightened scientific rationality and value freedom provide powerful legitimating discourses for the claims of its practitioners: namely, that their interventions in the prison (and elsewhere) are derived from the neutral but morally uplifting concern with deploying their benevolent expertise for the benefit of the less fortunate within and without the walls of penal and other institutions. First, I focused on being an ethnographer on prison hospital wings, the places Foucault called "the machine of the machine . . . where they send the ones that cannot be integrated into the machine and whom the machinery cannot succeed in assimilating according to its norms . . ." (quoted in Simon, 1974: 155–56). Second, the chapter considers a number of broader ethical questions that were generated as a result of the research. Third, it analyzes the changing role of the state and its relationship to critical research. Finally, it highlights the need to develop a Gramscian-based, alliance-led, idealistic research agenda in order to confront the pessimistic pragmatism that dominates contemporary criminology's world-view. In my view this development is necessary if those who work in the discipline are to avoid becoming, in the words of Max Weber "specialists without spirit and sensualists without heart" (quoted in Wolin, 1989: xxiv).

## Being There

"Prisoners are whinging, whining bastards." (Prison Health Care Officer, Field Notes)

Lisa Maher's (1997: Appendix) powerful and moving analysis of the dynamics of gender, race, and resistance in a Brooklyn drug market highlighted a number of issues that influence and underpin ethnographic research methodology and the deep emotions such research generates. Maher's rich and subtle description of her methodology (derived, it should be noted, from anthropology rather than criminology) resonates with the dynamics of researching the "messy business" of prison health care. Her research involved the "active construction of an ongoing story" which in turn meant that she was acting as a "record keeper" for the powerless. In addition, she argues that "being there" means acknowledging "the politics of domination and the power relations that inhere in ethnographic encounters" (ibid.: 207– 9). Thus,

> Establishing and maintaining a field presence is not about gaining a season's, or even a lifetime, pass to the exotic world of the "other." It is about creating and sustaining a world 'between' ourselves and those we study. . . . Ideally, the knowledge that emerges from this encounter is dialogic rather than monologic: it is "knowledge produced in human interaction." (ibid: 213)

In my own research, I encountered prisoners who were in the hospital wings because they were physically ill, psychologically distressed, had attempted suicide, or simply needed psychological and sometimes physical protection from the everyday ravages of the general prison culture. They were thus near the bottom of the prison hierarchy. Conducting the research—"being there"—was often a gruelling experience which was saturated by a sense of outrage, not only at the abject and corrosive physical conditions in which the prisoners were detained and examined, but also at the often callous, off-hand and brutally capricious medical treatment they received, treatment which Michael Vaughn and Linda Smith (1999) have described as "penal harm medicine":

> Prison Health Care Officer: That prisoner whom you discharged is threatening to kill himself.
> Prison Doctor: Let him do it.
> Prison Health Care Officer: That's what I said.
> (Field Notes)
> I like coming to the prison, I don't get depressed, it's different from general practice. In general practice I don't get to shout at patients . . . .

(Prison Doctor, Field Notes)

[A potentially suicidal prisoner was moved into the hospital wing which meant that beds had to be moved around to accommodate him.]

First Prison Health Care Officer: What's this, another fuckin' wanker?

Second Prison Health Care Officer: Fuckin' hell, I hope there's not a fire in here tonight.

First Health Care Officer: They all want to kill themselves anyway.

(Field Notes)

Many of the prisoners were also at the sharp end of two interconnected processes of penal and psychiatric interpellation: they were not only prisoners but also prisoners who were physically and/or mentally ill. Therefore, their knowledge about the world was subjugated not simply because of their status as prisoners who by definition were mendacious, but as unhealthy people whose knowledge of their own condition was inferior to that of the medical professionals involved in assessing them. Their definition of reality was not once but twice removed from the "normal" definition of reality as expressed by the majority of staff and managers. The research was particularly concerned with recording the medical experiences of older prisoners and black prisoners whose knowledge had been further subjugated and circumscribed as a result of deeply embedded social divisions around age and "race." Rescuing this body of lay knowledge from "the enormous condescension of posterity," which Williams and Popay argue is "incumbent on those involved in public health research" (Williams and Popay, 1997: 70–71), was therefore an important element in the conduct of my research. The principal "record keepers" for the prisoners in the study had been the prison authorities in general and medical personnel in particular, who had constructed a particular definition of epidemiological "truth" with respect to their lives, Through the prisoners' dialogic encounters with me, the research gave them the opportunity to construct their own records with respect to their experiences of prison medical power.

An example of the clear differences between expert and lay knowledge can be seen in relation to smoking. The drive by health promotion experts to "responsibilize" prisoners by creating rational self-disciplined individuals who do not smoke was often challenged by the prisoners' knowledge of the prison regime and the impact of that regime on their everyday sense of well-being. Expert knowledge often failed,

> to recognise that prisoners will often smoke *more*, not *less*, or will *start* smoking never having done so before, in order to cope with the suffocating boredom that local prisons engender . . . .Those promoting healthy prisons also fail to confront the differentials in power which are central to modern penal regimes through the immense discretion given to staff which reinforces the subordination of the confined. This can be seen in relation to exercise, behaviour that the health promotion lobby would argue is essential for the individual's physical and psychological well being. In practice, individual officers can dictate if and when prisoners will be allowed out of their cells. (Sim, 2002; emphasis in the original)

Or as another prisoner succinctly expressed it,

> My medication was taken off me when I came in. That big [prison officer] said "What makes you think you've got a heart condition?" I said, "I think the heart by pass gave me a bit of a clue." (Field Notes)

## Ethics and Prison Research

In another brilliant ethnographic study also built around anthropological research methods, Nancy Scheper-Hughes's analysis of medicine, power and death in Brazil, points to the importance of developing an "ethical orientation" (Scheper-Hughes, 1992: 24) in the conduct of research. Space precludes an in-depth discussion of her insights, but three issues arising from her work have important implications for thinking more broadly about the relationship between ethics and the conduct of ethnographic research in prisons.

First, she argues that anthropology (and I would say criminology) should be conceptualized as an ethical and radical project underpinned by the personal accountability of the researcher, who is answerable to the "other"; in Scheper-Hughes's case, it was to those powerless men and women who were central to her research in Alto do Cruzeiro in Brazil. Thus she argues that "what may never be compromised are our personal accountability and answerability to the other" (ibid.). This strategy involves having a sense of morality that "does not belong to culture" but rather enables the researcher to "judge it" (Levinas, cited in ibid: 23).

These insights, in my view, raise profoundly important questions with regard to the conduct of prison research. For example, how can prison researchers be answerable to the "other," particularly with respect to disseminating their results to prisoners, given the structural relationship between criminology as a discipline and the state. This relationship has meant that those who have been allowed into prisons to conduct research are often expected to provide feedback to the institutions under study but rarely, if ever, prisoners themselves. Allowing research results to be disseminated is usually couched in terms of improving managerial efficiency or removing bad practices in a particular institution. Therefore, even if the researcher wants to be answerable to prisoners, their structural location as powerless "others" often means that, despite some exceptions (Liebling, 2001), being answerable to them can be difficult if not impossible. This issue has remained neglected in the literature on prison research where the ethical debate has focused on the need to be reflexively aware of the issues around confidentiality and anonymity. Being reflexively aware of these issues, of course, should be central to the conduct of prison (and other) research. However, in following the logic of Scheper-Hughes's position, it could be argued that this reflexivity should be the beginning and not the end for the development of an ethical framework, and that it is therefore crucial to generate a wider definition of the ethical dimensions of prison research; without this, the researcher simply becomes a conduit for feeding back data and information to prison managers and state gatekeepers while the confined, as ever, are left languishing on the sidelines, their powerlessness reinforced by the very processes that in theory are supposed to protect them as research subjects.

In addition, the ethical guidelines issued by professional organizations such as the British Society of Criminology encourage researchers to be "sympathetic to the constraints on organizations participating in research and not inhibit their functioning by imposing any unnecessary burdens on them." (British Society of Criminology, 1999: 2). Researchers are told they should

> seek to maintain good relationships with all funding and professional agencies in order to achieve the aim of advancing knowledge about criminological issues and to avoid bringing the wider criminological community into disrepute with these agencies. In particular, researchers should seek to avoid damaging confrontations with funding agencies and the participants of research which may reduce research possibilities for other researchers. (ibid.)

However, who defines what is a "good relationship," and what is a "damaging confrontation"? Furthermore, what happens if a researcher discovers that a prison is institutionally violent or virulently racist or homophobic or sexist and recognizes it as a place where a kind of ethical atavism prevails? What if individual officers are seen to be violent towards prisoners? Should they and their institution remain anonymous or have they forfeited that right? What guidance is the researcher given in these matters? The answer is very little, because criminology's claim to be a seeker of undiluted truth is based on a set of Enlightenment-driven domain assumptions and political presumptions in which prisons are conceptualized as ethically healthy places which occasionally become unhealthy due to the presence of individual "bad apples" and "bad practices." Therefore, a healthy equilibrium will be restored by the dissection and removal of the "bad apples"—which in fact rarely, if ever, happens—and through an injection of "best practice" into the main body of the institution's work, that is, dealing with prisoners. This narrow conceptualization of how prisons operate (and the research questions that flow from such a conceptualization) thus leaves the deeply embedded discretionary power and the punitive discourses that are integral to the landing culture of the prison officers virtually intact.

The second ethical issue Scheper-Hughes raises concerns the role of anthropological (and again I would say criminological) writing as a "site of resistance." Here she is referring to the role of the academic as a "negative worker" who diverts "the time owed to the factory, or in this case, to the academic institution into more human activities" and who writes books "against the grain." In this way, "we can disrupt expected roles and statuses . . . and subvert the law that puts our work at the service of the machine in the scientific, academic factory" (Scheper-Hughes, 1992: 25). This remains a key political and strategic point for critical academics in general and prison researchers in particular; for to think and act reflexively (and thus ethically) means making conscious decisions to remain outside of the often politically expedient concerns of the "academic factory." Thus, in their writings, critical prison researchers have linked the expanding prison system with wider developments in the political economy of advanced capitalism and with the intensification in the power of the national and international state to regulate and punish the transgressions of the powerless while simultaneously virtually ignoring the deviance of the powerful. For these writers the prison remains pivotal (as it was in previous moments of profound economic and political transformation, in the late eighteenth and nineteenth centuries) in the struggle to manage, maintain, and reproduce a social order that is both brutal and brittle, constraining and contradictory (Ryan and Sim, 1998; Welch, 1999; Beckett and Sasson, 2000; Sim, 2000). Thus their strategic response has been to engage with official data and subject them to critical deconstruction in order to build an alternative truth about the role and place of the prison in the structurally divided world of the early twenty-first century. This deconstruction therefore transgresses both official discourse and liberal analysis and has been as central to a critical research praxis around prisons as Marx's use of official sources such as *The Times, Telegraph* and *Economist* to build his case against the immiseration generated by the depredations of nineteenth-century capitalism (Wheen, 1999: 132).

Furthermore, in publishing their research results in different forums such as activist newsletters, disseminating the results to activist groups, and being involved in the management and policy-making structures of these groups, critical prison researchers have attempted to transgress the suffocating dyad of value freedom and political disengagement, the implicit and explicit valorization of which remains central to the definition of what constitutes the "proper" conduct of research:

> in utilising a complex set of competing, contradictory and opposition discourses, and providing support on the ground for the confined and their families, [radical organisations have] challenged the hegemony around prison that historically and contemporaneously has united state servants, traditional reform groups and many academics on the same pragmatic and ideological terrain. In a number of areas . . . such as deaths in custody, prison conditions, medical power, visiting, censorship and sentencing, these groups have conceded key points in the abolitionist argument and have moved onto a more radical terrain where they have contested the construction of state-defined truth around penal policy. (Sim, 1994a: 275–76)

Therefore, disseminating the results of this research to prison activist groups such as Inquest and to influential commentators such as Her Majesty's chief inspector of prisons has been an important, interventionist consideration for me rather than simply focusing on publishing in the restricted, hierarchical, and intellectually inflated world of academic journals. Importantly, however, it is a consideration which is taking place in a highly politicized context, where the insidious impact of the Research Assessment Exercise has meant that

> articles for civil libertarian journals, activist newsletters and quality newspapers have become secondary to publishing in "respectable" academic journals. There is clearly merit in writing for academic journals but when this becomes the principal goal on the road to generating funds for university and college departments then by definition interventionist work which is worth less in monetary terms but often more in political terms becomes secondary. (Hillyard and Sim, 1997: 68)

The third ethical issue identified by Scheper-Hughes relates to the role of researchers in "writing against terror" (Taussig, cited in Scheper-Hughes, 1992: 25). While it is very important to recognize the specific cultural and political context to which Scheper-Hughes is referring—particularly the institutionalization of repressive violence within the Brazilian state—her argument can nonetheless be applied to analyzing the role of academics in exposing the nature and extent of state-induced terror and violence in prison. Prison research has not only lacked a theory of such violence but, where it has been discussed, it has been conceptualized around a pathological "bad apple" theory of the state and its servants which has restricted and restrained theoretical and political advances in this area. As Richard Edney has argued,

> Prison officers who are violent towards prisoners are labelled as sadists or thugs who by virtue of being prison officers are able to given free rein to their hitherto violent impulses. Such stereotypes, although functioning as convenient intellectual shortcuts, take us little further in attempting to understand this cruelty. (Edney, 1997: 290)

Edney's point has been supported empirically in reports by various chief inspectors of prisons—who it should be noted have *not* been criminologists—which have highlighted the fear of, and actual, abuse suffered by prisoners in different institutions. In September 2001, in Dartmoor Prison, for example, "25% of those who felt unsafe on their first night in [the prison] did so because of the 'attitude of staff.'" Furthermore,

> We [the Inspectorate] believe that from these indications there was a pattern of verbally abusive behaviour at Dartmoor. Additionally, we were told many times that when in E Wing (Segregation Unit), prisoners could be heard screaming, shouts of "Don't kick me" and verbal insults shouted by staff, such as "Vermin to exercise." (Her Majesty's Chief Inspector of Prisons, 2002: 38)

Theoretically, Nicos Poulantzas has recognized that a comprehensive analysis of the state requires an understanding of how its "monopolization of legitimate violence remains the determining element of power even when such violence is not exercised in a direct and open manner" (Poulantzas, 1978: 62). In addition, he maintained that "there is something else to repression, something about which people seldom talk: namely, *the mechanisms of fear*" (ibid.: 83, emphasis in the original). Allied to this position, feminist writers such as Liz Kelly (1988: 76) have argued that utilizing the term "continuum" has allowed women to identify the many different forms of violence that they experience, such as "abuse, intimidation, coercion, intrusion, threat and force." Therefore, writing *against* rather than simply *about* the violence that inscribes many prisoners' accounts of everyday life in prison wings, including hospital wings, and thinking about this violence in the broader conceptual terms outlined by Poulantzas and Kelly would enable prison researchers to develop both a theoretical *and* an ethical framework for understanding and analyzing the nuances in the dynamics of power as they are played out in the everyday lives of the confined "other." It would also mean thinking about how the culture of the prison induces states of anxiety, and sometimes terror, that are detrimental to the health of prisoners. Conceptualizing the issue in this way presents a theoretical and political challenge to the individualized epidemiological model which remains the dominant paradigm within which the health of the confined is discussed and responded to. As one prisoner indicated during the course of my research,

> if you come across one officer who's confrontative you flounder by default and they've got you . . . The added stress in here is if you've got an officer who's confrontative you're just waiting to say or do the wrong thing . . . It's an awful feeling of oppression but there's also a tension there that you're just watching everything, you go up the stair to use the toilet, "what are you doing up here, who gave you permission to come up here?" . . . you're almost afraid to breathe . . . (Research Interview)

Finally, I want to come back to a point made by Lisa Maher in her research on the powerless women in the Brooklyn drug market, which also has important ethical implications for the conduct of critical prison research. Maher argues that in "being there" (in the field), researchers need to ensure that they do not promise the researched too much. As she notes,

> [T]he greater the intimacy, the greater the potential dangers and risk of exploitation. Moreover, such practices may also serve to raise the expectations of "positive intervention" on the part of women who, by comparison with the researcher, are relatively powerless. (Maher, 1997: 231)

Quoting Patai, she observes that "'the misuse of sentiment as a research tool' poses real dangers" (ibid.). During the course of my research there was often the danger that the desperate need felt by prisoners (and some staff members) to speak to me as someone who was outside of the suffocating control of the discretionary-based prison rules, perhaps coupled with my own sense of outrage at prisoners' physical and psychological treatment, could generate high expectations that I, as the "outsider," could be a vehicle for doing something for them as individuals or for prisoners collectively. Maher concludes that it is not only incumbent on researchers to avoid the dangers of exploitation that such intimacy might engender, but they should also recognize that the "inequities and hierarchical ordering" (ibid.: 213–14) which govern the lives of the powerless will not be overridden by the adoption of critical research methods which may themselves impose the additional burden of high expectations on the researched.

## Researching the Prison as a State Institution

In 1972 Stan Cohen and Laurie Taylor published *Psychological Survival*. The book was an ethnographic account of how men survived the searing psychological and emotional pains of long-term imprisonment in Durham's "H" Wing. Five years after it was published, they discussed the Home Office-instigated obstacles they encountered when attempting to publish their research. Cohen and Taylor described five strategies through which the Home Office attempted to control the research agenda: the centralization of power, the legalization of secrecy, the standardization of research, the mystification of the decision structure, and the appeal to the public interest (Cohen and Taylor, 1977: 77). These strategies crystallized and symbolized the restrictions they encountered as identifiably *critical* criminologists attempting to conduct prison research in the early to mid-1970s, restrictions which were unlikely to be imposed on research conducted by those who followed a more politically and academically acceptable trajectory built on a liberal perspective of gradual reform, a pluralist conceptualization of dispersed power and a positivist discourse of individual deviance. Moreover, for state servants, Cohen and Taylor's work lacked the scientific rigor and value freedom that they insisted should underpin criminological research. In short, it was too journalistic.

Cohen and Taylor's conflict with the Home Office captured a particular moment in the history of critical criminology with respect to thinking about the nature of power and the role of academics and intellectuals in confronting that power. They began their research in 1967, the year in which Howard Becker published his famous and influential article "Whose Side Are We On?" (Becker, 1967). Together with his subsequent debate with Alvin Gouldner concerning the relationship between fact, values, and truth in the conduct of social science research, Becker's article remains an important touchstone for contemporary prison researchers (Liebling, 2001). It is not the intention here to consider the nuances in the debate between Becker and Gouldner except to say that it is undeniable that the depth of the theoretical and political insights developed by these writers, the academic iconoclasm their work engendered and the influence it exerted has been profoundly important in the decades since Becker asked his now famous question. However, there is a broader point I want to make concerning this early work that unites Cohen and Taylor with Becker and Gouldner, and this point relates to the question of the state and its role in the conduct of critical research.

In terms of labelling theory it has become a sociological truism that theorists such as Becker lacked a theory of the state. This led to an analysis and a research agenda—what was later called a "criminology from below" (Sim et al., 1987: 7)—which maintained that the world should be seen from the perspective of the deviant.

There was little consideration in this work concerning the state or its operation, rather the theoretical debate was dominated by a vague and ill-defined conceptualization of the "control culture," a concept that was underpinned by labelling theory's idealistic focus on the male as a transgressive, 1960s, outlaw.

The path-breaking work of the early critical criminologists moved the debate on the state forward. In particular, as noted above, researchers such as Cohen and Taylor, who attempted to engage in critical work in the 1970s and 1980s, highlighted the obstacles that confronted and confounded them in their attempts not only to obtain access to institutions but also to obtain research funds in order to conduct the research in the first place. For prison abolitionists such as Thomas Mathiesen, the state was central to this smothering process in terms of defining who and what was legitimate, and conversely who and what was problematic, with respect to the conduct of research and the nature of the questions that researchers could ask:

> The modern state in the late capitalist social formation manifests itself . . . as the developer of a series of ideological conceptions and concrete strategies which define out, as a counterpart to the absorbent features which define in . . . it is precisely the development of the absorbent, defining-in side, which make the corresponding development of the defining-out counterpart possible: the more effectively absorbent and defining-in the state becomes, the more reasonable it will appear *to define out those who nevertheless are unwilling to conform*. (Mathiesen, 1980: 288; emphasis in the original)

In England and Wales, the process of "defining-in and defining-out" was (and is) reinforced by a combination of the Official Secrets Act and the libel laws whose threatened and actual use has been instrumental in both curtailing critical researchers and positioning them as subjects who have censored themselves in order to avoid costly and usually unwinnable court cases (Sim, 1990). Thus the power of the state to restrict critical research into the nature and impact of penal power through the processes described above has been a dominant feature in the social construction of the prison research agenda since the 1970s.

However, it is also very important to note that the state has never exercised total hegemony with regard to the construction and conduct of prison research. Why is this? Bob Jessop's analysis of the state provides some of the answers to this question. As he acknowledges, the state should not be conceptualized as a unified, unitary, coherent ensemble or agency. Instead, the boundaries of the state and its relative unity as an ensemble or agency would be contingent . . . In many cases we can expect to find several "rival" emergent "states" corresponding to competing state projects with no overall coherence to the operations of the state system . . . It is not the state which acts: it is always specific sets of politicians and state officials located in specific parts of the state system. (Jessop, 1990: 366–67)

Jessop's insights have particular relevance to the conduct of prison research in general and the research discussed in this chapter in particular, in that they help to explain why I as a critical researcher was able to gain access to the three institutions which I studied. First, the funding came from an independent research organization, the Nuffield Foundation. The fact that I had written extensively in this area was very important in establishing my credentials with the foundation. This work, while critical of prison health care, had also been recognized as an important contribution to the contentious and sometimes vitriolic debate around health care for the confined. Importantly, the foundation, while raising some initial concerns about the methodology, was immensely supportive of the research, and because it was not part of the Home Office, it recognized the difficulties that I was to encounter. Thus, who funds research remains a key question for critical researchers, particularly with respect to those non-state organizations that are willing to provide funds for research they consider to be socially and politically relevant.

Second, I wrote to various prison governors outlining the nature of the research and asked if they would like their particular prisons to be involved. A number of them reacted positively as did a number of health care staff, some of whom knew my work and the critical nature of it. Clearance to conduct the research came from the governors, the principal health care officers, and the senior doctors in the prisons that agreed to host the research. As it turned out they were also influenced by the fact that the research was concerned not only with prisoners' health care arrangements but also with occupational health issues around prison health care *staff*, a topic which had remained overwhelmingly under-researched. This aspect of the research supports Jessop's position, outlined above, that it was specific individuals located in specific parts of the overall system who were important in allowing the research to take place. This is not to say that there were no difficulties. Dealing with the Home Office proved to be a convoluted process. These convolutions were related to the question of methodology, particularly the Prison Service Health Advisory Group's desire to ensure that the methodology was "scientifically valid" (personal communication). The Health Research Ethics Committee for the Prison Service also wanted "to ensure that it [the research] meets ethical criteria for health research" (ibid.). One civil servant expressed the position more succinctly when he commented that "proposals are looked at to see if they are in the best interests of the Prison Service" (personal communication). Discussions with the Home Office began on 18 July 1997 and ended when I was finally given clearance four months later on 12 November 1997.

The difficulties in conducting research in prisons, of course, do not end with generating funds and obtaining access. Once in the field, as Lisa Maher (1997: Appendix) has argued, other issues arise: some are technical, in terms of being known and getting access to different groups for interviews; some are personal in terms of the impact of conducting research on the researcher's outside relationships and on his/her physical and psychological health; some are academic, in terms of maintaining the focus of the research during long periods of participant observation; some generate psychological dissonance because of the complex moral dilemmas that are thrown up during the course of research; some remain ongoing with respect to analyzing the data and disseminating the results; and some remain a continuing part of the researcher's life, for example leaving behind the subjects and integrating (if that is possible) back into a "normal" life after being involved in "the ethnographic mill, a mill that has a truly grinding power" (Stacey, cited in Maher, 1997: 229). It is not the intention here to explore these issues further but rather to reiterate the more general point, which is that for critical researchers it is important to recognize the contingencies and contradictions inherent in the funding and conduct of research. However it is also becoming increasingly clear that while the state's hegemony around the research process has remained incomplete, a number of recent developments may well generate further difficulties for critical researchers and hamper and restrict their ability to conduct research. The next section of this chapter considers some of these developments in general and the implications for researching prison health care in particular.

## New Openings, Old Closures

The control of research agendas has been further augmented and reinforced by the impact of neo-liberal discourses on higher education and the subsequent commodification of academic work. Obtaining research grants, writing research reports, and conducting evaluation studies have coalesced into the cult around which the academic soul is increasingly being judged and through which academic redemption is increasingly being sought. Be enterprising, obtain financial support *from whatever source*, and work in partnership with the local, national, and international state are the mantras chanted by those who manage educational institutions as they struggle with the eviscerating impact of budgetary cuts while often acting as agents and conduits in the brutal implementation of these cuts. This development has been reinforced by the calculated insidiousness of what Richard Leo has called "the pull of the policy audience." Although he is discussing police research and socio-legal scholarship, Leo's conclusions have a searing applicability with respect to the current state of criminological research and the active role played by academics in the construction of a discipline bereft of critical and humanist engagement:

> Little contemporary police scholarship is animated by a desire to understand or expose the workings of power, coercion and authority in police institutions. As police scholars internalise the interests and agendas of police leaders and policymakers, they become the advocates of police reform agendas and the quality of police scholarship becomes impoverished. Quick monographs, research reports and slapdash books seem to carry greater currency than ever in the field ... The policy audience fosters an uncritical acceptance of the status quo and thus diminishes the critical potential of scholarship. And when the policymaker's problems become the scholars' problems, scholarship becomes a means to an end rather than a pursuit for its own sake. (Leo, 1996: 867)

In prison research, these corrosive developments have been increasingly articulated and legitimated through the formulation and construction of research projects built on the reifying, state-defined discourses of "relevance" and "evaluation." This, in turn, is underpinned by the demand to forge research partnerships with agencies, *any* agencies, outside of higher education, who express an interest in conducting research on offenders. The state remains central to this process. As Pat Carlen has noted,

> in its "partnerships" with non-state agencies ... the state [has not] given up any of its power to punish—in order to be funded, programmes have to meet stringent accreditation criteria, most of which recognise only one type of positivistic "knowledge" in relation to "offending behaviour". ... Most of the programmes are based on cognitive behavioural approaches involving positivistic assumptions about criminogenic patterns of behaviour and faulty modes of thinking as well as on empiricist assumptions about how changes in thinking can be measured. (Carlen, 2002: 120–121)

Through this process, Carlen maintains, the prison is becoming:

> [A] lucrative and staple source of financing for many newcomers to the prison industry who appear not at all unwilling to legitimate the use of imprisonment by reference to the "effectiveness" of their "programmes" in reducing crime. The verity of the "programmers' claims to success" are often "proven" by dubious self-report questionnaire-evidence from prisoners that a programme "works"—usually in terms of changing prisoners' understanding of their offending behaviour. (Indeed, in view of all these "programmers" and "counsellors" claiming to have found the philosopher's stone in relation to changing offenders' behaviour it truly is amazing that the prisons have not been emptied by now!) (ibid.: 120)

These developments have impacted on researching prison health care. Increasingly, this research is being formulated within, and underpinned by, the apparently benevolent rubric of a state-inspired "partnership approach" that in turn has legitimated the involvement of local health authorities in prisons. So while it appears that the prison system is now becoming institutionally more open as it allows larger numbers of professionals to come through the gates, at the same time, these professionals, both academic and otherwise, legitimate an ideological closure as their research is based on epidemiological quantification concerning prisoners' health. However, even on their own terms, such data are problematic given the reluctance of the studied group to provide accurate information "to a stranger with a survey form" (Maher, 1997: 208). The result is that, "most of the criminologists and sociologists who painstakingly undertake epidemiological surveys on crime and substance abuse collect fabrications" (Bourgois, quoted in ibid.).

Furthermore, the drive towards epidemiological quantification is based on the discourse of narrowly focused health promotion schemes, the adaptive, rational, self-disciplined prisoner and also the "thoroughly ingrained thinking about risk" (Schiller, 1992: 249) which now dominates criminal justice policy in England and Wales. The uncritical acceptance of the concept of "risk" as "useful" means that the key question concerning "useful for whom to do what?" (ibid.)—which inevitably raises issues of power and powerlessness—remains on the theoretical and political margins, if it is considered at all.

This development also raises a number of very important issues that transcend the restricted conceptualization of ethics which, as I noted above, dominates the debate around prison research. For Pat Bracken and Phil Thomas, the utilization of evidence-based practice and the discourse of clinical effectiveness does not simply involve the neutral, value-free application of science to the study of health and ill-health, but also involves "respect, values and power. This is what we mean by 'ethics.' The real debate is not about whether practice should be based on evidence but about *whose* evidence should be used, and how that evidence was generated" (Bracken and Thomas, 2000: 22, emphasis in the original). Furthermore, as Diana Medlicott has argued, the refusal of state officials to engage with research evidence that they (and some academics) label as unscientific—by virtue of the fact that it is based on qualitative methodology—can also be seen in political and ethical terms:

> To cling to a position which dogmatically and uncritically asserts the negative worth of all qualitative research in turn amplifies its generalised lack of credibility, and may be extremely convenient for policy makers. In some circumstances, it may be termed a "politico-ethical refusal" for if the validity of all such research, regardless of its conduct and findings, can be established as worthless, then the policy and practice implications can be ignored. If . . . the findings appear to have a strong ethical dimension, rooted in universal human need, and therefore compelling on the grounds of natural justice, and yet they suggest change which is uncomfortable and/or costly in terms of a costs/benefits analysis, it is particularly useful to be able to mount a wilful refusal to consider social analysis, on the grounds that it is non-scientific, lacks credibility and is difficult to replicate. (Medlicott, 2001: 43)

One final important development which is influencing the nature and direction of prison research relates to the emergence of the private prison industry and the cloak of commercial confidentiality thrown over the activities of private companies operating in the public sphere. The recourse to commercial confidentiality means that basic information may not be forthcoming, thus directly influencing both the formulation of research hypotheses and *what* questions researchers are allowed to ask. Crucially, commercial confidentiality now extends beyond academic researchers and involves the denial of information to those state servants to whom prisons are, theoretically, accountable. This is illustrated below in the extract from a radio program broadcast in January 2002. The presenter, Brian Whitaker, quizzed Tony Cameron, the Chief Executive of the Scottish Prison Service, about the impact of commercial confidentiality on the ability of the Chief Inspector of Prisons, Clive Fairweather, to publish information about staffing levels in Kilmarnock Prison, Scotland's only private prison:

> Cameron: There is a great deal of both theory and practical evidence to suggest that commercial confidentiality is an extremely important component of the way in which the market operates.
>
> Whitaker: But it would seem that in this case you agreed that commercial confidentiality was more important than public access to information about staffing levels in Scotland's only private prison?
>
> Cameron: That's right.
>
> Whitaker: So commercial confidentiality was more important than public information in this case?
>
> Cameron: Indeed it was . . .
>
> Whitaker: But you know how many staff there are in Scotland's one private prison.
>
> Cameron: Well I don't, no.
>
> Whitaker: You don't?
>
> Cameron: No.
>
> Whitaker: But you're head of the Scottish Prison Service. Surely you know that?
>
> Cameron: That's right. I only know what the company have told us and have made publicly available. I don't know more than that. . . . (BBC Radio 4, 2002: 11–12)

## Conclusion: Moving Forward

> [T]he intellectual's error consists in believing that one can know without understanding and even more without feeling and being impassioned. (Gramsci, 1971: 418)

Gramsci recognized that hegemony is never a complete process, it has to be struggled over to be maintained and it can be lost. His distinction between two kinds of hegemony—"transformism" and "expansive hegemony"—is useful here. In the case of "transformism," the active elements of dissent and challenge are gradually but continuously absorbed into structures of domination; in the case of "expansive hegemony," those who challenge structures of domination articulate a progressive vision of social change which is augmented by the creation of a genuine "popular will" around economic and political issues and events (cited in Benney, 1983:

195–96). Through this distinction, Gramsci attempted to develop a social theory and political strategy that was alliance-led, where political and personal links were forged between progressive social movements and cultural forces so that the "common sense" which governed the perception and understanding of social issues was replaced with an alternative, hegemonic "good sense."

Gramsci's insights can be applied to the question of penal hegemony and social change in that the brittle nature of the prison's legitimacy, both internally with respect to prisoners (and many prison staff) and externally in terms of the institution's ability to do very much about crime, is always a matter of serious contestation and debate. Contesting the institution's legitimacy can therefore provide critical academics with an important ideological platform from which to launch alternative visions of state and social control through writing and campaigning.

Gramsci's theoretical legacy also means that critical researchers need to think about state servants not just in terms of their capacity for punitive repression but also with respect to those in their group who attempt to challenge the overwhelmingly masculine culture and the threat and use of psychological and physical violence that legitimates this culture and pervades the everyday life, cracks, and crevices of many institutions. The exceptions, those who stand outside of the "punitive obsession" (Playfair, 1971) underpinning the culture and are therefore "different" on account of their more benevolent attitude to prisoners or their desire to see that the prison rules are properly implemented, are often characterized as problematic. As one health care officer explained,

> The culture is in the brickwork in [here]. Staff culture—give them nothing. If an officer is good at his job and takes things on, people say what is he after, he is ambitious and therefore criticised. (Field Notes)

Thus, the presence of the "good screw" may just be enough at particular moments to ensure prisoners some dignity, while constraining the activities of his closest working colleagues who form part of a landing culture whose world-view is dominated by punishment, retribution, expediency, and the next wage packet. Can and should critical researchers connect with these individuals and their attempt to introduce and induce some humanity and dignity into that culture, with sometimes devastating consequences for themselves in terms of their physical and mental health and their career prospects? Indeed, do researchers have the theoretical, methodological, political, *and* personal vision and capacity to connect with them? What about those staff who genuinely believe in a more therapeutic model for dealing with the problems of the prison population? Do they represent the further encroachment of the therapeutic state or do critical researchers need to engage with the contradictory spaces that this perspective offers, as perhaps one way of breaking out of the punitive cul-de-sac that prisons still inhabit?

If critical researchers conceptualize penal institutions in these terms, it has important implications for the construction of a radical research agenda. In particular, it leads directly to a consideration of whose side the researchers are on and whose side they are not on. Thus, if a prisoner has been convicted of violence against women or of a racial or homophobic murder, how should critical researchers engage with him? The old sociological adage that critical criminologists should not only see the world from the perspective of the deviant but should also accept their world-view seems a much more problematic position to take compared with 30 years ago, especially when considered against the theoretical advances that have been made around the social construction of masculinity and femininity both within and without the walls of the prison (Sim, 1994b). Recognizing this problematic, and the complex questions that flow from it, represents an important challenge to critical criminology not only in theoretical terms but also in political and strategic terms: exactly with *whom* should critical academics connect in order to generate social policies that are expansive in the Gramscian sense and that will not be absorbed into the micro and macro structures of punitive domination that still underpin and legitimate the everyday world of the prison in the early twenty-first century?

It is important to note that raising these issues does not mean jettisoning the theoretical, political, and strategic analysis developed by critical prison researchers and others concerning the authoritarian nature of the state and the intensification in the power of state institutions to punish under neo-liberal social arrangements (Hall et al., 1978; Scraton, 1987; Sim, 1987). Equally, it does not mean compromising the theoretical concerns and political objectives of critical research which directly implicates state servants either by omission or design in the reproduction of the punitive, violent, and degrading practices that dominate the minds, actions and culture of many of those who work in local prisons in particular. Indeed, it is *precisely* because critical researchers conceptualize the issues in such terms that distinguishes them from liberal/administrative researchers, whose theoretical position invariably transforms the materiality of penal power into the presence or absence of "bad apples" among prison staff or the lack of "good practices" in individual prisons. More broadly, the fact that research remains an inherently political process and is *recognized* as such by critical researchers reinforces the distinction between them and the managerialism—both old and new—that underpins the work of their liberal/administrative counterparts. In the words of Maurice Punch:

> To a greater or lesser extent, politics suffuses all social scientific research . . . By *politics* I mean everything from the micropolitics of personal relations to the cultures and resources of research units and universities, the powers and policies of government research departments, and ultimately even the hand (heavy or otherwise) of the central state itself . . . All of these contexts and constraints crucially influence the design, implementation and outcomes of research . . . (Punch, 1998: 159, emphasis in the original)

Confronting the academic and political restrictions to which Punch alludes requires the possession of what E. P. Thompson called an "angry courage" (Thompson, 1980: 10). In addition, subverting these restrictions and transcending the pessimistic pragmatism that prevails in academic institutions also necessarily involve thinking in idealistic and utopian terms (Young, 1992; Lippens, 1995), which by definition leads to thinking more broadly in emancipatory terms. The insertion of a committed idealism into contemporary criminology might also undermine the "psychic numbing" (Lifton, 1987: 232) generated by an academic culture which is, as noted above, increasingly reliant on endless evaluation and epidemiological studies to justify its existence. Failure to confront this culture and the process that flows from it—what could be termed criminology as industry—is likely to ensure that this "industry" will become a permanent and insidious blot on the academic and political landscape.

## Acknowledgments

The research on which this chapter is based was funded by the Nuffield Foundation. I am very grateful to the foundation for its financial, organizational and emotional support. Thanks to those prisoners and staff who participated in the research. Thanks also to Steve Tombs and Dave Whyte for their patience and invaluable comments on an earlier draft of this chapter. Finally, thanks to those staff and students at the Department of Criminology, Keele University for their helpful comments at the seminar they attended in February 2001 where these ideas were first presented.

# Conclusion

13  STEVE TOMBS AND
DAVE WHYTE

# Unmasking the Crimes of the Powerful

## *Establishing Some Rules of Engagement*

*One can understand nothing about economic science if one does not know how power and economic power are exercised in everyday life. The exercise of power perpetually creates knowledge and, conversely, knowledge constantly induces effects of power. The university hierarchy is only the most visible, the most sclerotic and least dangerous form of this phenomenon. One has to be really naïve to imagine that the effects of power linked to knowledge have their culmination in university hierarchies. Diffused, entrenched and dangerous, they operate in other places than in the person of the old professor.* (Michel Foucault)

*The smart way to keep people passive and obedient is to strictly limit the spectrum of acceptable opinion, but allow very lively debate within that spectrum— even encourage the more critical and dissident views. That gives people the sense that there's free thinking going on, while all the time the presuppositions of the system are being reinforced by the limits put on the range of the debate!* (Noam Chomsky)

## For Political Economy

The attacks on New York's World Trade Center in 2001 and the response of Western states, led by the USA, have in some ways created greater obstacles to the scrutiny of the powerful. Those who oppose the global march of neo-liberalism have, in the "you are either with us or against us" period constructed since these attacks, risked being labelled as "terrorist sympathizers." In the USA, for example, vocal, university-based opponents of the US Government's use of punitive emergency powers and critics of the war in Afghanistan have been silenced and sacked for speaking out (Stanley, 2002). Of course, academic censorship is not a new phenomenon. But at present it has, as we outlined in our introduction, a compliant context in which to operate, and a ready momentum based on widespread academic self-regulation; in other words, current attempts to silence, discredit, and marginalize alternative views of the world are both elements in and symptoms of the political reconfiguration of university research.

As our introduction intimated, and as Pearce and Snider indicate,[1] the voices of opposition from within the universities are now more fragmented and isolated than in the 1960s, the decade that many view as a high point in university radicalism. Using research to confront political decision making is not an approach that has been particularly fashionable in social theory and analysis for at least a quarter of a century. The influence of postmodern theoretical frameworks which reject the "grand narratives" of the Enlightenment and of twentieth century thought involves, as Hillyard notes, a rejection of the modernist quest for "rationality," "truth," and justice. As the conceptual dinosaurs of modernism are rejected, emergent understandings of power have proved increasingly lacking in any real utility for those who are engaged in struggles with power—they are more concerned with describing power in highly abstract terms, having rather little to say about possibilities for the transformation, or even the reform, of existing power relations. One of the most obvious consequences of postmodern theoretical abstraction has been a deafening silence around the key social and political questions of our time (Philo and Miller, 2001).

The greatest challenge faced by those who wish to conduct research which presents an alternative to the neo-liberal view of the world may not necessarily be an intellectual one. After all, much of the theoretical justification both for the primacy of the market and for the strident pro-business stance of contemporary Western states is based upon updated versions of eighteenth and nineteenth century liberal economic and social theory—hence the "neo" bit. It is not difficult to challenge intellectually these variants of primitive and reductionist economism, whether the rational choice theorists in criminology or the "trickle-down" ideologues of classical economics. Much more difficult is breaking down the new common sense, the conventional wisdom of neo-liberalism, that has accumulated momentum in recent years—and, most centrally, the idea that "There is no Alternative" (TINA) to the global expansion of a neo-liberal capitalism. Confronting this mantra has become a necessary part of conducting critical research. In order to present alternatives to the neo-liberal world order, reference to empirical indicators and experience-based research may be powerful, but in order to challenge the theoretical basis of TINA—and the armory of crackpot theories used to sustain neo-liberal dominance—we need a theoretical perspective that has been constructed for this task.

For us, a Marxist political economy is the key way to confront the logic of TINA. "Political economy" as a *general* approach is a powerful one, transgressing disciplinary straitjackets "of politics, economics and international relations" (Gill and Law, 1988: xviii), and, importantly, requiring "analysis of the way in which *ideas* about what constitutes the political and the economic have emerged" (ibid.), in contrast to the ahistorical character of much of what currently passes for criminology or sociology. In short, political economy is crucial in that its integrated historical and international character forces us to recognize that there are always alternatives—things are, have been, and can be different. Marxist political economy shares these features, but is specifically organized around concepts and ideas that have greater (not, as is claimed, less or even no) relevance today than when first forged in the adolescent stage of capitalist development. The labor theory of value and the theory of surplus value, the necessarily antagonistic relationship between classes, and the inherent tendency of capitalism to expand destructively while at the same time reproducing the contradictions upon which it is founded, are all crucial tools for understanding and engaging with the trajectories of the world around us.

To interpret the world is not, of course, to change it. And so a Marxist *analysis* can only be a starting-point. Thus, within the context of this book, to understand the neo-liberal march through the state and civil society as creating the conditions for undermining critical bodies of knowledge is at the same time to appreciate the enormity of the task of reversing this trajectory. Critical academics have spent years erecting ways of looking at the world which, in a whirlwind quarter of a century, have been subjected to a withering assault. Snider's description of the "disappearance" of corporate crime (in this volume; see also Snider, 2000) is testimony to the ferocity of this attack. This is, therefore, an era in which academics may be less and less protected by intellectual foundations which once seemed impregnable within a particular subject area, but when exposed to the discipline of the market, more or less turn to sand. Berrington, Jemphrey and Scraton demonstrate how assumptions about the criminal justice system which are relatively established and uncontroversial in the context of academic criminology can be the subject of censorship when applied in policy settings. Their experience seems symptomatic of the status of academic research within a market voracious for policy-driven "knowledge."

## Bringing the State Back In

Whether or not the postmodern rejection of certain forms of theorizing has been, or remains, dominant, much contemporary Western social science has either been heavily influenced by or seems compelled to take seriously some of the central tenets of the postmodernist narrative. "Risk" theorists have been drawn into dialogue with post-modern analysis and have responded with the idea that we have reached a new "reflexive" phase in "modernity" rather than a new historical epoch (Beck, 1992). The postmodernist call to reject unitary or "grand" theoretical perspectives (metanarratives) has inspired "governmentality" theorists to move closer to an understanding of power as an almost ethereal force, so dispersed throughout the body of society that it has little relation to the traditional centers of political and economic decision making in capitalist social orders. As Coleman points out, what the risk and governmentality theorists of the academic "left" have in common is a failure to acknowledge in any detail the ways in which the state has played a key role in sustaining and intensifying the neo-liberal project. The state is increasingly understood as merely one player in a vast network. Within these new systems of "centerless politics" or "governance at a distance," the state as a site of power or struggle rarely features as the primary object of scrutiny. As Green notes, such analyses offer little in the way of tangible opportunities for opposition.

But the downgrading of the state as a basic object of analysis also represents a major theoretical misjudgement on the part of social-scientific and criminological adherents to such perspectives. For example, within criminology and criminal justice research, the "partnership" approach has not, despite the assumptions of some mainstream criminologists, led to a loosening of the state's hold over research agendas; instead it has allowed the state to enlist and reorganize academics and other professional groups into more effective means of promoting knowledge claims made by local and national state officials. Partnerships thus legitimate an ideological closure on the part of the state (Sim). Critical research must retain a concept of the state not only as a primary object of analysis, but also as a primary object of struggle. As Fooks argues, since capital has a virtual monopoly over knowledge about its own activities, it is often only regulatory authorities that can penetrate this monopoly. Therefore what the state knows and allows us to know is likely to become increasingly important. This is illustrative of the likelihood that the state in general, and the law in particular, will remain key pressure points for counter-hegemonic struggle. The contributors to this volume, without exception, implicitly or explicitly place the state at the center of their conception of power, while simultaneously detailing how power operates in a myriad of ways beyond the state.

If we are to find out how the harmful activities of the powerful are to be properly understood, a central task must be to understand how those activities are produced, sustained and given momentum by states. This requires a concrete appraisal of the expansion of the power of local, national, and international state structures, their ability to regulate markets, intervene, and mediate in struggles within and between social groups, and ultimately their primary role in structuring social relations. For example, Coleman's research perhaps would not have been possible without a nuanced conception of the local state, particularly in relation to the identification of the most influential individuals and primary definers in the emerging entrepreneurial city-state of Liverpool. Similarly, Power required a lucid awareness of the centers of material power in the state before attempting to explore the reconfiguration of state sovereignty and power in Ireland and Spain. In short, as Hillyard reminds us, those who research the crimes of the powerful have to understand accurately the networks of power that operate in a given society.

Taken together, the contributions to this volume are clear testimony to the need to move beyond an analysis of "*the* state," to avoid a view of the state as a fixed, monolithic, homogeneous entity. Recognizing the internal contradictions and conflicts that exist within and between various state agencies and departments, and indeed between individual state representatives, has been key to the research conducted by several contributors here, and has created both opportunities to exploit the research process and obstacles to it. Alvesalo and Virta document the tensions generated between different branches of the state in relation to one set of research findings (see also Alvesalo and Tombs, 2002). For Power, breaking through official versions of policy was made possible by conducting simultaneous interviews with two officials from different police agencies. Both Sim and Power note the advantages to be gained by identifying sympathetic individuals within the state; indeed, Sim reminds us that some of the most critical views of the UK prison system are actually contained in reports published by the British government.

The research described by the majority of contributors required some level of access to data sources controlled by states or corporations. Even if one can negotiate that access, the use of state data is problematic, as we, and Pearce, have indicated. More generally, "[b]y taking state categories as our point of departure, we are captured by the meanings given by the official system of registration" (Christie, 1997: 20). But access to alternative data that "counts" may be difficult to achieve unless researchers are contracted by the state to conduct research. The contributions by Alvesalo and Virta and by Berrington, Jemphrey and Scraton, indicate that working for or within the state without compromising the position of the researcher is possible *under particular conditions*. Of course, as both of those contributions show, considerable barriers—in the case of Berrington and colleagues, total censorship—were erected at the stage of publication and dissemination. Alvesalo and Virta's experience, however, illustrates that under certain conditions it is possible to work within the state with relative academic freedom. Again, the need to consider specificity in relation to states is confirmed.

Thus, the contributions to this volume, taken together, tell us something both about the research process and about how critical researchers should view the state. First, that when it comes to the state, there are no hard and fast rules of engagement: ways of engaging with and confronting state institutions are greatly contingent on specific social and political conditions. Second, engaging with capital often involves a simultaneous engagement with the state. Challenging the state, if it is effective, means challenging social relations of power that privilege private interests.

We should add a note of caution here. Our discussion of states and corporations as powerful actors and as the subjects of critical scrutiny is by no means intended to suggest that we conceptualize, or challenge state power and the power of corporate interests in identical ways: engaging with the state is a rather different task than engaging with corporations. Most contemporary states must still seek to sustain some appearance of accountability, and establish a range of mechanisms through which this might be pursued, at least formally. For example, we may seek to use states — via regulatory agencies, law, access to certain kinds of information — in struggles to control or mitigate the harmful activities of corporations. By contrast, corporations do not have the same "pressure points" or sites of struggle. Further, states enjoy certain formal coercive powers that may be used against dissidents, including critical academics, which corporations cannot quite match. Thus the character of struggles with corporations and struggles with states is always going to be different in certain respects. At the same time, and indeed as many contributions here document, any understanding of, or challenge to, the operation of power should not reify the formal separations between capital and the state.

## Beyond the "Ivory Tower"

Researching the powerful is a task that is not only made problematic by the elite, powerful organizations and individuals that we seek to research, but also by our own institutions. This is by no means a new problem for academic critics of the powerful. Sutherland's experience of university censorship (Geis and Goff, 1983) is echoed in Tweedale's account of how his university management vetted his manuscript and, supported by legal advice, demanded that, despite the successful conviction of T&N for health and safety *crimes*, its conduct should not be described as crime.

Yet if universities monitor knowledge production, it is also the case that their reputations are closely tied to, indeed rely upon, notions of impartiality and academic neutrality. However illusory such claims to value neutrality may be, the *discourse* of value neutrality is one which can be exploited by critical researchers. The lack of attention to crimes of the powerful represents a gaping hole within mainstream criminology. It is a gaping hole which can be justified neither theoretically nor empirically, and one which supposedly value-neutral organizations cannot sustain without exposing their highly dubious preference for research and teaching programs which do not challenge powerful interests. As Tweedale intimates, for entrepreneurial researchers working in environments that still, necessarily, place some premium on original and novel work, the study of the crimes of the powerful remains a glaring lacuna that remains to be filled.

Indeed, there remain some important advantages in continuing to conduct research from within universities. Not least of these is the fact that universities retain a status as powerful organizations in their own right, often linked with local state networks, partnerships, and government initiatives. Academics therefore possess a credibility and social status as individuals and this has the potential to open doors to other powerful groups. Coleman and Power were both able to exploit their status as academics in order to gain access to "hard to reach," powerful subjects. Indeed, there is no little irony that Coleman's access to the locally powerful was largely guaranteed as a result of the entrepreneurialism of his university as a key actor in the locally emergent state, with the consequent assumption that he, too, was "one of us." In a rather different way, Alvesalo and Virta were also able to use their status as university researchers, their ability to secure access to data being related to general perceptions of university research as posing no threat to the state (see also Power) and especially to sexist assumptions about the malleability of young, female researchers. Those assumptions were subverted by the researchers and opened avenues to data that might have been barred to more established researchers or to enquiries from non-academic institutions.

On the issue of funding, the contributions to this volume are again instructive. First, they reiterate the fact that, while funding for critical work is scarce, it is still possible to gain access to research grants: one key implication of this is that critical academics must not self-regulate by choosing not to apply for such grants. Thus, for example, Green's research on state crime was funded by the ESRC, while the Nuffield Foundation provided funds to make Sim's prison research possible—and the very prestige of this foundation may have contributed to his gaining access to gaols. As Snider notes of corporate crime research, important studies in criminology continue to be conducted without significant funding. Indeed, some of the research described here indicates methods by which critical work can proceed on the basis of negligible funding—witness, for example, Ballinger's de-/re-constructions and re-theorizations of existing state documents to reveal systematic forms of gendered state killing, or Fooks's analysis of the construction of "knowledge" within and around the financial services industry.

One of the overwhelming pressures that comes from within the university is, of course, the pressure for mainstream academic publication, and to some extent this is important for many university-based researchers, since we need the credibility that such publications bring, both within our own institutions and in our wider academic communities. This is all very well, but we are also aware that to make a contribution beyond those publications, to engage in public dissent and to conduct research that is socially and politically relevant, we also need to reach wider audiences. A project of social transformation needs more than relatively isolated academic discussion, no matter how "influential" this might be, and we need increasingly to look beyond our academic peers to publish for larger, more diverse audiences (Sim, this volume). Put crudely, a letter to a local newspaper, or three minutes on *Newsnight* or even a regional current affairs show will reach a far greater audience, and thus have the possibility of being a much more effective form of political intervention than even the most critical of articles published in a scholarly journal.

Indeed, as Tweedale has recently reminded us (Tweedale, 2000: 226–31, 251–56) and as Hillyard confirms, investigative journalists have often played a much more important role than academics in exposing corporate and state illegality and immorality. Notwithstanding the decline of investigative journalism and the increasing and well-documented corporate control of most forms of media (Monbiot, 2000b), this is a process that is by no means complete. Thus, as Hillyard notes, journalists may *still* often look for a story that academics ignore. Moreover, at particular moments and under certain conditions there may be space for critical voices to intervene and be heard in the mass media. Thus Coleman notes how he was able to gain considerable local, national, and international media interest in his critical and oppositional account of the use of city center CCTV cameras (without acceding to the demand for "horror-comedy"). The growth of international electronic media sources will provide numerous opportunities for this type of exposure. Of course, it is not unheard-of for academics to have their views and findings misrepresented and distorted for commercial advantage. Media attention may also be a double-edged sword in the sense that control over representation and editorial control is never guaranteed. Further, as Fooks notes, a major *obstacle* to his inquiry was the representation by the press of the pensions scandal as implying negligence and incompetence rather than criminal; a series of representations which reinforced the masking and distortion of the past criminal activities of the corporations involved. A related problem is, of course, that a great deal of the work described in this volume is simply deemed un-newsworthy (Tombs and Whyte, 2001; see Alvesalo and Virta on "newsworthiness"). Ironically, Green, in the particular context she was researching, was able to use this to her advantage to gain access to Turkish state institutions, whose representatives calculated that her research would not be published in Turkey.

Quite different from the use of various forms of mass media is another, perhaps more obvious, mechanism through which we must disseminate our findings regarding the nature and prevalence of corporate and state illegality—namely, our teaching of students. Many contributors here note the relative dearth of textbooks around these issues. This is all the more reason for us to adopt the "strategy" of feminist criminologists over the past 25 years: to act upon the (important) demand of most commentators upon university teaching that our research must inform our teaching; to introduce into introductory levels sessions on corporate and state crimes; to build towards the inclusion of discrete modules, units, and streams in these topics; and thereby to create the demand from students for texts for which publishing houses are greedy, as well as to increase the possibility that some of our graduate students will take these issues with them into their own workplaces or research and teaching activities. Alvesalo and Virta's experience of seeing their work on corporate crime change a student's life may be extremely rare, but we all have *some* effect on the ways in which students view and act within the world (surely one of the reasons that we all teach). We certainly must not replicate in our teaching the collective marginalization of the harms and crimes produced by powerful actors.

## Beyond Value-Freedom, For Partisan Objectivity

To continue to produce critical research in the midst of the current neo-liberal assault upon the universities, it is increasingly important for researchers to be linked to counter-hegemonic struggle: to workers' organizations, political and social movements, pressure groups, and community organizations that are committed to challenging state and corporate power. This begins, of course, within the university. The processes of marketization and commodification that we described in our introduction have swept through all aspects of university life, affecting the pay and conditions of all those who work within and support universities—and we must recognize that struggles to preserve the pay and conditions of, for example, our technicians or cleaners or administrative staff, are struggles to defend remaining vestiges of humanity and dignity within our workplaces. Indeed, given the contemporary lip-service paid to the mantra of "the student experience," then our struggles alongside other workers must also be fought in the name of preserving the infrastructure of a better rather than poorer experience for those students.

To identify and then align ourselves with progressive political organizations, to seek their support and/or approval, may raise problems for objective research. But first we must be clear that this is a feature of all forms of research, though one that is rarely recognized by those that conduct "official" research. Accusations of *bias* or *subjectivity* are rare where organizations have granted access on their own terms or even funded research. On the contrary, close associations with wealthy funders, especially when it comes to large corporations and government departments are often worn as badges of honor, or credibility (McClung Lee, 1978). At the same time such associations reinforce the pretensions of the badge-wearer to be the guardian of more robust and more objective knowledge.

So a partisan research project is not, of course, free from the problems engendered by viewing the world from a particular perspective. But such problems—rooted as they are in the pretensions around objectivity—are at least mitigated where researchers recognize, describe, and are open about the perspective from which their research commitments, questions, and modes of analysis and dissemination originate. Put simply, we can start to value objectivity in social research only after we recognize that much of the research conducted in Western liberal democracies—particularly research that relies upon the consent or support of large organizations—is highly partisan in the first place. The historical development of the social sciences has been inseparable from "partisanship" (Hobsbawm, 1998: 179–80).

To some extent, recognizing the inevitability of partisan research, one way or the other, involves, as Sim argues, being answerable to the "other"—or in more general terms which reflect the concerns of this book, being answerable to the relatively powerless. In other words, we should not conduct research in league with powerful groups, nor should we communicate our research exclusively to such groups; our methods of communication must reflect a critical partisanship, and a commitment to audiences beyond the universities.

Recognizing and reading social research in these terms is for us, therefore, not simply an echo of Becker's famous call for a partisan sociology in 1967, when he argued for a sociology that declared itself on the side of the powerless underdog. In his response to Becker, Gouldner noted that this perspective had little potential to challenge the social reformist agenda of mainstream sociology. Declaring oneself "on the side of the powerless" may have little meaning unless it involves an assault on the powerful (Gouldner, 1973: 51). Indeed, independent from, but perhaps influenced by, the Becker/Gouldner debate, feminist research has since developed overtly partisan standpoint positions in order to present critiques of, and engage with, patriarchal power structures. The power of a standpoint position is illustrated well by Ballinger, who uses a feminist standpoint to show that the (British) state was criminally culpable in the executions of three women. Given that these cases were not aberrations, it is likely that the state was equally culpable in the execution of more women. In this study, the standpoint adopted by the author—in particular, the problematization of gender—has been used, carefully, to re-examine state "truths" and construct a powerful case for the expansion of definitions of state crime.

For us, adopting a "standpoint" must mean working in alliance with, or as part of, progressive social movements. Research which strives to attain an organic quality is, for all of the reasons outlined above, more likely not only to be effective in challenging power, but also to be effective in producing an alternative account which reveals hidden processes and experiences. For example, Sim noted that health promotion experts embarking on enthusiastic smoking-prevention campaigns do not possess the elementary level of inside knowledge required for understanding what every prisoner knows: it is the unique combination of intense stress and boredom created by local prison regimes that encourages smoking and turns non-smokers into smokers. Adopting a partisan objectivity often allows the researcher to see what remains obscured to others.

The development of organic links between research and progressive social movements is also becoming irresistible for highly practical reasons, particularly for those concerned with researching questions of power. As funding opportunities are increasingly closed off to those who do not wish to conduct research that has a use value for capital or for government departments, developing links with social movements, trade unions, and campaigning organizations may involve considerable benefits for researchers. Just as teaching and writing are enriched by involvement in movements, campaigning organizations and progressive movements themselves need trained researchers and intellectuals (Epstein: 2001: 201). Indeed, we would go further. For all the deterioration in working conditions and the relative decline in academic pay in higher education in recent years (see Woodward, 2002a, b, c), university academics, particularly those (albeit a diminishing number) on full-time permanent contracts, are in a relatively privileged position, with access to skills and resources that we have a duty to use for those groups and individuals denied access to, or lacking, such privileges. As Philo has recently noted, "There are very few groups of people in the country [the UK] now who are trusted. Politicians aren't trusted, journalists aren't very much trusted. Academics are one of the very few groups who are trusted to tell the truth and they ought to tell the truth" (speaking on *Talking Point*, Radio 4, 12 July 2000).

The significance of developing mutually supportive relationships between critical academics and counter-hegemonic movements is both desirable and necessary. The neo-liberal assault upon the universities has, in one sense, rattled the turrets of the ivory tower and raised the stakes for critical research to be openly partisan. Researchers who refuse to chase large grants or engage in policy evaluations are increasingly vulnerable to the disciplinary labor process mechanisms described in our introduction. This degree of vulnerability means that it is ever more important for critical academics to be involved with organizations that can give them some collective strength and "real world" credibility, and also increases the importance of being involved in networks of critical academics. The doctrine of market populism assigns a morally elevated status to those who produce "socially relevant" work. Within the contexts in which we work, organic links also allow critical researchers to claim this very same morally elevated status, through work which engages directly with contemporary social problems and is directed explicitly towards the development of a more just and humane social order. Within British criminology, for example, the contemporary mantra is policy-relevant research, which translates as research of immediate utility for the powerful—but we can and must use and subvert this language, engaging with policy in alliance with the relatively powerless.

Working towards social justice via academic activity which exposes corporate and state crimes and harms means engaging in two broad types of tasks, namely, the long-term exposure of the contradictions inherent in neo-liberal "common sense" (which our disciplines play a key role in producing and reproducing); and the making of strategic interventions at moments of crisis. On the basis of this volume, such activities would entail, among other things, the abandoning of pretensions to value neutrality; developing "organic" relationships with oppositional groups; recognizing the nature of particular struggles/moments; reflecting constantly and critically on the ways in which the outcomes of research may be used *and* misused; utilizing the credibility and voice granted to academics; avoiding various forms of financial or institutional straitjackets; and engaging in interventions in our own workplaces and in the public sphere, as academics and activists.

We may long have to suffer a capitalist world, one which exploits, distorts, maims, and kills. But while capitalism is defined by certain essential features, as a system it is neither unified nor homogenous: any examination of capitalist social orders, both historically and indeed contemporaneously, makes it clear that capitalist forms of production may be organized in a series of quite different ways within a variety of political and social "shells," producing quite different effects. Power affects people's lives differently, in ways that matter—and a key element in the struggle to attenuate power is the ability to subject it to critical scrutiny. There *are* alternatives. The *raison d'etre* of critical research is precisely to establish such alternatives.

## Note

1. Where an author is cited with no reference given, the reference is to a chapter in this text.

# Bibliography

Adams, S. (1984) *Roche versus Adams,* London: Jonathan Cape.

Agee, P. (1983) *British Intelligence and Covert Action,* Dingle, Ireland: Bandon.

Ainley, P. (1998) Higher Education in a Right State: professionalising the proletariat or proletarianising the professions, in Jary, D. and Parker, M., eds., *The New Higher Education: issues and directions for the post-Dearing university,* Stoke on Trent, England: Staffordshire University Press.

Alasuutari, P. (1998) *An Invitation to Social Research,* London: Sage.

Alexander, C.R. (1999) On the Nature of the Reputational Penalty for Corporate Crime: evidence, *Journal of Law and Economics,* 42 (1), April.

Alford, B.W.E. (1973) *W.D. and H.O. Wills and the Development of the UK Tobacco Industry 1786–1965,* London: Methuen.

Alletzhauser, A. (1990) *The House of Nomura: the rise to supremacy of the world's most powerful company,* London: Bloomsbury.

Alvesalo, A. (1999) A Sitting Duck or a Trojan Horse? Critical Criminology, Control, and White Collar Crime, *The Critical Criminologist,* 9 (2).

Alvesalo, A. and Laitinen, A. (1994) *Perspectives on Economic Crime,* University of Turku, Finland: Publications of the Faculty of Law, Criminal Law and Judicial Procedure, Series A: 20.

Alvesalo, A., Laitinen, A. and Virta, E. (1995) *Tukien Varassa (Depending on Subsidies),* Helsinki: Ministry of the Interior.

Alvesalo, A. and Tombs, S. (2002) Working for Criminalisation of Economic Offending: contradictions for critical criminology? *Critical Criminology,* 10 (4).

Alvesalo, A. and Tombs, S. (2001a) Can Economic Crime Control Be Sustained? *Innovation: the European Journal of the Social Sciences,* 14 (1).

Alvesalo, A. and Tombs, S. (2001b) The Emergence of a "War" on Economic Crime: the case of Finland, *Business and Politics,* 3 (3).

Alvesalo, A. and Tombs, S. (2001c) Working for Criminalization. Contradictions for critical criminology? paper presented to the European Group for the Study of Deviance and Social Control, Venice, 6–8 August.

Amnesty International (2001) *Stopping the Torture Trade*, London: Amnesty International.

Anderson, P. (1977) The Antinomies of Antonio Gramsci, *New Left Review*, 100, January/February.

Arber, S. (1993) Designing Samples, in Gilbert, N., ed., *Researching Social Life*, London: Sage.

Arrigo, B. (2000) Critical Criminology's Discontent: the perils of punishing and a call to action, *The Critical Criminologist*, http://sun.soci.niu.edu/~critcrim/critschool/barrigo.html.

Ashworth, W. (1986) *The History of the British Coal Industry. Volume 5. 1946–1982: The Nationalised Industry*, Oxford: Oxford University Press.

Asmal, K. ed. (1985) *Shoot to Kill? International lawyers' inquiry into the lethal use of firearms by the security forces in Northern Ireland*, Dublin, Ireland: Mercier Press.

Atkinson, R. (1999) Discourses of Partnership and Empowerment in Contemporary British Urban Regeneration, *Urban Studies*, 36 (1).

Aubert, F. (1952) Norwegian Businessmen and Attitudes to Violations of Price and Rationing Regulations, *American Journal of Sociology*, 58.

Audit Commission (1996) *Misspent Youth: young people and crime*, London: Audit Commission.

Ayata, S. (1996) Patronage, Party and State: the politicization of Islam in Turkey, *Middle East Journal*, 50 (1).

Baldwin, J. and McConville, M. (1977) *Negotiated Justice*, Oxford: Martin Robertson.

Balleisen, E.J. (1996) Vulture Capitalism in Antebellum America: the 1841 Federal Bankruptcy Act and the exploitation of financial distress, *Business History Review*, 70.

Ballinger, A. (2000) *Dead Woman Walking*, Aldershot, England: Ashgate.

Bamberg, J.H. (2000) *British Petroleum and Global Oil 1950–1975: the challenge of nationalism*, Vol. 3, Cambridge: Cambridge University Press.

Bamberg, J.H. (1994) *The History of the British Petroleum Company: Vol. 2, the Anglo-Iranian years 1928–1954*, Cambridge: Cambridge University Press.

Barker, T.C. (1977) *The Glassmakers Pilkington: the rise of an international company 1826–1976*, London: Weidenfeld and Nicolson.

Barker, T.C., Campbell, R.H., Mathias, P., and Yamey, B.S. (1971) *Business History*, London: Historical Association.

Barnett, A. (2000) Labour Charged with Excessive Secrecy, *The Observer*, 6 August.

Barnett, H. (1995) Can Confrontation, Negotiation, or Socialization Solve the Superfund Enforcement Dilemma? in Pearce, F. and Snider, L., eds., *Corporate Crime: contemporary debates*, Toronto: University of Toronto Press.

Barnett, H. (1994) *Toxic Debts and the Superfund Dilemma*. Chapel Hill, N.C.: University of North Carolina Press.

Barnett, R. (1994) *The Limits of Competence: knowledge, higher education and society*, Buckingham, England: Society for Research into Higher Education and Open University Press.

Barnett, C. and Low, M. (1996) Lingua Franca: international publishing and the academy as public sphere, paper presented to the British Sociological Association Annual Conference, University of Reading, 4 April.

Barr, N. (2001a) International Student Funding Comparisons: the UK, http://www.guardian.co.uk/Archive/Article/0,4273,4273668,00,html, accessed October 2001.

Barr, N. (2001b) International Student Funding Comparisons: the USA, http://www.guardian.co.uk/Archive/Article/0,4273,4273669,00,html, accessed October 2001.

Barry, A., Osbourne, T. and Rose, N., eds. (1996) *Foucault and Political Reason: liberalism, neoliberalism and rationalities of government*, London: UCL Press.

BBC Radio 4 (2002) *File on 4* Transcript, program transmitted on 22 January, Manchester, England: BBC.

BBC Radio 4 (2001) *File on 4* Transcript, program transmitted on 6 February, http://www.bbc.co.uk/radio4.

Beck, U. (1992) *Risk Society: towards a new modernity,* London: Sage.

Beck, U., Giddens, A. and Lash, S. (1994) *Reflexive Modernization. Politics, Tradition and Aesthetics in the Modern Social Order,* Cambridge: Polity.

Becker, H. (1967) Whose Side Are We On? *Social Problems,* 14 (3).

Beckett, K. and Sasson, T. (2000) *The Politics of Injustice: crime and punishment in America,* London: Pine Forge Press.

Beder, S. (1997) *Global Spin. The corporate assault on environmentalism,* Totnes, England: Green Books.

Belknap, J. (2001) *The Invisible Woman: gender, crime and justice,* Second Edition, Belmont, Calif.: Wadsworth Publishing Company.

Benney, M. (1983) Gramsci on Law, Morality and Power, *International Journal of the Sociology of Law,* 11.

Benson, M., Cullen, F. and Maakestad, W. (1991) *Local Prosecutors and Corporate Crime: final report,* Washington, D.C.: US National Institute of Justice.

Benson, M., Cullen, F. and Maakestad, W. (1988) District Attorneys and Corporate Crime: surveying the prosecutorial gatekeepers, *Criminology,* 26 (3).

Benson, M. and Walker, E. (1988) Sentencing the White-Collar Offender, *American Sociological Review,* 50.

Bergalli, R. (1997) The New Order in Spain and an Hispanic Perspective on the History and Meaning of Social Control, in Bergalli, R. and Sumner, C., eds., *Social Control and Political Order: European perspectives at the end of the century,* London: Sage.

Berrington, E. (2001) *Surviving the Media: a critical analysis of press reporting of disaster and tragedy,* unpublished Ph.D. thesis, Lancaster University, England.

Bittlingmayer, G. (1996) Antitrust and Business Activity: the first quarter century, *Business History Review,* 70.

Blair, T. (1999) *Romanes Lecture,* Oxford, 2 December.

Blankenship, M., ed. (1993) *Understanding Corporate Criminality,* New York: Garland.

Bliss, M. (1974) *A Living Profit: studies in the social history of Canadian business,* Toronto: McClelland and Stewart.

Block, A. (1993) Defending the Mountaintop: a campaign against environmental crime, in Pearce, F. and Woodiwiss, M., eds., *Global Crime Connections: dynamics and control,* Toronto: University of Toronto Press.

Blundell, W. (1976) Equity Funding: I did it for the jollies, in Moffitt, D., ed., *Swindled! Classic Business Frauds of the Seventies,* Princeton, N.J.: Dow Jones Books.

Bolger, A. and Croft, J. (2001) Countrywide Hit by Housing Market Downturn, *Financial Times,* 9 March.

Boliver, D. (1993) Endowments May Not Pay Off Loans, *The Guardian,* 6 January.

Bolton, D. (1988) *Death on the Rock,* London: Thames Television.

Bosely, S. (2000) $2m Plot to Discredit Smoking Study Exposed, *The Guardian,* 7 April.

Bourdieu, P. (1988) *Homo Academicus,* Cambridge: Polity Press.

Bower, T. (1996) *Maxwell: The Final Verdict,* London: Harper Collins.

Bower, T. (1991) *Maxwell: The Outsider,* London: Heinemann.

Boyd, A. (1984) *The Informers,* Dublin, Ireland: Mercier.

Bracken, P. and Thomas, P. (2000) Putting Ethics before Effectiveness, *Open Mind,* 102, March/April, 22.

Braithwaite, J. (1995) Corporate Crime and Republican Criminological Praxis, in F. Pearce and

L. Snider eds., *Corporate Crime: Contemporary Debates*, Toronto: University of Toronto Press.

Braithwaite, J. (1994) A Sociology of Modelling and the Politics of Empowerment, *British Journal of Sociology*, 45 (3).

Braithwaite, J. (1984) *Corporate Crime in the Pharmaceutical Industry*, London: Routledge and Kegan Paul.

Brewer, J.D. and Magee K. (1991) *Inside the RUC: routine policing in a divided society*, London: Clarendon Press.

British Coal Respiratory Disease Litigation (1998) *Griffiths and Others and British Coal Corporation before Hon. Mr Justice Turner*, Judgement, 23 January.

British Society of Criminology (1999) *Code of Ethics for Researchers in the Field of Criminology*, www.lboro.ac.uk/departments/ss/bsc/council/CODEETH.HTM.

Brodeur, P. (1985) *Outrageous Misconduct: the asbestos industry on trial*, New York: Pantheon Books.

Brown, B. (1995) *CCTV in Town Centres: three case studies*. Police Research Group Paper 68, London: Home Office.

Brown, S. (1997) What's the Problem Girls? CCTV and the gendering of public safety, in Norris, C., Moran, J., and Armstrong, G., eds., *Surveillance, Closed Circuit Television and Social Control*, Aldershot, England: Ashgate.

Bruun, N. (2001) Kuka Omistaa Tiedon (Who Owns Knowledge), *Tieteessä Tapahtuu 2*, http://www.tsv.fi/ttapaht/012/bruun.htm, accessed 7 December 2001.

Bryman, A., ed. (1988) *Doing Research in Organisations*, London: Routledge.

Burk, K. (1989) *Morgan Grenfell 1838–1988: the biography of a merchant bank*, Oxford: Oxford University Press.

Cain, M. (1990a) Realist Philosophy and Standpoint Epistemologies or Feminist Criminology as a Successor Science, in Gelsthorpe, L. and Morris, A., eds., *Feminist Perspectives in Criminology*, Milton Keynes, England: Open University Press.

Cain, M. (1990b) Towards Transgression: new directions in feminist criminology, *International Journal of the Sociology of Law*, 18.

Cain, M. (1986) Realism, Feminism, Methodology and Law, *International Journal of the Sociology of Law*, 14.

Calavita, K. and Pontell, H. (1991) Other People's Money Revisited: collective embezzlement in the savings and loan and insurance industries, *Social Problems*, 38 (1), February.

Calavita, K. and Pontell, H. (1990) Heads I Win, Tails You Lose: deregulation, crime and crisis in the savings and loan industry, *Crime and Delinquency*, 36 (3), July.

Calavita, K., Pontell, H. and Tillman, R. (1997) *Big Money Crime*, Berkeley: University of California Press.

Calavita, K., Tillman, R. and Pontell, H. (1997) The Savings and Loan Debacle, Financial Crime, and the State, *Annual Review of Sociology*, 23.

Cantor, D. (1992) Contracting Cancer? The politics of commissioned histories, *Social History of Medicine*, 5.

Carlen, P. (2002) Carceral Clawback, *Punishment and Society*, 4 (1).

Carlen, P., ed. (1985) *Criminal Women*, Cambridge: Polity.

Carson, W.G. (1980a) The Institutionalization of Ambiguity: early British Factory Acts, in Geis, G. and Stotland, E., eds., *White-Collar Theory and Research*, Beverly Hills, Calif.: Sage.

Carson, W.G. (1980b) The Other Price of Britain's Oil: regulating safety in off-shore installations in the British sector of the North Sea, *Contemporary Crises*, 4.

Carson, W.G. and Martin, B. (1974) *The Factory Acts*, London: Martin Roberson.

Carter, H. (2002) Police Chief "Treated like Sacrificial Lamb," *The Guardian*, 19 January.

Castells, M. (2000) Materials for an Exploratory Theory of the Networked Society, *British Journal of Sociology,* 51 (1), January/March.

Castells, M. (1997) *The Power of Identity,* London: Blackwell.

Caudill, H.M. (1977) Dead Laws and Dead Men: manslaughter in a coal mine, *Nation,* 226.

Cavendish, A. (1990) *Inside Intelligence,* London: Collins.

Cayley, D. (1998) *The Expanding Prison: the crisis in crime and the search for alternatives,* Toronto: Anansi Press.

Cayne, B., ed. (1991) *New Webster's Dictionary and Thesaurus of the English Language,* New York: Lexicon Publications Inc.

Centre for Corporate Accountability (2002) *Corporate Crime Update 1,* London: CCA/Unison.

Chadwick, K. and Scraton, P. (2001) Critical Research, in McLaughlin, E. and Muncie, J., eds., *The Sage Dictionary of Criminology,* London: Sage.

Chambliss, W. (1995) State Organised Crime—The American Society of Criminology Presidential Address, in Passas, N., ed., *Organized Crime,* Aldershot, England: Dartmouth.

Chandler Jr., A.D. (1990) *Scale and Scope: The Dynamics of Industrial Capitalism,* Boston: Harvard University Press.

Chandler Jr., A.D. (1977) *The Visible Hand: the managerial revolution in American business,* Boston: Harvard University Press.

Chandler Jr., A.D. (1962) *Strategy and Structure: chapters in the history of American industrial enterprise,* Cambridge, Mass.: MIT Press.

Chapman, S.D. (1991) Review of Hobson (1990), *Business History,* 33, January.

Chapple, C. (1998) *Dow Corning and the Silicon Breast Implant Debacle: a case of corporate crime against women.* Thousand Oaks, Calif.: Sage.

Chernow, R. (1998) *Titan: the life of John D. Rockefeller Sr.,* New York: Random House.

Chitnis, A. and Williams, G. (1999) *Casualisation and Quality.* Mimeo, London: NATFHE.

Christian, W. (1999) Toxic Purity: the progressive era origins of America's Lead paint poisoning epidemic, *Business History Review,* 73.

Christie, N. (1997) Four Blocks against Insight: notes on the over-socialisation of criminologists, *Theoretical Criminology,* 1 (1).

Christie, N. (1993) *Crime Control as Industry. Towards GULAGS, Western style?,* London: Routledge.

Church, R.A. (1969) *Kenricks in Hardware: a family business 1791-1966,* Newton Abbot, England: David and Charles.

City Safe (2000) *Liverpool Citizens Panel: community safety survey,* Liverpool: Safer Merseyside Partnership.

Clapp, B.W. (1994) *An Environmental History of Britain since the Industrial Revolution,* London: Longman.

Clarke, M. (1998) *Citizens Financial Futures: the regulation of retail financial investment in Britain,* Aldershot, England: Ashgate.

Cleary, E. (1984-86) Jabez Spencer Balfour (1843-1916), in Jeremy, D.J. and Shaw, C. eds., *Dictionary of Business Biography,* 1, London: Butterworths.

Clegg, S. (1989) *Frameworks of Power,* London: Sage.

Clinard, M. (1952) *The Black Market.* New York: Holt Rinehart Winston.

Clinard, M. and Yeager, P. (1980) *Corporate Crime,* New York: Free Press.

Clinard, M. and Yeager, P. (1978) Corporate Crime: issues in research, *Criminology,* 16 (2).

Clinard, M., Yeager, P., Brissette, J., Petrashek, D. and Harries, E. (1979) *Illegal Corporate Behavior,* Washington, D.C.: U.S. Department of Justice.

Cochran, P.L. and Nigh, D. (1987) Illegal Corporate Behavior and the Question of Moral

Agency: an empirical examination, in Frederick, W. and Preston, L., eds., *Research in Corporate Social Performance and Policy, Volume 9,* Greenwich, Conn.: JAI Press.

Cohen, M. (1991) Corporate Crime and Punishment: an update on sentencing practice in the federal courts, 1988–90, *Boston University Law Review,* 71 (March).

Cohen, M. (1989) Corporate Crime and Punishment: a study of social harm and sentencing practice in the federal courts, *American Criminal Law Review,* 26, Winter.

Cohen, N. (1999) *Cruel Britannia,* London: Verso.

Cohen, S. (2000) *States of Denial,* London: Polity Press.

Cohen, S. (1981) Footprints on the Sand: a further report on criminology and the sociology of deviance in Britain, in Fitzgerald, M. et al., eds., *Crime and Society. Readings in history and theory,* London: Routledge and Kegan Paul.

Cohen, S. and Taylor, L. (1972) *Psychological Survival: the experience of long-term imprisonment,* Harmondsworth : Penguin.

Cohen, S. and Taylor, L. (1977) Talking about Prison Blues, in Bell, C. and Newby, H., eds., *Doing Sociological Research,* London: George Allen and Unwin.

Cohen, W., Florida, R. and Goe, W. (1994) *University Research Centre in the United States,* Pittsburgh: Carnegie Mellon University Press.

Coleman, C. and Moynihan, J. (1996) *Understanding Crime Data: haunted by the dark figure,* Buckingham, England: Open University Press.

Coleman, D.C. (1969–80) *Courtaulds: an economic and social history,* 3 Volumes, Oxford: Clarendon Press.

Coleman, J. (1989) *The Criminal Elite: the sociology of white-collar crime,* New York: St. Martin's Press.

Coleman, R. and Sim, J. (2000) "You'll Never Walk Alone": CCTV surveillance, order and neoliberal rule in Liverpool city center, *British Journal of Sociology,* 51 (4).

Coleman, R. and Sim, J. (1998) From the Dockyards to the Disney Store: risk, surveillance and security in Liverpool city center, *International Review of Law, Computers and Technology,* 12 (1), March.

Coleman, R., Sim, J. and Whyte, D. (2002) Power, Politics and Partnerships: the state of crime prevention on Merseyside, in Edwards, A. and Hughes, G., eds., *Community Crime Prevention,* Cullompton, England: Willan.

Collinge, C. and Hall, S. (1997) Hegemony and Regime in Urban Governance: towards a theory of the locally networked state, in Jewson, N. and MacGregor, S., eds., *Transforming Cities: contested governance and new spatial divisions,* London: Routledge.

Collins, P.H. (1990) *Black Feminist Thought,* Boston: Unwin Hyman.

Collinson, P. (1999) So Poorly Endowed, *The Guardian,* 6 March.

Consumers' Association (1999) *Endowment Mortgages,* http://www.which-net.org.uk/endowmentmortgages/html.

Consumers' Association (1998) *Endowment Mortgages,* http://www.which-net.org.uk/endowmentmortgages/html.

Cooper, C. and Cartwright, S. (1995) *Mental Health and Stress in the Workplace: a guide for employers,* London: HMSO (not available—report printed and subsequently withdrawn by the Department of Health).

Cotterrell, R. (1984) *The Sociology of Law,* London: Butterworths.

Cowie, I. (1995) Money-Go-Round: debt misery blamed on endowments. Many housebuyers have been trapped needlessly by negative equity says new research, *Daily Telegraph,* 21 January.

Cox, H. (2000) *The Global Cigarette: origins and evolution of British American Tobacco, 1880–1945,* Oxford: Oxford University Press.

CPT (2001) *Report to the Turkish Government on the Visit to Turkey Carried Out by the European*

*Committee for the Prevention of Torture and Degrading Treatment or Punishment (CPT) from 19 to 23 August 1996 and Response of the Turkish Government,* Strasbourg: European Union.

Crace, J. (2001) Free and Fair, *The Guardian, Education Supplement,* 29 May.

Cranston, R. (1982) Regulation and Deregulation: general issues, *University of New South Wales Law Journal,* 5.

Crawford, A. (1998) *Crime Prevention and Community Safety: politics, policies and practices,* Harlow, England: Longman.

Crawford, A. (1997) *The Local Governance of Crime: appeals to community and partnership,* Oxford: Clarendon.

Cressey, D. (1953) *Other People's Money: a study in the social psychology of embezzlement,* Glencoe, Ill.: Free Press.

Cresswell, J. (1998) Improving North Sea Safety, *Petroleum Review,* September.

Crewe, I. (1974) Introduction: studying elites in Britain, in Crewe, I., ed., *Elites in Western Democracy,* London: Croom Helm.

Croall, H. (2001) *Understanding White-Collar Crime,* Buckingham, England: Open University Press.

Croall, H. (1998) *Crime and Society in Britain,* London: Longman.

Croall, H. (1992) *White Collar Crime,* Buckingham, England: Open University Press.

Crowther, C. (2000) Thinking about the "Underclass": towards a political economy of policing, *Theoretical Criminology,* 4 (2).

Currie, J. (1998) Introduction, in Currie, J. and Newson, J., eds., *Universities and Globalisation,* Thousand Oaks, Calif.: Sage.

Currie, J. and Newson, J., eds. (1998) *Universities and Globalisation. Critical perspectives,* Thousand Oaks, Calif.: Sage.

Dalton, A.J.P. (1979) *Asbestos Killer Dust,* London: BSSRS Publications.

*Daily Telegraph* (1995a) City Comment: Penny drops and the game is up, 12 January.

*Daily Telegraph* (1995b) City Comment: Endowments looking terminally ill, 31 January.

Daly, K. (1989) Gender and Varieties of White-Collar Crime, *Criminology,* 27.

Darby, J. (1997) The Environmental Crisis in Japan and the Origins of Japanese Manufacturing in Europe, *Business History,* 39, April.

Davenport, P. (1986) I Did My Duty over Stalker Inquiry, Says Anderton, *The Times,* 2 September.

Davenport-Hines, R.P.T. (2001) *The Pursuit of Oblivion: a global history of narcotics 1500–2000,* London: Weidenfeld and Nicolson.

Davenport-Hines, R.P.T. (1984) *Dudley Docker: the life and times of a trade warrior,* Cambridge: Cambridge University Press.

Davenport-Hines, R.P.T. and Slinn, J. (1992) *Glaxo: a history to 1962,* Cambridge: Cambridge University Press.

Davies, N. (1999) *Ten-Thirty-Three: the inside story of Britain's secret killing machine in Northern Ireland,* Edinburgh: Mainstream Publishing.

Davies, S. (1996a) *Big Brother: Britain's web of surveillance and the new technological order,* London: Pan Books.

Davies, S. (1996b) The Case Against: CCTV should not be introduced, *International Journal of Risk, Security and Crime Prevention,* 4 (1).

Davis, M. (1990) *City of Quartz: excavating the future in Los Angeles,* London: Verso.

Davis, M.L. (1998) *The Dark Side of Fortune: triumph and scandal in the life of oil tycoon Edward L. Doheny,* Berkeley, Calif.: University of California Press.

Dearing, R. (1997) *Higher Education in the Learning Society,* London: HMSO.

Department for Education and Employment (2000) *Blunkett Rejects Anti-Intellectualism and Welcomes Sound Ideas,* news release, 2 February.

Dickson, B. (1999) Miscarriages of Justice in Northern Ireland, in Walker, C. and Starmer, K., eds., *Miscarriages of Justice: a review of justice in error,* London: Blackstone Press.

Dillon, M. (1988) *The Dirty War,* London: Hutchinson.

DiMento, J., Geis, G. and Gelfand, J. (2000–2001) Corporate Crime Liability: a bibliography, *Western State University Law Review,* 28.

Doern, B.G. (1995a) *Fairer Play: Canadian competition policy institutions in a global market.* Policy Study Number 25, Toronto: C.D. Howe Institute.

Doern, B.G. (1995b) Sectoral Green Politics: environmental regulation and the Canadian pulp and paper industry, *Environmental Politics,* 4.

Doern B.G. and Wilks, S. eds. (1998a) *Comparative Competition Policy: national institutions in a global market,* Oxford: Clarendon Press.

Doern B.G. and Wilks, S. (1998b) Conclusions: international convergence and national contrasts, in Doern, G.B. and Wilks, S., eds., *Comparative Competition Policy: national institutions in a global market,* Oxford: Clarendon Press.

Doherty, F. (1986) *The Stalker Affair,* Dublin, Ireland: Mercier Press.

Donnelly, R. (2002) Academics say Casement's Diaries Genuine following Forensic Examination, *Irish Times,* 13 March.

Dorril, S. and Ramsey, R. (1991) *Smear! Wilson and the secret state,* London: Fourth Estate.

Douglas, M.T. (1985) *Risk Acceptability According to the Social Sciences,* New York: Russell Sage.

Dowie, M. (1977) Pinto Madness, *Mother Jones,* 2.

Dyer, C. (2002) Silence Please, *The Guardian,* 9 January.

Dyer, C. (2000) Home Office Censors Report from Anti-Torture Group, *The Guardian,* 13 January.

Eagleton, T. (1996) *Literary Theory. An Introduction.* 2nd Edition, Oxford: Blackwell.

Edelhertz, H. (1970) *The Nature, Impact and Prosecution of White-Collar Crime,* Washington, D.C.: National Institute for Law Enforcement and Criminal Justice.

Edelhertz H. and Overcast, T., eds. (1982) *White Collar Crime: an agenda for research,* Lexington, Mass.: D.C. Heath.

Edney, R. (1997) Prison Officers and Violence, *Alternative Law Journal,* 22 (4), December.

Edwards, J. (1997) Urban Policy: the victory of form over substance, *Urban Studies,* 34 (5/6).

Edwards, M. (1998) Commodification and Control in Mass Higher Education: a double edged sword, in Jary, D. and Parker, M., eds., *The New Higher Education: issues and directions for the post-Dearing University,* Stoke-on-Trent, England: Staffordshire University.

Edwards, S. (1989) *Policing "Domestic" Violence,* London: Sage.

Edwards, S. (1987) "Provoking Her Own Demise": from common assault to homicide, in Hanmer, J. and Maynard, M., eds., *Women, Violence and Social Control,* London: Macmillan.

Edwards, T. and Miller, H. (1998) Change in Mass Higher Education: university, state and economy, in Jary, D. and Parker, M., eds., *The New Higher Education: issues and directions for the post-Dearing University,* Stoke-on-Trent, England: Staffordshire University Press.

Eisenschitz, A. and Gough, J. (1998) Theorising the State in Local Economic Governance, *Regional Studies,* 32 (8).

Epstein, B. (2001) Corporate Culture and the Academic Left, in Philo, G. and Miller, D., eds., *Market Killing: what the free market does and what social scientists can do about it,* London: Pearson Education.

ESRC (1999) *Annual Report 1998/99,* http://www.esrc.ac.uk/esrccontent/publicationslist/arep9899/report9899.html.

Evans, G.R. (2001) The Integrity of UK Academic Research under Commercial Threat, *Science as Culture,* 10 (1).

Fairclough, N. (2000) *New Labour, New Language?* London: Karia Press.

Faith, K. (1993) *Unruly Women,* Vancouver: Press Gang Publishers.

Faligot, R. (1983) *Britain's Military Strategy in Ireland: the Kitson experiment,* Dingle, Ireland: Brandon.

Fallon, I. and Strodes, J. (1983) *DeLorean: the rise and fall of a dream-maker,* London: Hamish Hamilton.

Fanning, D. (1984–86) Clarence Charles Hatry (1888–1965), in Jeremy, D.J. and Shaw C., eds., *Dictionary of Business Biography,* Volume 3, London: Butterworths.

Fay, S.J. (1998) Tough on Crime, Tough on Civil Liberties: some negative aspects of Britain's wholesale adoption of CCTV surveillance during the 1990s, *International Review of Law, Computers and Technology,* 12 (2).

Feeley, M. and Simon, J. (1994) Actuarial Justice: the emerging criminal law, in Nelken, D., ed., *The Futures of Criminology,* London: Sage.

Ferguson, N. (1999) *The House of Rothschilds,* London: Weidenfeld and Nicolson.

Ferrier, R.W. (1982) *The History of the British Petroleum Company, Vol. 1,* Cambridge: Cambridge University Press.

Finlay, A. (1999) Whatever You Say Say Nothing: an ethnographic encounter in Northern Ireland and its sequel, *Sociological Research Online,* 4 (3), http://www.socresonline.org.uk/socre sonline/4/3/finlay.html.

Fitzpatrick, T. (2001) Critical Theory, Information Society and Surveillance Technologies, paper presented to European Group for the Study of Deviance and Social Control, British Section Conference, Lincoln, England, April.

Flynn, L. (1992) *Studded with Diamonds and Paved with Gold: miners, mining companies and human rights in Southern Africa,* London: Bloomsbury.

Fooks, G. (1997) *The Serious Fraud Office: a political history,* Unpublished Ph.D. thesis, University of Southampton, England.

Foot, P. (1989) *Who Framed Colin Wallace?* London: Macmillan.

Forgacs, D., ed. (1988) *A Gramsci Reader,* London: Lawrence and Wishart.

Fortune (2001) *Global 500. The World's Largest Corporations.* http://www.fortune.com/in dexw.jhtml?channel=list.jhtmlandlist_frag=list_global500.jhtmlandlist=19, accessed March 2002.

FOS (2001a) *Mortgage Endowment Complaints: assessment guide,* London, FOS.

FOS (2001b) *Ombudsman News,* February 2001, http://www.financial-ombudsman.org.uk/publications/ ombudsman-news/investment/ab, accessed 17 July 2001.

FOS (2001c) *Ombudsman News,* August 2001, London: FOS.

Foucault, M. (1980) *Power/Knowledge: selected interviews and other writings, 1972–1977* (ed. C. Gordon and trans. by C. Gordon, L. Marshall, J. Mepham and K. Soper), New York: Pantheon.

Foucault, M. (1979) *Discipline and Punish: the birth of the prison* (trans. A. Sheridan), New York: Vintage.

Friedrichs, D. (1996) *Trusted Criminals. White collar crime in contemporary society,* Belmont, Calif.: Wadsworth Publishing Company.

FSA (2001a) *Endowment Mortgage Complaints,* London: FSA.

FSA (2001b) *Endowment Mortgages: seven out of ten households have taken no action,* press release, FSA/PN/086/2001, http://www.FSA.gov.uk/pubs/press/2001/086.html

FSA (2000a) *FSA Factsheet: your endowment mortgage—what you need to know,* London: FSA.

FSA (2000b) *Progress Report on Mortgage Endowments,* London: FSA.

FSA (1999a) *Endowment Mortgages—what to do if you are worried,* FSA/PN/084/1999, 26 August, London: FSA.

FSA (1999b) *Endowments: the FSA's conclusions and actions,* FSA/PN/136/1999, 21 December, London: FSA.

FSA (1999c) *Is an Endowment Mortgage Right for You?* London: FSA.

FSA (1997) *Consumer Complaints,* London: FSA.

Furbey, R. (1999) Urban "Regeneration": reflections on a metaphor, *Critical Social Policy,* 14 (4), November.

Fyfe, N.R. (1995) Crime, Space and Society: key research themes, findings and questions in the 1990s, *Scottish Geographical Magazine,* 111 (3).

Fyfe, N.R. and Bannister, J. (1996) City Watching: CCTV surveillance in public spaces, *Area,* 28 (1).

Garland, D. (1994) Of Crimes and Criminals: the development of criminology in Britain, in Maguire, M., Morgan, R. and Reiner, R., eds., *The Oxford Handbook of Criminology,* Oxford: Oxford University Press.

Garrard, J. (1987) *The Great Salford Gas Scandal of 1887,* Manchester, England: British Gas North Western.

Geiger, R. (1992) The Dynamics of University Research in the United States: 1945–90, in Whiston, T. and Geiger, R., eds., *Research and Higher Education: the United Kingdom and the United States,* Buckingham, England: The Society for Research into Higher Education and Open University Press.

Geis, G. (1967) The Heavy Electrical Equipment Antitrust Cases of 1961, in Clinard, M. and Quinney, R., eds., *Criminal Behaviour Systems,* New York: Holt, Rinehart Winston.

Geis, G. and Goff, C. (1983) Introduction, in Sutherland, E., *White Collar Crime: the uncut version,* London: Yale University Press.

Geis, G., Meier, R. and Salinger, L., eds. (1995) *White Collar Crime: classic and contemporary views,* New York: Free Press.

Geis, G. and Stotland, E. (1980) *White Collar Crime Theory and Research,* Beverly Hills, Calif.: Sage.

Gelbspan, R. (1997) Hot Air on Global Warming: science and academia in the service of the fossil fuel industry, *Multinational Monitor,* 18 (11), November.

Gerber, J. (1990) Enforced Self-Regulation in the Infant Formula Industry: a radical extension of an impractical proposal, *Social Justice,* 17 (1).

Giddens, A. (1991) *Modernity and Self-Identity,* Cambridge: Polity.

Giddens, A. (1990) *The Consequences of Modernity,* Cambridge: Polity.

Gill, P. (1994) *Policing Politics: Security Intelligence and the Liberal Democratic State,* London: Frank Cass.

Gill, S. and Law, D. (1988) *The Global Political Economy,* Hemel Hempstead, England: Harvester Wheatsheaf.

Glantz, S., Slade, J., Bero, L.A., Hanauer, P. and Barnes, D.E., eds. (1996) *The Cigarette Papers,* Berkeley, Calif.: University of California Press.

Glasberg, D.S. and Skidmore, D.L. (1998) The Role of the State in the Criminogenesis of Corporate Crime: a case study of the savings and loan crisis, *Social Science Quarterly,* 79 (1), March.

Gold, T.L. (1969) Roles in Sociological Field Observation, in McCall, G.J. and Simmons, J.L., eds., *Issues in Participant Observation: A text and reader,* Reading, Mass.: Addison-Wesley.

Gold-Biss, M. (1994) *The Discourse on Terrorism. Political Violence and the subcommittee on security and terrorism, 1981–1986,* Peter Lang: New York.

Goldson, B. (2001) New Punitiveness: the politics of child incarceration, in Muncie, J., Hughes, G. and McLaughlin, E., eds., *Youth Justice: critical readings in history, theory and policy,* London: Sage.

Goodall, F. et al., eds. (1997) *International Bibliography of Business History,* London: Routledge.

Goodman, J. and Pringle, P. (1974) *The Trial of Ruth Ellis,* London: David and Charles.

Goss, J. (1996) Disquiet on the Waterfront: reflections on nostalgia and utopia in the urban archetypes of festival market places, *Urban Geography,* 17 (3).

Gottfredson M. and Hirschi, T. (1990) *A General Theory of Crime,* Stanford, Calif.: Stanford University Press.

Gouldner. A.W. (1975) *For Sociology: renewal and critique in sociology today,* London: Pelican.

Gouldner, A.W. (1970) *The Coming Crisis of Western Sociology,* London: Heinemann.

Graham, S. (2000) The Fifth Utility, *Index on Censorship 194,* 29 (3), May/June.

Gramsci, A. (1996) *Selections from Prison Notebooks,* London: Lawrence and Wishart.

Gramsci, A. (1971) *Selections from Prison Notebooks,* London: Lawrence and Wishart.

Green, E. (2001) Is It Cold Out There? Economic history in a business climate, in Hudson, P., ed., *Living Economic and Social History,* Glasgow, Scotland: Economic History Society.

Green, E., and Moss, M. (1982) *A Business of National Importance: the Royal Mail shipping group, 1902–1937,* London: Methuen.

Green, P. (2002) Turkish Jails, Hunger Strikes and the European Drive for Prison Reform, *Punishment and Society,* 4 (1).

Green, P. (2000) Criminal Justice and Democratisation in Turkey: the paradox of transition, in Green P. and Rutherford A., eds., *Criminal Policy in Transition,* Oxford: Hart Publishing.

Green, P. and Ward, T. (2000) State Crime, Human Rights and the Limits of Criminology, *Social Justice,* 27 (1).

Greer, S. (1995) *Supergrasses: a study in anti-terrorist law enforcement in Northern Ireland,* London: Clarendon Press.

Gregory, M. (1994) *Dirty Tricks,* Boston: Little Brown.

Griffiths, R. (1998) Making Sameness: place marketing and the new urban entrepreneurialism, in Oatley, N., ed., *Cities, Economic Competition and Urban Policy,* London: Paul Chapman.

Groombridge, N. and Murji, K. (1994) As Easy as AB and CCTV? *Policing,* 10 (4).

Hagan, J. and Bumiller, K. (1983) Making Sense of Sentencing: a review and critique of sentencing research, in Blumstein, A., Cohen, J., Martin, S. and Tonry, M., eds., *Research on Sentencing: the search for reform, Volume 2,* Washington, D.C.: National Academy Press.

Hagan, J. and Nagel, I. (1982) White-Collar Crime, White-Collar Time, *American Criminal Law Review,* 20.

Hagan, J., Nagel, I. and Albonetti, C. (1980) Differential Sentencing of White–Collar Offenders, *American Sociological Review,* 45.

Hainsworth, P. (1994) Climate of Concern: Northern Ireland. Review Essay, *Crime, Law and Social Change,* 23.

Hakman, M. (1993) *Sata Konkurssia.* Verotarkastuksiin ja Asiantuntijalausuntoihin Perustuva Tutkimus Konkursseihin Liittyvistä Rikoksista (*One Hundred Bankruptcies—A study of criminality connected with bankruptcy situations),* National Institute of Legal Policy Research publications 121/1993. Helsinki, Finland: National Institute of Legal Policy Research.

Hall, S. (1997) The Work of Representation, in Hall, S., ed., *Representation: cultural representations and signifying practices,* London: Sage.

Hall, S. and Scraton, P. (1981) Law, Class and Control, in Fitzgerald, M., McLennan, G. and Pawson, J., eds., *Crime and Society: readings in history and theory,* London: Routledge and Kegan Paul.

Hall, S., Critcher, C., Jefferson, T., Clarke, J. and Roberts, B. (1978) *Policing the Crisis: mugging, the state and law and order,* London: Macmillan.

Hall, T. and Hubbard, P. (1998) Afterword: mappings of the entrepreneurial city, in Hall, T. and Hubbard, P., eds., *The Entrepreneurial City: geographies of politics, regime and representation,* Chichester, England: John Wiley and Sons.

Hall, T. and Hubbard, P. (1996) The Entrepreneurial City: new urban politics, new urban geographies, *Progress in Human Geography*, 20 (2).

Hamilton, V.L. and Sanders, J. (1996) Corporate Crime through Citizens' Eyes: stratification and responsibility in the United States, Russia, and Japan, *Law and Society Review*, 30 (3).

Hannah, L. (1983) *The Rise of the Corporate Economy*, London: Methuen.

Hannah, L. and Ackrill, M. (2001) *Barclays*, Cambridge: Cambridge University Press.

Hansen, H. (1995) *Konkursryttere. Gjengangere in Dobbel Forstand. (Research on Economic Crime, Report 25)*, Oslo, Norway: Norges forskningsråd.

Haraway, D. (1988) Situated Knowledges: the science question in feminism and the privilege of partial perspective, *Feminist Studies*, 14 (3).

Harding, S. (1991) *Whose Science, Whose Knowledge? Thinking from women's lives*, Milton Keynes, England: Open University Press.

Harding, S. (1987) Conclusion: epistemological questions, in Harding S., ed., *Feminism and Methodology*, Milton Keynes, England: Open University Press.

Harding, S. (1986) *The Science Question in Feminism*, Milton Keynes, England: Open University Press.

Harkin, G. (2000) Plotting with Killer Stone, *Sunday People*, October 22.

Harris, J.R. (1998) *Industrial Espionage and Technology Transfer: Britain and France in the Eighteenth Century*, Aldershot, England: Ashgate.

Hartsock, N. (1990) Foucault on Power: A theory for women?, in Nicholson, L.J., ed., *Feminism/Postmodernism*, London: Routledge.

Hartung, F. (1950) White-Collar Offenses in the Wholesale Meat Industry in Detroit, *American Journal of Sociology*, 56.

Harvey, L. (1990) *Critical Social Research*, London: Unwin Hyman.

Harvie, D. (2000) Alienation, Class and Enclosure in UK Universities, *Capital and Class*, 71.

Hay, C. (1999) *The Political Economy of New Labor*, London: Unwin Hyman.

Hay, C. (1996) *Re-stating Social and Political Change*, Buckingham, England: Open University Press.

Haydon, D. and Scraton, P. (2000) "Condemn a Little More, Understand a Little Less": the political context and rights implications of the domestic and European Rulings in the Venables-Thompson case, *Journal of Law and Society*, 27 (3).

HEFCE (1999) *Analysis of the 1999 Financial Forecasts and Annual Operating Statements, Report 99/69, circulated to heads of HEFCE-funded institutions and heads of DENI-funded universities*, Bristol, England: HEFCE.

Heidensohn, F. (1986) *Women and Crime*, Basingstoke, England: Macmillan.

Henhan, R. (2000) Some Alternative Strategies for Improving the Effectiveness of the English Prison Ombudsman Scheme, *Howard Journal of Criminal Justice*, 39 (3), August.

Henry, S. and Milovanovic, D. (1996) *Constitutive Criminology. Beyond postmodernism*, London: Sage.

Heper, M. (1992) The Strong State as a Problem for the Consolidation of Democracy: Turkey and Germany compared, *Comparative Political Studies*, 25 (2), July.

Heper, M. (1985) *The State Tradition in Turkey*. Hull, England: Eothen Press.

Her Majesty's Chief Inspector of Prisons for England and Wales (2002) *HM Prison Dartmoor. Report of an unannounced follow-up inspection 17–21 September 2001*, London: Home Office.

Herrnstein, R.J. and Murray, C.J. (1994) *The Bell Curve: intelligence and class structure in American life*, New York: Free Press.

Hill, C.W., Kelley, P.C., Agle, B.R. et al. (1992) An Empirical Examination of the Causes of Corporate Wrongdoing in the United States, *Human Relations*, 45 (10).

Hillyard, P. and Sim, J. (1997) The Political Economy of Socio-Legal Research, in Thomas, P., ed., *Socio-Legal Studies*, Aldershot, England: Dartmouth.

Hilton, M. (2001) Review of Cox (2000), *Business History*, 43, April.

Hoberg, G. (1998) North American Environmental Regulation, in Doern, G.B. and Wilks, S., eds., *Changing Regulatory Institutions in Britain and North America* Toronto: University of Toronto Press.

Hobsbawm, E. (1998) *On History*, London: Abacus.

Hobsbawm, E. (1994) *Age of Extremes: The short twentieth century 1914–1991*, Harmondsworth, London: Penguin.

Hobson, D. (1990) *The Pride of Lucifer: the unauthorised biography of a merchant bank*, London: Hamish Hamilton.

Hochstedler, E. ed. (1984) *Corporations as Criminals*, Beverly Hills, Calif.: Sage.

Hodgson, G. (1984) *Lloyd's of London: a reputation at risk*, London: Allen Lane.

Hogg, D. (1989) *Statement at the Committee Stage of the Debate on the Prevention of Terrorism (Temporary Provisions) Bill*, 17 January.

Hogwood, B. (1998) Regulatory Institutions in the United Kingdom: increasing regulation in the shrinking state, in Doern, G.B. and Wilks, S., eds., *Changing Regulatory Institutions in Britain and North America* Toronto: University of Toronto Press.

Holroyd, F. and Burbridge, N. (1989) *War without Honour*, Hull, England: Medium.

Holstein, J.A. and Gubrium, J.F. (1997) Active Interviewing, in Silverman, D., ed., *Qualitative Research—theory, method and practice*, London: Sage.

Home Office (2002) *Research Development Statistics Department Publications*. April, London: Home Office RDS.

Home Office (2000a) *Crime Reduction Programme: crime reduction index*, 20th March. http://www.homeoffice.gov.uk/crimprev/cri_index.htm, accessed 20 March 2001.

Home Office (2000b) *Guidance Document. Anti-social behaviour orders*, http://www.homeoffice.gov.uk/cdact/asbo.htm, accessed 22 May 2001.

Home Office (2000c) *Research Development and Statistics Research Programme: business plan, 2000/01*, http://www.homeoffice.gov.uk/rds/resprog1.htm, accessed 16 October 2000.

Home Office (1994) *CCTV: Looking Out for You*, London: Home Office

Hooper, D. (2000) *Reputations under Fire: winners and losers in the libel business*, London: Little, Brown.

Hough, M. and Mayhew, P. (1983) *The British Crime Survey First Report Home Office Research Study No. 16*, London: HMSO.

Hudson, B. (2000) Critical Reflection as Research Methodology, in Jupp, V., Davies, P. and Francis, P., eds., *Doing Criminological Research*, London: Sage.

Hughes, G. (1998) *Understanding Crime Prevention: social control, risk and late modernity*, Buckingham, England: Open University Press.

Hughes, G. (1996) The Politics of Criminological Research, in Sapsford, R., ed., *Researching Crime and Criminal Justice*, Milton Keynes, England: Open University Press.

Hughes, M. (1995) Endowment Mortgages a Bad Bet, Warns Watchdog, *The Guardian*, 29 April.

Huhtamäki, A. (1994) *White Collar Bank Crime in Finland: a study of insider abuse and outsider fraud as cause to banking crisis in Finland—with comparison to Sweden and to the USA (English Summary)*, Helsinki, Finland: Painatuskeskus Oy.

Human Rights Watch (1999) *World Report 1999*, London: Human Rights Watch.

Hunt, A. (1994) Governing the Socio-Legal Project: or what do research councils do? *Journal of Law and Society*, 21.

Hunter, T. (1995) Norwich Union Pulls Out of Endowment Mortgages, *The Guardian*, 11 June.

Hunter, T. (1991a) Crackdown on Endowment Mortgages, *The Guardian*, 10 September.

Hunter, T. (1991b) Why Borrowers Need Home Truth on Endowment Loans, *The Guardian*, 14 September.

Hunter, T. and Pandya, N. (1993) Endowment Loans Get Kiss of Death from Society Chief, *The Guardian*, 14 August.

Hutton, W. (1995) *The State We're In*, London: Jonathan Cape.

*Iltalehti* (1994) Jäätteenmäki is Talking through Her Hat, 31 August.

Inman, P. (2001) Only One in 10 Recalls Endowment Caution, *The Guardian*, 3 July.

Institute of Actuaries (1999) *Report of the Endowment Mortgages Working Party*, London: Institute of Actuaries.

Jackall, R. (1988) *Moral Mazes: The World of Corporate Managers*, New York: Oxford University Press.

Jacoby, N. (1977) *Bribery and Extortion in World Business: a study of corporate political payments abroad*, New York: Macmillan.

Jacoby, R. (2000*) The Last Intellectuals: American culture in the age of academe*. Second Edition, New York: Basic Books.

Jacoby, R. (1999) *The End of Utopia: politics and culture in an age of apathy*, New York: Basic Books.

Jemphrey, A. and Berrington, E. (2000) Surviving the Media: Hillsborough, Dunblane and the press, *Journalism Studies*, 1 (3).

Jenkins, P. (2001) Endowment Hopes Boosted, *The Financial Times*, 7 July.

Jeremy, D.J. (2001) Business History and Strategy, in Pettigrew, A., Thomas, H., and Whittington, R., eds., *Handbook of Strategy and Management*, London: Sage.

Jeremy, D.J. (1998) *A Business History of Britain, 1900–1990s*, Oxford: Oxford University Press.

Jeremy D.J., and Tweedale, G. (1994) *Dictionary of 20th Century Business Leaders*, London: Bowker Saur.

Jessop, B. (1990) *State Theory*, Cambridge: Polity.

Johnson, P. (1987) *Goldfields: a centenary portrait*, London: Weidenfeld and Nicolson.

Jones, A. (1991) *Women Who Kill*, London: Gollancz.

Jones, E. (2001) *The Business of Medicine: the extraordinary history of Glaxo*, London: Profile Books.

Jones, E. (1995) *True and Fair: a history of Price Waterhouse*, London: Hamish Hamilton.

Jones, R. (2001) Half Lloyds TSB Endowments in Trouble, *The Guardian*, 2 June.

Jupp, V. (1989) *Methods of Criminological Research*, London: Unwin Hyman.

Jupp, V., Davies, P. and Francis, P. (2000) *Doing Criminological Research*, London: Sage.

Jupp, V. and Norris, C. (1993) Traditions in Documentary Analysis, in Hammersley, M., ed., *Social Research: philosophy, politics and practice*, London: Sage.

Justice (1989) *Report on Miscarriages of Justice*, London: Justice.

Kelly, L. (1988) *Surviving Sexual Violence*, Cambridge: Polity.

Kelsey, J. (1998) Privatizing the Universities, *Journal of Law and Society*, 25 (1).

Kiander, J. and Vartia, P. (1996) The Great Depression of the 1990s in Finland, *Finnish Economic Papers*, 9 (1).

Kishun, R. (1998) Internationalisation in South Africa, in Scott, P., ed., *The Meanings of Mass Higher Education*, Buckingham, England: Open University Press.

Klein, N. (2000) *No Logo*, London: Flamingo.

Kniffin, K. (1997) Serving Two Masters: university presidents on two boards, *Multinational Monitor*, 18 (11), November.

Knightley, P. (1981) *The Vestey Affair*, London: Macdonald Futura.

Knightley, P., Evans, H., Potter, E. and Wallace, M. (1980) *Suffer the Little Children: the story of thalidomide,* London: Futura.

Kogan, M. and Kogan, D. (1983) *The Attack on Higher Education,* London: Kogan Page.

Korander, T. (1999) "Policezation" and Zero Tolerance in Finland, paper presented to the American Society of Criminology Annual Meeting, Toronto, Canada, 17–20 November.

Korander, T. (1998) Katujen Nollatoleranssi, Tilastojen Kelvottomuus ja Ongelmien Poliisisointi (Zero Tolerance, the Incompetency of Statistics and the Policezation of Problems), *Oikeus* (4).

Korander, T. (1994) *Suomalaisten Turvallisuuden Kokeminen ja Suhtautuminen Poliisiin 1993 (Finns' Experience of Security and Attitudes towards the Police 1993),* Helsinki, Finland: Ministry of the Interior.

Kramer, R. (1992) The Space Shuttle Challenger Explosion: a case study of state-corporate crime, in Schlegel, K. and Weisburd, D., eds., *White Collar Crime Reconsidered,* Boston: Northeastern University Press.

Kramer, R.C. (1989) Criminologists and the Social Movement Against Corporate Crime, *Social Justice,* 16 (2).

Kransdorff, A. (1998) *Corporate Amnesia: keeping know-how in the company,* London: Butterworth-Heinemann.

Kvale, H. (1996) *Interviews,* Beverly Hills, Calif.: Sage.

Kynaston, D. (1999) *The City of London: illusions of gold 1914–1945,* London: Chatto and Windus.

Labour Party (1996) *Tackling Youth Crime: reforming youth justice,* London: Labour Party.

Lacey, N. (1994) Introduction: making sense of criminal justice, in Lacey, N., ed., *A Reader in Criminal Justice,* Oxford: Oxford University Press.

Lacey, N., Wells, C. and Meure, D. (1990) *Reconstructing Criminal Law,* London: Weidenfeld Paperbacks.

Lahti, R. (1983) Finland. National Report, *Revue Internationale de Droit Penal,* 54.

Laitinen, A. and Alvesalo, A. (1994) *Talouden Varjopuoli (The Dark Side of the Economy),* Helsinki, Finland: Ministry of the Interior.

Lappi-Seppälä, T. (1998) *Regulating the Prison Population. Experiences from a long-term policy in Finland.* National Institute of Legal Policy Research Communications 38, Helsinki, Finland: National Institute of Legal Policy Research.

Lashmar, P. (2001) The Stalker Affair, *Violations of Rights in Britain Series,* 3 (27).

Latham, R. (2000) Social Sovereignty, *Theory, Culture and Society,* 17 (4).

Lee, M. and Ermann, M.D. (1999) Pinto "Madness" as a Flawed Landmark Narrative: an organizational and network analysis, *Social Problems,* 46 (1).

Lee, R. (1993) *Doing Research on Sensitive Topics,* London: Sage.

Lees, S. (1996) *Carnal Knowledge,* London: Hamish Hamilton.

Leigh, L. H. (1969) *The Criminal Liability of Corporations in English Law,* London: Weidenfeld and Nicolson.

Leigh, D. (1980) *The Frontiers of Secrecy,* London: Junction Books.

Leishman, F., Loveday, B. and Savage, S. (2000) *Core Issues in Policing,* London: Longman.

Leo, R. (1996) Police Scholarship for the Future: resisting the pull of the policy audience, *Law and Society Review,* 30 (4).

Leppard, D., Walsh, G., Gardner, N. and Nuki, P. (1999) Mortgage Bosses Face Probe, *The Times,* 25 July.

Lester, V.M. (1995) *Victorian Insolvency: bankruptcy, imprisonment for debt, and company winding-up in nineteenth century England,* Oxford: Oxford University Press.

Liebling, A. (2001) Whose Side are we On? Theory, practice and allegiances in prisons research, *British Journal of Criminology,* 41 (3).

Lifton, R. (1987) *The Future of Immortality and Other Essays for a Nuclear Age*, New York: Basic Books.

Lindsay, K. (1979) *Ambush at Tully West: the British intelligence services in action*, Dundalk, Ireland: Dunrod Press.

Lippens, R. (1995) Critical Criminologies and the Reconstruction of Utopia, *Social Justice*, 22.

Lipsey, Lord (2000) Ruling by Research, *Social Sciences—news from the ESRC*, May 2000, www.esrc.ac.uk/news1.html.

Lliars of London, www.lliarsoflondon.com, accessed 2001.

Loader, I. (1996) *Youth, Policing and Democracy*, London: Macmillan.

Lofquist, W. (1993) Legislating Organizational Probation: state capacity, business power and corporate crime control, *Law and Society Review*, 27 (4).

Lofquist, W. (1992) *Crafting Corporate Crime Controls: the development of organizational probation and its implications for criminology*. Unpublished Ph.D. dissertation, University of Delaware.

Lofquist, W., Cohen, M. and Rabe, G., eds. (1997) *Debating Corporate Crime*, Academy of Criminal Justice Sciences, Cincinnati, Ohio: Anderson.

Lukes, S. (1974) *Power. A radical view*, London: Macmillan.

Lynn, M. (1991) *Merck v. Glaxo: the billion-dollar battle*, London: Heinemann.

Lynxwiler, J., Shover, N. and Clelland, D. (1984) Determinants of Sanction Severity in a Regulatory Bureaucracy, in Hochstedler, E., ed., *Corporations as Criminals*, Beverly Hills, Calif.: Sage.

Maakestad, W. (1981) A Historical Survey of Corporate Homicide in the United States: could it be prosecuted in Illinois? *Illinois Bar Journal*, August.

MacLeod, G. and Goodwin, M. (1999) Space, Scale and State Strategy: rethinking urban and regional governance, *Progress in Human Geography*, 23 (4).

Maguire, M. (1997) Crime Statistics, Patterns and Trends: changing perceptions and their implications, in Maguire, M., et al., eds., *The Oxford Handbook of Criminology*, Second Edition, Oxford: Clarendon Press.

Maher, L. (1997) *Sexed Work*, Oxford: Clarendon Press.

Mäkelä, K. (2001) *Talouselämän Rikokset, Rikosoikeus ja Kriminaalipolitiikka –Empiirinen ja Rikosoikeusteoreettinen Tutkimus Rauenneista Konkursseista. (Economic Crimes, Criminal Law and Criminal Policy)*. Suomalaisen lakimiesyhdistyksen julkaisuja, E-sarja No 4, Helsinki, Finland: Suomalainen Lakimiesyhdistys.

Mann, K., Wheeler, S. and Sarat, A. (1980) Sentencing White-Collar Offenders. Symposium: white-collar crime, *American Criminal Law Review*, 17 (4).

Marchak, P. (1991) *The Integrated Circus: the new right and the restructuring of global markets*, Montreal: McGill-Queen's.

Marks, L. and Van den Bergh, T. (1990) *Ruth Ellis: a case of diminished responsibility?* Harmondsworth, England: Penguin.

Marrer, J. and Patten, C. (1976) The Correlates of Consultation: American academics in the real world, *Higher Education*, 5.

Marx, K. (1979) A Critical Analysis of Capitalist Production, in *Capital Volume 1* (trans. Samuel Moore and Edward Aveling), New York: International Publishers.

Marx, K. and Engels, F. (1970) *The German Ideology: part 1*, London: Lawrence and Wishart.

Mathiesen, T. (1986) The Politics of Abolition, *Contemporary Crises*, 10.

Mathiesen, T. (1980) *Law, Society and Political Action*, London: Academic Press.

McCahill, M. (1998) Beyond Foucault: towards a contemporary theory of surveillance, in Norris, C., Moran, J. and Armstrong, G., eds., *Surveillance, Closed Circuit Television and Social Control*, Aldershot: Ashgate.

McClintick, D. (1976) The Biggest Ponzi Scheme: a reporter's journal, in Moffitt, D., ed. *Swindled: classic business frauds of the seventies.* Princeton, N. J.: Dow Jones Books.

McClung Lee, A. (1978) *Sociology for Whom?* New York: Oxford University Press.

McCraw, T.K. and Cruikshank, J.L., eds. (1999) *The Intellectual Venture Capitalist: John H. McArthur and the work of the Harvard Business School, 1980–1995,* Boston, Mass.: Harvard Business School Press.

McDonald, H. (2001) Murder Probe "Blocked to Protect Police Informer," *The Observer,* 11 November.

McGuffin, J. (1974) *Guineapigs,* Harmondsworth, England: Penguin Books.

McKendy, J. (1992) Ideological Practices and the Management of Emotions: the case of wife abuse, *Critical Sociology,* 19.

McLaughlin, E. (1996) Political Violence, Terrorism and Crimes of the State, in Muncie, J. and McLaughlin, E., eds., *The Problem of Crime,* London: Sage/Open University Press.

McLean, I. and Johnes, M. (2000) *Aberfan: government and disasters,* Cardiff, Wales: Welsh Academic Press.

McNamee, F. and Ruane, C. (1991) *Report of the Public Inquiry into the Killing of Fergal Caraher and the Wounding of Mícheál Caraher 30th December 1990,* Dublin, Ireland: Irish National Congress.

McNeill, S. (1996) Getting Away with Murder, *Trouble and Strife,* 33, Summer.

Medlicott, D. (2001) *Surviving the Prison Place: narratives of suicidal prisoners,* Aldershot, England: Ashgate.

Menzies, R. and Chunn, D. (n.d.) *Discipline in Dissent: Canadian academic criminology at the millennium,* unpublished monograph.

Messerschmidt, J. (1997) *Crime as Structured Action,* Thousand Oaks, Calif.: Sage.

Michael, J. (1982) *The Politics of Secrecy: confidential government and the public right to know,* Harmondsworth, England: Penguin.

Michalowski R. (1985) *Order, Law and Power,* New York: Random House.

Michie, R. (1999) *The London Stock Exchange: A history,* Oxford: Oxford University Press.

Miliband, R. (1973) *The State in Capitalist Society,* London: Quartet.

Miller, J. and Glassner, B. (1997) The "Inside" and the "Outside": finding realities in interviews, in Silverman, D., ed., *Qualitative Research — Theory, Method and Practice,* London: Sage.

Mills, C. Wright (1967) *Power, Politics & People: The Collected Essays of C. Wright Mills,* New York: Oxford University Press.

Milne, S. (1994) *The Enemy Within: the secret war against the miners,* London: Pan.

Ministry of Interior (1992) *Result Orientated Plan of the Police 1993–1996,* Helsinki, Finland: Sisäasiainministeriö.

Mitchell, A., ed. (2001) *The Amazon Journal of Roger Casement,* Dublin, Ireland: Lilliput Press.

Mock L. and Rosenbaum, D. (1988) *A Study of Trade Secrets Theft in High Technology Industries,* Washington, D.C.: U.S. National Institute of Justice.

Molotch, H. and Logan, J. (1985) Urban Dependencies: new forms of use and exchange in US cities, *Urban Affairs Quarterly,* 21.

Monbiot, G. (2000a) Big Business as Seen on TV, *The Guardian,* 14 December.

Monbiot, G. (2000b) *Captive State: the corporate takeover of Britain,* London: Macmillan.

Monbiot, G. (1998) Unsafe to Criticise, *The Guardian,* 21 May.

Monbiot, G. (1997) Law and the Profits of PR, *The Guardian,* 21 August.

Moore, C. (1966) *The Kincora Scandal: political cover-up and intrigue in Northern Ireland,* Dublin, Ireland: Marino Books.

Morera, E. (1990) *Gramsci's Historicism: a realist interpretation,* London: Routledge.

Moss, M.S. (2000) *Standard Life, 1825–2000: the building of Europe's largest mutual life company,* Edinburgh, Scotland: Mainstream.

Mullin, J. (2000) Was an IRA Informer So Valuable That Murder Was Committed to Protect Him? *The Guardian,* 25 September.

Muncie, J. and McLaughlin, E., eds. (1996) *The Problem of Crime,* London: Sage/Open University Press.

Murphy, D. (1991) *The Stalker Affair and the Press,* London: Unwin Hyman.

Murray, R. (1998) *State Violence: Northern Ireland 1969–1997,* Dublin, Ireland: Mercier Press.

Murray, R. (1997) *The SAS in Ireland,* Dublin, Ireland: Mercier Press.

Muttitt, G. and Lindblom, H. (forthcoming) *Degrees of Capture: an examination of the relationship between universities, the oil and gas industries and climate change,* Oxford: Corporate Watch.

Nader, R. (1965) *Unsafe at Any Speed,* New York: Grossman.

Naffine, N. (1996) *Feminism and Criminology,* Philadelphia: Temple University Press.

Needleman M. and Needleman, C. (1979) Organizational Crime: two models of criminogenesis, *Sociological Quarterly,* 20 (4).

Nelken, D. (1997) White-Collar Crime, in Maguire, M., Morgan, R. and Reiner, R., eds., *The Oxford Handbook of Criminology,* Oxford: Clarendon Press.

Nelken, D., ed. (1994a) *White-Collar Crime,* Aldershot, England: Dartmouth.

Nelken, D. (1994b) White-Collar Crime, in Nelken, D., ed., *White-Collar Crime,* Aldershot, England: Dartmouth.

Nevins, A. (1953) *Study in Power: John D. Rockefeller, industrialist and philanthropist.* Two Volumes, New York: Scribners.

Nevins, A. (1940) *John D. Rockefeller: the heroic age of American enterprise.* Two Volumes, New York: Scribners.

Newman, D. (1953) Public Attitudes towards a Form of White-Collar Crime, *Social Problems,* 4, January.

Newson, J. and Buchbinder, H. (1988) *The University Means Business,* Toronto: Garamond Press.

Ní Aoláin, F. (2000) *The Politics of Force: conflict management and state violence in Northern Ireland,* Belfast, Northern Ireland: Blackstaff Press.

Nichols, T. and Beynon, H. (1977) *Living with Capitalism,* London: Routledge.

Nicholson, L.J., ed. (1990) *Feminism/Postmodernism,* London: Routledge.

Niiniluoto, I. (2001) Julkisuusperiaate ja Tutkimustulosten Salailu (The Principle Of Publicity and the Secrecy Of Scientific Results), *Tieteessä tapahtuu* 2, http://www.tsv.fi/ttapaht/012/nii niluoto.htm, accessed 7 December 2001.

NIO (1990) *The Stevens' Inquiry: Statement in the House of Commons today by the Secretary of State, Rt. Hon. Peter Brooke, MP,* Belfast, Northern Ireland: NIO.

Norris, C. (1996) *Reclaiming Truth. Contributions to a critique of cultural relativism.* London: Lawrence and Wishart.

Norris, C. and Armstrong, G. (1998) Introduction: power and vision, in Norris, C., Moran, J. and Armstrong, G., eds., *Surveillance, Closed Circuit Television and Social Control,* Aldershot, England: Ashgate.

Oakley, A. (1981) Interviewing Women: a contradiction in terms, in Roberts, H., ed., *Doing Feminist Research,* London: Routledge and Kegan Paul.

Oc, T. and Tiesdell, S. (1997) *Safer City Centres: reviving the public realm,* London: Paul Chapman Publishing.

O'Connor, J. (1973) *The Fiscal Crisis of the State,* New York: St Martin's Press.

O'Dowd, L. (1990) New Introduction, in Memmi, A., *The Colonizer and the Colonized,* London: Earthscan.

OFT (1995a) *Endowment Mortgages,* London: OFT.

OFT (1995b) *Mortgage Repayment Methods,* London: OFT.

Oikeusministeriö (1996) *Ehdotus Hallituksen Esitykseksi Ulosmittauksen Tehostamista Koskevaksi Lainsäädännöksi (Motion of a Governmental Proposal to Reform the Law on Execution Proceedings).* Helsinki, Finland: Oikeusministeriön lainvalmisteluosasto.

Oikeusministeriö (1983) *Taloudellisen Rikollisuuden Selvittelytyöryhmän Mietintö (The Report of the Working Group on Economic Crime),* Helsinki: Oikeusministeriön lainvalmisteluosaston julkaisu.

Orr, L. (1997) Globalisation and the Universities: towards the market university?, *Social Dynamics,* 23 (1).

Ovetz, R. (1996) Turning Resistance into Rebellion: student movements and the entrepreneurialisation of the universities, *Capital and Class,* 58.

Passerini, L. (1986) Oral Memory of Fascism, in Forgacs, D., ed., *Rethinking Italian Fascism: capitalism, populism and culture,* London: Lawrence and Wishart.

Paternoster, R. and Simpson, S. (1996) Sanction Threats and Appeals to Morality: testing a rational choice model of corporate crime, *Law and Society Review,* 30.

Paternoster, R. and Simpson, S. (1993) A Rational Choice Theory of Corporate Crime, in Clarke, R. and Felson, M., eds., *Routine Activities and Rational Choice: advances in criminological theory,* New Brunswick, N.J.: Transaction.

Paulus, I. (1974) *The Search for Pure Food: a sociology of legislation in Britain,* London: Martin Robertson.

Pearce, F. (1990) Commercial and Conventional Crime in Islington, *Second Islington Crime Survey,* London: Economic and Social Research Council.

Pearce, F. (1976) *Crimes of the Powerful,* London: Pluto Press.

Pearce, F. and Snider, L., eds. (1995) *Corporate Crime: contemporary debates,* Toronto: University of Toronto Press.

Pearce, F. and Tombs, S. (2001) Crime, Corporations and the "New" Social Order, in Potter, G., ed., *Controversies in White-Collar Crime,* Cincinnati, Ohio: Anderson.

Pearce, F. and Tombs, S. (1998) *Toxic Capitalism: corporate crime and the chemical industry,* Aldershot, England: Dartmouth.

Pearce, F. and Tombs, S. (1996) Hegemony, Risk and Governance: "'social" regulation and the US chemical industry, *Economy and Society,* 25 (3), August.

Pearce, F. and Tombs, S. (1991) Policing Corporate "Skid Rows." A reply to Keith Hawkins, *British Journal of Criminology,* 31 (4).

Pearce, F. and Tombs, S. (1990) Ideology, Hegemony and Empiricism: compliance theories of regulation, *British Journal of Criminology,* 30 (4).

Peppin, P. (1995) Feminism, Law and the Pharmaceutical Industry, in Pearce, F. and Snider, L., eds., *Corporate Crime: contemporary debates,* Toronto: University of Toronto Press.

Perraton, J., Goldblatt, D., Held, D. and McGrew, A. (1997) The Globalization of Economic Activity, *New Political Economy,* 2 (2).

Phillips, D. (1994) *The Research Mission and Research Manpower. Universities in the Twenty First Century: a lecture series,* London: Paul Hamlyn Foundation, National Commission on Education and Council for Industry and Higher Education.

Philo, G. and Miller, D. (2001) Introduction, in Philo, G. and Miller, D., eds., *Market Killing. What the free market does and what social scientists can do about it,* London: Pearson Education.

PIA (2000a) *1999 Disclosure Report,* London: PIA.

PIA (2000b) *Interest Only Mortgages. Regulatory Update 80.* London: FSA.

PIA (1999) *1998 Disclosure Report,* London: PIA.

Pickering, S. (2001) Undermining the Sanitized Account. Violence and emotionality in the field in Northern Ireland, *British Journal of Criminology,* 41 (3), Summer.

Playfair, G. (1971) *The Punitive Obsession,* London: Victor Gollancz.

Pollak, O. (1950) *The Criminality of Women,* Philadelphia: University of Pennsylvania Press.

Pontell, H., Calavita, K. and Tillman, R. (1994) Corporate Crime and Criminal Justice System Capacity: government response to financial institution fraud, *Justice Quarterly* 11 (3), September.

Pope, H. and Pope, N. (1997) *Turkey Unveiled: Ataturk and After,* London: John Murray.

Post, J. (1998) *Research in Corporate Social Performance and Policy. Volume 15,* Stamford, Conn.: JAI Press.

Poster, M. (1997) *Cultural History and Postmodernity Disciplinary Readings and Challenges,* New York: Columbia Press.

Poulantzas, N. (1978) *State Power Socialism,* London: Verso.

Poulantzas, N. (1970) *Fascism and Dictatorship,* London: New Left Books.

Poveda, T. (1992) White-Collar Crime and the Justice Department: the institutionalization of a concept, *Crime, Law and Social Change,* 17.

Power, C. (2003) *A Critical Examination of the Normalisation of Special Powers within the European Union and their Impact on Operational Policing,* unpublished Ph.D. thesis, Edge Hill College of Higher Education, England.

Presdee, M. and Walters, R. (1998) The Perils and Politics of Criminological Research and the Treat to Academic Freedom, *Current Issues in Criminal Justice,* 10 (2).

Prince, M. (1988) *God's Cop: The Biography of James Anderton,* London: Frederick Muller.

Pringle, P. (1998) *Dirty Business: Big Tobacco at the Bar of Justice,* London: Aurum Press.

Proctor, R.N. (2000) Review of Harlow, G.E., ed. (1998), *The Nature of Diamonds,* Cambridge/New York; Cambridge University Press, in *Isis,* 91.

Punch, M. (1998) Politics and Ethics in Qualitative Research, in Denzin, N. and Lincoln, Y., eds., *The Landscape of Qualitative Research,* London: Sage.

Punch, M. (1996) *Dirty Business: exploring corporate misconduct. Analysis and cases,* London: Sage.

Punch, M. (1993) Observation and the Police: the research experience, in Hammersley, M., ed., *Social Research: philosophy, politics and practice,* London: Sage.

Ramsey, R. (1996) Of Conspiracies and Conspiracy Theories: the truth buried by the fantasies, *Political Notes,* 128.

Ramsey, R. (2000) Getting It Right: the security agencies in modern society, *Lobster,* 41.

Raphael, A. (1994) *Ultimate Risk,* London: Banham.

Raw, C. (1977) *Slater Walker: an investigation of a financial phenomenon,* London: Deutsch.

Raw, C. et al. (1971) *Do You Sincerely Want to Be Rich? Bernard Cornfeld and IOS: An International Swindle,* London: Deutsch.

RCCP (1953) *Royal Commission on Capital Punishment 1949–1953 Report,* London: HMSO.

Reader, W.J. (1970–75) *Imperial Chemical Industries,* two volumes, Oxford: Oxford University Press.

Reasons, C. and Goff, C. (1980) Corporate Crime: a cross-national analysis, in Geis, G. and Stotland, E., eds., *White-Collar Crime Theory and Research,* Beverly Hills, Calif.: Sage.

Reed, M. (1989) *The Sociology of Management,* New York: Harvester Wheatsheaf.

Reeve, A. (1998) The Panopticisation of Shopping: CCTV and leisure consumption, in Norris, C., Moran, J. and Armstrong, G., eds., *Surveillance, Closed Circuit Television and Social Control,* Aldershot, England: Ashgate.

Reiman, J. (1998) *The Rich Get Richer and the Poor Get Prison,* Boston: Allyn and Bacon.

Reiss, A. and Tonry, M. (1993) Organizational Crime, in Tonry, M. and Reiss, A., eds., *Beyond the Law: crime in complex organizations,* Chicago: University of Chicago Press.

Ricci, D. (1984) *The Tragedy of Political Science: politics, scholarship and democracy*, New Haven, Conn.: Yale University Press.

Richardson, K.M. (1984–86) Ernest Terah Hooley (1859–1947), in Jeremy D.J. and Shaw C., eds., *Dictionary of Business Biography*, London: Butterworths.

Rigakos, G.S. (1999) Risk Society and Actuarial Criminology: prospects for a critical discourse, *Canadian Journal of Criminology*, 41 (2).

Risse, T., Ropp, S. and Sikkink, K., eds. (1999) *The Power of Human Rights: international norms and domestic change*, Cambridge: Cambridge University Press.

Rivers, J. (1998) Chomsky Warns of Corporate Secrecy Threat, *Times Higher Education Supplement*, 20 November.

Rix, B., Walker D., and Brown, R. (1997) *A Study of Deaths and Serious Injuries Resulting from Police Vehicle Accidents, AH312*, London: Home Office.

Robb, G. (1992) *White Collar Crime in Modern England: Financial Fraud and Business Morality, 1845–1929*, Cambridge: Cambridge University Press.

Robertson, G. (1999) *The Justice Game*, London: Vintage Books.

Robinson, J. (2001) *Prescription Games: money, ego and power inside the global pharmaceutical industry*, New York: Simon and Schuster.

Rock, P. (1994) The Social Organisation of British Criminology, in Maguire, M., Morgan, R. and Reiner, R., eds., *The Oxford Handbook of Criminology*, Oxford: Oxford University Press.

Rock, P. and Holdaway, S. (1998) Thinking about Criminology: "facts are bits of biography," in Holdaway, S. and Rock, P., eds., *Thinking about Criminology*, London: UCL Press.

Rodriguez, L. and Barlow, D. (1999) Structural Contradictions and the U.S. Sentencing Commission — the development of federal organizational sentencing guidelines, *Crime, Law and Social Change*, 32 (2).

Rogers, A. (1997) *Secrecy and Power in the British State: a history of the Official Secrets Act*, London: Pluto.

Rolston, B. (2000) *Unfinished Business: state killings and the quest for truth*, Belfast, Northern Ireland: Beyond the Pale.

Rolston, B. (1998) Crimes of Passion: sociology, research and political violence, *Irish Journal of Sociology*, 8.

Roniger, L. and Gne-Ayata, A. (1994) *Democracy, Clientelism and Civil Society*, Boulder, Colo.: Lynne Reiner.

Rose, N. (1996) The Death of the Social? Refiguring the territory of government, *Economy and Society*, 26.

Rossi, P., Waite, E., Bose, C.E. and Berk, R.E. (1974) The Seriousness of Crimes: normative structure and individual differences. *American Sociological Review*, 39, April.

Rowell, A. (1996) *Green Backlash. Corporate subversion of the environment movement*, London: Routledge.

Ruggiero, V. (1994) Corruption in Italy: an attempt to identify the victims, *Howard Journal of Criminal Justice*, 33 (4).

Ryan, M. and Sim, J. (1998) Power, Punishment and Prisons in England and Wales 1975–1996, in Weiss, R. and South, N., eds., *Comparing Prison Systems*, Amsterdam: Gordon and Breach.

Rynbrandt, L.J. and Kramer, R.C. (1995) Hybrid Nonwomen and Corporate Violence: the silicone breast case, *Violence against Women*, 1 (3).

Said, E. (1981) *Covering Islam: how the media and the experts determine how we see the rest of the world*, New York: Pantheon.

Salmi, J. (1993) *Violence and Democratic Society. New approaches to human rights*, London: Zed Books.

Salter, B. and Tapper, T. (1994) *The State and Higher Education,* Ilford, England: Woburn Press.

Sampson, A. (1987) *Black and Gold—tycoons, revolutionaries and apartheid,* London: Hodder and Stoughton.

Sampson, A. (1982) *The Money Lenders: bankers in a dangerous world,* London: Coronet Books.

Sampson, A. (1977) *The Arms Bazaar,* London: Coronet Books.

Sampson Report (1986) *Report of the Investigation by Chief Constable Colin Sampson, Q.P.M., into Allegations of Misconduct against Deputy Chief Constable John Stalker of the Greater Manchester Police,* West Yorkshire Police.

Sanders, A. (1997) Criminal Justice: the development of criminal justice research in Britain, in Thomas, P., ed., *Socio-Legal Studies,* Aldershot, England: Dartmouth.

Sanderson, M (1972) *The Universities and British Industry 1850–1970,* London: Routledge and Kegan Paul.

Sarantakos, S. (1998) *Social Research.* 2nd edition, London: Macmillan.

Sawicki, J. (1991) *Disciplining Foucault,* London: Routledge.

Sawyer, R. (1997) *Roger Casement's Diaries 1910: The black and the white,* London: Pimlico.

Sayar, S. (1977) Political Patronage in Turkey, in Gellner, E. and Waterbury, J., eds., *Patrons and Clients,* London: Duckworth.

Scheper-Hughes, N. (1992) *Death without Weeping,* Berkeley: University of California Press.

Schiffrin, A. (2000) *The Business of Books,* London: Verso.

Schiller, N.G. (1992) What's Wrong with This Picture? The hegemonic construction of culture in AIDS research in the United States, *Medical Anthropology Quarterly,* 6 (3).

Schlegel, K. and Weisburd, D., eds. (1992) *White-Collar Crime Reconsidered,* Boston: Northeastern Press.

Schlesinger, P. and Tumber, H. (1995) *Reporting Crime: the media politics of criminal justice,* Oxford: Clarendon.

Schrecker, T. (2001a) From the Welfare State to the No-Second-Chances State, in Boyd, S., Chunn D. and Menzies, R., eds., *[Ab]using Power: The Canadian Experience,* Halifax: Fernwood.

Schrecker, T. (2001b) Using Science in Environmental Policy: can Canada do better? in Parson, T., ed., *Governing the Environment: persistent challenges, uncertain innovations,* Toronto: University of Toronto Press.

Scott Report (1996) *Report of the Inquiry into the Export of Defence Equipment and Dual-Use Goods to Iraq and Related Prosecutions,* London: HMSO.

Scraton, P., ed. (1997) *"Childhood" in "Crisis"?,* London: UCL Press.

Scraton, P. (1985) *The State of the Police,* London: Pluto Press.

Scraton, P., ed. (1987) *Law, Order and the Authoritarian State,* Milton Keynes, England: Open University Press.

Scraton, P. and Chadwick, K. (1991) The Theoretical and Political Priorities of Critical Criminology, in Stenson, K. and Cowell, D., eds., *The Politics of Crime Control,* London: Sage.

Scraton, P., Jemphrey, A. and Coleman, S. (1995) *No Last Rights: The denial of justice and the promotion of myth in the aftermath of the Hillsborough disaster,* Liverpool: Liverpool City Council/Alden Press.

Scraton, P., Sim, J. and Skidmore, P. (1991) *Prisons under Protest,* Milton Keynes, England: Open University Press.

Searle, G.R. (1998) *Morality and the Market in Victorian Britain,* Oxford: Oxford University Press.

Sears, A. and Morera, C. (1994) The Politics of Hegemony: democracy, class struggle and social movements, *Transformations,* 1.

Seidler, L., Andrews, F. and Epstein, M. (1977) *The Equity Funding Papers: The anatomy of a fraud,* New York: John Wiley.

Shapiro, S. (1990) Collaring the Crime, Not the Criminal: considering the concept of white-collar crime, *American Sociological Review,* 55 (June).

Shapiro, S. (1985) The Road Not Taken: the elusive path to criminal prosecution for white collar offenders, *Law and Society Review,* 19.

Shapiro, S. (1983) The New Moral Entrepreneurs: corporate crime crusaders, *Contemporary Sociology,* 12.

Shapiro, S. (1980) *Thinking about White-Collar Crime,* Washington, D.C.: National Institute of Justice.

Shaw, C. (1984–86) Horatio William Bottomley (1860–1933), in Jeremy, D.J. and Shaw C., eds., *Dictionary of Business Biography,* London: Butterworths.

Shearing, C.D. and Stenning, P.C. (1996) From the Panopticon to Disney World: the development of discipline, in Muncie, J., McLaughlin, E. and Langan, M., eds., *Criminological Perspectives: a reader,* Milton Keynes, England: Open University Press.

Shiells, D. (1991) The Politics of Policing: Ireland 1919–1923, in Emsley, C. and Weinberger, B., eds., *Policing Western Europe—politics, professionalism and public order, 1850–1940,* New York: Greenwood Press.

Short, E. and Ditton, J. (1995) Does CCTV Affect Crime? *CCTV Today,* 2 (2), Spring.

Shover, N. (1998) White Collar Crime, in Tonry, M., ed, *Handbook on Crime and Punishment,* New York: Oxford University Press.

Shover, N. (1980) The Criminalization of Corporate Behaviour: federal surface coal mining, in Geis, G. and Stotland, E., eds., *White-Collar Crime Theory and Research,* Beverly Hills, Calif: Sage.

Shover, N. and Bryant, K. (1993) Theoretical Explanations of Corporate Crime, in Blankenship, M., ed., *Understanding Corporate Criminality,* New York: Garland.

Shover, N., Clelland, D.A. and Lynwiler, J. (1986) *Enforcement or Negotiation: constructing a regulatory bureaucracy,* Albany, N.Y.: State University of Albany Press.

Showstack-Sassoon, A. (2000) *Gramsci and Contemporary Politics. Beyond pessimism of the intellect,* London: Routledge.

Sim, J. (2002) The Future Organisation of Prison Health Care: a critical analysis, *Critical Social Policy,* 22 (2).

Sim, J. (2000/01) The Victimised State, *Criminal Justice Matters 42,* Winter.

Sim, J. (2000) "One Thousand Days of Degradation": New Labour and old compromises at the turn of the century, *Social Justice,* 27 (2).

Sim, J. (1994a) The Abolitionist Approach: a British perspective, in Duff, A., Marshall, S., Dobash R.E. and Dobash, R.P. eds., *Penal Theory and Practice,* Manchester, England: Manchester University Press.

Sim, J. (1994b) Tougher Than the Rest? Men in prison, in Newburn, T. and Stanko, E.A., eds., *Just Boys Doing Business?,* London: Routledge.

Sim, J. (1990) *Medical Power in Prisons,* Milton Keynes, England: Open University Press.

Sim, J. (1987) Working for the Clampdown: prisons and politics in England and Wales, in Scraton, P., ed., *Law, Order and the Authoritarian State,* Milton Keynes, England: Open University Press.

Sim, J., Ruggiero, V. and Ryan, M. (1995) Punishment in Europe: perceptions and commonalities, in Ruggiero, V., Ryan, M. and Sim, J., eds., *Western European Prison Systems,* London, England: Sage.

Sim, J., Scraton, P. and Gordon, P. (1987) Introduction: crime, the state and critical analysis, in

Scraton, P., ed., *Law, Order and the Authoritarian State,* Milton Keynes, England: Open University Press.

Simon, D. and Eitzen, D. (1999) *Elite Deviance.* 4th edition, Boston: Allyn and Bacon.

Simon, J. (1974) Michel Foucault on Attica: an interview, *Telos,* 19.

Simpson, C., ed. (1998a) *Universities and Empire. Money and politics in the social sciences during the cold war,* New York: the New Press.

Simpson, C. (1998b) Universities, Empire and the Production of Knowledge: an introduction, in Simpson, C., ed., *Universities and Empire. Money and politics in the social sciences during the cold war,* New York: The New Press.

Simpson, S. (1997) *Why Corporations Obey the Law,* New York: Cambridge University Press.

Simpson, S. (1992) Corporate Crime Deterrence and Corporate Control Policies: views from the inside, in Schlegel, K. and Weisburd, D., eds., *Essays in White Collar Crime,* Boston: Northeastern Press.

Simpson, S. (1987) Cycles of Illegality: antitrust violations in corporate America, *Social Forces,* 64.

Simpson, S. (1986) The Decomposition of Antitrust: testing a multi-level longitudinal model of profit squeeze, *American Sociological Review,* 51: 859–875.

Simpson, S. and Koper, C. (1992) Deterring Corporate Crime, *Criminology,* 30 (3).

Simpson, S., Paternoster, R. and Piquero, N. (1998) Exploring the Micro-Macro Link in Corporate Crime Research, *Research in the Sociology of Organizations,* 15.

Sisäasiainministeriö (1997) *Talousrikollisuuden ja Harmaan Talouden Torjunta Suomessa. Talousrikostorjunnan Vuosiraportti (Report on the Control of Economic Crime and the Grey Economy),* Helsinki, Findland: Sisäasiainministeriö.

Sisäasiainministeriö (1994) Sisäasiainministeriö Tiedottaa. Vain Murto-Osa Talousrikollisuuden Aiheuttamista Vahingoista Tuomitaan (Only a Fraction of Known Damages Caused by Economic Crimes are adjudged) 9 August, Helsinki, Finland: Ministry of the Interior.

Sisäasiainministeriö (1992) *Poliisin Tulossuunnitelma (Result Orientated Plan of the Police) 1993-1996,* Helsinki, Finland: Ministry of the Interior.

Sivanandan, A. (1990) *Communities of Resistance: writing on black struggles for socialism,* London: Verso.

Slapper G. and Tombs, S. (1999) *Corporate Crime,* London: Longman.

Slaughter, S. (1998) National Higher Education Policies in a Global Economy, in Currie, J. and Newson, J., eds., *Universities and Globalisation,* Thousand Oaks, Calif.: Sage.

Slaughter, S. and Leslie, L. (1997) *Academic Capitalism: politics, policies and the entrepreneurial university,* Baltimore: John Hopkins University Press.

Smart, C. (1995) *Law, Crime, and Sexuality,* London: Sage.

Smart, C., ed. (1992) *Regulating Womanhood,* London: Routledge.

Smart, C. (1990) Feminist Approaches to Criminology, or Postmodern Woman meets Atavistic Man, in Gelsthorpe, L. and Morris, A., eds., *Feminist Perspectives in Criminology,* Milton Keynes, England: Open University Press.

Smart, C. (1989) *Feminism and the Power of Law,* London: Routledge.

Smart, C. and Smart, A., eds. (1978) *Women, Sexuality and Social Control,* London: RKP.

Smith, D. (1974) *Who Rules the Universities?* New York: Monthly Review Press.

Smith, D.E. (1987) *The Everyday World as Problematic,* Milton Keynes, England: Open University Press.

Smyth, M. and Moore, R. (1996) Researching Sectarianism, in Smyth, M., ed., *Three Conference Papers on Aspects of Segregation and Sectarian Division,* Derry, Northern Ireland: Templegrove Action Research Limited.

Snider, L. (2000) The Sociology of Corporate Crime: an obituary (or: whose knowledge claims have legs?) *Theoretical Criminology,* 4 (2).

Snider, L. (1998) Towards Safer Societies, *British Journal of Criminology,* 38 (1).

Snider, L. (1996) Options for Public Accountability, in Mehta, M., ed., *Regulatory Efficiency and the Role of Risk Assessment,* Kingston, Ontario, Canada: School of Policy Studies, Queen's University Press.

Snider, L. (1993) *Bad Business: Corporate Crime in Canada,* Toronto, Canada: Nelson.

Snider, L. (1991) The Regulatory Dance: understanding reform processes in corporate crime, *International Journal of Sociology of Law,* 19.

Snider, L. (1990) Co-operative Models and Corporate Crime: panacea or cop-out? *Crime and Delinquency,* 36 (3).

Soley, L. (1998) The New Corporate Yen for Scholarship, in Simpson, C., ed., *Universities and Empire. Money and politics in the social sciences during the cold war,* New York: The New Press.

Sorensen, J., Grove, H. and Sorensen, T. (1980) Detecting Management Fraud: the role of the independent auditor, in Geis, G. and Stotland, E., eds., *White-Collar Crime Theory and Research,* Beverly Hills, Calif.: Sage.

Sparks, R., Bottoms, A. E. and Hay, W. (1996) *Prisons and the Problem of Order,* Oxford: Clarendon.

Stalker, J. (1988) *Stalker,* London: Harrap.

Stankiewicz, R. (1986) *Academics and Entrepreneurs: developing university-industry relations,* London: Frances Pinter.

Stanley, E. (2002) An Attack on Truth? in Scraton, P., ed., *Beyond September 11th: an anthology of dissent,* London: Pluto.

Stanley, L. and Wise, S. (1983) *Breaking Out,* London: Routledge and Kegan Paul.

Statewatch (1999) France: Ertzaintza Denied Hot Pursuits by French, *Statewatch,* 9 (5), September–October.

Stauber, J. and Rampton, S. (1995) *Toxic Sludge Is Good for You: lies damn lies and the public relations industry,* Monroe, Maine: Common Courage Press.

Stenson, K. (1998) Beyond Histories of the Present, *Economy and Society,* 27 (4), November.

Stotland, E., Brintnall, M., L'Heureux, A. and Ashmore, E. (1980) Do Convictions Deter Home Repair Fraud? in Geis, G. and Stotland, E., eds., *White-Collar Crime Theory and Research.* Beverly Hills: Sage.

Suomen Hallitus (Finnish Government) (2001) *Valtioneuvoston Periaatepäätös Toimintaohjelmaksi Talousrikollisuuden ja Harmaan Talouden Vähentämiseksi 2.6.2001. (Decision of Principle on the Action Plan to Reduce Economic Crime and Grey Economy 2.6.2001),* Helsinki, Finland: Suomen Hallitus.

Suomen Hallitus (Finnish Government) (1998) *Valtioneuvoston Periaatepäätös 22.10.1998 Toimintaohjelmaksi Talousrikollisuuden ja Harmaan Talouden Vähentämiseksi Vuosina 1999–2001. (Decision of Principle on the Action Plan to Reduce Economic Crime and Grey Economy 22.10.1998),* Helsinki, Finland: Suomen Hallitus.

Suomen Hallitus (Finnish Government) (1996) *Valtioneuvoston Periaatepäätös Toimintaohjelmaksi Talousrikollisuuden ja Harmaan Talouden Vähentämiseksi 1.2.1996 (Decision of Principle on the Action Plan to Reduce Economic Crime and Grey Economy) 1.2.1996,* Helsinki, Finland: Suomen Hallitus.

Suomen Hallitus (Finnish Government) (1995) Pääministeri Paavo Lipposen hallituksen ohjelma 13.4.1995 (Prime Minister Paavo Lipponen's Governments Programme 13.4.1995), Helsinki, Finland: Suomen Hallitus.

Suomen Tietotoimisto STT (Finnish news agency STT) (1995) *KTM:n yritystukia tutkinut poliisi ei usko suuriin konnuuksiin (The Investigator Researching the Subsidies of The Ministry Of Trade and Industry Doesn't Believe that There are Great Rip-Offs),* 26 January, Helsinki, Finland.

Suomen Tietotoimisto STT (Finnish news agency STT) (1994) *Talousrikollisuudesta Yhteiskun-nalle 14 Miljardin Lasku—oikeusjärjestelmän vaikea puuttua organisaatiorikollisuuteen (A 14 Billion Bill to the Society Caused by Economic Crime—the justice system has difficulties in confronting organizational crime)*, 9 August, Helsinki, Finland.

Suontausta, S. and Hämäläinen, H. (2000) *Raportti Rauenneista Konkursseista. (Report on Discontinuation of Bankruptcies due to Lack of Funds)*, Helsinki, Finland: Oy Edita Ab.

Supple, B. (1970) *The Royal Exchange Assurance: a history of British insurance 1720–1970*, Cambridge: Cambridge University Press.

Sutherland, E.H. (1983) *White-Collar Crime: the uncut version*, New Haven, Conn.: Yale University Press.

Sutherland, E.H. (1977) White Collar Criminality, in Geis, G. and Meier, R., eds., *White Collar Crime*, New York: Free Press.

Sutherland, E.H. (1949) *White-Collar Crime*, New York: Holt, Rinehart and Winston.

Sutherland, E.H. (1940) White-Collar Criminality, *American Sociological Review*, 5, February.

Swain, H. (1999) Jobs Insecurity Spreads, *The Times Higher Education Supplement*, 10 December.

Swigert, V. and Farrell, R. (1980–81) Corporate Homicide: definitional processes in the creation of deviance, *Law and Society Review*, 15 (1).

Swyngedouw, E. (1996) Reconstructing Citizenship, the Re-scaling of the State and the New Authoritarianism: closing the Belgian mines, *Urban Studies*, 33 (8).

Szockyi, E. and J. Fox, eds. (1996) *Corporate Victimization of Women*, Boston: Northeastern University Press.

Szwajkowski, E. and Figlewicz, R. (1998) Corporate Crime: the case for a database of cases on anticompetitive behavior, *Research in Corporate Social Performance and Policy*, 15.

Tappan, P. (1947) Who Is the Criminal? *American Sociological Review*, 12.

Taylor, I. (1997) Crime, Anxiety and Locality: responding to the "condition of England" at the end of the century, *Theoretical Criminology*, 1 (1).

Taylor, K. (1990) *The Poisoned Tree: the untold truth about the police conspiracy to discredit John Stalker and destroy me*, London: Sidgwick and Jackson.

Taylor, P. (1987) *Stalker: the search for the truth*, London: Faber and Faber.

Taylor, P. (1984) *The Smoke Ring: tobacco, money and multinational politics*, London and Sydney, Australia: Sphere Books.

Taylor, P. (1980) *Beating the Terrorists? Interrogation in Omagh, Gough and Castlereagh*, Harmondsworth, England: Penguin.

Taylor, R. (1988) Social Scientific Research on the "Troubles" in Northern Ireland, *Economic and Social Review*, 19.

Terkel, S. (1972) *Working*, New York: Avon.

*The Daily Telegraph* (1995a) City Comment: endowments looking terminally ill, 31 January.

*The Daily Telegraph* (1995b) City Comment: penny drops and the game is up, 12 January.

Thomas, P., ed. (1997) *Socio-Legal Studies*, Aldershot, England: Dartmouth.

Thompson, B. (1981) *Structural and Organizational Forces in the Etiology of Corporate Crime*, unpublished Ph.D. dissertation, Western Michigan University.

Thompson, E.P. (1980) *Writing by Candlelight*, London: Merlin.

Thompson, E.P. (1970) *Warwick University Ltd*, Harmondsworth, Middlesex, England: Penguin.

Thomson, A. (2001) Does Labour Come Up Smelling of Red Roses?, *The Times Higher Education Supplement*, 11 May.

Tilley, N. (1998) Evaluating the Effectiveness of CCTV Schemes, in Norris, C., Moran, J. and Armstrong, G., eds., *Surveillance, Closed Circuit Television and Social Control*, Aldershot, England: Ashgate.

Tilley, N. (1993) *The Prevention of Crime against Small Businesses: The Safer Cities experience, CPU 45,* London: Home Office.

Tillman, R. (1999) *Broken Promises,* Boston: Northeastern University Press.

Tillman, R., Calavita, K. and Pontell, H. (1997) Criminalizing White-Collar Misconduct, *Crime, Law and Social Change,* 26.

Tillman, R. and Pontell, H. (1995) Organizations and Fraud in the Savings and Loan industry, *Social Forces,* 73 (4).

Tillman, R. and Pontell, H. (1992) Is Justice "Collar-Blind"? Punishing Medicaid provider fraud, *Criminology,* 30 (4).

Tombs, S. (2002) Understanding Regulation? *Social and Legal Studies,* 11 (1).

Tombs, S. (1999) Death and Work in Britain, *The Sociological Review,* 47 (2), May.

Tombs, S. (1996) Injury, Death and the Deregulation Fetish: the politics of occupational safety regulation in United Kingdom manufacturing industries, *International Journal of Health Services,* 26 (2).

Tombs, S. and Whyte, D. (2001) Media Reporting of Crime: defining corporate crime out of existence?, *Criminal Justice Matters,* 43, Spring.

Tomlinson, M. (1998) Walking Backwards into the Sunset: British policy and the insecurity of Northern Ireland, in Miller, D., ed., *Rethinking Northern Ireland: Culture, Ideology and Colonialism,* London: Longman.

Tonry, M. and Reiss, A.J., Jr., eds. (1993) *Beyond the Law: crime in complex organizations. Crime and Justice, Volume 18,* Chicago: University of Chicago Press.

Townshend, C. (1983) *Political Violence in Ireland,* Oxford: Clarendon Press.

Travis, A. (2001) Focus Shifts to Repeat Criminals, *The Guardian,* 6 July.

Travis, A. (1994) Ministers Suppress Research, *The Guardian,* 4 July.

Tunnel, K., ed. (1993) *Political Crime in Contemporary America: a critical approach,* New York: Garland.

Turk, A.T. (1982) *Political Criminality—the defiance and defence of authority,* Beverly Hills, Calif.: Sage Publications.

Tweedale, G. (2000) *Magic Mineral to Killer Dust: Turner and Newall and the asbestos hazard,* Oxford: Oxford University Press.

Tweedale, G. (1990) *At the Sign of the Plough: Allen and Hanburys and the British pharmaceutical industry, 1715–1990,* London: John Murray.

Tweedale G. and Jeremy, D.J. (1999) Compensating the Workers: industrial injury and compensation in the British asbestos industry, 1930s-1960s, *Business History,* 41, April.

Urban, M. (1992) *Big Boys' Rules,* London: Faber and Faber.

Valtionvarainministeriö (1995) *Harmaan Talouden Selvitystyöryhmän Loppuraportti (Final Report of the Research Committee on the Grey Economy),* Helsinki, Finland: Treasury.

Vaughan, D. (1998) Rational Choice, Situated Action and the Social Control of Organizations, *Law and Society Review,* 32 (1).

Vaughan, D. (1997) Rational Choice, Situated Action and the Social Control of Organizations, in Ewick, P., Saft, A. and Kagan, R., eds., *Social Science, Legal Scholarship, and the Law,* New York: Russell Sage and University of Chicago Press.

Vaughan, D. (1996) *The Challenger Launch Decision,* Chicago: University of Chicago Press.

Vaughan, D. (1983) *Controlling Unlawful Organizational Behavior,* Chicago: University of Chicago Press.

Vaughan, D. (1982) Toward Understanding Unlawful Organizational Behavior, *Michigan Law Review,* 80.

Vaughan, D. (1979) *Crime between Organizations: a case study of Medicaid provider fraud,* unpublished Ph.D. thesis, Ohio State University.

Vaughn, M. and Smith L. (1999) Practicing Penal Harm Medicine in the United States: prisoners' voices from jail, *Justice Quarterly*, 16 (1).

Vick, D.W. and Campbell, K. (2001) Public Protests, Private Lawsuits, and the Market: the investor response to the McLibel case, *Journal of Law and Society*, 28 (2).

Vidal, J. (1997) *McLibel: Burger Culture on Trial*, London: Macmillan.

Virta, E. (2000) Do Penniless White Collar Offenders Steal, Batter Others and Drink-Drive?, *Turku Law Journal*, 1.

Virta, E. (1999) A Thief is a Criminal Who Has Not Had Time to Start a Company, in Laitinen, A. and Olgiati, V., eds., *Crime-Risk-Security. Publications of the Faculty of Law, Joint Studies Publications. B Series No. 8*, Turku, Finland: University of Turku.

Virta, E. (1998) Talousrikoksista Epäiltyjen Toiminta Yritysmaailmassa—Taustoista ja Maksuhäiriöistä (The Functioning of Economic Crime Suspects in Business), *Velkakierre—tutkimuksia luottoalalta*, 20.

Virta, E. and Laitinen, A. (1996) *Talousrikostuomioihin Liittyvä Perintä (The Collection of the Costs Adjudged in Economic Crime Cases). Police Department Publication 4/1996*, Helsinki, Finland: Ministry of the Interior.

Walker, C. and Starmer, K., eds. (1999) *Miscarriages of Justice: a review of justice in error*, London: Blackstone Press.

Walker, M. (1986) *With Extreme Prejudice*, London: Canary Press.

Walklate, S. (1998) *Understanding Criminology*, Buckingham, England: Open University Press.

Wallis, N. (1986) MI5 Smear Scandal Exposed, *The Star*, 19 July.

Walters, R. and Presdee, M. (1999) The Politics of Conducting Critical Evaluations—the "policing of knowledge," *Criminology Aotearoa/New Zealand*.

Ward, T. and Green, P. (2000) Legitimacy, Civil Society and State Crime, *Social Justice*, 27 (4).

Weinberg, S. (1989) *Armand Hammer: the untold story*, Boston: Little Brown.

Weir, R. (1995) *The History of the Distillers Company, 1877–1939*, Oxford: Oxford University Press.

Weisburd, D., Chayet, B. and Waring, E. (1990) White-Collar Crime and Criminal Careers: Preliminary Findings, *Crime and Delinquency*, 36 (3).

Weiss, L. (1997) Globalisation and the Myth of the Powerless State, *New Left Review*, 225, September/October.

Welch, M. (1999) *Punishment in America: social control and the ironies of punishment*, London: Sage.

Wheeler, S., Mann, K. and Sarat, A. (1988) *Sitting in Judgment: the sentencing of white-collar criminals*, New Haven, Conn.: Yale University Press.

Wheeler, S., Weisburd, D. and Bode, N. (1982) Sentencing the White-Collar Offender: rhetoric and reality, *American Sociological Review*, 50.

Wheeler, S., Weisburd, D., Waring, E. and Bode, N. (1991) *Crimes of the Middle Class*, New Haven, Conn.: Yale University Press.

Wheeler, S., Weisburd, D., Waring, E. and Bode, N. (1988) White-Collar Crimes and Criminals, *American Criminal Law Review*, 25.

Wheen, F. (1999) *Karl Marx*, London: Fourth Estate.

Whitebloom, S. and Atkinson, D. (1993) Large Calls for Disclosure of Commission, *The Guardian*, 9 July.

Whitty, N., Murphy, T. and Livingstone, S. (2001) *Civil Liberties Law: the Human Rights Act era*, London: Butterworths.

Whyte, D. (2000) Researching the Powerful: towards a political economy of method? in King, R. and Wincup, E., eds., *Doing Research on Crime and Justice*, Oxford: Oxford University Press.

Whyte, D. (1999) *Power, Ideology and the Regulation of Safety in the Post-Piper Alpha Offshore Oil Industry,* unpublished Ph.D. thesis, Liverpool John Moores University.

Whyte, D. (1998) *Power, Corruption and Lies: the world according to the UK oil and gas industry,* paper presented to the OILC National Conference, Aberdeen, Scotland, 30 May.

Wigmore, B. (1986) Power of the Masons—myth or a menace? *The People,* 13 July.

Wilks, S. (1998) Utility Regulation, Corporate Governance and the Amoral Corporation, in Doern, G.B. and Wilks, S., eds., *Changing Regulatory Institutions in Britain and North America,* Toronto: University of Toronto Press.

Williams, G. (1992) *Changing Patterns of Finance in Higher Education,* Buckingham, England: Society for Research into Higher Education and Open University Press.

Williams, G. and Popay, J. (1997) Social Science and Public Health: issues of method, knowledge and power, *Critical Public Health,* 7 (1/2).

Williams, P. and Dickinson, J. (1993) Fear of Crime: read all about it? *British Journal of Criminology,* 33 (1), Winter.

Wilson, C. (1954) *History of Unilever.* Two Volumes, London: Cassell.

Winckler, J. (1987) The Fly on the Wall in the Inner Sanctum: observing company directors at work, in Moyser, G. and Wagstaffe, M., eds., *Research Methods for Élite Studies,* London: Allen and Unwin.

Wing Lo, T. (1993) The Politics of Social Censure: corruption and bourgeois liberation in communist China, *Social and Legal Studies,* 2 (2).

Winter, R. (1995) The University of Life Plc: the "industrialisation" of higher education? in Smyth, J., ed., *Academic Work: the changing labour process in higher education,* Buckingham: Society for Research into Higher Education and Open University Press.

Wintour, P. (2002) Targeting the After-School Criminals, *The Guardian,* 22 March.

Wolin, R. (1989) Introduction, in Habermas, J., *The New Conservatism,* Cambridge: Polity.

Woodiwiss, M. (1992) The Passing of Modernism and Labour Rights: lessons from Japan and the United States, *Social and Legal Studies,* 1 (4).

Woodward, W. (2002a) Universities in Crisis, *The Guardian,* 20 May.

Woodward, W. (2002b) Universities in Crisis, *The Guardian,* 21 May.

Woodward, W. (2002c) Universities in Crisis, *The Guardian,* 22 May.

Woolf, M. (1998) Civil Servants are Told to Turn Spy, *The Observer,* 3 May.

Worrall, A. (1990) *Offending Women,* London: Routledge.

Wright, D. (1995) Use Spare Cash to Reduce Endowment Mortgages, *The Times,* 15 January.

Wright-Mills, C. (1967) The Cultural Apparatus, in Horowitz, I., ed., *Power, Politics and People: the collected essays of C. Wright Mills,* Oxford: Oxford University Press.

Yeager, P. (1991) *The Limits of Law: the public regulation of private pollution,* Cambridge: Cambridge University Press.

Young, P. (1992) The Importance of Utopias in Criminological Thinking, *British Journal of Criminology,* 32 (4).

Zey, M. (1993) *Banking on Fraud: Drexel, junk bonds and buyouts,* New York: Aldine de Gruyter.

Zimring, F. and Hawkins, G. (1993) Crime, Justice and the Savings and Loan Crisis, in Tonry, M. and Reiss, A., eds., *Beyond the Law: crime in complex organizations,* Chicago: University of Chicago Press.

Zuege, A. (1999) The Chimera of the Third Way, in Panitch, L. and Leys, C., eds., *Necessary and Unnecessary Utopias: the Socialist Register 2000,* Rendlesham: The Merlin Press.

Zukin, S. (1996) Cultural Strategies of Economic Development and the Hegemony of Vision, Merryfield, A. and Swyngedouw, E., eds., *The Urbanisation of Injustice,* London: Lawrence and Wishart.

# Contributors

Anne Alvesalo works as a Senior Researcher in the Police College of Finland. Her present research is concentrated on the problems of policing economic crime in Finland, which she has studied extensively, and on which she has published several books and articles, both sole-authored and co-authored with Ahti Laitinen, Erja Virta and Steve Tombs. Her other area of interest is legal theory, and in 1997 she published a book on the American critical legal studies movement, *Critical Legal Studies—a critical approach* to law (Helsinki, Lakimiesliiton kustannus: 1997).

Anette Ballinger is a Lecturer in Criminology at Keele University. Her research interests include gender, history, and punishment. Her most recent publication is *Dead Woman Walking: executed women in England and Wales 1900–1955* (Ashgate: 2000).

Eileen Berrington is a Lecturer in Critical Criminology at the Centre for Studies in Crime and Social Justice at Edge Hill University College and Course Leader for the BA (Honours) in Critical Criminology. She was formerly Research Officer for the West Lancashire Association of Disabled People (WLAD). Her publications include *The Life of the People* and *The Voice of the People* (WLAD/Edge Hill University College, 1996, co-authored with David Johnstone and Linda Cartwright). Her doctoral research focused on media representations of crisis disaster and tragedy. She has a number of publications in this area, including (with Ann Jemphrey and Phil Scraton) "Intimate Intrusions? Press Freedom, Private Lives and Public Interest," *Communications Law* (1998) and "Surviving the Media: Hillsborough,

Dunblane and the press," *Journalism Studies* (with Ann Jemphrey, 2000). Her current research focuses on gendered representations of violence.

Roy Coleman is a Lecturer in Criminal Justice at Liverpool John Moores University, and has just completed a Ph.D. thesis entitled *Surveillance, Power and Social Order: a case study of CCTV in Liverpool*. Previously he has taught at the Open University and Edge Hill University College. He gained his MA in Crime, Deviance and Social Policy from the University of Lancaster in 1991. Roy has published in the *British Journal of Sociology, International Review of Law, Computers and Technology, Social & Legal Studies,* and *Sociology*.

Gary Fooks is a Senior Lecturer in Criminology at South Bank University. His research interests include white collar crime and the policing of public displays of poverty.

Penny Green is Professor of Law and Criminology at the School of Law, University of Westminster. She is on the INQUEST Board of Trustees and the editorial board of the *British Journal of Criminology*. Her current research interests include natural disasters and state crime—specifically the 1999 Kocaeli earthquake—torture, state corporate crime, human rights, and criminal justice in Turkey. Her published work includes *The Enemy Without: Policing and Class Consciousness in the 1984–85 Miners' Strike* (Open University Press, 1990), *Drug Couriers: an International Perspective* (Quartet, 1996), *Drugs, Trafficking and Criminal Policy: the Scapegoat Strategy* (Waterside, 1997) and, with Andrew Rutherford, *Criminal Policy in Transition* (Hart, 2000). She is currently co-authoring a book on state crime with Tony Ward.

Paddy Hillyard is Professor of Social Administration and Policy at the University of Ulster. He is a former Chair of Liberty (the National Council for Civil Liberties) and of the editorial board of *Social and Legal Studies*. He has written widely on the administration of justice, civil liberties and social policy. His publications include *Law and State: The Case of Northern Ireland and Ten Years on in Northern Ireland* (with Kevin Boyle and Tom Hadden, Martin Robertson, 1975 and Cobden Trust, 1980), *The Coercive State: The Decline of Democracy in Britain* (with Janie Percy-Smith, Fontana, 1987), and *Suspect Community: People's Experience of the Prevention of Terrorism Acts in Britain* (Pluto Press, 1993). He is currently completing a book on the Taylor/Stalker affair.

Ann Jemphrey is Research Co-ordinator in the Centre for Studies in Crime and Social Justice at Edge Hill University College. Previously a researcher on the Hillsborough project, she has contributed to *Hillsborough and After: The Liverpool Experience* (Coleman, S., Scraton, P. and Skidmore, P.; CSCSJ/Liverpool City

Council, 1990) and is co-author of *No Last Rights: the Denial of Justice and the Promotion of Myth in the Aftermath of the Hillsborough Disaster* (Liverpool City Council/Alden Press, 1995, with Phil Scraton and Sheila Coleman). She co-authored (with Eileen Berrington and Phil Scraton), "Intimate Intrusions? Press Freedom, Private Lives and Public Interest" in *Communications Law* (1998) and co-authored (with Eileen Berrington), "Surviving the Media: Hillsborough, Dunblane and the press" in *Journalism Studies* (2000).

Colm Power has recently completed a Ph.D. thesis titled *A Critical Examination of the Normalisation of Special Powers within the European Union and Their Impact on Operational Policing.* He is Principal Researcher for *"Room to Roam: Britain's Irish Travellers,"* a major research project based at St. Mary's College Strawberry Hill and funded by the National Lotteries Charities Board, and is the author of *Our Histories, Our Futures* (Irish Centre Housing, 1999).

Phil Scraton is Professor of Criminology and Director of the Centre for Studies in Crime and Social Justice at Edge Hill University College. His research interests include the application of critical theory; police powers and accountability; incarceration and punishment; controversial deaths; the regulation of gender and sexuality; the criminalisation of children and young people. He has published widely and his books include: *Causes for Concern* (Penguin, 1984, ed. with Paul Gordon); *The State of the Police* (Pluto, 1985); *The State v The People* (Blackwell, 1985, ed. with Phil Thomas); *Law, Order and the Authoritarian State* (Open University Press, 1987, ed.); *In the Arms of the Law* (Pluto 1987, with Kathryn Chadwick); *Prisons Under Protest* (Open University Press, 1991, with Joe Sim and Paula Skidmore); *No Last Rights* (LCC/Alden Press, 1995 with Ann Jemphrey and Sheila Coleman); *Childhood in "Crisis"?* (UCL Press 1997, ed.); *Hillsborough: The Truth* (Mainstream, 1999, revised 2000); *Beyond September 11:An Anthology of Dissent* (Pluto, 2002, ed.); *Disaster, Trauma, Aftermath* (Lawrence and Wishart, forthcoming, with Howard Davis).

Joe Sim is Professor of Criminology in the Centre for Social Science, Liverpool John Moores University. His publications include *Medical Power in Prisons* (Open University Press, 1990), *British Prisons* (Blackwell, 1982, with Mike Fitzgerald), *Prisons under Protest* (Open University Press, 1991, with Phil Scraton and Paula Skidmore) and *Western European Penal Systems* (Sage, 1995, co-edited with Vincenzo Ruggiero and Mick Ryan). His latest research is concerned with the further exploration of medical power in prisons.

Laureen Snider is a Professor of Sociology at Queens University, Kingston, Ontario, and Board Member of the Vancouver Centre for Corporate Accountability. She has written extensively on corporate crime, on agendas of punishment and modern states, and on the significance of social movements such as feminism. Among her numerous publications are *Bad Business: Corporate Crime in Canada* (Nelson, 1993), and, as editor with Frank Pearce, *Corporate Crime: Contemporary Debates* (University of Toronto Press, 1995). Her main articles include "Constituting the Punishable Woman: Atavistic Man Incarcerates Postmodern Woman," *British Journal of Criminology*, 2002, "Crimes Against Capital: Discovering Theft of Time," *Social Justice* (Law, Order and Neo Liberalism), 2001, "The Sociology of Corporate Crime: An Obituary," *Theoretical Criminology*, 2000, and "Towards Safer Societies," *British Journal of Criminology*, 1998.

Steve Tombs is a Professor of Sociology, Liverpool John Moores University. He has a long-standing interest in the incidence, nature, and regulation of corporate crime. His main recent publications are *Corporate Crime* (Longman, 1999), with Gary Slapper, and *Toxic Capitalism: corporate crime and the chemical industry* (Ashgate, 1998; Canadian Scholars' Press, 1999), with Frank Pearce, and he has recently completed co-editing a text, *Risk, Management and Society* (Kluwer-Nijhoff, 2000), with Eve Coles and Denis Smith. He has been Chair of the UK Centre for Corporate Accountability since it was founded in 1999.

Geoffrey Tweedale is a Reader in the Centre for Business History at Manchester Metropolitan University Business School. His most recent publication is *Magic Mineral to Killer Dust: Turner & Newall and the Asbestos Hazard* (Oxford University Press, 2nd edition, 2001). He is currently researching the history of a range of occupational health issues, including dust diseases in the cotton, coal, steel, pottery, and refractories industries.

Erja Virta works as a Senior Planning Officer in the Authority Co-operation Development Project. She has a licentiate degree from the Faculty of Law at the University of Turku, and obtained her master's degree from the Turku School of Economics and Business Administration. She has been a researcher in several empirical research projects and has written books and articles on business security, tax law, insurance fraud, and especially economic crime.

Dave Whyte is a Lecturer in Criminology at the University of Leeds. He teaches and writes on issues relating to corporate crime and the regulation of business, transnational criminal justice systems, and the construction of criminological knowledge. His research on those topics has appeared in a range of edited collections, websites and journals, including *Corporate Watch, Critical Criminology, Journal of Law and Society, Policy and Politics, Risk Management, Social and Legal Studies, Studies in Political Economy*, and *www.peoplenotprofit.co.uk*. He is currently completing *Safety Crimes* (Willan), with Steve Tombs.

# Index